KEEP YOUR EAR TO THE GROUND

KEEP YOUR EAR TO THE GROUND

A HISTORY OF PUNK FANZINES IN WASHINGTON, DC

JOHN R. DAVIS

Washington, DC · press.georgetown.edu

Cataloging-in-Publication Data is on file with the Library of Congress:

978-1-64712-635-3 (paperback)
978-1-64712-636-0 (ebook)

This paper meets the requirements of ANSI/NISO Z39.48-1992 (Permanence of Paper).

26 25 9 8 7 6 5 4 3 2 First printing

EU GPSR Authorized Representative
LOGOS EUROPE, 9 rue Nicolas
Poussin, 17000, LA ROCHELLE, France
Email: Contact@logoseurope.eu

Printed in the United States of America

Cover design by Faceout Studio, Spencer Fuller
Interior design by Faceout Studio, Paul Nielsen

Front cover images:
Wreckless Eric reading *The Infiltrator*, photograph courtesy of Mary Leary
Jello Biafra reading *Capitol Crisis*, photograph courtesy of Xyra Harper-Cann
Susan Springfield reading *Vintage Violence*, photograph by Jonathan Wallen

Back cover image: Ian MacKaye reading *Touch & Go*, photograph by Tesco Vee

To M, m, and n.

CONTENTS

FOREWORD

Emily Flake

THE FIRST TIME I ever laid my hands on a fanzine, I was fourteen years old. Skulking around the Record Breaker in Manchester, Connecticut, I hoped nobody would sniff me out as a poser and banish me from the store. My sense of punk rock at the time was rudimentary at best. I could see little pieces, here and there, but I had no idea of the shape or the scope of the thing. I just knew that whatever it was, I wanted it. That day, when I came across the April 1992 issue of the San Francisco–based punk fanzine *Maximum Rocknroll*, it was the first concrete artifact from a planet whose transmissions I'd only just begun to tune into.

Of course, that April 1992 issue of *MRR* was the "April Fool's" issue. Not being familiar with the material that its columns and articles lampooned, I swallowed it whole and wondered if being punk rock meant I had to be cool with columnist Mykel Board raising legal defense funds through NAMBLA. I was—how shall I put this—an extremely gullible dork at fourteen, and when the May issue came out, I realized the joke was on me. As an adult and a humor professional today, however, I commend them for their commitment to the bit. Recently, I found a digitized version of that April issue online and, flipping through it, I can still feel the excitement I felt thirty-two years ago, flipping through the real thing. Everything about it was exactly what I had been looking for then.

That fall, I started high school and flung myself at the punks, desperate to be taken in. I've never had the patience or wherewithal to learn a musical instrument, even by punk rock standards, so participating in the scene by joining a band was out. But I'd been making my own little publications since I was a child, and I'd seen kids selling or trading fanzines at the shows I'd started attending. My pathway to scene citizenship seemed obvious. My first effort was a half-letter sized number called *Brick*, about which I remember little (except that, to my horror, I might have had some Ayn Rand–adjacent nonsense in there? I told you I was a gullible dork). A boy I liked said nice things about it, which is basically the teen equivalent of a Pulitzer.

But my real baby was my second title, *Puddle Jumper Weather Stomper*. *PJWS* was half-legal sized, objectively the most satisfying of all fanzine sizes. I'd figured out a thing or two about how to achieve the anarchic but surprisingly design-savvy look of the time. Letraset lettering to use in the layout was prohibitively expensive and hard to find, but photocopying fonts out of type sample books at various sizes was a good workaround. I got a job at the local library, where many of my fellow scenesters worked, providing me access to visual material in the form of a huge cache of old *Life* magazines. Crucially, our boss let us use the copy machine free, or at least failed to stop us when we stole the copy key. I made three issues (plus a fourth, as a lark in college), and I still think I was never better at graphic design than when I did it by hand, with scissors and a glue stick.

My scene was based in central Connecticut, in the ex-mill towns and suburbs that floated uneasily between Boston and New York, two towns with terrifying meathead scenes for which most of the nice kids from Connecticut were ill-suited. We orbited around Studio 158 outside Willimantic, but when I first started going to shows, most of the kids kept their eyes fixed west toward California—I knew about the punk scene at Gilman Street long before I could have found the East Bay on a map. But we also had a healthy respect for the punk community located in Washington, DC. We'd been born too late for a lot of it, but Fugazi, Jawbox, and Shudder to Think had a fanbase among me and mine. Once, a girl friend of mine got ahold of Ian MacKaye's phone number, called it, said something salacious when he answered, and hung up screaming. I guess we'd missed the memo about not fucking?

Fugazi played the University of Connecticut in September of 1993—that show being another artifact of my youth that I can summon in full from the internet. Guitarist/vocalist Guy Picciotto scolds the crowd for (say it with me) dancing too hard—would it even be a Fugazi show without such a scolding?—pointing out that they'd been doing this for a decade. "I saw them before that even, when they were Minor Threat," a man next to me said, raising his eyebrows at me. "Ew," I responded. "What are you, thirty?!"

By the time I was a senior, tastes in my regional scene had shifted away from the (surprisingly extremely commercially viable!) pop punk of the East Bay label Lookout! Records to chain-wallet screamo that aped the abstemious screech of Fugazi without coming anywhere close to the fun of their rhythm section. I drifted in another direction, toward the tender mercies of whatever twee nonsense K Records was up to (it's fine, I'm rolling my eyes, too). I wrote my high school junior thesis on underground business and media, and I can tell you from the vantage point of middle age that while I may have been a massive dork, the passion and excitement I felt for that world of sui generis arts and letters put me on a very clear path for the rest of my life.

Looking through the pages of the zines in this book, I still feel that excitement. While some of the titles are unfamiliar to me, the tone and energy are not, and the design vernacular still feels like the language I love the most (1990s dependence on ellipses aside, God bless). Nothing I do and nothing I am now would have happened without that kindling spark of the fanzine world. You can draw a thick, straight line from my love of fanzines to my eventual work for altweeklies (RIP) and *The New Yorker*. Newsprint ink and copier toner is an indelible part of my blood. And I didn't even have to write a check to NAMBLA to get there.

ACKNOWLEDGMENTS

PROFOUND THANKS TO Hope LeGro, my editor, for her patience, guidance, and vision; to past and present colleagues in the University of Maryland Libraries, for their support, editing, advice, and enthusiasm, such as Stephen Henry, Vin Novara, Ben Jackson, Jessica Grimmer, and many others; to folks like Jeff Krulik, Ian MacKaye, James Schneider, Guy Picciotto, Sharon Cheslow, Richard Harrington, and others who helped connect me with people for the interviews, research, and image permissions that went into this book; to Sara Baum for transcription prowess and kind encouragement; to Amanda Hardt Sorensen, for skilled assistance helping me organize my research, which was an important step in this process; to all who assisted in helping me obtain images and other materials for research, including those at institutions like the DC Public Library, the National Gallery of Art, the University of Maryland–Baltimore County's Albin O. Kuhn Library and Special Collections, Yale University's Beinecke Rare Book and Manuscript Library, the Chicago History Museum, Cornell University, New York University, the Library of Congress, and beyond; to all the photographers and fanzine creators who permitted me to use their works in this book and who created these amazing documents in the first place; to everyone who allowed me to interview them for this book; to all involved in DC punk for building and maintaining this inspiring and inclusive community; to my friends for sharing their fandom, camaraderie, humor, and guidance with me along the way; to my parents for imparting a love of music and writing, as well as supporting my musical and fanzine creation efforts; and finally, to Mollie, Mira, and Naomi, thank you for being who you are (which includes encouraging me from start to finish as I worked on this book!) and for making this life such a good one.

—John Davis

The author at age sixteen, center, in a light green shirt with back to the camera, watching Fugazi perform at Fort Reno Park in DC on August 9, 1993. From the collection of Dischord Records, photographer unknown. Used by permission.

INTRODUCTION

THE CHU FAMILY MINIVAN cruised south down 16th Street NW in Washington, DC, on a chilly, early spring evening. I was fifteen years old and on my way to my first punk concert, peering out the curtained backseat window as the houses of Sixteenth Street Heights rolled past. My best friend, Dan, had just obtained his driver's license and, better yet, was allowed to borrow his parents' brown Toyota MasterAce Surf for the night. A group of us, chattering in nervous anticipation, were piled into the trapezoid-shaped van for the ride from suburban Montgomery County, Maryland, down to Sanctuary Theater in DC's Columbia Heights neighborhood. It was April 4, 1992, and we had tickets to see that night's Fugazi, L7, and Bikini Kill concert.

Throughout the preceding year, those same friends introduced me to the music of Fugazi, and other punk bands from DC—like Minor Threat, Gray Matter, Jawbox, Rites of Spring, the Nation of Ulysses, and so many others—through the usual methods of mixtapes and word of mouth. As an avid reader then of mainstream music magazines like *Rolling Stone* and *Spin*, I had already read some about punk rock and enjoyed flagship bands like the Clash and the Sex Pistols, but none of it spoke to me the way that DC punk did.

Donning headphones in my bedroom and listening to Minor Threat's *Complete Discography* compact disc for the first time was the moment of realization: "Oh, so *this* is punk rock!" Punk's possibilities were illuminated as soon as the portentous opening power chord of "Filler" gave way to the full band, hurtling through the song in just over 90 galvanizing seconds. "You call it religion," the band's vocalist, Ian MacKaye, shouted, "you're full of shit!" I listened, eyes and mind wide, immediately eager to talk with my friends about this amazing music. DC punk bands were as fast and fierce as they were intelligent and innovative. Somehow, the songs were rich with melodic hooks despite embracing chaos, rejecting the edgeless laminar flow of much turn-of-the-1990s rock music. Equally optimistic and angry, this was music that made sense amid a confounding world.

Much as I loved the records I had heard from DC's punk scene, I still had never been to a show until that April night in 1992. Opening the heavy doors of Sanctuary Theater, I was enveloped by an aromatic wave of humidity generated by the crowd packed into the church. It rushed over and past me, out into the cold air, initiating me into this new realm. Pushing into the crowded hallway, the clamor and crush were intimidating, yet strangely magnetic. Then, once the music started, any lingering doubts disappeared.

Bikini Kill—nearing the end of their temporary relocation to DC from Olympia, Washington, but still advertised on the show's flier as "from Washington, DC"—opened the concert, making them the first punk band I ever saw live. This was a hard act for the rest of my life to follow, although

I inaccurately presumed then that every group from the subculture must be this thrilling and threatening.[1]

L7, the ferocious alternative rock band from Los Angeles, followed on the bill and were also unforgettable. Their set ended with guest Slymenstra Hymen of GWAR—a horror-influenced metal band from Richmond—expectorating fire out over the crowd, spawning a malodorous smoke that hovered in the room until Fugazi took the stage.

Fugazi was transcendent, performing with a klieg light intensity for the duration of their set. The band's communion with the crowd was authentic and reciprocal, so different from the mainstream arena rock concerts I had attended as a kid. Also intriguing were the audience members lining the edges of the stage, dancing and singing along mere feet away from the band. How was this possible? Security staff at those arena concerts would *never* have allowed fans to get that close, of course. At Sanctuary Theater, though, there was no uniformed security staff at all. The relationship between the band and its fans was one of mutual respect and trust. It was evident from a few minor moments of tension within the crowd that if anyone violated that unspoken contract, the community addressed it itself. Looking around the space, you could see that any number of fans were essential parts of the show's ecosystem—the photographers in the front row, the ticket takers at the entrance, the activists sitting at tables distributing literature on veganism and political issues. The concert itself was a benefit for groups fighting to maintain reproductive rights for women. People were not there as passive recipients of entertainment, but as part of a symbiotic fellowship presenting actionable alternatives to mainstream thought.

Fanzines, also known as zines, are the fan-made, small-run periodicals that were so vital for connecting punks before the internet transformed fandom. Although I later learned that numerous zine creators distributed their works at the April 4 show, I was too overwhelmed by the concert's bounty of stimuli to notice at the time. Just a few weeks later, however, I came across some fanzines that older kids at my high school had published, featuring interviews with punk bands from DC like Bikini Kill, Nation of Ulysses, Unrest, and Circus Lupus. The form reified the accessibility and freedom I sensed at the Fugazi show, demonstrating that its relationship to the music it covered was complementary, not adjunctive. Sure, bands were a main draw to the subculture, but fanzines made it clear that fans were equally critical to the relevance and sustainability of punk, influencing dialogues without asking for permission to do so. Seeing my peers say whatever they wanted to say in print was enthralling, and I wanted to do the same.

I began publishing my own punk fanzine in the fall of 1993, a practice I continued through my teenage years and into my mid-twenties. When I first heard Minor Threat two years earlier, I felt an urgent need to connect with others about this exciting music. Now, through fanzines, I had my canvas to do so. As ambitious to find a place in the DC punk scene as I was then, my introversion often made it challenging for me to talk with people I did not already know. Publishing a fanzine, however, made that so much easier, as I felt I now had a legitimate reason to approach bands or record labels. Even better, selling my publication at shows or sending them out to other zines for review often sparked friendships, many of which I still have today.

Crucially, for me, it broadened the network of people I called upon when booking shows for my bands or when I needed help putting out our records. Ultimately, playing music took up so much of my time that, by 2002, I was unable to continue publishing fanzines. The rise of the internet and the questionable relevance of print fanzines in this new reality was an additional deterrent to continuing. I proceeded to tour constantly as a member of the bands Q and Not U, Georgie James, and Title Tracks until 2011, before the discouraging financial realities facing most touring musicians led me to eventually pursue a master's degree in library and information science (MLIS) with hopes of building a career as an archivist.

By 2014, I had my MLIS and was a few months into working as an archivist at the University of Maryland's Special Collections in Performing Arts (SCPA). In my new profession, I sought projects that prompted the passion I so readily felt as a musician and fanzine editor. When I learned of the Riot Grrrl archival collection at New York University and the zine collections that institutions like Duke University, the University of Iowa, and Barnard College had built, the same enthusiasm and purpose animating my first two decades in punk came flooding back.

I proposed an idea to SCPA's then-curator, Vin Novara—who also had drummed for bands on Dischord Records, DC punk's defining record label—that SCPA start an archival collection of punk fanzines from DC. Vin observed that there was an increasing interest in scholarly research on punk and popular music, so I was given the go-ahead to curate a collection, which swiftly bloomed into one of SCPA's most popular. The DC punk and indie fanzine collection consists of more than one thousand titles—about half from the DC area, with the rest published elsewhere but featuring significant coverage of DC punk bands. Before long, we added an oral history component, gathering interviews with dozens of DC punk fanzine creators active from the mid-1970s into the twenty-first century. Many of those interviews are drawn from in the pages ahead.

Recent years have seen a number of compelling documentaries, exhibitions, books, and podcasts centered on DC punk, but the focus was mostly on bands. As I acknowledged, musicians are the indispensable centerpiece of the community, but this subculture is still composed of interdependent facets. Without the photographers, concert promoters, volunteers, audio engineers, showgoers, record stores, and other key elements, *there is no punk scene*.

This book examines another of those integral, yet underexplored, parts of DC punk—fanzines and the fans who made them. Punk fanzines were particularly necessary in the pre-internet era of the subculture, providing a public space for creativity, accountability, and connection. More recently, though far fewer in number, print fanzines still provide a tactile, much-needed alternative to the electronic screens and unbounded scrolling that most fans absorb their information on the punk community from.

I titled this book not only as a nod to the lyrical hook of Three's "Swann Street"—perhaps my favorite song to ever come out of DC—but also in reference to the important role that punk fanzine editors play as documenters, truth-tellers, and diviners of the scene. To keep one's ear to the ground, of course, refers to maintaining awareness of what is coming, the distant approach of something meaningful. Indeed, this is what fanzine editors do. Their fandom is a manifestation of a punk subculture in DC that remains thriving after nearly half a century. Part of why it remains vibrant relates to the restless impulse that Three's Geoff Turner captured in his song. From a fanzine creator's perspective, that motivation is to not be complacent or cynical, but to instead pay attention to what is here in the present and to listen closely for what is on the way. "Well, I don't care how picturesque or incomplex your life gets," he sang. "The ground's unsolid, don't forget, now keep your ear to the ground."

John R. Davis, 2025
Silver Spring, Maryland

1. Bikini Kill's performance was described in vivid detail by Sara Marcus in her 2010 book *Girls to the Front: The True Story of the Riot Grrrl Revolution*. Marcus grew up in Montgomery County at the same time I did, just a few towns over from where I lived. During those years, she copublished the zine *Out of the Vortex*.

The Roots of DC's Punk Fanzines

PUNK ROCK IS ABOUT CONNECTION without artifice, its ethos ostensibly centered on critiquing or razing anything broadening the gulf between performers and fans. Upon its arrival in the 1970s, punk urgently sought to reconnect rock and roll with the vitality and immediacy of its earliest days. This felt imperative for believers in rock's kinetic, yet waning, promise. By the mid-1970s, everything from drum solos to hospitality riders had lengthened intemperately in the wake of rock's ascent to pop culture dominance. Likewise, the increasingly massive scale of concerts by rock's leading bands was antithetical to genuine synthesis, rendering audiences an anonymous monolith seemingly there just to roar on cue rather than inspire a band's performance through the alchemical kinship born in smaller venues.

Punk, however, rejected what had become rock's characteristic traits, whether it was progressive rock's primacy of virtuosity or soft rock's stultifying mellowness. Instead, punk asserted attributes like authenticity, humor, energy, and amateurism over the self-indulgence and insularity of established rock groups like Led Zeppelin, the Eagles, and Pink Floyd.[1] The rock star paradigm positioned itself as an elite status, worthy of worship, and nearly unobtainable. Punk opposed this, opening itself to anyone with the desire to take part. As one rock critic observed of punk's contrarian fervor in spring 1977, "rock has had generational crises before, but never one so serious or heated as this."[2] Punk's egalitarian, do-it-yourself ethic sparked an amateur media ecosystem within the subculture built on outlets like mixtapes, freeform college radio broadcasts, and other outlets obviating rock music's gatekeepers.[3]

A critical piece of that punk network was fanzines, which embody music's solitary *and* communal joys, while platforming fiercely individual voices that nevertheless yearned to connect with like-minded others. Punk zines serve as material proof of the community's core tenet that "anyone can do it," offering zine publishers a reciprocal connection to a greater body and a chance to report on the subculture while shaping it.[4] If zines are a way out of tedium and powerlessness, they are also a way in for their creators to communicate fleeting waves of frustration or inspiration that might otherwise have dissipated into the past.

Fanzines—a portmanteau of "fan" and "magazine" coined by science fiction fanzine creator Louis Russell Chauvenet in 1940—are unlike regular music magazines in that they eschew the ambition of reaching a broad audience.[5] Zine publishers do not need to compromise on what they cover to chase higher circulation rates and advertising dollars. They are free to offer *their* visions of music that matters, and *their* opinions on which voices need to be heard or which ideas are worth exploring. Fanzines are created to reach, and potentially build, that small group of fans out there, waiting to commune.

"Zines are as much about the communities that arise out of their circulation as they are artifacts of personal expression," author and scholar Stephen Duncombe wrote.[6] The connections made between fans bind these communities together, accelerating the group's growth. Indeed, "fandom is a way of life," as an old slogan asserts, and the personal relationships developed among fans can feel as rewarding as the expression of fandom itself. "Primarily, the rewards of belonging to science fiction fandom are friendships," one science fiction fan and writer observed. "My wife and I have been fans for over thirty years, and our social life is almost entirely with other fans."[7]

When punk arrived, new fanzines all over the world cropped up to cover it, like *Punk* in New York City, *Sniffin' Glue* in London, *Pulp* in Australia, *Search and Destroy* in San Francisco, and *Flipside* and *Slash* in Los Angeles. These zines reveled in the liberation of amateurism, breathlessly documenting the new music repudiating the establishment. Punk fanzines flaunted their disruptive aesthetics, gleefully eschewing the polish of mainstream rock magazines like *Rolling Stone* that typically ignored or dismissed punk.

Punk's loathing of established mores is, ironically, a convention in the avant-garde. Whether it was Futurists, Stuckists, Dadaists, or Lettrists, the rejection of orthodoxy animated numerous movements. Fanzines, though, were another tradition—albeit a newer one—that punk tapped into, satisfying its urge for autonomy, connection, and identity. "Fanzines show a combination of independence and responsibility not easily found elsewhere in our culture," observed psychologist and author Fredric Wertham: "Editorial writers have more freedom of expression than a person who writes for a commercial magazine or publisher. And they not only state frankly what they think, and experiment with form, they can also discuss freely and intelligently their differing views and beliefs."[8]

As I explore in this chapter, fanzines coming from DC's punk subculture are built on a foundation laid through decades of experimentation and subversion in art, fan, and underground communities, fueled by the universal yearning to be seen, heard, and acknowledged. Early fanzines from the comic book and science fiction communities lit the way, while everything from the Dada art movement, *MAD Magazine*, the Situationist International, and the underground counterculture newspapers of the 1960s built the path to punk zines.

DC's punk community coalesced in 1976 with bands like the Slickee Boys and Overkill working to steer local rock music away from the light, post-hippie sounds of Starland Vocal Band and similar popular outfits. For those who subscribe to DC's naggingly persistent reputation as "a government town" or "a city of transients" deficient in creative culture,[9] this region was an unlikely site for punk to prosper as it has. However, that lingering misconception of the city's character is "a product of racism [that] reinforces the disenfranchisement of the city's predominantly African American population," according to the author and scholar Blair Ruble.[10] It also diminishes the wealth of culture coming from the DC area, "one of the most vibrant centers of African American culture in the country," as educator and writer Maurice Jackson noted.[11] The enormous

Figure 1.1 Kim Kane and Howard Wuelfing of the Slickee Boys, circa 1978. Photo by Don Hamerman, Don Hamerman collection of performing arts photographs, Special Collections in Performing Arts, University of Maryland Libraries. Used by permission.

contributions made by musicians like Duke Ellington, Marvin Gaye, Billy Taylor, Roberta Flack, Chuck Brown, and many others are undeniable. The same can be said for the visual art scene that took off in the latter half of the twentieth century on a wave of inventive artists—Gene Davis, Alma Thomas, Morris Louis, Anne Truitt, Sam Gilliam, Rockne Krebs, and Cool "Disco" Dan, to name a few.[12]

Despite that routine diminution of the majority of people living, working, and creating in the DC area, culture has long flourished there. Along with jazz, bluegrass, and go-go music, punk rock is one of DC's musical specialties. The hundreds, if not thousands,[13] of fanzines generated by DC area punk fans attest to the impact of the music the scene has produced—from the foundational bands of the 1970s, through the hardcore explosion of the early 1980s, the renaissance of Revolution Summer in 1985, the extraordinary popularity of Fugazi, the influential Riot Grrrl movement that exploded in the early 1990s, and on into the twenty-first century, still pulsing with purpose and innovation.

By early 1977, shortly after the earliest rumblings of the nascent DC punk scene, a local punk fanzine community started to take slow, but lasting, root with the publication of *It's Only a Movie* and *Vintage Violence*, the first two local zines to align themselves with the incipient punk movement. Like so much about punk, these early DC fanzines represented both a culmination *and* a beginning. Before we explore the history of DC punk fanzines, though, there is a spectrum of influences to consider.

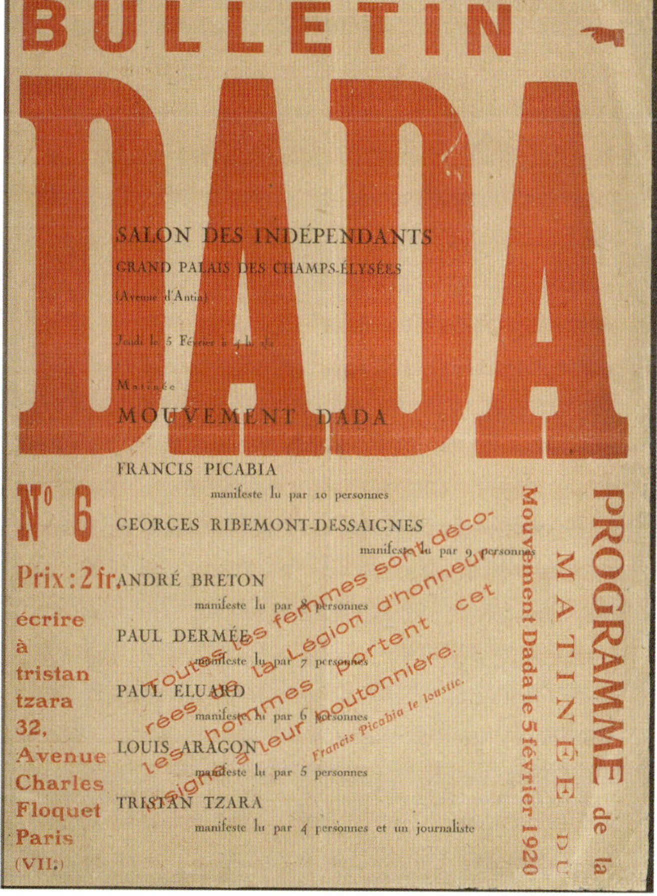

Figure 1.2 Raoul Hausmann's *Der Dada*, number 3 (Berlin, 1919) and Tristan Tzara's *Dada*, number 6 (Zurich, 1920). Courtesy of the National Gallery of Art Library, Gift of Thomas G. Klarner. Used by permission.

Dada, Situationists, and Punk

One can go back centuries to find examples of print materials used to circulate subversive art and ideas on a grassroots level, like chapbooks, little magazines, and broadsides. A reasonable starting point for understanding punk zines could be the anarchic publications coming out of Dada, the international art movement that thrived from the early 1910s into the 1920s. The pleasingly dissonant blend of playfulness and darkness found in those titles reverberated through punk fanzines created decades later. Dada's "violation of traditional artistic categories—art and nonart, medium and its domain," as well as its embrace of the concept that "art might be assembled from the stuff of modern life itself" strongly informed the cut-and-paste, antielitist, *détournement*-loving punk graphics of the 1970s.[14] "Dada had a direct impact on the visual language of fanzines and specifically those produced during the punk period beginning in 1976," the writer and historian Teal Triggs observes: "Illustrations and advertisements were cut out of the newspapers and popular magazines of the time, and re-presented using collage techniques. The collage approach, which juxtaposed 'found' imagery with photographs and texts, reinforced the Dadaists' attack on the dominant culture of the time."[15]

The photomontage technique, mastered by German Dadaist Hannah Höch, was another central part of punk's aesthetic, likely influenced by the 1976 publication of art historian Dawn Adès' book *Photomontage*. Adès' work "[offered] punk agitators a crash course in the history and practice of radical image making," and its lessons are reflected in Linder Sterling's iconic graphics for the British punk band Buzzcocks.[16] Punks' use of collages and photomontages "generated an 'aesthetic of rebellion' matching the Dadaists' contempt for bourgeois sensibilities," Triggs noted.[17]

A line of clever disruption runs from Dada through the Lettrist International and Situationist International movements of the 1950s and 1960s and on to punk in the 1970s. The lettrists and the situationists, two French avant-garde art and political groups, spawned multiple serials, such as *Potlatch* from the former and both *Internationale Situationniste* and *The Situationist Times* from the latter. The groups' activities helped establish the technique of *détournement* as a tool to creatively subvert mainstream imagery, stripping it of its power and repurposing it to broadcast new meanings. Roughly translated to mean "hijacking," *détournement* is "what postmodernism would come to understand as a deliberate, politicized use of irony and pastiche," as arts scholar Amy J. Elias defined it: "It was a method of interpretation and reinterpretation: reordering pre-existing materials in order to expose their banality or their function within a system of spectacular control and creatively reconstructing them in the service of authenticity. . . . Instead of naturalizing existing reality, it denaturalized and parodied it to expose and counter alienation."[18]

Figure 1.3 Hannah Höch, *Cut with the Kitchen Knife Dada Through the Last Weimar Beer-Belly Cultural Epoch in Germany*, 1919. Used by permission.

Author and cultural theorist Sadie Plant noted that "these methods were essentially reworkings of those employed by the Dadaists and surrealists, extended by the situationists to every area of social and discursive life."[19] A significant portion of the punk aesthetic was built on this technique, particularly in the hands of British artist Jamie Reid. Developed during his time operating *Suburban Press*—a radical political magazine running from 1970 to 1975 that provided "a bridge between the hippie press and punk fanzines"—Reid's skills with *détournement* led to his creation of the "ransom note" lettering and iconoclastic visuals of the Sex Pistols, shocking mainstream Britain in 1977.[20] Artwork for the band's "God Save the Queen" single exemplified this aesthetic, depicting Queen Elizabeth II with her eyes and mouth crudely obscured by cut-and-paste artwork bearing ransom note lettering. This brickbat was emblematic of punk's broader aims. "Punk was also a *détournement* of the culture industry and an attack on the notions of originality, genius, and talent," Plant wrote. "Undermining the music industry's monopolistic overproduction of 'superstars,' punk generated the confidence that anyone could make music in the same way that Dada had insisted that everyone could be a poet or an artist."[21]

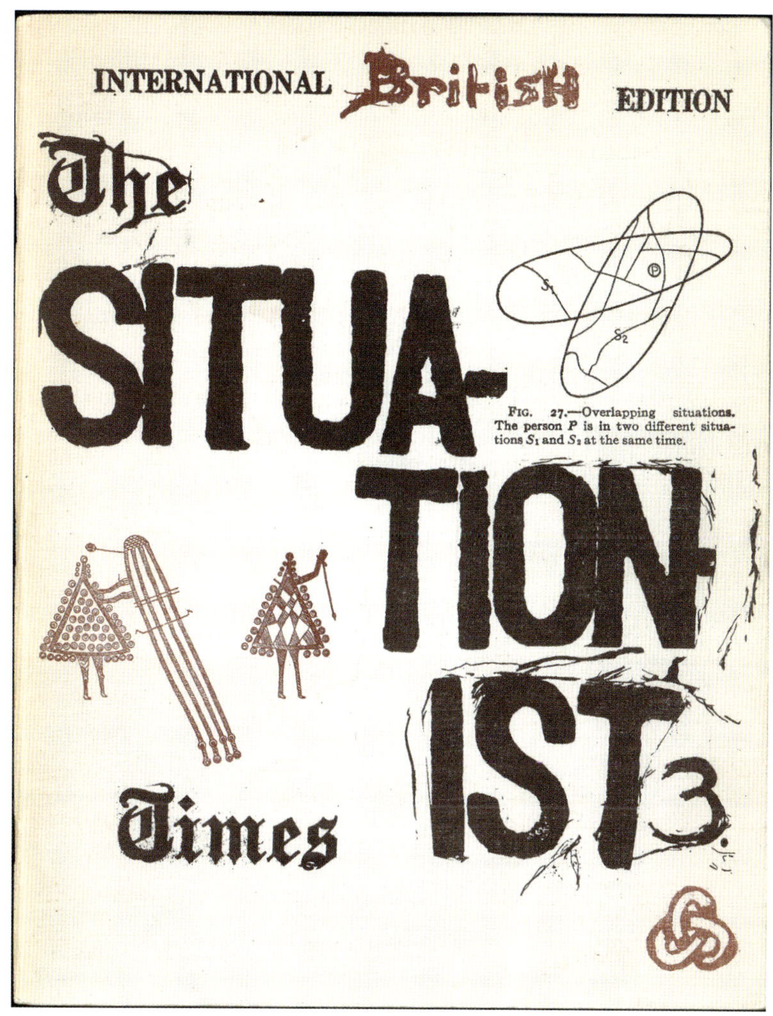

Figure 1.4 *The Situationist Times*, issue 3, 1963. Used by permission.

For all their much-discussed connection to the Situationists, however, the Sex Pistols' vocalist, John Lydon (known as Johnny Rotten when he was a member of the band), was dismissive of drawing much inspiration from it, later referring to the movement as "a ludicrous proposition":

> *It all reads nicely, but it's an intellectual entertainment, really. Look, if the Situationists achieved what they wanted, they would be very unhappy and they would have to be Situationists all over again. It's a never-ending process. So, I keep myself well out of that particular way of ruining your life. But you've got to see the fun in those ideas. You just learn what you can from them, and walk away laughing, because these people are hopeless idiots. It's just like that wonderful line in that Roxy Music song, "Really Good Time": "You're well-educated, . . . with no common sense."*[22]

Punk ultimately endured a significant degree of recuperation—the neutering of a radical idea by the establishment through appropriation and assimilation into the mainstream—particularly through the new wave music genre, a polished, punk-adjacent strain of rock that was easily integrated into the establishment of the late 1970s and early 1980s via bands like the Cars and the Police. The massive mainstream success in the early to mid-1990s of punk-rooted alternative rock bands like Nirvana and Green Day sanded the edges off punk further, even as it opened the gates to a multitude of new, young participants. "Just as Dada anti-art hangs in the galleries and surrealist dreams sell cars," Plant observed, "the Situationists joined every other failed critique and abandoned their weapons on the battlefield where their slogans were captured for T-shirts."[23]

The whimsically profound slogans the Situationists spray-painted onto walls around Paris—"be realistic: demand the impossible" or "never work!"—still bear a mysterious, amusing resonance, while *détournement* endures as a familiar, if clichéd, punk signifier on fliers, clothing, art, and fanzines. Reid even updated one of his more scandalous iterations of the Queen Elizabeth II *détournement*—in which swastikas were emblazoned over her eyes—in 2017 to feature the image of American president Donald Trump in place of the Queen.

Fanzines Before Punk

The "for fans, by fans" elements of fanzines are generally credited to have come from the science fiction and comic book fanzines generated by those flourishing fan communities, beginning in the first half of the twentieth century. Early fanzines like *The Comet* (the first amateur sci-fi fanzine, appearing in 1930[24]), *Fantasy News*, and *Comic Collectors' News* served as hubs where enthusiasts could interact, initially through correspondence, and later through fan conventions that became an established part of the subcultures.[25] The personal connections between fans generated by fanzines and conferences were a large part of fandom's appeal. Those mimeographed or hectographed publications helped forge the template for rock fanzines later in the twentieth century.[26]

By the mid-1960s, rock and roll was a primary form of popular music. Prominent coverage of it, however, was still generally in the hands of establishment critics who, when they found any words of praise for rock and roll, were wont to—as in one infamous instance—praise the Beatles using technical musical terms like "aeolian cadences,"[27] or dither over whether the group's harmonies were diatonic or pandiatonic.[28] These were gestures of respect from the establishment toward the Beatles, but were offered in terms impenetrable for most pop fans. That was the point, of course, as the usage of this technical jargon served as a code, conveying to older music fans (and nonfans, too) that at least *some* of this new music might be worthy of sharing a breath with Liszt or Stravinsky.

Musician and critic Mick Farren pointed out that not all rock coverage was as swaddled in establishment clothes—or any clothes, even:

> *Some of the very first writing about the "new" rock music appeared in girlie mags like Escapade (who had actually published Jack Kerouac in 1959) and Cavalier, who ran one of the very first non-specialist magazine pieces on Bob Dylan—referring to him as "The Charisma Kid." The T&A writers had no problem with their young and underpaid scribes writing about rock & roll. It gave them fast copy to fill the spaces between the nudie spreads.*[29]

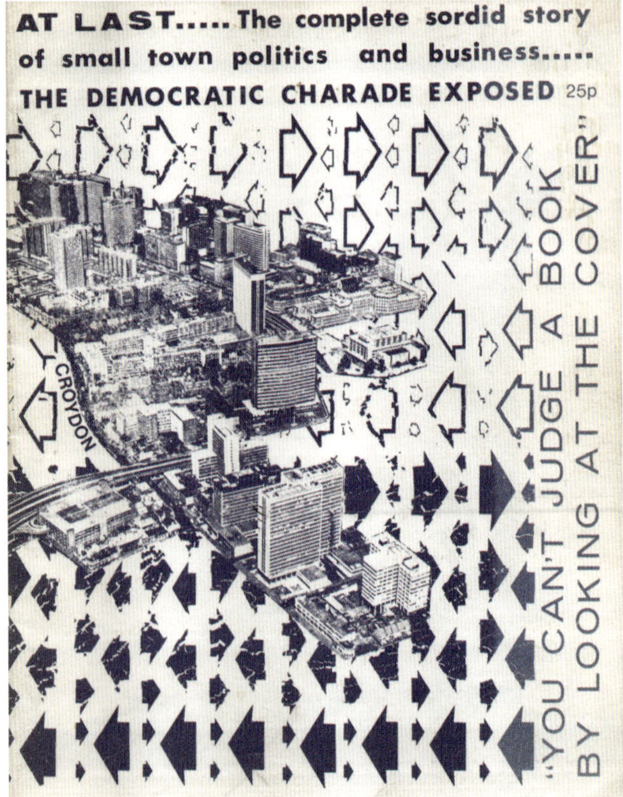

Figure 1.5 *Suburban Press*, issue 6, 1974. Used by permission.

Farren also credited Ralph Gleason and Jim Delehant, two somewhat unlikely sources, as journalists who helped legitimize rock and roll writing. By the 1960s, Gleason was an established jazz and popular music critic for the *San Francisco Chronicle* who evinced a respect for rock that was generally absent among his fellow critics. This ultimately led him to mentor Jann Wenner, a young journalist with whom he cofounded *Rolling Stone*, a magazine that swiftly became an authoritative, if myopic, voice in rock criticism. Delehant, meanwhile, was a "radical writer" who assumed a lead editorial position at *Hit Parader*, previously an innocuous magazine focused on teenage culture. Delehant "instigated the revolutionary policy of treating rock & roll as if it mattered," Farren declared.

Seemingly inspired by both the dearth of high-quality rock and roll coverage and the few examples of when it *was* done with intelligence and conviction, a few rock and roll fans took it upon themselves to communicate about this music in their own words. Rather than seek approval from older arbiters of musical taste, they published rock fanzines,

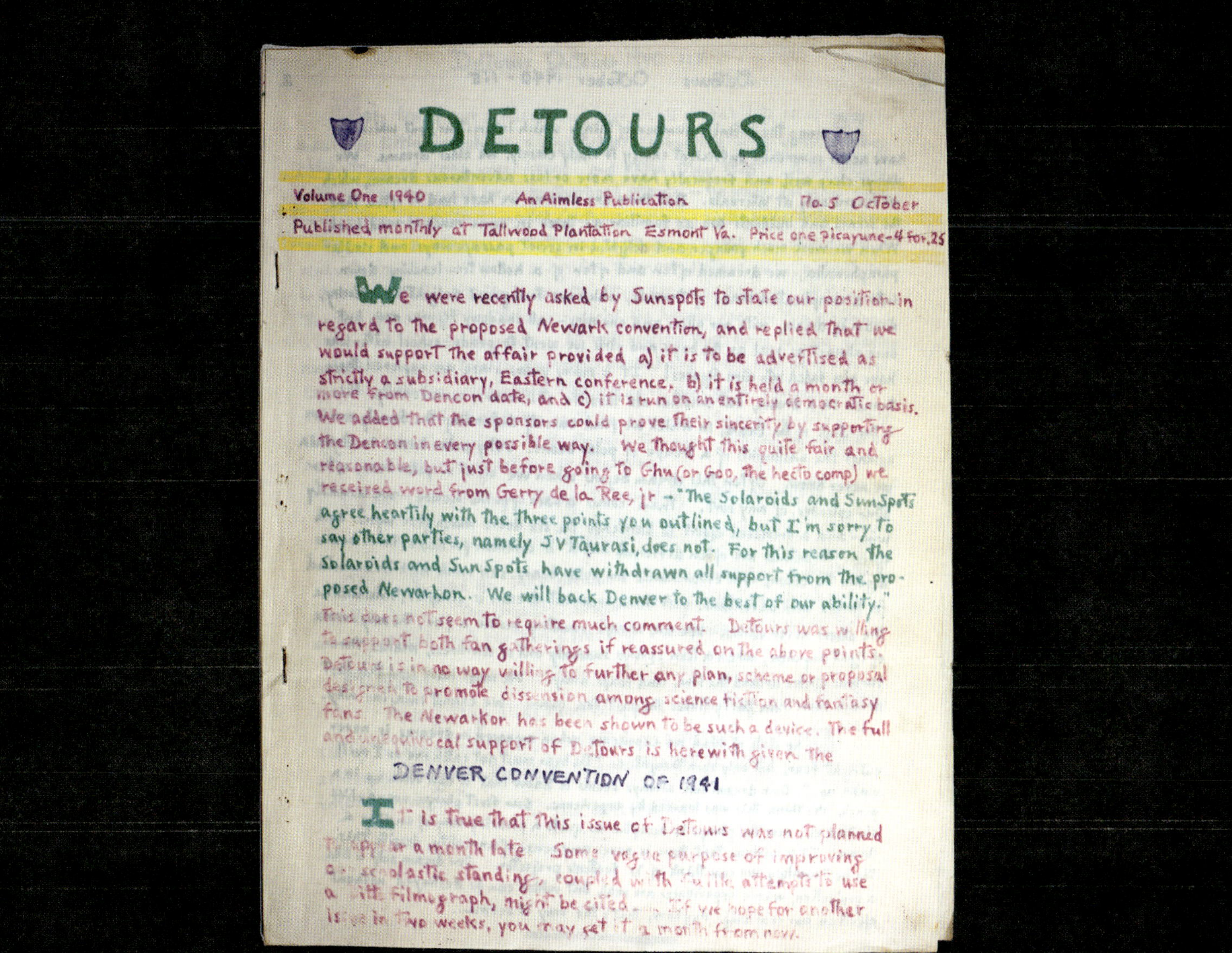
DETOURS

Volume One 1940 An Aimless Publication No. 5 October

Published monthly at Tallwood Plantation Esmont Va. Price one picayune—4 for .25

We were recently asked by Sunspots to state our position in regard to the proposed Newark convention, and replied that we would support the affair provided a) it is to be advertised as strictly a subsidiary, Eastern conference. b) it is held a month or more from Dencon date, and c) it is run on an entirely democratic basis. We added that the sponsors could prove their sincerity by supporting the Dencon in every possible way. We thought this quite fair and reasonable, but just before going to Ghu (or Goo, the hecto comp) we received word from Gerry de la Ree, jr — "The Solaroids and SunSpots agree heartily with the three points you outlined, but I'm sorry to say other parties, namely J V Taurasi, does not. For this reason the Solaroids and SunSpots have withdrawn all support from the proposed Newarkon. We will back Denver to the best of our ability." This does not seem to require much comment. Detours was willing to support both fan gatherings if reassured on the above points. Detours is in no way willing to further any plan, scheme or proposal designed to promote dissension among science fiction and fantasy fans. The Newarkon has been shown to be such a device. The full and unequivocal support of Detours is herewith given the

DENVER CONVENTION OF 1941

It is true that this issue of Detours was not planned to appear a month late. Some vague purpose of improving our scholastic standing, coupled with futile attempts to use a little filmograph, might be cited.... If we hope for another issue in two weeks, you may get it a month from now.

Figure 1.7 Top left: *Mojo Navigator*, issue 9, October 17, 1966. Top right: Greg Shaw at the mimeograph machine, circa 1966. Bottom left: *Who Put the Bomp!*, summer 1974. Bottom right: *Bomp!*, March 1978. Used by permission.

as elegant in their simplicity as they were crude in technique. *Crawdaddy!* and *Mojo Navigator*—both launched by sci-fi fanzine creators and published out of San Francisco—are two oft-cited founding rock fanzines.

Paul Williams' *Crawdaddy!* is considered the first rock fanzine, although it soon developed into a more "professional" magazine. "The fact that Williams explicitly stated that the entire contents were copyrighted underlined [his] aim for mainstream recognition," Triggs argued.[30] *Mojo Navigator*, created by Greg Shaw and David Harris, was minimal in its presentation—early issues typically consisted of typewritten text and a few subtle psychedelic doodles to illuminate the manuscript—and focused intently on San Francisco's burgeoning rock scene. *Mojo Navigator*'s fourteen-issue run only lasted from 1966 to 1967, but its impact was significant, considering what Shaw went on to accomplish.

After the publication of Shaw's short-lived zine *Mojo Entmooter*—a nod to his earlier creations, *Mojo Navigator* and *Entmoot*, the latter a fanzine dedicated to fantasy author J. R. R. Tolkien—the rock fanatic debuted a new fanzine in 1970. Dismayed by the increasingly leaden state of rock music, Shaw created a zine celebrating rock and roll's rambunctious early days. *Who Put the Bomp* was devoted to the first decade or so of the genre, extolling the virtues of the British Invasion, surf music, rockabilly, and pioneers like Elvis Presley, Little Richard, and Buddy Holly. In the pages of *Who Put the Bomp*, Shaw would proclaim a new spin on an old motto—"rock is a way of life"—while including contributions from a slew of names who became synonymous with the new wave of rock criticism in the 1970s: Greil Marcus, Lester Bangs, Richard Meltzer, Alan Betrock, and others.

Shaw distributed the first issue of *Who Put the Bomp* through an amateur press association—also known as an APA—that he participated in. APAs generally consisted of a group of people agreeing to each create a fanzine and have a central editor distribute them among the group, with members subsequently sharing feedback with each other.[31] Shaw stated that *Who Put the Bomp* was "designed as an alternative to the mainstream music press,"[32] and the zine (its title shortened to *Bomp!* by later issues) grew through the 1970s, even spawning a record label.

That label—Bomp! Records—issued recordings from Flamin' Groovies, Iggy Pop, 20/20, the Last, and other notable punk and power pop bands. Bomp! helped seed the ground for the mid-decade punk explosion, as well as the power pop boom that followed in the late 1970s and early 1980s, led by the Knack and their epochal pop hit "My Sharona." *Who Put the Bomp* was joined in the first half of 1970s by other new rock fanzines, including *Denim Delinquent*, *Bam Balam*, *Flash*, and *Back Door Man*. They offered substantial coverage of protopunk bands—the Velvet Underground, the Stooges, New York Dolls, and MC5, among others—while casting an approving eye back on the garage rock of the 1960s, mapping out the music that eventually become canonical.

Underground Newspapers of the 1960s and 1970s

Rock fanzines of the late 1960s, like *Mojo Navigator*, were part of a network of underground publications, led by independent newspapers, eschewing the spoonful of sugar that had helped the Beatles' subversion go down easier earlier that decade. American publications like the *Los Angeles Free Press* (founded in 1964), the *East Village Other* (1965), and the *Berkeley Barb* (1965) or British titles like *International Times* (1966) flaunted their antiauthoritarian attitudes, exploring radical politics, sex, and drugs with a voice employing liberal use of profanity and sexual images. These elements combined to create a reading experience continuing the "[timeless] attitude of épater *le bourgeois*,"[33] which suffused the avant-garde from the French Decadent poets through Stravinsky's *Le Sacre du printemps*, Dada, the Futurists, the Surrealists, the Beats, the situationists, and others whose proud alterity reshaped art and society.

G. L. van Roosbroeck, in his 1927 history *The Legend of the Decadents*, explained an important element of the avant-garde's essence, found later at the core of hippie and punk subcultures:

> *To be misunderstood was a glory. The "average man" only understands what resembles him, and to be applauded by him would have been only a*

sign of a similarity, distasteful to every spiritual aristocrat. The attitude of the so-called Decadent was then something else and something more than merely an attempt at "astonishing the bourgeois." It was an unequivocal way of affirming his aesthetic individualism, denied to him in the name either of science or of Democracy. It was a way of affirming his right to create an aristocratic art, the delectation of a minority, even when the majority did not approve of its existence.[34]

The underground press of the late 1960s reflected the tumultuous period it covered, with coverage of countercultural groups like the Yippies, Black Panthers, Weathermen, and the Diggers mingling with a mélange of comics, drug references, art, astrology, and, critically, intergroup communication. Specific numbers were hard to pinpoint but, by 1971, it was estimated that cumulative readership of underground newspapers was in the tens of millions.[35] Dada and the surrealists directly influenced the creatively disruptive approach employed by much of the underground press. Ben Morea, cofounder of Black Mask—a 1960s art group that later changed its name to Up Against the Wall Motherfucker[36]— spoke to that earlier artistic and philosophical influence on his group's eponymous publication: "Not only did we want to follow the direction of Surrealism and Dada, but we made it even more political. . . . We were also interested in Constructivism, and really interested in all the art movements of the modern twentieth century. We saw the layout as being an important tool, equal to the words."[37]

Figure 1.8 *Chicago Seed*, volume 4, number 13, with the illustration of a skull wearing a Statue of Liberty crown by Karl-Heinz Meschlach, March 1970.

Abe Peck of the *Chicago Seed* echoed the impact of those earlier art movements, but also cited Paul Krassner and his satirical magazine, *The Realist*, as a more immediate influence on the newspapers of the late 1960s. "Krassner, to me, was kind of the godfather of the underground press [because of] his attitude about Dadaism and [his] ability to laser into psychedelic mind-set issues of how to think about politics and about government," Peck declared.[38] Before starting *The Realist*, Krassner worked for *MAD Magazine*, the iconic humor periodical whose gonzo parodies of popular culture later led musician, poet, and protopunk trailblazer Patti Smith to remark "after *MAD*, drugs were nothing."[39] Krassner's response to his unofficial role as a "godfather of the underground press"—that he "[demanded] a blood test"[40]—drolly deflected credit, but his ambitions for *The Realist* were earnest. His goal was "to try to communicate without compromise," Krassner explained. "The mission statement was, in effect, a combination of entertainment and the First Amendment."[41]

That same mix of irreverent humor and urgent politics coursed through the underground press that followed in the late 1960s and early 1970s, but years of government harassment and financial challenges took their toll. Damage was done from within, too, as underground newspaper staffs often fractured under the strain of their collective organizational structures and from the pervasive sexism that stifled women's contributions.[42] Most underground papers stopped publication by the mid-1970s, with some participants scattering to the emerging network of alternative weekly newspapers and to publications with a focus on specific issues like women's and gay rights.[43] Despite the downbeat conclusion of the period, Morea testified to the importance of the short-lived era: "[The underground press] was essential then. It meant connecting the dots. What happened in the 1960s, I wouldn't say couldn't have happened without the underground press, but the underground press was a vital part of it, period."[44]

Underground Press and Rock Fanzines in DC

The civil rights movement in the United States and activism against the Vietnam War made DC a political nexus in the 1960s and early 1970s. Musically, the area buzzed, as well, with major touring acts passing through constantly and local rock bands like the Hangmen, the Cherry People, Claude Jones, Crank, the Fallen Angels, and several others gaining notice during this period. The urgency and purpose of that time manifested through numerous alternative publications from the DC area. These titles are typically not as heralded today in histories of the subject as peers from San Francisco, Los Angeles, or New York City are, but Washingtonians undeniably made consequential contributions, particularly within the network of underground newspapers.

The city's first underground tabloid newspaper, aptly titled *Underground,* debuted in 1966. According to the author and historian Dale Brumfield, however, "the only resemblance *Underground* shared with the more commonly known papers of the underground press was its name and membership in the Underground Press Syndicate."[45] Primarily interested in publishing a newspaper that ran articles expressing a variety of viewpoints, especially "information that is usually not believed by editors and most readers,"[46] *Underground* focused less on the issues related to sex and drugs commonly found in other underground papers and, instead, delved into politics and activism. As became typical for participants in the counterculture press, *Underground* publisher Tom DeBaggio, along with his staff and distributors, received harassment from authorities and

Figure 1.9 *Washington Free Press*, volume 2, number 42, October 15–31, 1968. Used by permission.

their enablers via disruption of distribution, arrests, and threats of violence.[47]

Later in 1967, DeBaggio tired of the opposition and ceased publishing *Underground*. Despite its brief run, *Underground* established DC as a home for the underground press, although it was the *Washington Free Press* that picked up *Underground*'s mantle and positioned itself as DC's definitive underground newspaper in the 1960s. Both papers were a part of the Underground Press Syndicate (UPS), a content-sharing alliance between underground papers facilitating "the free exchange of articles, news stories, and reviews among underground papers, [drawing] a broad range of New Left, counterculture, and youth-oriented papers into its fold," wrote historian John Campbell McMillian. Founded in 1966, the UPS boasted a combined readership of approximately 250,000 by the next year, not factoring in the likelihood that each issue was read by more than one person.[48]

Washington Free Press had also premiered in 1966 but closed shortly thereafter. It returned, however, in March 1967, and became "the bible of the DC counterculture scene," according to the *Washington Post*.[49] Richard Harrington's long career in DC journalism began by answering phones at the *Washington Free Press*, ultimately leading him to *Quicksilver Times*, *Unicorn Times*, and the pop critic position at the *Washington Post*. He and concert promoter Michael Schreibman also cofounded the arts publication *Woodwind* in 1972, a fleeting but influential link between the underground press of the late 1960s and DC's burgeoning music press in the mid to late 1970s. Harrington recalled the importance of the *Washington Free Press* to DC's late-1960s counterculture: "It was impossible to find papers like the *Berkeley Barb* or anything like that in DC. So, the *Washington Free Press*, when it arrived . . . that was impactful, because it was free and rebellious and, you know, it printed swear words, and it had pictures of naked people. And it was rebellious, at a time where rebelliousness was a definite 'plus' culturally."[50]

Figure 1.10 *Quicksilver Times*, volume 4, number 2. Special Collections in Performing Arts, University of Maryland Libraries. Used by permission.

As DC journalist John Kelly later explained, the *Washington Free Press*'s "young, progressive staff adhered to a few bedrock principles: for civil rights, against the war, for recreational drugs."[51] Its cofounder and editor, William Blum, later recalled a sign someone posted on the wall of the newspaper's office asserting that "Grammar Is Bourgeois," noting that he "was the only one who cared about the quality of the writing."[52] One can only hope the sign was posted with tongue in cheek and, indeed, the writing in the *Washington Free Press* was usually concise and informative, if rife with hippie jargon. Their writings were a primary way relevant information and analysis from outside the mainstream circulated through DC's counterculture.

Like many underground newspapers, the *Washington Free Press* was partially supported by advertising from major record labels. The September 1–14, 1968, issue features a Peter, Paul and Mary advertisement adjacent to one promoting the Joint Possession, a local head shop, while an article on curfew law—helpfully illustrated with photographs of police officers, a piglet, and a group of young people lounging near what appears to be DC's Dupont Circle Fountain—sits across the fold, urging readers to "stand up for the very laws that protect you." Major label support evaporated by early 1969, however, when government pressure convinced labels like Columbia Records to shift their advertising dollars elsewhere, rendering Columbia's "The Man Can't Bust Our Music" promotional campaign from December 1968 as dishonest as it was laughable.[53]

With funds dwindling, lawsuits percolating, and government pressure increasing, the *Washington Free Press* eventually met the same fate as other colleagues in the underground press. The final issue appeared in December 1969, although its circulation was at twenty-five thousand, a peak for the publication.[54] "We had all the different communists arguing among themselves: the Trotskyites, the

Leninites, the Stalinists," cofounder Art Grosman recalled of one internal argument, typical of the environment within the newsroom. "My only interest was just getting the word out about the counterculture that was going on."[55]

Quicksilver Times was another noteworthy underground newspaper in DC's counterculture, founded by former *Washington Free Press* contributors. First published in June 1969, *Quicksilver Times* was "much more radical than the *Free Press*," remembered Harrington.[56] Incredibly, one of its significant contributors and "most agitating voices,"[57] known as Sal Ferrera, was an undercover CIA operative. This was a "pervasive" tactic that led to "90 percent of all intelligence gathered on the New Left movement [being] the work of infiltrators and informants," wrote Brumfield.[58] In 1969, the FBI even anonymously distributed its own ersatz underground newspaper, the *Rational Observer*, on DC campuses. This clumsy attempt at sowing confusion proclaimed its mission was "not to stifle dissent but to expose charlatans of the right, left and middle, whether they be in government, industry, clergy, labor or the academic world." According to Brumfield, articles in the *Rational Observer* often "read more like 'Hints from Heloise' than expositions of the evils of the New Left." One news item implored readers to avoid drugs and, instead, "turn on to your rabbi, minister, priest, and yes, your parents, for help in solving your hang-ups."[59]

As bumbling as some of these interference efforts were, more potent obstacles emerged for underground press publications. "We can't seem to find a printer anywhere in Washington or in suburban Maryland or Virginia," *Quicksilver Times* cofounder Terry Becker complained in 1970. He noted how some print shop employees "thought the paper was obscene and subversive and definitely not American" and, therefore, refused to take part in the printing of the newspaper.[60] Several DC punk fanzines in the decades ahead ran into this barrier, too, before the accessibility of photocopiers diminished the gatekeeping powers of conservative printers later in the 1990s.

Ultimately, much of what stymied the success of the underground press in the United States was self-imposed. As McMillian noted, "In their organization and content, most underground newspapers mirrored the sexism and homophobia of the dominant culture."[61] This was one of the factors pushing participants in the burgeoning women's and gay liberation movements away from contributing to most underground newspapers. In DC, as it occurred throughout the country, some of those people created their own publications, focusing on issues mattering to their more specific communities. The first issue of *off our backs* was dated February 27, 1970, and immediately set to work covering the women's liberation movement with "a spirit of iconoclasm, looseness, and humor."[62] The title was chosen to "[reflect] our understanding of the dual nature of the women's movement," an editorial in the first issue explained:

> *Women need to be free of men's domination to find their real identities, redefine their lives, and fight for the creation of a society in which they can lead decent lives as human beings. At the same time, women must become aware that there would be no oppressor without the oppressed, that we carry the responsibility for withdrawing the consent to be oppressed. We must strive to get off our backs, and with the help of our sisters to oppose and destroy that system which fortifies the supremacy of men while exploiting the mass for the profit of the few.*[63]

off our backs endured for decades, publishing its final issue in 2008. Cofounder Marilyn S. Webb described *off our backs* as "a quintessential child of the 1960s—born of enthusiasm, a pinch of planning, and a lot of idealistic vision." It was "a very important publication," Harrington recalled. "I'd see stories that would shock me or surprise me or interest me."[64] Like the publications that emerged from punk and so many other subcultures, Webb explained that *off our backs* was inspired by the lack of representation of authentic issues that mattered to women in the mainstream media, stating that "we wanted our own newspaper for women with issues women were concerned about."[65]

Likewise, members of DC's gay community took action against the dearth of substantive coverage related to them in either the mainstream or the underground press. *The Gay Blade* debuted on October 5, 1969, later changing its name to the *Washington Blade* in 1980. As of 2025, the publication still informs and supports DC's gay community. Also, in 1971, a group of lesbian feminists that split from *off our backs*—due to feeling "pressured to suppress their lesbian politics"[66] while participating in the newspaper's production—created their own publication, *The Furies*. Running until May 1973, the newspaper and the eponymous collective behind it was "pivotal in presenting [a] lesbian presence to the women's movement and legitimizing lesbian feminism as a political issue," according to Brumfield.[67] DC's Black gay and lesbian communities were served by *Blacklight*, founded by Sidney Brinkley and published from 1979 through 1985. *Blacklight*'s circulation reached seven thousand copies, which were mostly distributed through libraries, bookstores, and bars.[68] Marion Barry, DC's mayor from 1979 to 1991 and, later, from 1995 to 1999, praised *Blacklight* in 1982 as "a publication that speaks to the vitality of the cultural, artistic, and political growth of this community."[69]

Unlike the active underground newspaper scene, rock fanzines created by DC-area residents were scarce leading up to punk. Two notable rock zines created by DC music participants did not last long as publications, but their creators each went on to make an impact. *Hype*, initially known as *Hyperion*, started as a "general interest publication" in the early 1970s when its creator, Mark Jenkins, was a high school student in Alexandria, Virginia.[70] "I don't remember exactly when the first issue came out," Jenkins explained, "but I was interested in the technologies that were available." Jenkins reproduced his zine's early issues—typically in runs under one hundred copies—using a ditto machine, also known as a spirit duplicator:

> *With the ditto machine, you inscribed or typed onto a master, and that came up in a color. The color that was most often used in schools was purple. And then you put it on and the alcohol took it off and transferred it to sheets of paper until there was no more ink left and you couldn't do any more. So, that limited the number of copies you could make. But what I discovered was there were other colors, and you could put different backings in when you were drawing or typing, and you could have a multicolor page.*[71]

Figure 1.11 *Hype*, fall–winter 1974 issue. Used by permission.

When Jenkins moved to Annapolis, Maryland—about 30 miles outside DC—to attend St. John's College, he found work at "what St. John's considered its weekly newspaper, although it wasn't a newspaper." Jenkins recalled: "There were no reporters; it was sort of a grab bag of things. And in a rather punk fashion, they printed everything that was submitted by a member of the community. So, what I learned there was mostly how to run the [offset printing] press and make plates and that sort of thing."[72]

Early issues of *Hype* included writings from Lester Bangs and Richard Meltzer, though Jenkins notes these were articles that had been "rejected other places or [that Bangs and Meltzer] thought were not good enough to publish in a real magazine." Still, the inclusion of writers like Bangs and Meltzer in his zine was meaningful to Jenkins, as "*Creem* was probably the bible at that point," referring to the irreverent rock magazine that frequently published both Bangs' and Meltzer's criticism. Jenkins met other notables through the production of *Hype*, particularly other young "fanzine kids" like musician Jon Tiven and future entrepreneur and founder of Lotus Software Mitch Kapor ("Probably the wealthiest person to come out of that scene," Jenkins wryly observed).[73] The switch from the "general interest publication" *Hyperion* to the music fanzine *Hype* occurred as the protopunk era was in full swing "and music was getting more interesting," Jenkins explained. "[Also,] as the publication became more widely known and distributed, most of the response was from other music-fanzine types and most of the writing I received was about music."[74]

Jenkins applied his knowledge of offset printing to the last three issues of *Hype*, with the final one coming in late 1974. Unlike previous issues that were offset printed onto regular paper, that concluding issue was on newsprint and featured the New York Dolls on the cover, along with writings on protopunk mainstays like the Stooges, Lou Reed, and Kim Fowley. "I distributed it in New York and Boston and sent it to people I knew who were in college various places around the country," Jenkins explained, "[but] it just turned out to be too complicated, too expensive, to ever do again." Jenkins subsequently worked and wrote for a variety of DC area newspapers in the 1970s and early 1980s, like *Newsworks*, the *Washington Tribune*, *Chronicle of Higher Education*, and *Unicorn Times*. The period from 1979 to 1981 saw him back in the world of fanzines, contributing writing and production work to the DC punk zines *Descenes* and *Discords*. Later in the 1980s, Jenkins established himself as one of DC's most prolific and insightful critics, finding frequent bylines in the *Washington Post* and *Washington City Paper* up to the present, offering his thoughtful, direct analysis of music and art.

Groffiti, another DC area rock fanzine, was first published by Skip Groff in 1973. Groff started out as a disc jockey in the late 1960s before becoming a record promoter for RCA Records. He also worked with the pioneering doom metal band Pentagram at the start of their career, producing and

Figure1.12 Left: *Groffiti*, issue 10, 1974. Right: Skip Groff in Slickee Boys T-shirt, circa 1979, photographer unknown.

releasing their first two singles on his one-off labels, Boffo Socko and Gemini, in 1973 and 1974. *Groffiti* was printed on government legal-sized paper (slightly smaller than standard legal-sized paper at 8.5 inches by 13 inches), folded, and bound. Groff initially envisioned *Groffiti* as a tip sheet modeled on the DC area record producer and promoter Bobby Poe's *Pop Music Survey*, rounding up music news from a perspective more focused on the music business than fandom. "It became a fanzine later on, because the tip sheet thing was going to be based on having record companies buy advertising, and that didn't pan out," Groff said. "And by the time I started doing the first couple of issues that were basically a fanzine type thing, a guy named Geof O'Keefe from Pentagram, who was the drummer of the group . . . was helping me out with writing a lot of articles. And he and I were into very similar things in terms of the British groups of the 1960s. We were both Roy Wood and the Move fans."[75]

Loaded with articles and discographies related to 1960s rock bands, with the occasional nod to then-contemporary music like Suzi Quatro, *Groffiti* reads like a stripped-down version of *Who Put the Bomp*. "The early issues [of *Groffiti*] were similar in scope and nature [to] what they were trying to do," Groff agreed of the comparison. "They became much more of a full magazine later on in the years." After opening Hit and Run Records with business partner Al Ercolani in Kensington, Maryland, on June 25, 1977, Groff debuted a new fanzine the next month that maintained *Groffiti*'s look and feel. *Hit and Run* compiled music news and reviews alongside a lengthy list of albums for sale from the new store. Aside from including one of the first Slickee Boys interviews to see print, *Hit and Run* was also notable for featuring writings from Howard Wuelfing and Mike "Livewire" Heath, two of the earliest DC punk fanzine creators.

Groff split from Hit and Run Records that September, however, opening Yesterday & Today Records a few minutes up the road in Rockville. The new store quickly became a locus for DC's punk scene. "It was definitely one of those record stores that people came [to] from afar,"[76] recalled the influential DC musician Ian MacKaye, whose work in the bands Minor Threat, Embrace, and Fugazi, among others, helped shape punk rock globally from 1980 on.

Groff established another record label, Limp Records, in 1978, and this one lasted longer than previous efforts. Limp documented DC punk's first-wave heights in the late 1970s and early 1980s, releasing music from the Slickee Boys, Razz, the Shirkers, DCeats, and others. Limp's 1978 compilation *:30 Over DC~~Here Comes the New Wave!* captured the charmingly inchoate nature of DC punk and new wave that year, as the bands featured (Half Japanese, the Slickee Boys, the Penetrators, Nurses, White Boy, Tina Peel, Chumps, and more) vary wildly in intensity, charisma, tone, and vision.

Consequentially, Groff used his music business expertise to mentor a group of young punks who shopped at Yesterday & Today, including MacKaye, helping them set up a record label in 1980. Dischord Records quickly became DC punk's flagship label, as it remains into the twenty-first century. Yesterday & Today customer, author, and musician Henry Rollins testified: "You can't tell the story of Dischord and not mention Skip. You can't. He's inextricably woven into this great American independent label narrative. Because you can't tell the story about independent music without talking about Dischord and Ian and Minor Threat and Fugazi . . . and Rites of Spring . . . and ad infinitum. Skip is in that. Like he's *in* it. He's in the infrastructure."[77]

1976: Punk Fanzines Arrive

As decades of influences coalesced into punk rock by the mid-1970s, fanzines separated by thousands of miles were there to cover it. January 1976 saw the debut of *Punk*, a zine from New York City that helped cement the pairing of the word "punk" with the new music scene taking shape behind the likes of the Ramones, Talking Heads, and Television, whose names all appeared in that first issue. The "punk rock" tag percolated throughout the early 1970s, spotted in publications like *Creem*, as well as the establishment newspaper the *New York Times*. Its lack of definition, however, allowed *Punk*'s creators John Holmstrom, Ged Dunn, and Legs McNeil to shape it how they saw fit. "We may not have invented the word punk, but we put it on the map . . . by describing the music and the scene in words and pictures with an authentic feel," Holmstrom wrote later.[78]

Punk was heavily influenced by comix, the underground expansion of what was permissible in the comic format. Notable artists like Robert Crumb, Trina Robbins, Barbara Mendes and Art Spiegelman all published comix, an art-form that made "comic books an adult commodity," author and academic Charles Hatfield wrote:

> *The singular genius of the underground comic books was the way they transformed an object that was jejune and mechanical in origin into a radically new kind of expressive object, a vehicle for the most personal and unguarded of revelations . . . convey[ing] an unprecedented sense of intimacy, rivaling the scandalizing disclosures of confessional poetry but shot through with fantasy, burlesque, and self-satire.*[79]

Comix artist Bill Griffith was a particular influence on Holmstrom. Spiegelman and Griffith visited a class Holmstrom enrolled in on "comics, cartoons, and humor" at the School of Visual Arts in New York City. Holmstrom recalled that the "visit really stuck with me afterward" and he subsequently corresponded with Griffith. "The artistic freedom that self-publishing offered was something that intrigued me," Holmstrom remembered, "and his letters encouraged me to publish my own work."[80]

The impiety and iconoclasm of comix made an impression on many punk musicians and artists. "Comix and rock n' roll are the highest art forms," Patti Smith declared in *Punk*'s second issue, in March 1976. Holmstrom's comix-inspired artwork is found throughout *Punk* and was central to the zine's aesthetic. *Punk* also employed the use of photo comics—known as fumetti—to great effect. Imminent punk idols like Joey Ramone, Debbie Harry, and Richard Hell were photographed—often by Roberta Bayley, who shot the Ramones' iconic debut album cover—acting out pulpy storylines then laid out like comic book frames, projecting the comics aesthetic directly onto the New York City punks. The accomplished graphic designer Milton Glaser, perhaps best known for creating the "I ❤ NY" logo, reportedly once picked up a copy of *Punk* and, "visibly shaken"—presumably by the zine's skill and imagination—sat down and said, "these guys could put me out of business."[81]

New York Rocker, another formative punk publication, premiered shortly after *Punk* in February 1976. Initial issues featured early coverage of New York punk bands like the Ramones, Television, and Suicide, as well as other emerging American bands like the Nerves, a power pop trio from California featuring three gifted songwriters—Jack Lee, Peter Case, and Paul Collins. Published by the one-time *Who Put the Bomp* contributor Alan Betrock,[82] *New York Rocker*'s larger format and cleaner layouts had a marked influence on the music fanzine and arts newspaper hybrids proliferating in the late 1970s and 1980s. In DC alone, titles from that period like *Descenes*, *The Infiltrator*, and *Discords* were all clearly indebted to *New York Rocker*'s visual and editorial approach, while still effectively establishing their own voices.

Aside from the debuts of *Punk* and *New York Rocker*, another profoundly influential fanzine emerged in 1976.

Figure 1.13 *Punk*, issue 1, January 1976, art by John Holmstrom. Beinecke Rare Book and Manuscript Library, Yale University. Used by permission.

Created by a young British bank clerk named Mark Perry, *Sniffin' Glue* appeared that July and was "a genius piece of DIY and one of the ultimate punk statements," according to author and journalist John Robb.[83] As the "first punk fanzine to represent the punk movement visually in Britain,"[84] *Sniffin' Glue* had an immediate impact, with "literally hundreds of titles [emerging] from towns, cities and suburbs across the UK from 1976–77 [that] followed the *Sniffin' Glue* template: fervid text with cut 'n' paste imagery that was Roneo-stenciled,[85] or Xeroxed to be sold for minimal cost at gigs, school, college, or in local record shops."[86]

Perry was inspired by the Ramones—the zine's title derived from the band's song "Now I Wanna Sniff Some Glue"—and the Sex Pistols, but especially so by the lack of accessible punk magazines. "I was always asking [the record shop] if they'd got any magazines about punk and the Ramones," he remembered. "They would say, 'no, we haven't,' and as a joke the guy from there said, 'Why don't you just go and start your own one?' So, I said, 'Yeah, I will.' So, I went home that night and tapped it out."[87]

Initial print runs of *Sniffin' Glue* started at 50 copies but, by the fanzine's final issue, circulation peaked at 20,000. "To do a fanzine you didn't even need a typewriter," Perry explained. "Shane MacGowan did a fanzine inspired by *Sniffin' Glue*.[88] He called it *Bondage* and he used to have a go at us 'cause we used a typewriter! He just scrawled it in a pen. That was more punk than us."[89]

Just as punk fanzines proliferated rapidly around the world in the late 1970s after the debut of pioneers like *Punk*, *New York Rocker*, and *Sniffin' Glue*, the nascent punk subculture in DC prompted its own burst of fanzines beginning in late 1976 and into 1977, starting with *It's Only a Movie* and *Vintage Violence*. Building from the inspirations of the previous half-century, knowingly or not, a handful of young punk rock fanatics in the DC area put their passions onto the page, continuing one tradition while starting another that ran into the next century.

Notes

1. Dave Laing, *One Chord Wonders: Power and Meaning in Punk Rock* (Milton Keynes, UK: Open University Press, 1985), 146.
2. Larry Rohter, "Punk: Rock Music in the Second Generation—What's the Nastiest Four-Letter Word in Pop Today?" *Washington Post*, May 1, 1977.
3. Kathrin Fahlenbrach, Erling Sivertsen, and Rolf Werenskjold. *Media and Revolt: Strategies and Performances from the 1960s to the Present* (New York: Berghahn, 2014), 366.
4. Pete Dale, *Anyone Can Do It: Empowerment, Tradition and the Punk Underground* (Farnham, UK: Ashgate, 2012), 69.
5. Teal Triggs, *Fanzines: The DIY Revolution* (San Francisco: Chronicle Books, 2010), 10.
6. Stephen Duncombe, *Notes from Underground: Zines and the Politics of Alternative Culture* (London: Verso, 1997), 44.
7. Robert Coulson, "Fandom as a Way of Life," in *Science Fiction Fandom*, edited by Joseph L. Sanders, Contributions to the Study of Science Fiction and Fantasy 62 (Westport, CT: Greenwood Press, 1994), 11–13.
8. Fredric Wertham, *The World of Fanzines: A Special Form of Communication* (Carbondale: Southern Illinois University Press, 1973), 130.
9. Francine Cary, *Washington Odyssey: A Multicultural History of the Nation's Capital* (Washington, DC: Smithsonian Books, 2003), xiii.
10. Blair A. Ruble, *Washington's U Street: A Biography* (Washington, DC: Woodrow Wilson Center Press, 2012), xvii.
11. Maurice Jackson and Blair A. Ruble, *DC Jazz: Stories of Jazz Music in Washington, DC* (Washington, DC: Georgetown University Press, 2018), 1.
12. John Anderson and American University Museum, *Making a Scene: The Jefferson Place Gallery—September 5–October 22, 2017, American University Museum at the Katzen Arts Center, Washington, DC*, edited by Lee Flemming (Washington, DC: Alper Initiative for Washington Art, American University Museum, 2017).
13. With the number of fanzines lost to the dustbin of time, a precise count is impossible.
14. Leah Dickerman, Brigid Doherty, Centre Georges Pompidou, National Gallery of Art (DC), and Museum of Modern Art (New York), *Dada: Zurich, Berlin, Hannover, Cologne, New York, Paris* (Washington and New York: National Gallery of Art in Association with DAP / Distributed Art Publishers, 2005), 8.
15. Triggs, *Fanzines*, 5.
16. Rick Poynor, "Graphic Anarchy in the UK," in *Oh So Pretty: Punk in Print 1976–80* (London: Phaidon Press, 2016), 21.
17. Triggs, *Fanzines*.
18. Amy J. Elias, "Psychogeography, Détournement, Cyberspace," *New Literary History* 41, no. 4 (2010): 825.
19. Sadie Plant, *The Most Radical Gesture: The Situationist International in a Postmodern Age* (London: Routledge, 1992), 145.
20. Triggs, *Fanzines*, 49.
21. Plant, *Most Radical Gesture*.
22. David Gavan, "Thinking Outside the Box: PiL's John Lydon Interviewed," *The Quietus*, March 4, 2010, https://thequietus.com/articles/03833-reformed-john-lydon-johnny-rotten-of-public-image-limited-pil-and-sex-pistols-interview.
23. Plant, *Most Radical Gesture*, 146.
24. Triggs, *Fanzines*, 17.
25. Matthew Pustz, *Comic Book Culture: Fanboys and True Believers* (Jackson: University Press of Mississippi, 1999), 30.
26. Mimeographing and hectographing were printing processes often utilized to print small-run publications in the time before photocopiers, although both processes still have niche uses.
27. Ian MacDonald, *Revolution in the Head: The Beatles' Records and the Sixties*, 3rd ed. (Chicago: Chicago Review Press, 2007), 98.
28. Francis Kenny, *The Making of John Lennon* (Bloomington, IN: Red Lightning Books, 2018), 119.

29. Suzy Shaw, Mick Farren, and Greg Shaw, *Bomp! Saving the World One Record at a Time* (Los Angeles: Ammo, 2007), 18.
30. Triggs, *Fanzines*.
31. Bernadette Bosky, "Amateur Press Associations: Intellectual Society and Social Intellectualism," in *Science Fiction Fandom*, edited by Joseph L. Sanders, Contributions to the Study of Science Fiction and Fantasy 62 (Westport, CT: Greenwood Press, 1994), 181.
32. Shaw Farren, and Shaw, *Bomp!*, 93.
33. Dave Laing, "Listening to Punk," in *The Subcultures Reader*, editeed by Ken Gelder and Sarah Thornton (London: Routledge, 1997), 455–56.
34. G. Leopold Van Roosbroeck, *The Legend of the Decadents* (New York: Institut des Études Françaises at Columbia University, 1927), 3.
35. Bob Ostertag, "The Underground Press: A History," in *Power to the People: The Graphic Design of the Radical Press and the Rise of the Counter-Culture, 1964–1974*, edited by Geoff Kaplan (Chicago: University of Chicago Press, 2013), 169.
36. The group's name was inspired by a line from Amiri Baraka's poem "Black People."
37. Sean Stewart, *On the Ground: An Illustrated Anecdotal History of the Sixties Underground Press in the US* (Oakland: PM Press, 2011), 16.
38. Stewart, 28.
39. Maud Lavin, "Neuman's Own," *New York Times*, September 14, 2003.
40. Harrison Smith, "Paul Krassner, Countercultural Ringmaster and Leader of the Yippies, Dies at 87," *Washington Post*, July 22, 2019.
41. Stewart, *On the Ground*, 9.
42. John Campbell McMillian, *Smoking Typewriters: The Sixties Underground Press and the Rise of Alternative Media in America* (New York: Oxford University Press, 2011), 174–75.
43. Ostertag, "Underground Press," 190.
44. Stewart, *On the Ground*, 186.
45. Dale M. Brumfield, *Independent Press in DC and Virginia: An Underground History* (Charleston, SC: History Press, 2015), 18.
46. Brumfield.
47. Brumfield, 22.
48. McMillian, *Smoking Typewriters*, 73.
49. Washingtonpost.com, "Counterculture Wars: Remembering One of the District's First Alternative Papers," November 1, 2016; "Gale in Context: Opposing Viewpoints," https://link.gale.com/apps/doc/A468594968/OVIC?u=umd_um&sid=OVIC&xid=85bf2d58.
50. Richard Harrington, interview by the author, September 10, 2019.
51. Washingtonpost.com, "Counterculture Wars."
52. Brumfield, *Independent Press*, 27.
53. Peter Doggett, *There's a Riot Going On: Revolutionaries, Rock Stars, and the Rise and Fall of the 60s* (Edinburgh: Canongate, 2007), 220.
54. Brumfield, *Independent Press*, 45.
55. Washingtonpost.com, "Counterculture Wars."
56. Harrington, interview.
57. Harrington.
58. Brumfield, *Independent Press*, 45.
59. Brumfield, 98.
60. F.X. Boyle, "The Gang-Bang on the Underground Press," *Avant Garde*, May 1970, 46–47.
61. McMillian, *Smoking Typewriters*, 11.
62. Carol Anne Douglas and Fran Moira. "*off our backs*: the First Four Decades," in *Insider Histories of the Vietnam Era Underground Press*, edited by Ken Wachsberger (East Lansing: Michigan State University Press, 2011), 157.
63. Douglas and Moira, 157–58.
64. Harrington, interview.
65. Marilyn S. Webb, "*oob* and the Feminist Dream," in *Insider Histories of the Vietnam Era Underground Press*, edited by Ken Wachsberger (East Lansing: Michigan State University Press, 2011), 185.
66. Douglas and Moira, "*off our backs*," 162.
67. Brumfield, *Independent Press*, 83.
68. "Blacklight: DC Public Library, People's Archive," no date, https://thepeoplesarchive.dclibrary.org/repositories/2/digital_objects/1323.
69. Marion Barry, letter to editor, *Blacklight*, 4, no. 1, October 1982.
70. Mark Jenkins, email to the author, February 8, 2020.
71. Mark Jenkins, interview with the author, April 27, 2018.
72. Jenkins.
73. Tiven was a member of the Big Star satellite band Prix, among other elements of his long career.
74. Jenkins, email.
75. Skip Groff, interview with the author, September 19, 2017.
76. Ian MacKaye and Skip Groff, interview with the author, December 13, 2018.
77. Henry Rollins, interview with the author, January 3, 2019.
78. John Holmstrom and Bridget Hurd, *Punk: The Best of Punk Magazine* (New York: !t, 2012), 1.
79. Charles Hatfield, *Alternative Comics: An Emerging Literature* (Jackson: University Press of Mississippi, 2005), 7.
80. Holmstrom and Hurd, *Punk*, 3.
81. Mark Jacobson. *Teenage Hipster in the Modern World: From the Birth of Punk to the Land of Bush—Thirty Years of Millennial Journalism* (New York: Grove Press, 2005), 17.
82. Betrock also launched a fanzine in 1971 called *JAMZ*, which was another key prepunk title.
83. John Robb, *Punk Rock: An Oral History*, edited by Oliver Craske (Oakland: PM, 2012), 203.
84. Teal Triggs, "Scissors and Glue: Punk Fanzines and the Creation of a DIY Aesthetic," *Journal of Design History* 19, no. 1 (2006): 69–83, www.jstor.org/stable/3838674.
85. Roneo duplicating machines were a low-cost way to make copies in the 1970s.
86. Subcultures Network, *Ripped, Torn and Cut: Pop, Politics and Punk Fanzines from 1976* (Manchester: Manchester University Press, 2018).
87. Robb, *Punk Rock*, 204.
88. Shane MacGowan later achieved international fame as the vocalist for the Pogues.
89. Robb, *Punk Rock*, 206.

Wake Up, Washington! 1976–1979

PUNK FANZINES BEGAN PUBLISHING in the DC area by the end of 1976, but a few local alternative newspapers were a beat ahead of them. The short-lived *Washington Newsworks* ran a small item on the Slickee Boys earlier that year,[1] as did *Unicorn Times*, a monthly music newspaper founded in 1973 by Elliot Ryan. Richard Harrington joined *Unicorn Times* as editor by 1976 and the paper soon established itself as a central source for DC music coverage. "[Ryan] was a schemer, and he wasn't sure what the scheme was," Harrington recalled of *Unicorn Times*' early years. "But then I came in and, pretty much right away, I started adding some depth to it because of the writers. It took a while for the design to catch up with the writing but, again, it was all about the writers."[2]

Among those journalists was Myron Bretholz, who wrote an ecstatic concert review of the band Overkill in the July 1976 issue of *Unicorn Times*. Overkill, later described by *Descenes* and *Discords* fanzine editor Howard Wuelfing as "DC's first modern 'punk' act," was formed in November 1975.[3] As rock magazine *Trouser Press* observed in a 1979 report on DC's growing punk and new wave scene, Overkill appeared "virtually out of nowhere, taking the city by surprise, if not by storm."[4] Bretholz's review documented an Overkill performance at the Keg, a nightclub in DC's Glover Park neighborhood, just north of Georgetown. A recording of that concert survives and, while much of the music plays to modern ears like a clever rock group with slightly serrated edges, a punky cover of the Velvet Underground's "Rock & Roll" stands out. Overkill's vocalist, Barney Jones, playfully altered Lou Reed's lyrics, replacing "she started dancing to that fine, fine music" with "she started dancing to that punk rock music"—among the more obvious clues that Overkill was not the Keg's typical booking. When hecklers mocked the band's Roxy Music and Music Machine covers, demanding to hear something by Alice Cooper instead, Jones dispatched them with a terse "get a haircut." Bretholz's review was unequivocal: "Overkill is doing punk-rock. . . . In a city where a Dan Fogelberg show would probably sell out a month in advance, punk-rock, my friends, is radical."[5,6]

The Slickee Boys, too, appeared in *Unicorn Times* throughout 1976, primarily via advertisements they placed, one of which referred to the group as DC's "No. 1 Punk Beat Rockers." Their self-released debut EP, *Hot and Cool*, appeared in summer 1976, but it only somewhat sounds "punk" when compared with the genre. Similar elements to those at the heart of the Ramones—garage rock, surf, bubblegum pop, and a mordant sense of humor—are present, but if the Ramones were an unrelenting laser beam, the Slickee Boys were a kitschy neon sign flickering in a bar window, beckoning you inside.

The Slickee Boys lacked the monomaniacally propulsive, four-on-the-floor approach the Ramones used to help forge punk's identifiable sound. The absence is glaring when

Figure 2.1 Left: Richard Harrington, circa 1978. Right: Urban Verbs on the cover of *Unicorn Times*, March 1979. Photos by Don Hamerman. Used by permission.

holding up *Hot and Cool* as a punk record, yet the band's defiant attitude, bold visual aesthetic, and ragged musical technique affirm its place as DC's first punk release. Vocalist Martha Hull's performance on "What a Boy Can't Do" (a cover of "What a Girl Can't Do" by the 1960s DC garage pioneers the Hangmen) exuded swagger and charisma, while guitarist Kim Kane's cover artwork mixed a pop art palette with influences from time he spent in South Korea as a youth.

That period abroad bore a strong influence on Kane's creative output, inspiring him to name the Slickee Boys after a term used by American soldiers in reference to local spivs they purchased contraband from.[7] Kane incorporated Japanese artist Katsushika Hokusai's "The Great Wave off Kanagawa" into *Hot and Cool*'s artwork, and then drew on another aspect of Asian culture when christening his independent record label. Dacoit Records, named after packs of roving bandits that plundered parts of India and Burma, was the home for several Slickee Boys releases (sometimes in consort with Skip Groff's Limp Records) before the band landed with the Minneapolis indie, Twin/Tone, for its 1983 album *Cybernetic Dreams of Pi*.

The Slickee Boys and Overkill founded a scene that expanded quickly through the end of 1976 into 1977, with bands like Razz, the Controls, the Look, and White Boy gaining notice. Charlie McCollum of the *Washington Star* acknowledged at the time that there was "a budding punk rock scene locally" but warned that "without a myopic New York press to boost them—as happened with the CBGB[8] bands—it's doubtful that any of these groups will ever make a splash beyond Georgetown."[9] Fanzines might not have been the very first to refer in print to DC's emerging punk scene, but a fall 1976 appearance by the Slickee Boys in a local fanzine called *It's Only a Movie* marked the start of an enduring symbiosis.

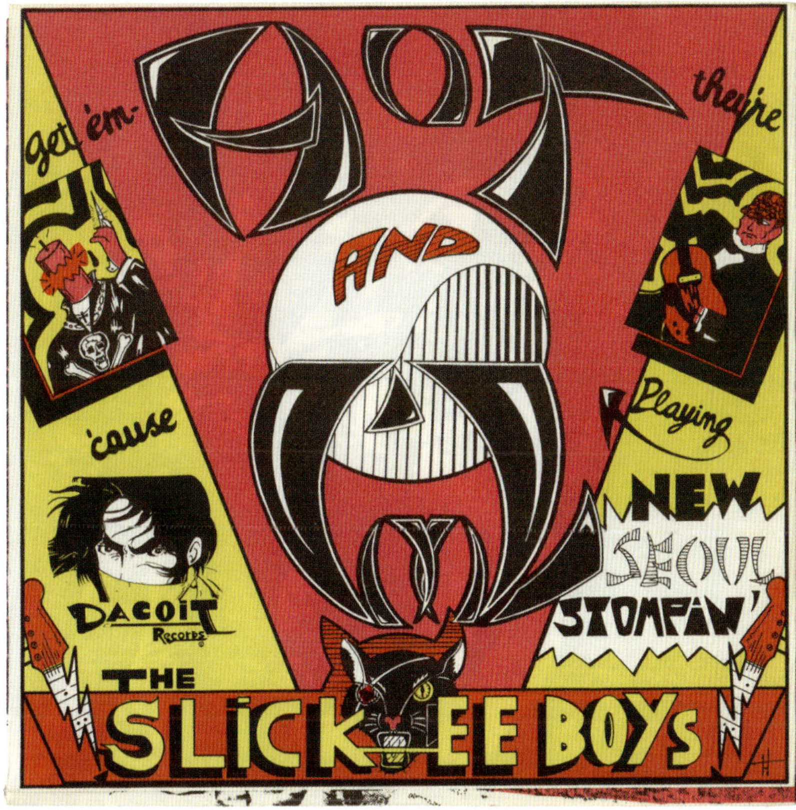

Figure 2.2 The Slickee Boys, *Hot and Cool*, 7-inch EP, 1976, designed by Kim Kane. Used by permission.

It's Only a Movie

The October 1976 issue of *Creem* included a humble invitation toward the end of its "Letters to the Editor" section that served as the kernel of a scene that still thrives. Norm DeValliere, a teenage science fiction and rock music fan from Fairfax, Virginia, asked for "reviews and articles about intelligent groups by intelligent writers," which would appear in his new fanzine. DeValliere quickly forgot about the *Creem* letter, but eventually started receiving submissions in the mail. He was initially perplexed, but one of his correspondents reminded him of his call for submissions in *Creem*. "So, then I'm like, 'Oh, now I guess I feel obligated to follow through on what I was going to do and publish this magazine,'" he laughed, recalling the situation in a 2020 interview.[10]

DeValliere initially named his fanzine *Break On Through* after a song by the late 1960s rock band the Doors. Soon enough, he swapped the title for *It's Only a Movie*, which he insisted was not inspired by an album of the same name by British progressive rock band Family. "I simply thought it was a somewhat more tasteful name than *Rotten Teeth* or *Grimace*," he wrote in "a little rambling editorial" near the front of the first issue, published around November 1976.[11] The first issue of DeValliere's "Journal of Avant Garde Culture," as its cover proclaimed, consisted almost entirely of reviews and doodles. The editorial content is a mixed bag—reviews of singer-songwriter Warren Zevon and folk-rock guitarist Roy Harper are as prominent as the zine's coverage of punk rock. However, due to its prominent and fannish coverage of punk, it can be considered DC's first punk fanzine. Yvonne Carr contributed a prescient record review within of the Ramones' recently released debut album, accurately stating that "the Ramones are the masters of something new to come."

That first issue also included a half-page feature review of the Slickee Boys, whom DeValliere first heard on WGTB-FM, Georgetown University's radio station. "I'd

Figure 2.3 *It's Only a Movie*, issues 1 and 2, 1976. Used by permission.

say my ties to the DC punk scene was purely from listening to WGTB," DeValliere said. "That station was just such a revelation to me." WGTB DJ Steve Lorber's show, *Mystic Eyes*, particularly connected DeValliere to happenings in the District, less than 20 miles from Fairfax. "I dug it, for sure," he remembered, singling out *Mystic Eyes*' steady diet of "the garage band sound, like the stuff on Lenny Kaye's *Nuggets* album" for helping to shape his musical tastes.

Hot and Cool provided DeValliere a tantalizing glimpse of developments just up the road. "Yes folks, there is rock and roll in the nation's capital," DeValliere trumpeted in his review. "The Slickee Boys are the best regionally oriented, nationally unrecorded band that I have heard," he wrote, calling them "better than anything on the *Live at CBGB* LP [or] Television's single "Little Johnny Jewel." DeValliere described the four-song EP as "great, short, fast, economical, [and] two minutes long with no excess at all," all attributes at the heart of the new punk subculture. "These guys are a weird solution of street punk attitudes, science fiction word games and Oriental flavoring," he continued, in the now outdated parlance of the time. "Very 'crypto-anarchic,' definitely unique, definitely rock and roll."[12]

For the second issue of *It's Only a Movie*, DeValliere declared his zine was "a member of the NVAAGPEP, the Northern Virginia Association of Avant Garde Punk Editors & Publishers, a society dedicated to the organization and hype of everything avante garde or punk." DeValliere cited his earlier science fiction fandom as a source for this cheeky creation. "I was trying to be funny," DeValliere explained: "Because as far as I knew, I was the only one, you know? So, it would be like, 'Oh, yeah. We're part of this big association.' [laugh] And it was like, 'Yeah. I'm the president. And treasurer. And—' You know? . . . It was just totally whimsical."[13]

The second issue waded further into punk in coverage and aesthetic, although it remained broad in its rock coverage, offering writings on well-known musicians like Robert Palmer and Ted Nugent amid reviews and news items on the Ramones, Patti Smith, and the Gizmos. An interview with Blue Öyster Cult, the New York rock band then riding high on their hit "(Don't Fear) the Reaper," included praise for punk—"I think it's great; . . . I find it to be a really healthy thing," drummer Albert Bouchard enthused—and, more specifically, for the Ramones and the Dictators. Regarding the former, "they have a good imagination and they have a pop consciousness in their music," while the latter New York group was described as "the hottest thing in the US."[14] Blue Öyster Cult's connections to Patti Smith and the Clash ultimately cemented them as fellow travelers to early punks—even if their music was not particularly in step—with this interview among the earliest records of that association.

By late 1977, DeValliere left the DC area for the western United States with his family, completing two more issues before ceasing publication. "I satisfied my obligation to my three or four subscribers," he said, "[so it was] like, 'OK, I'm going to do something else.'" Copies of those final two issues are lost to time, according to DeValliere, but they included more of the same mix of reviews and illustrations. DeValliere acknowledged the influence of *Punk* and *New York Rocker* on his early efforts, recalling "those, I read a lot. . . . I do remember corresponding with those guys [from *Punk*] a lot, but a lot of it was just . . . idiotic conversations, probably," he laughed. Although punk music was not something DeValliere followed in subsequent years, its lessons stuck. "It's sort of just like the punk philosophy in general, just the whole DIY bit," he stated. "Expertise isn't everything. Virtuosity isn't everything."[15]

Vintage Violence

It's Only a Movie's impact lingered, as one of its readers was inspired to start a zine of his own. Michael Heath, a self-described "schmucky suburban kid from Burtonsville, Maryland," began corresponding with DeValliere after reading his zine. "I still have a letter from [DeValliere] that has a photo of Dagmar Krause, the singer from Slapp Happy, on the front of it," Heath recalled in a 2019 interview. Remembering *It's Only a Movie* as "quite excellent," Heath cited it and "what was going on in London" via fanzines like *Sniffin' Glue* as big parts of why he started *Vintage Violence*, first published in March 1977.[16]

Heath was initially turned on to more esoteric forms of rock earlier in the 1970s by Skip Groff's "Heavy Metal Thunder" radio show on WINX-AM—a small but influential radio station that broadcast from Rockville, Maryland—and by rock magazines like *Creem*, *Rock Scene*, and *Hit Parader*. "*Hit Parader* was really such a gateway," Heath remembered:

> *Lisa and Richard Robinson were the editors, and they brought in all these amazing writers like Lenny Kaye, and even people like . . . Jayne County, and Richard Hell, to write for them. And Lisa was very much into what was going on in New York at the time, and was avid and very vocal and literate about what was going on in '74, '75, '76 in New York. And then* Rock Scene *was kind of a hipper version of* 16 *magazine. It was all photos, and . . . they would have these features like, "The Ramones Do Laundry" [laugh] or "Debbie [Harry] and Chris [Stein of Blondie] go get a slice of pizza" [laugh] or something like that.*[17]

Through *Hit Parader*, Heath became aware of the Ramones, but it was a pair of articles in local publications that cinched his interest in the band. "There were two consecutive reviews that I remember coming out within, like, a week of each other in DC," he said:

> *One was Howard Wuelfing writing for some free paper saying, "This music is like a hydrogen bomb dropped on Herman's Hermits." [laugh] And then concurrently with that was this guy Richard Harrington who was the just—ugh!—don't get me started about Richard Harrington! But he also reviewed the Ramones record [in the* Washington Post*] and he said, "It is empty music for empty minds." And I said, "Oh! [snaps fingers] I've got to go out and get it now!" [laugh] And I did. I didn't really get [the music] at first, but I appreciated it.*[18]

Harrington's actual negative appraisal of the Ramones—"It is music for the empty spaces of the mind"[19]—did not appear in print until October 1977, well after Heath covered the Ramones in *Vintage Violence*, so it is likely he conflated Harrington's 1977 review with one that ran in the *Washington Post* after the band's concerts at DC's Childe Harold in October 1976. There, Harrington dismissed the Ramones as "perhaps the worst of the New York punk bands" and "only the latest pretenders in a long line of musical successors to the New York Dolls and Iggy and the Stooges."[20] Harrington eventually came around, however. "I didn't get them," he conceded decades later:

> *Hardly an unusual situation for a critic to miss something. And later on, maybe even [laughs] as it was explained to me by people like Mark [Jenkins] and Howard [Wuelfing] and other people in their writings, I got to really appreciate what they were doing, and the charms and the musical strength and power of it. But at the Childe Harold, I clearly missed the boat.*[21]

By fall 1976, when Heath enrolled at the University of Maryland in College Park, he ventured further into punk, a terrain expanding swiftly as new bands and publications cropped up each month. A newsstand in the university's student union carried the British music magazine *Melody Maker*, which usually would not arrive until a few weeks after the publication date. "The first issue I saw of *Melody Maker* there was the famous cover of the Pistols caught in a fistfight . . . in the audience at the Nashville Rooms in London," Heath said:[22]

> *And it was, "Oh, those guys. Hmm. Let me check this out." And then a later issue reviewed the 100 Club Punk Festival in London. [The music journalist] Caroline Coon was very, very much into that scene and very articulate about it and made it sound really, really fascinating and attractive. And she was also writing that it's not just music; it's also fashion. Or anti-fashion in the case of, you know, Malcolm [McLaren] and Vivienne [Westwood] and Don Letts and the guy who ran Boy [John Krivine].*[23]

Heath borrowed copies of *Bomp!* and *Trouser Press* from his friend and future *Vintage Violence* contributor Jeff Zang, broadening his awareness of the flood of new music coming out. Much like DeValliere, Heath was a regular *Mystic Eyes* and WGTB listener, "which was pretty much *the* first place I heard a lot of what was coming out of the American underground, whether it was New York or Cleveland, with bands like Pere Ubu, or London," Heath recalled. Lorber also introduced Heath to the Slickee Boys, whom Heath first saw perform at My Friend's House, a venue near the University of Maryland:

> *They were playing 1960s British and American garage covers, . . . stuff like "What A Boy Can't Do" by the Hangmen.*[24] *. . . I thought they were great and I started hanging out with them. [Kim Kane] was way much more ahead of the curve or hip to things than I was at the time, and was getting all these zines. . . . John Holmstrom's Punk and I think he was also getting* Sniffin' Glue*, too. And I would go over to his house after school some afternoons, and he would play me all this latest stuff.*[25]

Already inspired, Heath was further motivated to create his own fanzine as he learned about Mark Perry and *Sniffin' Glue*. Perry was "just this guy who was a bank clerk, who was a total music fan [and] not seeing what he was listening to and what he was into . . . represented as vividly or as passionately as he felt it in the mainstream music press." Heath wrote an overview of the new punk subculture, but it was rejected by two University of Maryland publications—*The Diamondback* and *Argus*—he had submitted it to. "I think [*Argus*] said 'Oh, nobody's going to care about this stuff in six months," Heath laughed. Recalling the story of Perry's trip to a record store where the clerk told him to go make his own fanzine, Heath reached a similar conclusion—"I said, 'I'll do it myself.'"[26]

Named after the 1970 John Cale album, *Vintage Violence* developed into more of a pure punk fanzine during its fifteen-month run than *It's Only a Movie* ever had. DeValliere remarked that "Mike was definitely more of a real part of that" punk scene in DC.[27] The first issue, mimeographed onto letter size paper and stapled together, saw coverage of the Ramones, Blondie, and Stiff Records mingle with that

Figure 2.4 *Vintage Violence*, issue 1, March 1977; and issue 2, April 1977. Published by Michael Layne Heath. Used by permission.

of punk-friendly rockers like Brian Eno, Phil Manzanera, Flamin' Groovies, and David Bowie. Most profound, from a local perspective, was "DC Rockers: Sleepytime Time Is Over!," Heath's article on DC punk's stirrings as 1976 led into 1977. While *Unicorn Times* continued offering some coverage of DC's embryonic punk community, typically in Steve Lorber and Mark Jenkins' "Teenage News" column, Heath wrote the first extended scene report in a DC punk fanzine.

There was not much to talk about yet, but Heath neatly encapsulates the subculture's launch in DC. "Already the stirrings of a scene, not unlike New York, are beginning," he wrote. Heath first reported the bad news that Overkill was "barely limping along" now that "charismatic lead singer"[28] Barney Jones had left for college. He followed, however, with a rundown of bands containing various musicians who would be at the heart of the community for the rest of the 1970s and, for some, beyond.

Heath tabbed the Slickee Boys as one of the city's top two bands, noting that the group's "watchword is 'energy'" as they knocked out "hard edged rock and roll, no fat, and later with the lettuce." Heath's clumsy acclaim for Hull—"a gutsy little hussy [that] looks like a talented Ruby Starr"[29]—is a rare sour note, betraying the influence of *Creem* and the casual sexism endemic in rock and roll. His acclaim for the male band members is less awkward, remarking that as "nice as they may be offstage," onstage they are "the meanest looking bunch since the old Pretty Things—real tough guys." Kane contributed to the reviews section, submitting an approving assessment of a March 1977 concert by New Zealand art rock band Split Enz at DC's Cellar Door.

Heath evocatively describes his choice for the other top band in the local scene, the Look, as "art deco in sound." The Look's bassist, Howard Wuelfing (later of Nurses and the *Descenes* and *Discords* fanzines); drummer Chris Thompson (a WGTB disc jockey who later drummed for Tiny Desk Unit and wrote for *The Infiltrator*); and guitarist Robert Goldstein all ultimately played meaningful roles in developing DC's punk scene.[30] Heath lavished praise on vocalist Teamon Treadway, writing that he "cuts a mean figure" while "standing practically still, in a suit and tie, shrieking then moaning then whispering like death, he's playing for keeps, and damned if it don't show."[31] As the *Washington Post* noted in its own local punk roundup, published in May 1977, the Look were "not so much punks, as arty primitivists."[32]

True punks or not, the Look were "causing a lot of excitement among their small legion of fans."[33] Treadway soon left the band, however, and, after one more concert with Patricia Ragan on vocals, the Look was defunct by later in spring 1977.[34] A small trove of demos and live recordings exist as proof of the band's brief tenure, but nothing was released commercially. Existing recordings document an intriguing band for the period, knocking out covers of Richard Hell, the Stooges, the Velvet Underground, Roky Erickson, and the Ramones, while mixing in some original material like "Control," an ominous yet tuneful composition from Wuelfing.[35] "We practiced a lot and we were pretty sharp," Wuelfing recalled in 2018. "I think we had an interesting repertoire for a band that was basically a cover band."[36]

Goldstein played a central role in the early DC punk and new wave scene as guitarist for Urban Verbs, which were formed in 1978. Urban Verbs traversed edges of the mainstream that no other band from the first wave of DC punk and new wave reached, signing with Warner Bros. Records and, briefly, attaining an association with musician and producer Brian Eno, who said he "was tremendously impressed" by the band.[37] Goldstein's role in helping to establish the Atlantis Club, one of the few venues available for local punk bands to perform at during the late 1970s, was even more consequential for the DC scene than Urban Verbs. The Atlantis was short-lived and plagued by controversy—with Heath occasionally at the center of it—during its run from 1978 to 1979. It reopened in 1980, however, as the 9:30 Club, and established itself as a flagship venue for independent and adventurous music in DC.

Heath concluded that ten-page first issue with the declaration that his zine operated "under one motivation: the love of real live rock and roll." As he put it: "It's the hope of

Figure 2.5 Left: Mike Heath, circa 1980. Photo by Nancy Sprandel. Right: *Vintage Violence*, issue 4, 1977. Published by Michael Layne Heath. Used by permission.

the staff here that people will get into what it's all about and that *Vintage Violence* will become an important fanzine 'all for the love of rock and roll.' For all the mess-ups in typing and all else that may be wrong with the magazine, it's done for that love of the music."

A second issue followed in April 1977, feeling like an extension of the first. Heath assembled an aesthetically identical, twelve-page mimeographed collection of hand-lettered headlines and typewritten articles on punk, again focusing mostly on happenings outside DC. Despite DC's signs of life, London and New York remained where the action was in early 1977. A significant portion of the issue centers on the comeback of former Stooges vocalist Iggy Pop and his new solo debut record, *The Idiot*. Reviews of the Damned, Talking Heads, and Television are of interest, but the most notable writing in the second issue is Heath's detailed review of a concert by the Controls.

The Controls were another founding piece of DC's punk scene, although they never recorded and rarely performed. One concert at DC's American University, however, was described as "exciting, original, daring"[38] and "fucking fantastic."[39] Vocalist Roddy Frantz, backed by the drummer Josh Shufflin, started the performance with "deadpan readings" of a series of poems from Allen Ginsberg and Sylvia Plath, along with the liner notes to the Velvet Underground's debut album. Guitarist Keith Campbell and bassist Dave Arnold took the stage, with the band receiving "huge applause" before launching into a set highlighted by covers from "old (and not so old) masters" like the Kinks, John Cale, and the Ramones, while debuting original material like "Raygun" and "Subways." Heath's description of Frantz's stage presence is transporting: "Rod Frantz sang in his strangled chicken voice, looking for all the world like Beaver Cleaver's next-door neighbor. Bouncing on his heels when he really gets into the music, making little windmill guitar gestures, now and then jiggering around the stage shadow boxing, Frantz has a very interesting stage stance."

A malfunctioning public address system inspired another of the set's memorable moments, with Frantz wandering from one dormant microphone to the next, shouting

Figure 2.6 Advertisements posted by the Razz in *Unicorn Times*, June and July 1978. Artwork by Michael Reidy. Used by permission.

in vain before throwing a microphone stand off the stage. Heath dubbed the performance "incredible," doubting that "the people there that night will forget the Controls any time soon." Campbell soon reappeared in DCeats and Black Market Baby, while Frantz fronted Urban Verbs, bringing along his lyrics to "Subways."

Heath took an extended trip to Los Angeles in summer 1977, discovering the new punk zine *Slash*, visiting Greg Shaw's Bomp! record store, and watching the Ramones sign albums for fans in a suburban shopping mall parking lot. Heath scrapped a third issue of *Vintage Violence* that he had started before his trip—"the great lost issue," he recalled[40]—filling the time between issues with a new, short-lived "micromegazine," as he called it. *Return to Whatever* was two sheets of corner-stapled paper bearing a barrage of news from throughout the flowering punk subculture. "Jonathan Richman's 'Roadrunner' is top 10 in Europe," Heath reported, before pinballing on to more fragments like "where is Patti Smith's book?" and "Ted Niceley of Razz getting married?" *Return to Whatever*'s breathless tone captured that thrilling period in 1977 when punk rock fully arrived with astonishing force and purpose.

Issue four of *Vintage Violence* finally appeared that December, bearing Dennis Morris's photo of the Sex Pistols' Johnny Rotten—appropriated by Heath from another magazine—on its cover. "Johnny Wishes You & Yours a Happy Xmas," smirked a handwritten headline beneath the image of Rotten, his arms held in a Christ-like pose. The writings within were another step forward for *Vintage Violence*, led by a lengthy "manifesto" from musician Rob Kennedy on the Sex Pistols' *Never Mind the Bollocks* album and an effusive review of the Ramones' *Rocket to Russia* by former Look vocalist Patricia Ragan. The latter favorably positioned the Ramones' "Americanness" against their "Limey" punk peers across the Atlantic. "The Ramones are about FUN and . . . the Limeys (wacky as they are) don't know bee from bullfoot about having REAL FUN," Ragan declared.[41]

Heath, meanwhile, contributes his own historic writings in praise of another foundational group for the DC punk scene. Razz had toiled in DC's rock scene since 1971, cycling through band members before settling into their "classic lineup"[42] by 1977, with vocalist Michael Reidy, guitarists Abaad Behram and Bill Craig, bassist Ted Niceley, and drummer Doug Tull. This iteration established an exciting strain of rock music in DC with sounds that were not "punky, unless you begin by redefining punk rock," *Unicorn Times* discerned in June 1977. "Punky, yes, in performance. . . . Their music, however, is contrary to punk. It is professional and highly structured."[43] Once a hirsute bar band covering the Rolling Stones and Aerosmith, Razz overhauled its aesthetic through a series of confrontational, darkly humorous advertisements Reidy created to promote their concerts in local publications, as well as a more aggressive performance style centered on Reidy's antics.

In the first significant coverage of the band in a DC punk fanzine, Heath praised them extensively, asserting that "Razz is one of the best rock and roll bands DC has,"[44] while also comparing them with the Who at their mod peak in 1965. Heath notes that, like the Slickee Boys, Razz does not fit in with the increasingly "de rigueur punque outfits" already codifying by the end of 1977. "They ain't the Saturday morning cartoon show," Heath enthuses. "They're the kids who watched rock and roll TV whenever the Stones or [Yardbirds] or Animals were on, vowing that someday they'd be up there, too." The group's debut single, "C. Redux," allowed Razz to join Slickee Boys—whose new album, *Separated Vegetables*, Heath favorably reviewed in that same issue—at the front of DC's growing scene. Overkill, the Controls, and the Look made an impression on the few who saw them in concert, but their impact could not equal groups like Razz, the Slickee Boys, and White Boy—a bizarre father-and-son punk band from DC—all of whom released records that circulated outside the area.

Vintage Violence's final two issues were published in the first half of 1978, exhibiting a more kinetic aesthetic than earlier issues had. Heath attributed this to the increasing influence of staff members Rob Kennedy and Caki Kallas, romantic partners who "brought so much experience to the table, to the page," Heath recalled. "They were slightly older than me, but they had . . . much older, richer experience than I did, at the time," Heath remembered. "Rob was a . . . great writer and Caki, with her artistic comic skills and whatnot." Kallas, in particular, left her mark on these final two issues, with her striking, angular hand-lettering

Figure 2.7 *Vintage Violence,* issues 5 and 6, 1977–78. Published by Michael Layne Heath. Used by permission.

and illustrations throughout each issue, aligning *Vintage Violence* with the punk aesthetic more than ever. "We were on fire, just passionate about what was coming over from England and coming up from New York and out of DC, and Cleveland, San Francisco, LA," Heath said.

In addition to features on Urban Verbs and the New York City punk band Dead Boys, issue five covered the deteriorating relationship between the DC punk scene and the Atlantis Club, which began canceling concerts and banning bands from its premises due to having "offended" the audience, according to club co-owner Paul Parsons.[45] A multidate engagement at the Atlantis by the Cramps, the garage-punk trailblazers from New York City, was cut short due to disagreements between the band and venue over money, primarily. Parsons described the Cramps as "not healthy," to which the Cramps' singer Lux Interior later responded, "I'm gonna have to do some jogging."

Vintage Violence's coverage of the contretemps led to tensions between Heath and the Atlantis staff, which were detailed in issue six. After alleging that Atlantis staff were "harassing representatives" of *Vintage Violence* and "following *VV* personnel to restrooms, refusing entry to dressing rooms for interviews, and generally making a writer's work—already a hassle—into a hassling bitch," Heath described his ejection from a Mumps concert at the club. Heath and "two conspirators [had] in a rash moment . . . lit a joint" in the Atlantis's pinball room. Security was called and Heath, though not his friends, was thrown out of the club. While being ejected, Heath overheard Atlantis staff complaining about his outspoken criticisms of the venue—"he's lucky he got in here at all after what he wrote about us and said on the radio"—leading him to believe he had been singled out for expressing his opinions. "Does freedom of the press exist at the Atlantis, or is the first amendment just another swampwater cocktail napkin?" he asked at the end of the editorial. Kennedy, too, had his own run-in with the Atlantis staff, leading to him being placed in handcuffs by security before being "booted out the door."[46]

Fueled by incidents like this, along with how often bands and fans were dissatisfied in their dealings with the club, a boycott ensued, and the club eventually went out of business. Despite its poor reputation, the Atlantis

Figure 2.8 Mary Leary of *The Infiltrator*, circa winter 1977. Photographer unknown.

played a pivotal role in the punk community's development, serving as a rare venue that hosted punk rock bands while the scene found its legs. Now an award-winning author and critic, Elizabeth Hand was an avid reader of *Vintage Violence* and a participant in DC's late 1970s scene, a period she said was "vibrant and a hell of a lot of fun!" She described the scene at the Atlantis as "small at the start, more like a party than a bar or club." A community was building, however, in which Hand immersed herself. "I worked at the National Air & Space Museum, and in the summers my shift ended at 9," she recalled, "so I walked across the Mall to the club every night and stayed there till closing." Hand submitted a Dead Boys review to *Vintage Violence* during this period, too, but did not hear back, "so I probably just got discouraged" and forgot about it.[47] Decades later, Heath found the submission and sent it to Hand. "I read it, and I was like, 'Wow, I definitely could have done this, if I'd just been braver or smarter or more connected,'" Hand recalled in 2018. "I had the chops. It wasn't great criticism, by a long shot, but for the time and for how old I was, it was fine. It was one of the roads not traveled. It was probably for the best."[48]

The remainder of *Vintage Violence*'s final issue—including interviews with Billy Idol, Richard Hell, and Jeff Dahl, along with plenty of comics and hand-lettered text by Kallas—offered little clue that *Vintage Violence* was ending. "There was no major argument; . . . it just ran its course," Heath recalled. "Rob was getting more involved in his music;[49] . . . it was kind of just a mutual drifting apart."[50] Despite his zine's anticlimactic ending, Heath remained in music journalism, eventually writing for *Record Collector News* and *Perfect Sound Forever*, as well as editing *My Week Beats Your Year*, a book of collected interviews with Lou Reed. He also contributed to DC punk fanzines in the wake of *Vintage Violence*, including *The Infiltrator*, a new zine that would make an outsized impact on the scene.

The Infiltrator Arrives

The Infiltrator was the work of Mary Leary, who typically wrote under the pseudonym of Marie Provost, a nod to the late silent film actress Marie Prevost. Prevost had been immortalized in Nick Lowe's 1977 power pop gem "Marie Provost [*sic*]," which riffed upon the urban legend—popularized by Kenneth Anger's *Hollywood Babylon* book—that Prevost perished of acute alcoholism (which was true) and was then eaten by her dog (which was not true).[51] Aside from the desirable anonymity the pseudonym gave, going by Marie Provost "meant we could call it 'Hungry Dachshund Productions,' which I thought was really, really fun," Leary recalled.[52]

"I just have never really thought of myself seriously as like a punk rocker, because I'm into too much stuff," Leary explained. "If it's rock and roll, I probably like it." That said, *The Infiltrator* was a big step forward for DC's punk scene and its fanzines, with sharp visuals and a standard of writing exceeding most punk zines anywhere. Leary had "picked up the ball that [*Vintage Violence*] dropped and ran big-time with it," Heath enthused. "It had great graphics, a lot of them done by Michael Reidy from the Razz. Great writers. It was just brilliant." Before moving to DC, Leary lived in Spain and New York City, both of which expanded her tastes in music and art. "I went to one of the first shows maybe Patti Smith ever did," Leary said. "I lucked into, at the age of 19, getting introduced to and hanging out with what would turn into the beginning of the new wave scene. . . . You could use the word 'punk' if you want."

Leary participated in DC's rock scene throughout the 1970s, witnessing the Controls cover the Ramones' "53rd and 3rd" at one party or Martha Hull's pre–Slickee Boys rock band Lady at another. A job as an assistant buyer at Bialek's Discount Records and Books in the Dupont Circle neighborhood furthered her musical knowledge, offering early exposure to the innovative punk and new wave records appearing. This fed into a DJ gig at the Keg where, once again, Steve Lorber served as a conduit within the young scene. Lorber heard Leary's DJ sets and asked if she would be interested in a show on WGTB. Leary took over a spot there and thrived in the free-form format, which made it all the more painful when Georgetown University shut down WGTB in January 1979. The school's administration cited financial reasons, but the station's "gay and lesbian programming and abortion-counseling public service announcements were more controversial," along with WGTB's unwillingness to air Georgetown basketball games, Mark Andersen and Mark Jenkins reported in *Dance of Days*, their book on the DC punk scene's first two decades.

With WGTB gone, Leary thought of a new way to continue the station's advocacy for alternatives to mainstream music. "There was no way for a lot of what was exploding at that time to be covered," Leary said. "So, it struck me as very important to do something that sort of carried on from this amazing station." Leary cited *Vintage Violence*, *Creem*, and *New York Rocker* as elements of what she wanted to do with her new zine, but a continuation of WGTB's spirit seemed the paramount influence. Collaborating with artist Kevin MacDonald—who went on to a remarkable career as a visual artist before passing away in 2006—on the zine's deft blend of professional presentation and handmade verve, Leary launched *The Infiltrator*. Leary chose the name because "I think because I liked the idea that we would go in anywhere and cover anything, or we would try to," she said.

Figure 2.9 Issues 1 and 2 of *The Infiltrator*, 1979. Published by Mary Leary. Used by permission.

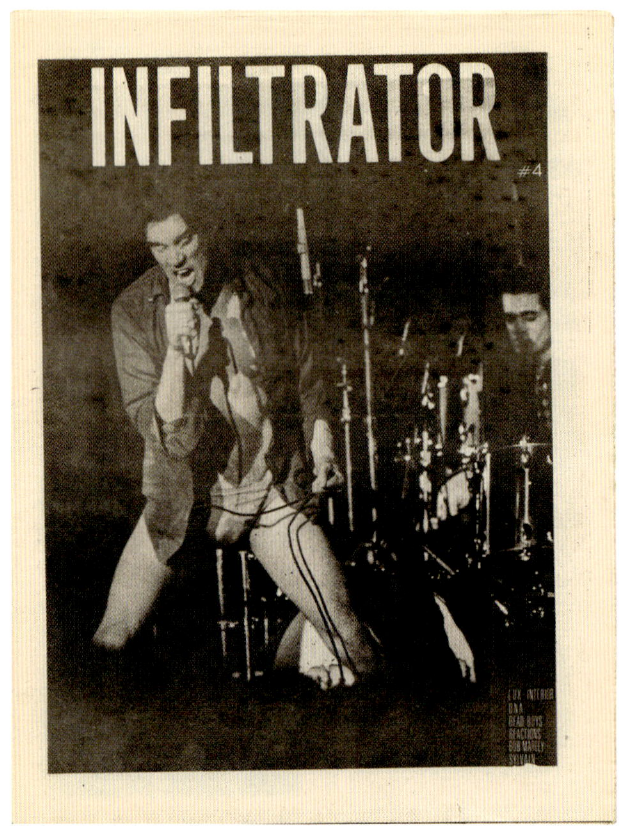

Figure 2.10 Issues 3 and 4 of *The Infiltrator,* 1979. Published by Mary Leary. Used by permission.

The first issue saw a fairly diverse mix of music coverage, from interviews with roots rockers NRBQ and studio musician Ron Riddle to a beautifully laid out interview with the Clash, conducted by former WGTB disc jockey Xyra Harper. Another article, tracing the development of Urban Verbs, was cowritten by Leary and musician Bob Boilen. The latter cofounded the band Tiny Desk Unit around this time and, later, achieved renown as host of NPR's *All Songs Considered* program. Rounded out by a lengthy postmortem on WGTB and coverage of jazz and reggae music alongside rock, punk, and new wave writings, *The Infiltrator*'s first issue is a successful realization of Leary's goal to crystallize what made WGTB special.

The zine only improved, however, as the second issue's layout was bolder and its writing more confident. Aside from interviews with internationally known figures like the reggae musician Peter Tosh, erstwhile Velvet Underground member John Cale, and Roxy Music's Phil Manzanera, coverage of DC's growing punk scene captures the excitement building locally. Former *Vintage Violence* contributor Rob Kennedy's urgent extolling of a new, lightning-fast punk band to emerge from the DC scene is notable, as well as riven with imagery inspired by the recent partial meltdown at Pennsylvania's Three Mile Island nuclear facility. "Bad Brains seeping out of suburban split levels like radioactive iodine seeping from split reactor cores; as deadly, not as subtle," Kennedy writes. "Do not expect President Carter to drop by to reassure us—he does not care about these Bad Brains, but will someone please erase their graffiti from the Corcoran Art School, it messes up the clean white walls." [53]

An in-depth interview with DCeats—featuring Keith Campbell of the Controls, Martha Hull of Slickee Boys, and two members of Overkill—joins Rick Reck's overview of "the Washington School of New Music," as he put it.[54] A supportive review by Chris Thompson of *Air Time*, a new single on Limp Records by the Razz (who had recently appended "the" to their band's name), is also included. Punk's heart might have beat stronger in a few other regional scenes during the late 1970s, but *The Infiltrator*'s coverage of the DC community indicated that the city's pulse was far from faint. "I just think it was an amazing cultural scene to be in," Leary recalled:

> *Partly because Washington DC, is such a mecca for people from so many different places, . . . and it always had so much diversity, in my opinion. So, the culture reflects that. And if it's pre-Reagan, Carter years—there were still grants for performance art and shit, man. You could still talk people into giving you money for doing all kinds of wacky things. Which is wonderful. To me, DC, in a way, in the 1970s, just [felt] like an extension of all the possibilities of the 1960s.*[55]

The third and fourth issues of *The Infiltrator,* both published in the latter half of 1979, shifted to a larger, tabloid newspaper format with impressive results. The third issue, with an amusing image of the Razz's Michael Reidy hanging dramatically from what appeared to be a high precipice, cut back slightly on the previous issue's page count. The spacious format, though, allowed for more arresting graphics, complementing coverage of the rapidly expanding punk and new wave scenes. "I think we went to newsprint partly because it was cheaper, and partly because we could realize our dream of being more like a *New York Rocker* or *FILE*,"[56] Leary said.[57] *The Infiltrator* remained eclectic in its coverage, seamlessly juxtaposing features on soul duo Sam & Dave, progressive rock guitarist Robert Fripp, and the British punk band 999.

The Slickee Boys reconvened after a short break necessitated by band member departures—including Hull and Wuelfing—and reached new heights creatively. Singer Mark Noone highlighted the remodeled lineup, writing two outstanding songs on the group's self-titled EP, which Limp Records issued later in 1979. "Gotta Tell Me Why" and "Forbidden Alliance" (the latter cowritten with guitarist Marshall Keith) were of an advanced quality previously unmet by DC punk and new wave bands. At last, the Slickee Boys were equals with many of their out-of-town peers. "This band has moved from the minor leagues of competent, fun bands to join the ranks of DC's finest," Leary wrote in that third issue. A two-page spread featuring a collage of Slickee Boys photos, lyrics, and drawings cemented the feeling that the band and their distinctive aesthetic were secure at the center of a scene that seemed boundless.

The fourth issue, with a snarling Lux Interior on its cover, extended the look and tone of the third issue. Copious reviews of commercial recordings and concerts were illustrated with compelling photographs from contributors like Rebecca Hammel, Mike Tanner, and Hank Numb. WGTB's catholic sensibilities lingered in *The Infiltrator* with mostly positive results, but an interview with John Cipolina of the 1960s psychedelic rock band Quicksilver Messenger Service felt incongruous alongside interviews with rising new wave groups like the B-52s from Athens, Georgia, and the new DC band Insect Surfers. As the 1970s ended, *The Infiltrator* was cresting. Although its circulation never exceeded 1,000, its impact on the scene was significant thanks to Leary's intelligent, authoritative work. Feedback from within the subculture was "really, really enthusiastic," she remembered. "People just thought it was great. But, again, we're talking a scene of maybe two hundred people."

Descenes

Another important DC punk fanzine started in 1979. This one, *Descenes,* was the work of Howard and Tina Wuelfing, a married couple who moved to DC from the New York–New Jersey area in 1975.[58] Around the time of *Descenes'* inception, Howard Wuelfing departed the Slickee Boys and started a new band, Nurses, whose spare, garage-influenced power pop served as a bridge between DC punk's first and second waves. By January 1979, the first issue of *Descenes,* with Mr. Ott of White Boy on its cover, was on the street. As *Unicorn Times* wrote of *Descenes* when word of initial production on the zine first circulated in late 1978, "all this is being done for lotsa love and no money."[59]

Descenes' mission was to build a punk scene in DC, much as *New York Rocker* had accomplished in its respective locale. "It seemed like a lot of what [*New York Rocker* was] doing was having people from the bands write about each other," Wuelfing said later. "And they just wrote about New York bands that no one had heard about. I thought it was a good idea. We just adapted it to DC."[60] Tina Wuelfing worked a day job at *The Chronicle of Higher Education,*[61] enabling the duo to lay out each new issue with professional typesetting equipment—"without that free production

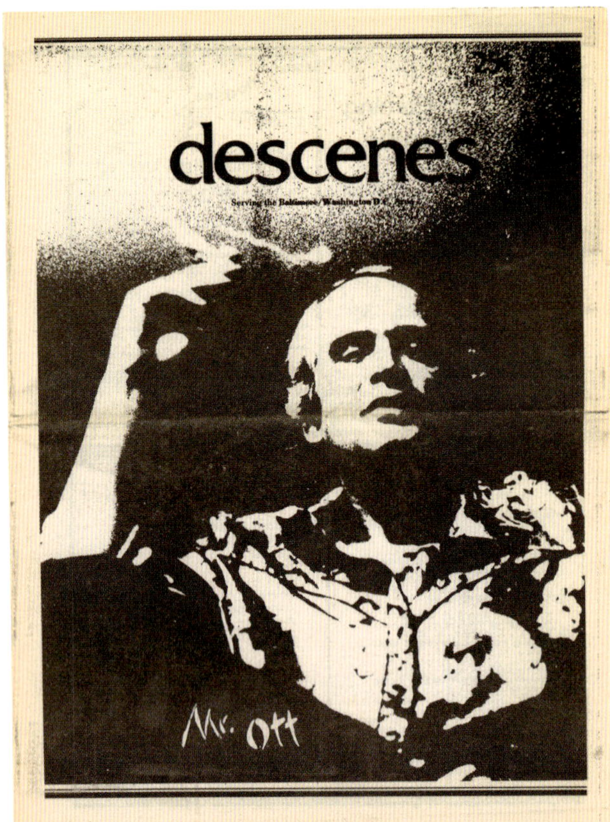

Figure 2.11 Issues 1 through 4 of Descenes, 1979. Published by Howard and Tina Wuelfing. Used by permission.

work of hers the whole thing could NOT have existed at all," Wuelfing attested.[62]

Howard Wuelfing was inspired by zines like *Bomp!* and the writing of the rock journalists Robert Christgau, Lester Bangs, Richard Meltzer, and Nick Tosches, not to mention his own time spent in the early years of New York City's punk scene. "I think those writers had helped to cultivate the sensibility that blossomed into punk across the board," he stated. "I have a whole theory about how the early fanzine nation gave birth pretty directly to punk, as a fair amount of people went from being fanzine writers and editors and publishers to running bands—Andy Shernoff from The Dictators being a prime example, along with Phast Phreddie and Metal Mike Saunders from the Angry Samoans."[63]

Throughout its six-issue run, ending in 1980, *Descenes* evinced the same sharp wit and savvy ear its inspirations did. The first issue was sixteen pages of no-frills music reporting, less polished than *The Infiltrator*, but not as rudimentary as early issues of *Vintage Violence*. The debut resembles a cleaned-up version of the *Washington Free Press*, with neat rows of text indicating aspirations towards professionalism, while shadowy photographic reproductions and a sarcastic attitude recall an earlier era in the underground press. The optimism is palpable in Howard Wuelfing's earnest opening editorial. "Our purpose is simple: we hope to promote fun in the greater Washington area by lending whatever support we can to the formation of a vital, ongoing community of exciting/excited rock and rollers," he wrote. "We hope to make this a lively and timely publication, hopefully as provocative and pleasurable as the music it supports."

White Boy, among the handful of bands at the core of DC's new scene, dominated the issue, with nearly half its pages centered on the group. Founded in the spring of 1977, the duo made for an unlikely sight. James Kowalski, a besuited, middle-aged businessman; and his teenage son, Glenn—operating under the stage names Mr. Ott and Jake Whipp, respectively—were joined by a rotating cast of backing musicians. White Boy's music—a shambolic mix of vocals cloaked in horror movie reverb, boogie rock guitar solos, and lyrics that took great pains to convey that they were composed in bad taste—was divisive, at best. "'What's this stuff on your plate?' Ott intones on the band's debut single, "I Could Puke." "Eat it all up! Looks like, smells like, tastes like puuuuuuke!" White Boy's influence, though limited, was ultimately lasting, making an impression on future genre icons Ian MacKaye and Henry Rollins.[64] "When I was in eighth or ninth grade, . . . I bought that [single] from a friend of mine in junior high school and they really predated everybody," MacKaye remembered. "They put out their own records and everything."[65]

Descenes' interview with White Boy displays the stark personality differences between father and son, which invert stereotypical familial dynamics. The elder Ott injects chaos, offering prurient yarns and a disdain for propriety, while the younger Whipp answers seriously, expressing a desire to be more professional with his music. "I had this pair of underwear hidden in my cape with brown shoe polish smeared on all of the strategic places, and at the end of the song I fired it at somebody in the audience," Ott laughingly recalled of the band's performance of "Rotten Crotch Disaster" at their debut concert. "We scared them shitless," Ott bragged about the concert, a house party for high school students, which began with him screaming into the microphone: "Good evening and FUCK YOU!"[66]

Another anecdote reveals, despite Ott's intentions, the oft-denigrated Paul Parsons of the Atlantis Club getting something right: "He told us that he didn't like that our roadies were all kids," Ott complained. "You know, 14, 15, and he was trying to sell beer and he's—I don't know—'fraid that they might drink some or maybe afraid that they wouldn't drink some, because they were under age." Ott's unseemly behavior might have amused some at the time, but his story has an ugly conclusion that left behind numerous victims. In the 1990s, years after White Boy disbanded, Ott was arrested and convicted of multiple sexual crimes against children,[67] sending him "to jail for life," according to Skip Groff.[68]

The standout portion of *Descenes*' first issue is a hand-drawn "family tree" of the new DC punk scene, drawn in the style of Pete Frame.[69] This pedigree tree, credited to the Wuelfings, traced the roots of the Slickee Boys, DCeats, Urban Verbs, Nurses, and other then-current DC punk and new wave bands back to the relatively antediluvian late 1960s. Here, in the centerpiece of this first issue, *Descenes* created a simple, yet comprehensive, visualization of the

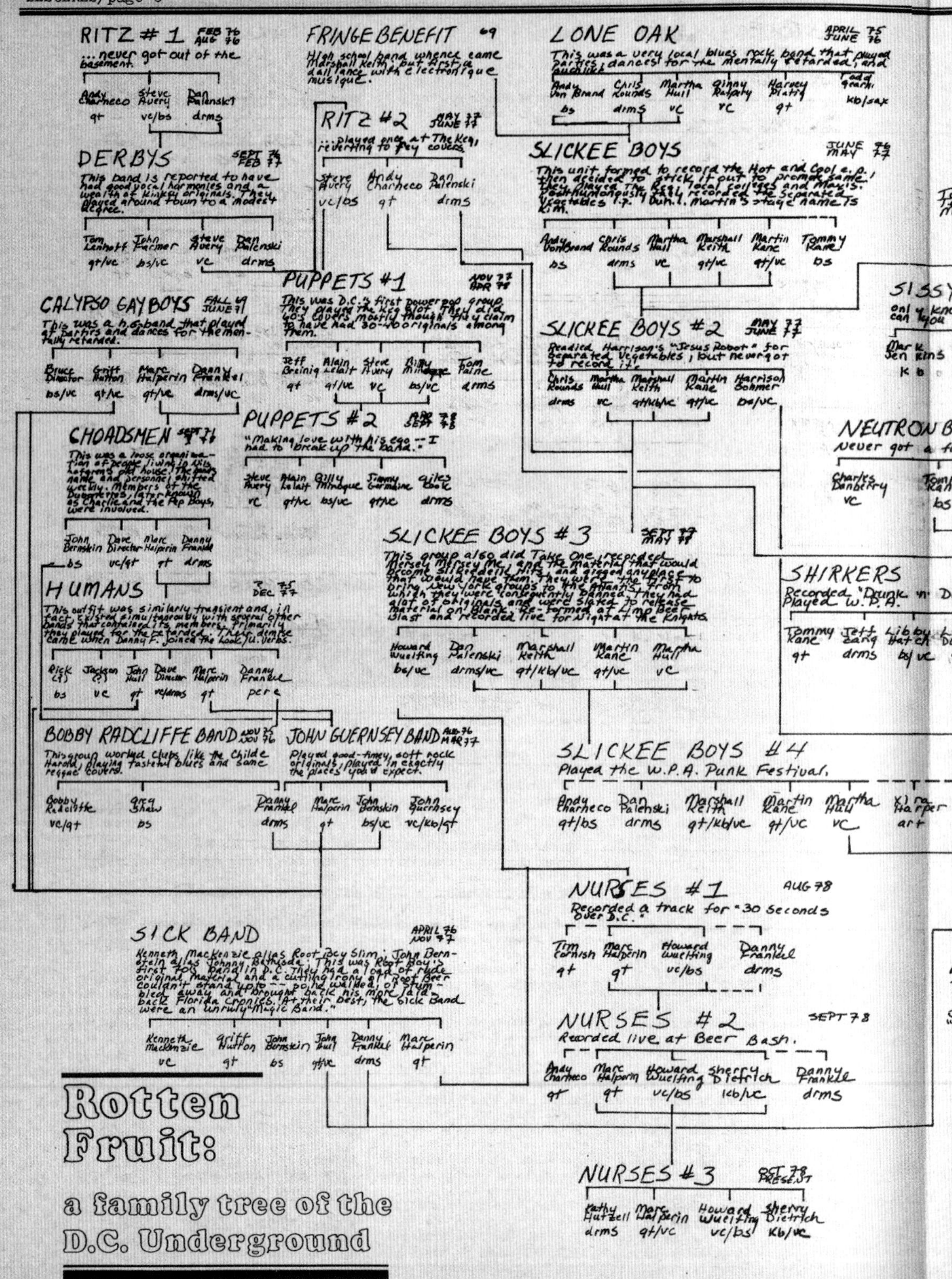

Figure 2.12 "Rotten Fruit: A Family Tree of the DC Underground," *Descenes*, issue 1, 1979. Used by permission.

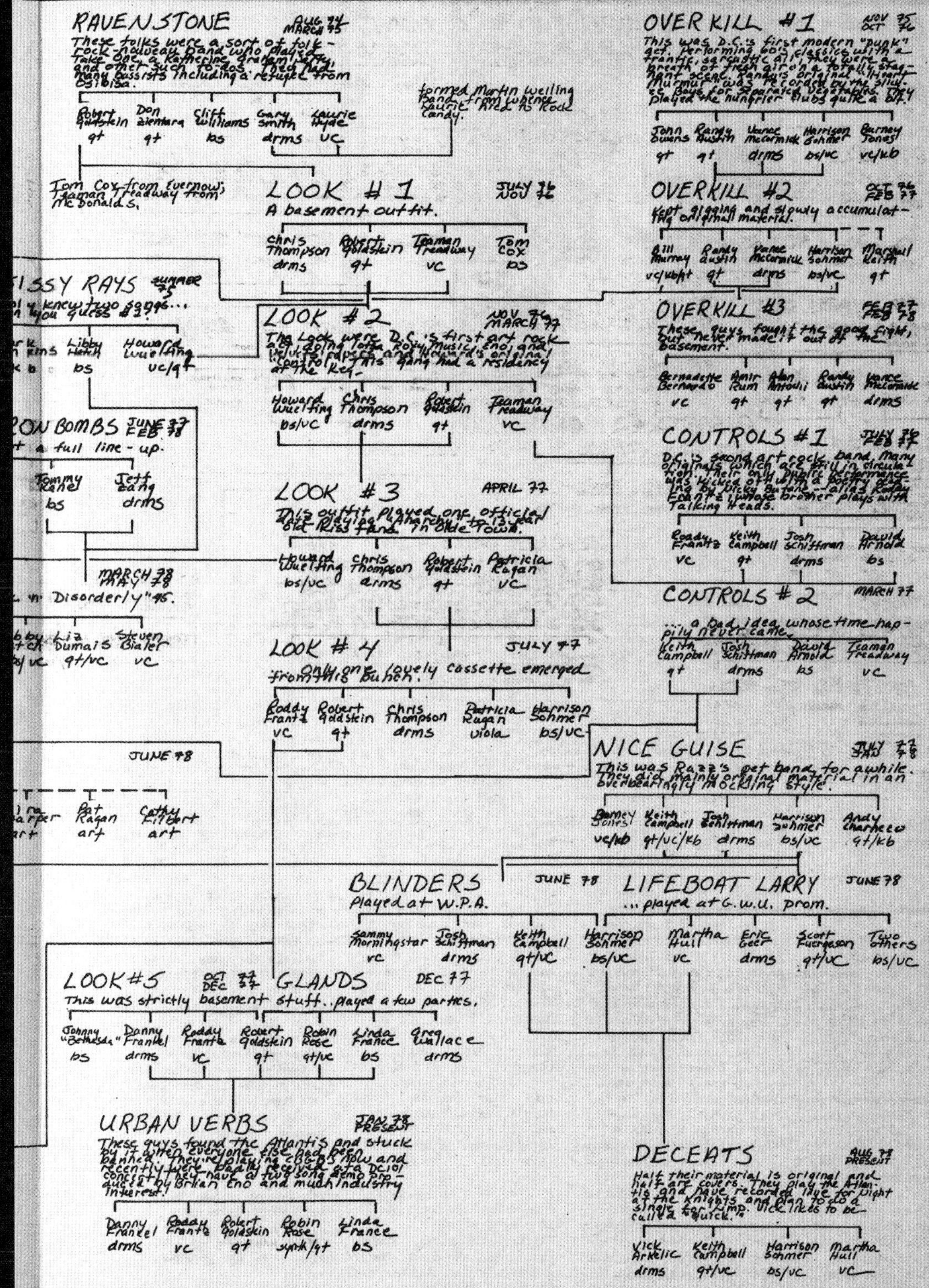

RAVENSTONE
AUG 74 MARCH 75
These folks were a sort of folk-rock-nouveau band who played Take One, a Katherine Graham soiree, and other such to-dos. They had many bassists including a refugee from Osibisa.
Robert Goldstein gt
Don Zientara gt
Cliff Williams bs
Gary Smith drms
Laurie Hyde vc
formed Martin Welling Band from Lubing Laurie. Also to Rock Candy.
Tom Cox from Evernow; Teaman Treadway from McDonald's.
OVERKILL #1
NOV 75 OCT 76
This was D.C.'s first modern "punk" act. Performing 60's classics with a frantic, sarcastic air, they were a breath of fresh air in a totally stagnant scene.
John Owens gt
Randy Austin gt
Vance McCormick drms
Harrison Sohmer bs/vc
Barney Jones vc/kb
LOOK #1
JULY 76 NOV 76
A basement outfit.
Chris Thompson drms
Robert Goldstein gt
Teaman Treadway vc
Tom Cox bs
OVERKILL #2
OCT 76 FEB 77
Kept gigging and slowly accumulating original material.
Bill Murray vc/kb/gt
Randy Austin gt
Vance McCormick drms
Harrison Sohmer bs/vc
Marshall Keith gt
SISSY RAYS
SUMMER 75
Libby Hertl bs
Howard Wuelfing vc/gt
LOOK #2
NOV 76 MARCH 77
The Look were D.C.'s first art rock act, doing lotsa Roxy Music, Eno and Velvets, and Howard's original. This gang had a residency at the Keg.
Howard Wuelfing bs/vc
Chris Thompson drms
Robert Goldstein gt
Teaman Treadway vc
OVERKILL #3
FEB 77 FEB 78
These guys fought the good fight, but never made it out of the basement.
Bernadette Bernardo vc
Amir Rum gt
Alan Antoshi gt
Randy Austin gt
Vance McCormick drms
RON BOMBS
JUNE 77 FEB 78
t a full line-up.
Tommy Kane bs
Jeff Bang drms
CONTROLS #1
JULY 76 FEB 77
D.C.'s second art rock band. Many originals which are still in circulation. Their only public performance was kicked off with ... Roddy Frantz, whose brother plays with Talking Heads.
Roddy Frantz vc
Keith Campbell gt
Josh Schiffman drms
David Arnold bs
LOOK #3
APRIL 77
This outfit played one official date.
Howard Wuelfing bs/vc
Chris Thompson drms
Robert Goldstein gt
Patricia Ragan vc
MARCH 78 MAY 78
"... 'n' Disorderly"
Liz Dumais gt/vc
Steven Bialer vc
CONTROLS #2
MARCH 77
... a bad idea whose time happily never came.
Keith Campbell gt
Josh Schiffman drms
David Arnold bs
Teaman Treadway vc
LOOK #4
JULY 77
Only one lovely cassette emerged from this bunch.
Roddy Frantz vc
Robert Goldstein gt
Chris Thompson drms
Patricia Ragan viola
Harrison Sohmer bs/vc
JUNE 78
NICE GUISE
JULY 77 JAN 78
This was Razz's pet band for awhile. They did mainly original material in an overbearingly mocking style.
Barney Jones vc/kb
Keith Campbell gt/vc/kb
Josh Schiffman drms
Harrison Sohmer bs/vc
Andy Charneco gt/kb
Pat Ragan art
Cathy Kilbert art
BLINDERS
JUNE 78
Played at W.P.A.
LIFEBOAT LARRY
JUNE 78
... played at G.W.U. prom.
Sammy Morningstar vc
Josh Schiffman drms
Keith Campbell gt/vc
Harrison Sohmer bs/vc
Martha Hull vc
Eric Geer drms
Scott Furgeson gt/vc
Two others bs/vc
LOOK #5
OCT 77 DEC 77
GLANDS
DEC 77
This was strictly basement stuff.. played a few parties.
Johnny "Bethesda" bs
Danny Frankel drms
Roddy Frantz vc
Robert Goldstein gt
Robin Rose gt/vc
Linda France bs
Greg Wallace drms
URBAN VERBS
JAN 78 PRESENT
These guys found the Atlantis and stuck ... Recently were ... received at a DC101 concert. They have a two song demo produced by Brian Eno and much industry interest.
Danny Frankel drms
Roddy Frantz vc
Robert Goldstein gt
Robin Rose synth/gt
Linda France bs
DECEATS
AUG 78 PRESENT
Half their material is original and half are covers. They play the Atlantis and have recorded live for Night at the Knights and plan to do a single for Limp. Vick likes to be called "Quick."
Vick Arkelic drms
Keith Campbell gt/vc
Harrison Sohmer bs/vc
Martha Hull vc

overlapping musical false starts and one-offs populating DC punk's early days. It illustrated how, in many ways, punk was a point on a musical and cultural continuum, rather than the sui generis explosion it often felt like.

Three more issues of *Descenes* followed in 1979, maintaining the first issue's granular focus on DC's small, but promising, punk subculture. The second issue included interviews with the Slickee Boys, the Young Turds, and Da Chumps, along with an addition to the first issue's family tree. This time, the drawing appended a rundown of White Boy's various live incarnations, along with details on the latest lineup of the Slickee Boys and a newer band called No Joe, which included singer and songwriter Mark Hoback and musician and producer Don Zientara.[70] Considering the popularity of the Razz, their absence from both editions of the family tree is glaring although, aside from a couple of reviews, *Descenes* tended not to cover them in depth.

By the third issue of *Descenes*, published in July 1979 and with DCeats on its cover, the zine's impact was evident. Even Andy Schwartz, editor of *New York Rocker*, wrote in to offer praise, describing *Descenes* as "one of the best-put-together and best-written [fanzines] I've seen." Schwartz remarked that "the simplicity and cleanliness of the layout reminded me of the earliest issues of *NY ROCKER*, and the whole thing exuded the same kind of sense of excitement and discovery at what's going on in your own backyard." The placement of Schwartz's correspondence at the top of the "Letters" section indicated the Wuelfings' pride in having received it, but the letter that followed was an equally resonant endorsement. This message, written in telegram-terse prose, was from David Thomas, vocalist for the Ohio-based Pere Ubu, already a highly influential postpunk band. "DC sounds like it's getting serious," he declared. "Keep up the good work."

Descenes final issue of 1979 appeared in December, with Half Japanese on the cover. Mark Jenkins' interview with David and Jad Fair, the brothers at the core of the Uniontown, Maryland, band, was conducted following their second-ever live performance. David Fair lost interest in the interview about halfway through and walked out—"I'm not rude. I'm a nice guy, but I'm gonna go upstairs and watch the bands"—but the interview is one of the earliest documents of a group that could rightly claim significant credit for the lo-fi, outsider, DIY nature of indie rock in the years ahead. The brothers also provided a list of their essential records, offering a blueprint for understanding where they stood in 1979. Alongside protopunk standards like the Stooges, Velvet Underground, MC5, and New York Dolls are less expected choices like Tapper Zukie's "Man Ah Warrior" and Armand Schaubroeck Steals' "Ratfucker."[71]

Another highly influential band at the beginning of its career highlighted in this issue is Bad Brains. Dave Findley's article finds him hanging out with "the only Black punk band in DC" at their home in "an unassuming suburban rambler" in Forestville, Maryland. After a discussion of the band's roots in jazz fusion, their contempt for disco, and affection for the Ramones, the band picked up their instruments, offering a private concert featuring songs, such as "Don't Need It," that redefined punk. "I realize I am being blown away," Findley wrote with odd detachment. "The sound is well-honed, original, and powerful." A powerful creative force had arrived in DC's scene. "Some people think the new wave is dying, but more of my friends are getting into it," vocalist H. R. said. "I think it's just getting started."

The years 1976 through 1979 saw the birth of DC's punk scene, growing out of a cauldron of influences years in the making. The diversity in aesthetic of the scene's fanzines mirrored the inchoate state of the city's punk community. The more daring, artistic air of *The Infiltrator* sat as comfortably alongside the spare, newspaper-like *Descenes* as it did the rough, proudly amateur look that *It's Only a Movie* and early issues of *Vintage Violence* presented. Divergent as their appearances could seem, all of DC's first-wave fanzines were on a mission to establish and promote a scene rivaling those in New York, Los Angeles, and London. Their hopes were about to be realized.

Notes

1. Mark Andersen and Mark Jenkins. *Dance of Days: Two Decades of Punk in the Nation's Capital*, updated and expanded 4th ed. (Brooklyn: Akashic Books, 2009), 13.
2. Richard Harrington, interview with the author, September 10, 2019.
3. Howard Wuelfing, "Rotten Fruit: A Family Tree of the DC Underground," *Descenes* 1:1, 1979, 8.
4. Jim Green and Steve Lorber, "America Underground: Capitol Radio (& Clubs, Bands, Etc.)," *Trouser Press*, 6:8, 1979, 48–50.
5. Myron Bretholz, "Overkill at the Keg," *Unicorn Times*, 3:12, 1976, 28.
6. Fogelberg was the quintessential example of the soft rock singer / song-

writers dominating popular music in the mid-1970s.

7. Andersen and Jenkins, *Dance of Days*.
8. CBGB was a music venue in New York City closely identified with the earliest punk and new wave bands like the Ramones, Blondie, Television, and Talking Heads.
9. Georgetown is a neighborhood in DC known for its wealthy residents, as well as its active shopping and entertainment district. In the 1960s and 1970s, in particular, the neighborhood was one of DC's primary locations for music venues. Charlie McCollum, "Has There Ever Been a Washington Sound?" *Washington Star*, January 23, 1977.
10. Norm DeValliere, telephone interview with the author, February 11, 2020.
11. *It's Only a Movie*, issue 1, 1976, Fairfax, VA.
12. Norm DeValliere, "The Slickee Boys," *It's Only a Movie*, issue 1, 1976, 4.
13. DeValliere, telephone interview.
14. *It's Only a Movie*, Issue 2, 1977, 6.
15. DeValliere, telephone interview.
16. Michael Layne Heath, interview with the author, January 6, 2019.
17. Heath.
18. Heath.
19. Richard Harrington, "Ramones: Empty Punk," *Washington Post*, October 12, 1977.
20. Harrington.
21. Harrington, interview.
22. Heath is likely referring to the August 7, 1976, issue.
23. Heath, interview.
24. The Hangmen were one of the DC area's premier garage bands in the 1960s. Their signature song, "What A Girl Can't Do" (covered by the Slickee Boys with Martha Hull on vocals as "What A Boy Can't Do"), was a regional hit, hitting number one on Arlington, VA, radio station WEAM's top 40 chart on February 7, 1966. As *Garage Hangover* explained, when the band appeared at the Giant Music store in Falls Church, Virginia, the turnout was so massive that police were called to break up the "near-riot," which was highlighted by fainting teenagers and hundreds of dollars in property damage.
25. Heath, interview.
26. Heath.
27. DeValliere, telephone interview.
28. Michael Heath, "DC Rockers: Sleepytime Time Is Over," *Vintage Violence*, issue 1, March 1977, 8–9.
29. Ruby Starr was a vocalist most notable for her work with the Southern Rock band Black Oak Arkansas in the 1970s.
30. Tiny Desk Unit was on the more experimental end of the new wave scene, releasing an LP and an EP on 9½ x 16" Records, and performing often during its run from 1979 to 1981.
31. Heath, "DC Rockers."
32. Larry Rohter, "Punks on Parade: The Local Scene," *Washington Post*, May 1, 1977.
33. *Vintage Violence*, issue 1, March 1977, Fairfax, VA.
34. Howard Wuelfing, email to the author, September 2, 2019.
35. "Control" was reincarnated as a Slickee Boys song when Wuelfing joined that band.
36. Howard Wuelfing, phone interview with the author, September 11, 2018.
37. Sharon Conway, "Urban Verbs: Still Waiting for That Big-Time Contract," *Washington Post*, February 19, 1979.
38. Marie Provost, "The AU Connection," *The Infiltrator*, 1:1, 1979, 34.
39. Michael Heath, "The Controls: March 25, American U.," *Vintage Violence*, 1:2, 1977, 9.
40. Heath, interview.
41. Patricia Ragan, "Rock and Ramone over with *Rocket to Russia*," *Vintage Violence*, 1:4, 1977, 5.
42. Mark Opsasnick, *Rock the Potomac: Popular Music and Early-Era Rock and Roll in the Washington, DC, Area* (Saint Petersburg: BookLocker, 2019), 731.
43. Valerie Suzanne Flynn, "Razz Is Back," *Unicorn Times*, June 1977, 14.
44. Michael Heath, "Razz Redux," *Vintage Violence*, 1:4, 1977, 13.
45. Michael Heath, "The Story from the Atlantis," *Vintage Violence*, 1:5, 1978, 7–8.
46. Heath, interview.
47. Elizabeth Hand, email to the author, November 25, 2018.
48. Jason Heller, "Elizabeth Hand on Her 5 Favorite Books About Music," AV Club, April 20, 2016, https://music.avclub.com/elizabeth-hand-on-her-5-favorite-books-about-music-1798246869.
49. Kennedy was a member of Da Chumps and, later, Half Japanese, among other bands.
50. Heath, interview.
51. Eve Golden, *Golden Images: 41 Essays on Silent Film Stars* (Jefferson, NC: McFarland, 2001), 140.
52. Mary Leary, interview with the author, January 4, 2019.
53. The Corcoran School of the Arts and Design was a hub for many of the scene's early participants. Robert Kennedy, "At 3 Mile River," *The Infiltrator*, 1:2, 1979, 10.
54. This is a possible nod to the Washington Color School movement of the 1950s to the 1970s, which drew the art world's eye to DC via vivid abstract expressionist paintings by Morris Louis, Gene Davis, Alma Thomas, and others.
55. Leary, interview.
56. *FILE Megazine* was a Canadian arts and culture periodical that was published from 1972 to 1989.
57. Leary, interview.
58. Wuelfing, personal communication, September 11, 2018.
59. Anonymous, "The Word," *Unicorn Times* 6, no. 2 (November 1978): 8.
60. Wuelfing, personal communication.
61. Tina Wuelfing, later known as Tina Cargile, died in September 2010.
62. Howard Wuelfing, email to the author, September 24, 2018.
63. Wuelfing, personal communication.
64. Henry Rollins, in-person interview with the author, Los Angeles, January 3, 2019.
65. Ian MacKaye, interviewed by David Ensminger, *Left of the Dial*, 1:1, 2001, 37–51.
66. Howard Wuelfing, "Talking Trash with White Boy," *Descenes*, 1:1, 1979, 7.
67. Anonymous, "Molester Denied Plea," *Washington Post*, September 9, 1994.
68. James Sinks, "Skip Groff," Signaland, July 13, 2015, http://signaland.com/posts/2015/07/13.php.
69. Frame is a British music journalist and rock historian known for his detailed, well-researched pedigree charts that map out the origins and memberships of bands.
70. Zientara would soon be a critical player in DC punk through his production work with Bad Brains and the Dischord Records scene.
71. The former choice was Jad Fair's; the latter was David Fair's.

3

All Right, Here We Go, 1980–1981

DC'S PUNK COMMUNITY was still in its early stages as 1980 dawned, but divisions within the subculture had already developed between its first participants and a crop of new arrivals. By the end of 1980, first-wave DC punk fanzines like *The Infiltrator* and *Descenes* had published their final issues. Similarly, early standout bands like Urban Verbs were either stumbling—the rollout of their eponymous debut album that year for the major label Warner Bros. was essentially snuffed by a harsh review in *Rolling Stone*—or breaking up, as the Razz did at the end of 1979.[1] Meanwhile, a new group of younger punks appeared on the scene by late 1979, asserting their harder-edged take on the subculture.

Some older members of the punk community initially referred to the new arrivals with the sarcastic shorthand "Georgetown Punks" due to their frequent congregation in the shopping district of a wealthy neighborhood in Northwest DC. The younger punks, including members of bands like the Teen Idles and the Untouchables, were more enamored with the staggering power and speed of Bad Brains or the working-class grit of much British punk than they were the Razz's polished crunch or the arty detachment of Urban Verbs. As Ian MacKaye, bassist for the Teen Idles, later declared, namechecking the British band whose fierce mien was a core influence on the new punks, "I wanted to be Sham 69!"[2]

The Georgetown Punks soon had an additional nickname, irking them further—"Teeny Punks." This light-hearted, but dismissive, tag appeared in a review in the June 1980 issue of *Descenes*, contributed by *The Infiltrator*'s Mary Leary. Her assessment of a Bad Brains and Teen Idles concert at Madam's Organ in DC's Adams Morgan neighborhood expressed appreciation for the Teen Idles' exuberance and communal joy. However, after noting that the band's first set was a mess of "miserable sound, broken strings, and long delays between songs," she remarked upon the group and its friends:

> *Nevertheless, the teenie-punks [sic] held their hard-won places by the stage—drinking, laughing, showing off the spike-haired crew's delight in being packed together—it makes their number seem greater and keeps out the sad truth that "punk" modes of dress and behaviour have been "out" in London and New York for about two years—that (if anything, Mod is "in" to the Anglophile) they are behind the times—displaced people who haven't yet realized their individual importance; theirs is safety in the pack.*[3]

Leary offered backhanded praise of Teen Idles vocalist Nathan Strejcek, describing him as "a Beau Brummell who, if anything, should be mentioned for his clothes," before airing her perception that these new punks seemed to look backward instead of forward:

> *Here's the rub: like most of DC's punks, [Strejcek]'s*

Figure 3.1 The Teen Idles perform on the roof of Blitz, a short-lived punk boutique in the Georgetown neighborhood of DC. This concert occurred on September 27, 1980. Photo by Athena Angelos. From the collection of Dischord Records. Used by permission.

> *quite well-to-do. There's even a term for his ilk coined by Clare: "Georgetown Punks." Punk is in and punk is stylish and these kids don't give a shit if Grandaddy Punks, the Ramones, were suburban boys; they don't care if their music copies other punk and that what started the whole scene was the quest for something new. Undeterred, they emulate the British working-class punks down to the last snarl. Maybe that's why it's hard to take them seriously. Well, they're young—most of them—and I guess everyone has to believe in something.*

Although Leary's review went on to commend the band's "fast, exuberant, excited" second set of the night, MacKaye and his friends felt both aggrieved and motivated upon reading it. "Yeah, we took it hard," MacKaye remembered in 2018. "It's the kind of criticism where I don't see the point of it, honestly. I think we took it as a challenge: 'All right, here we go.'" Regarding the class tensions simmering throughout Leary's criticisms, MacKaye still bristled at the memory. "Nathan Strejcek was *not* well-to-do," he asserted. "That's just fucking bullshit. I think that's just the way [the first wave of DC punks] thought [of us]. I don't know why it would even matter."[4]

Leary's assessment rankled the younger punks, but older members of the scene minimized the idea of a rivalry. "It was significant to the kids; it wasn't significant to us," music writer and former *Hype* publisher Mark Jenkins recalled about the purported schism. "They felt, at various times, that they were being condescended to, or put down, or whatever, and that was certainly not intentional. And a lot of those bands actually had gigs as opening acts in '78, '79, and '80, for the 'older' bands—the bands of people between the ages of 22 and 26 or whatever. Nurses and Tru Fax &

Figure 3.2 David Arnson of the Insect Surfers, circa 1978. Photo by Don Hamerman, Don Hamerman collection of performing arts photographs, Special Collections in Performing Arts, University of Maryland Libraries. Used by permission.

the Insaniacs . . . frequently used the teenage bands as opening acts, and got them gigs in places where they technically weren't supposed to be, since [the venues] were serving alcohol."[5] MacKaye agreed that, although the younger scene felt "scared" and "intimidated" by the older punks, "there was a few that were nice. [Howard] Wuelfing was nice. Diana [Quinn] from Tru Fax was real nice. [Slickee Boys guitarist] Kim Kane was *great*. [Insect Surfers guitarist David] Arnson was all right."[6]

"On one hand, you're talking about teenagers, who are people who are looking to crystallize their sense of identity," Wuelfing later explained, describing the source of the divide: "So, they're very vulnerable and they're very sensitive. For whatever cultural tribe you decide to align with, that's the nature of being a teenager. And on the other hand, if you're a little bit older and you've been doing this thing, and you helped build it, . . . and suddenly all these new people come along and they're doing it a different way, you feel that they're calling into question what you're doing. And that's kind of natural, too."[7]

Leary vividly recalled her feelings from that era when interviewed in 2018: "I—along with lots of others—thought Bad Brains were brilliant," she stated, "[but] hardcore bands started attracting a different element/behavior, which seemed disconnected from a grass roots experience / sense of punk or new wave." That growing split in the scene led to tense exchanges between older punks and newer arrivals. "Fans of bands like the [Teen] Idles apparently had such a thin grasp of what had led to their existence," Leary remembered, "that David Arnson has reported being taunted by skinheads while putting up fliers in Georgetown—for being a 'hippie.'"[8]

Despite the significant role that the wild-haired Arnson had played in establishing the new wave wing of the DC music scene with the Insect Surfers' unpretentiously fun mashup of surf guitar and punk-inspired energy, his band was perceived by some Georgetown Punks as coming from a different musical culture. "They were a good band," MacKaye said later. "I mean, I knew Dave [but] I think at this point, we wanted to be taken seriously, and the Insect Surfers were definitely a band that was not serious in the sense that . . . they were goofy. You know, it was like B-52s. They were fun. And that is not what I was interested in."[9]

Arnson did not specifically recall being called a "hippie," but he did say that similar harassment was common and that it was "very typical to be putting up fliers in Georgetown for a show and then turn around and see, one block behind me, some hardcore punk ripping the flier off of the lamp pole!" Arnson's memories of that transitional period are flecked with the older punks' common perception that the younger punks' congregation in Georgetown implied a degree of privilege. "The hardcore punks—who were often very affluent—thought that anybody older than them was the enemy, because they could play clubs that served alcohol and were, therefore, some kind of sellout," Arnson said. "I remember once going into [Georgetown's] Biograph Theater to see *The Road Warrior* and outside being accosted by about ten hardcore punks who were saying 'Hey, are you in the Urban Verbs or something?!'"[10]

To Leary, an unwelcome shift had occurred. "For me, a very wild young woman who was usually going nuts in the front lines for any musician I liked, hardcore shows weren't much fun," she related. "Those front lines got taken over by angry young men who were much more violent. Before that, women could let themselves go at Cramps shows, for instance, with no worries. Everyone would just work around and with each other."[11]

Leary's discomfort was echoed in a June 1981 letter from a woman to *1981,* a local alternative newspaper.[12] The author declared "perhaps no other group in DC leaves one so stupefied as the 'Georgetown Punks,'" before detailing the sexual harassment she received from a group of younger punks on M Street, one of Georgetown's two primary thoroughfares. Upon hearing one of the bunch singing the Clash's "Guns of Brixton," the woman initially joined in the singalong, as she was "a Clash fanatic of long standing." As she reported, things turned ugly when one of the punks dropped his pants and, crudely distorting the song's lyrics, said to her 'grab my gun.' They then paraded past, . . . and the moment for me to kick the brat in the groin was gone." The letter's author complained that "Washington's punks represent the worst America has to offer," after relaying an anecdote about seeing a punk at the 9:30 Club wearing a jacket that "dripped 'blood' from the words 'I kill children' [on] the day the twenty-third Atlanta child victim had been buried."[13] Expressing the same class perceptions and criticisms of the Georgetown Punks that others employed, she concluded:

> *Having been brought up with the idea that money can buy anything, they have proceeded to buy a culture and then pretend they had a hand in its creation. Even at their age, they have learned well the method by which their elders and ancestors succeeded in obscuring the racial, sexual, and class roots of so much that has made history. . . . The anomaly of the G-town punks is nothing new. Rich kids have always known that all the Earth is theirs for the grabbing, including songs written about other people's struggle against oppression. Never having known any form of real oppression, they can only make them anthems to their own self-centered boredom. A G-town punk singing "Guns of Brixton" is like Reagan singing "Blowin' in the Wind"—a cruel, dangerous joke.*[14]

The Infiltrator Ends

The Infiltrator's final two issues continued mixing Leary's unabashed love for the thriving international punk and new wave scenes with her dedication to DC bands like Nurses, Tru Fax & the Insaniacs, and Insect Surfers. Praise for locals, though, was generally relegated to sections with provincial names like "Local Wax," rather than the larger features dedicated to acts from elsewhere like Roy Loney and Wreckless Eric. The "Critics Poll '79" section in the fifth issue distills the lock that music from outside DC seemed to have on the attention of the scene's tastemakers. Although a litany of local writers and scenesters—including Yesterday & Today Records owner Skip Groff, *Unicorn Times* music critic Joe Sasfy, and Record & Tape Exchange owner Bill Asp—list their favorite releases of 1979, few DC musicians earned mention. The section is instead packed with the likes of Graham Parker, Buzzcocks, the Cramps, and other nonlocals who have since joined the punk and new wave canons.

The Slickee Boys and the Razz are tabbed on several ballots, but little else from DC is honored. One might think something like the gritty "TV Violence" from the Killer Bees or the nervy pop of the Nurses' "Hearts"—two still-overlooked efforts from the 1979 DC scene—might deserve inclusion, but competition from outside the region proved fierce. Groff's list touts the Razz's "Love Is Love" and the Slickee Boys' "Gotta Tell Me Why," both of which he released on his own label, Limp Records. Groff swats away the seeming conflict of interest, saying they "are my fave songs of the year, not because I was involved in them, but I became involved with them because I thought they were the two best songs ever written in DC."[15]

Asp's rundown of his top 1979 releases overflows with enthusiasm for the astounding new music appearing that year. Albums by the Cure, Stiff Little Fingers, Soft Boys,

Figure 3.3 Issues 5 and 6 of *The Infiltrator*, 1980–81. Published by Mary Leary. Used by permission.

and Joy Division are among Asp's favorites, but no DC groups make the cut. Asp compensated for any oversight by later printing his own zine, *Washington Waves*, packing scads of local scene minutiae into one or two photocopied sheets of tabloid-sized paper throughout the latter months of 1980 and into 1981. The zine, generally distributed from Record & Tape Exchange, "was really a brilliant way for him to promote what he was selling at his store and to review local bands, especially the ones that he was working with at the same time," Arnson recalled about Asp, who died in 2004. "He was an amazing promoter and writer, although he was a bit of a curmudgeon and hated hated hated to schmooze, which sometimes put him at a disadvantage."[16]

While the dearth of DC bands on a "best of" list published by a punk and new wave fanzine from DC seems odd, it was less a repudiation of the scene than a symptom of the fact that few DC punk bands even released records in 1979, never mind created music that could be mentioned in the same breath as high-profile contemporaries from elsewhere, like XTC, Elvis Costello, and the Ramones. The year 1979 saw such an embarrassment of riches within the larger worlds of punk, power pop, and new wave that it is understandable the developing DC scene was overlooked, even by its champions. "The local scene was still interesting, but mostly around the psychobilly scene and bands who felt unapologetically idiosyncratic and original, such as the Chumps, the Velvet Monkeys, and Half Japanese," Leary recalled of her tastes circa 1980–81. "I think those sorts of bands were significant, for their role in linking the early new wave / punk attitude with what would morph into post-punk and classic alternative music. And for just continuing to make weird or different music with no apparent 'make it' motivation."[17]

Leary admitted that "in retrospect, I think we may have missed the boat on what for me is the most lasting and significant music/sound development to have happened from the early '80s—hip-hop. I don't know if anything like that had started in DC yet, but if it had, I'm bummed we weren't in on it."[18] Hip-hop did not have much of a foothold in DC in 1980; but go-go music, another underground genre emerging from Black culture, *was* already gaining notice in the region and occasionally mingled with punk. Go-go is "the beating heart of the 'Chocolate City,'" a galvanic hybrid of funk and hip-hop that, for many DC-area residents, became a defining part of the city's cultural identity.[19] Eye-catching, Day-Glo posters used to promote concerts were a distinctive hallmark of the go-go community, dotting the city like "fluorescent flags" that "asserted a territory of black economic, cultural and political power," as author and scholar Natalie Hopkinson wrote.[20] The genre was pioneered by groups like Chuck Brown & the Soul Searchers, Rare Essence, and Trouble Funk—the latter shared stages with DC hardcore punk bands and found coverage within punk fanzines like *Thrillseeker*. "We played with Minor Threat and other bands whose style was totally different from ours, but we always felt welcome," Trouble Funk's bassist, Big Tony Fisher, recalled in 2013. "What I do know about these two styles of music is that we both have that raw edge. Both are very free and open styles, and have a lot of room to allow the audience to take part fully in the live show."[21]

WASHINGTON WAVES 2

Published by Record & Tape Exchange of Virginia 821 N. Taylor Street Arlington VA 22203 (One block from METRO) 522-6497 or 241-0394 Submissions are welcome but obviously space is ltd. We may edit copy as it comes to us. C.1980

data panik Aw gee! DC's latest hope for the Great White Punk the TEEN IDLES have split up, two of the little misfits joining up with newly formed EX-TORTS. Limp Records will do the posthumous thing vinylly with an Ep of the lad's fun noise. Whilemean in the real world rumours abound regarding local power rock quartet and their all but confirmed label deal . . something about an image problem . . Speaking of images, IMP will presenting the notorious PLASMATICS on November 20th at the Ontario. There will be a game of russian roulette to determine the opening band for that evening's festivities Also IMP will be doing some bookings at 9:30 in the n to d future with MARTHA & THE MUFFINS and SQUEEZE being mentioned prominently. The main components of the Killer Bees have now started a new band called the KNOBS and the NURSES are looking to broaden the music horizon with the addition of a new guitarist. Congrats to TDU for upcoming New York (Hurrah) and Boston gigs; they will be showcasing MISSION OF BURMA at an upcoming date as part of the Boston arrangement. Heard the SLICKEES slayed them at Danceteria and have been invited back but that venue's future is cloudy due to liquor violations; said offenses caused cancellation of INSECT SURFERS gig there. The Surfers also had the promise of several opening gigs with the B-52's fall apart as NY management has decided on Kid Creole & the Coconuts for that role.

The Podboys did experience modest success on their recent road trip to the north, breaking new ground in Worcester and Salem in Massachusetts and in Portland, Maine. NYC gigs proved of interest to sources close to Armegeddon Records of the UK and Island Records stateside. Rumours: Slickees to rush release a new single (the old EP just hit the playlist of WHBI in NYC) and news of drummer Chris Thompson departure from TDU. Just a personal note here; We've had several calls about "will you cover this event/show/happening" We have no staff per se. If it's something you think should have some coverage be our guest to send it in.

d.c LIVE! R.E.M.- 9:30- 10/3/80

In the blink of an eye a new corps of art rockers comes to fruition in DC. REM's third ever gig gave sneakingly brief evidence to this process, incorporating snatches of Joy Division, Tom Verlaine, Echo and the Bunnymen, and Killing Joke and a lot of unexpected muscle in their approach; no dronovoid mess this! The rhythms pop and punch a la XTC but the hooks are absent (of course, this is art after all). REM's progress will be noted and their contemporaries should take heed: don't look back, someone may be gaining on you.

BREAKERS and SYNDROME - Reeks - 10/18/80

On two days notice, the Breakers - one of Baltimore's least known bands and probably its best - gave a crowd of 50 or so far more than its moneys' worth. the Breakers have a tight, clean sound with soaring harmonies and a keen sense of dynamics. They play well-constructed songs with such an infective exuberance that they just about force you to dance. The Breakers won't be little-known long.

Syndrome is a new Annapolis band. Their opening set kept everyone on their feet but showed little in the way of original material. Their covers (including 2 Neil Young songs! surely a first for Reeks) were performed mostly note for note. Still their few originals showed promise and the playing was solid.

BILLY & the SHAKES plus YOUNG PROFESSIONALS Desperado's - 10/27/80

The homegrown British invasion lives! Last month we gave the low-down on the Caves and this ish spots the very hot Billy and the Shakes. The Beatle cop is obvious, with several of the Fab's best sprinkled throughout their set, but the groups' perfectly rendered originals ("Mama's Little Girl" -their local single and "Desi Arnez") more than hold their own. Tight playing and the good-natured wise ass of the frontman Billy put the Shakes at the forefront of DC teen hop bands.

The Young Professionals on the other hand seem a bit too diffuse. The elimination of one of their girl singers has helped to focus the intents of the band to some degree but if the Young Pros' aim is contemporary electro-pop they need to concentrate more on more danceable melodies and hooks. They perform an outstanding rendition of a Buddy Holly classic "Well Alright" that made my evening!

EAR WAX The last few weeks have seen an explosion of new product on the import front with debut albums from several of our fave bands. The KILLING JOKE Lp (EG Records) met our expectations and more with a furious blend of punk-art wave fusion and the recent pop excursions of THE TEARDROP EXPLODES find realization on their Polydor Lp entitled "Kilamanjaro". Colin Newman of WIRE has a solo effort out on Begger's Banquet; "A-Z" returns to the textured minimalism of his group's earlier albums. Those who enjoyed the smooth posturings of UB40's recent disc will like-wise enjoy "The Label" by THE RELUCTANT STEREOTYPES on UK WEA and the party-minded can pick up on a new JOE "KING" CARRASCO album on Stiff. Late arrivals include COMSAT ANGELS first Lp and the "Luminous Basement" album from the TOURISTS replete with free single. New singles from SIMPLE MINDS with a ltd. flexi included; those in the know should find a bit of ecstasy in the debut 45 from the COLONEL; the legendary RICO does the classic "Sea Cruise" on a new offering from 2-Tone;Domestically two new ones from the electronic OUR DAUGHTER'S WEDDING and some ska-rock on NEW MATH's 2nd single (their first "Die Trying" was great!). POLY STYRENE formerly of X-Ray Spex goes goo-goo on her solo "Talk In Toytown". Punx should be pleased with the new UK DECAY single and ECHO & the BUNNYMEN triumph anew with "The Puppet" on Korova. COMING!:Discs from SPANDAU BALLET, FACTORY QUARTET (label sampler), BAUHAUS MODERN MAN (Ultravox proteges), BASEMENT 5, U2, THE BOOKS, PASSAGE, DURUTTI COLUMN, BERLIN BLONDES, OMID's 2nd Lp, ANDROIDS OF MU. Availabl from RECORD & TAPE EXCHANGE, Arlington and Falls Church. Arlington store 1 block from METRO Ballston station, call 522-6497 or 241-0394.

GIGS Nightclub 9:30 (393-0930)- DJ nights each Wednesday; SVT with Teen Idles; Y-Pants with Transfactor; DNA with Indoor Life; Insect Surfers and the Bongos; Tex Rabinowitz plus the Pin-ups; Bush Tetras; Who's Got the Funk #4; Video #6; Nona Hendryx. - DESPERADO'S (338-5220) Puppets with Pin-ups(F) and Dispensers(S); the Tools; Tex Rubinowitz; The Crank. - ONTARIO THEATRE - Plasmatics and Slickee Boys; Stranglers, Black Market Baby, Bad Brains + films; Iggy Pop, Joan Jett & Insect Surfers.- COLUMBIA STATION (667-2900)- Billy & the Shakes plus Pin-ups; Reactions and the Accused.- UMD (454-2803)- Ultravox plus Free Base; Rockpile plus Moon Martin.- PSYCHEDELLY (654-6611)- Reactions & Nightman; Billy & the Shakes and Dirty work; Tex Rubinowitz. REEKS (543-5433)- Accused, Breakers & Darkside; Young Professionals and Tru Fax & the Insaniacs; Warsaw Pak; the Charts; Dan Yody Band; Nurses. CHANCERY (789-0604)- Accused; Black Market Baby and Keen; Insect Surfers and Beex; Billy & Shake plus Puppets; Crank and Free Base and Tru Fax & the Insaniacs; Reactions.- CHILDE Harold (483-6702)- Nightman; Dirty Work, Trish Burton plus the Kids; Warsaw Pak; Premier International; Puppets plus Dispensers; Insect Surfers with the Caves(F) and Tony Perkins & Psychotics(S) BAYOU (333-2897)- Gang of 4 plus Pylon; Athletico Spizz 80 and 999.

WASHINGTON WAVES II

Figure 3.4 *Washington Waves*, issue 2, circa November 1980. Published by Bill Asp.

The sixth and final issue of *The Infiltrator* appeared in early 1981 and possessed a noticeable shift in tone from earlier efforts, both aesthetically and, seemingly, in its enthusiasm toward its own existence. More acrid in tone than previous issues, thanks primarily to the "What I Hate" motif throughout the issue via lists by Leary (who sarcastically, if tellingly, cites *The Infiltrator* on hers), artwork by Michael Reidy that détournes photos of "Leave It to Beaver" cast members and serial killer Charles Starkweather, and an article that vents about the likes of Elvis Costello, Howard Wuelfing, and the new wave; "What's this 'New Wave' crap?" pseudonymously named author Clone Ranger queries peevishly. "Ain't no New Wave; just a buncha amateur pop poseurs. Once again, the record companies are hyping more old shit as new shit."[22] Leary explained that "in a way, it was the most conceptual of all the issues; more informed by visual and performance art," adding that issue six's sardonic tone "fit in really well with a sort of black humor, ultimate punk ethos, I thought. 'What we hate' was just a way of turning the typical on-the-street question inside out."[23]

The casually acerbic tone of the final

issue was also influenced by a change in how the fanzine was duplicated. According to Leary, issue six was "the cheapest and easiest to produce, done totally on a Xerox machine" in a letter-sized format, unlike previous issues printed in a larger, more professional-looking tabloid newsprint format. Leary and her main graphic designer, Kevin MacDonald, "responded to [the new] format by being more fanzine-ish and less conventionally journalistic," she explained. "In other words, more fun, more goofy, more 'What do we feel like doing?'"

Leary shut down the zine following issue six's publication. Aside from her feeling that *The Infiltrator* had "served our purpose" by amplifying media conversation around local bands, the financial juggling inherent in running a small publication was increasingly onerous.[24] Fanzines with advertising, like *The Infiltrator*, could defray publishing costs somewhat but, eventually, there was not enough revenue to continue. "On a practical level, we were running out of gas for funding the thing," Leary conceded:

> *Between 1979 and 1980, some of the local bigwigs met with me at [music venue] dc space to suggest that* The Infiltrator *could become more of a successful, enduring publication by doing, say, a cover story on [the popular New York City new wave band] Blondie, [and] then selling a full-page, back cover ad to Blondie's record label.* The Infiltrator *had never "sold out" in that way—and the business end of the magazine was my weakest point. For me, there was no fun—or integrity—in such an approach. I pretty much responded with "You're kidding!"*[25]

Beyond financial concerns, the core of talented contributors buoying Leary's vision also became harder to bring back. "Each issue of *The Infiltrator* depended on the availability of unpaid staff who were willing to put in a fair amount of effort," she explained. On top of this, "the scene had changed a lot," she asserted. "It was more categorical/splintery than it had been in the beginning. I had shifted from doing more carefree, lower-paid work at a record store and printing press to more demanding, white-collar employment that made it harder to be out every night, seeing everything. And I was getting into and learning about all sorts of things—you know, growing."[26]

The Infiltrator was gone, but its influence lingered within the punk scene. Future Rites of Spring and Fugazi vocalist/guitarist Guy Picciotto was only in his early teens during *The Infiltrator*'s run, but "that one made a big impact on me and was very well executed," he remembered. "It looked great and supplied lots of information about local bands when a lot of what was going on was still somewhat of a mystery to me."[27] Leary's broadening horizons pulled her away from DC punk, but the growth of the local scene that *The Infiltrator* engendered conversely pulled more new people into its orbit.

DC-born author and television producer George Pelecanos recalled the area's rising punk and new wave community, which he was drawn to at the dawn of the 1980s. "[The DC scene] was exciting because it was new and, because we felt we were oddballs and outsiders in a way, the music spoke to us," he said. "Going out at night, I'd see bands at places like dc space and, of course, the old 9:30 [Club], and at spots like The Local Gentry on 8th Street SE. It wasn't so much chasing certain bands as it was being out at night and happening upon them. It was adventure."[28]

Descenes Departs

The vinyl debuts in 1980 of Bad Brains and the Teen Idles heralded the shift into a new era, as did additions to the hardcore punk scene like State of Alert (SOA)—featuring the vocalist Henry Garfield, who would join the Southern California hardcore band Black Flag in 1981 and subsequently change his last name to Rollins—and the Untouchables, fronted by Ian MacKaye's younger brother Alec, a powerful creative force of his own. Despite this rapid growth within the musical side of the scene, another linchpin zine folded in the summer of 1980.

Like *The Infiltrator*, *Descenes* produced two more issues in 1980 before quietly ceasing operations after its July issue. *Descenes*' devotion to the local scene ultimately led to burnout. "I think we had just really extensively covered the DC

Figure 3.5 Issues 5 and 6 of *Descenes*, June and July 1980. Published by Howard and Tina Wuelfing. Used by permission.

scene, and . . . bands weren't forming quick enough," Wuelfing remembered. "We didn't want to just keep covering the same bands over and over and over again. Unless everything broke up and reformed, like, every six months, we just ran out of subject matter."[29]

Months before the Wuelfings' zine ended, *Unicorn Times* already reckoned that "*Descenes* has, predictably enough, run into the brick wall dictated by its narrow (and narrow-minded) domain of appropriate subject matter. Increasingly, we are treated to articles on bands (Half Japanese, Loverspike, Snitch) who are seldom seen or heard."[30] Although the July 1980 issue of *Descenes*, featuring Tiny Desk Unit's Susan Mumford on its cover, did not announce itself as the finale, Wuelfing's displeasure with the local scene was obvious. That issue's fiery opening editorial overflowed with frustration:

> *In the very first* Descenes, *we dedicated ourselves to a number of "lofty" ideals, all basically aimed at aiding the local punk community. Now we'd like to amend that. Well, let's fuck it completely! Not that we aim to line our pockets and start promoting private interests, but we'll be damned if we're gonna serve what today's new wave community at large wants—non-analytical, non-controversial boosterite toadying, and of all sorts of boring, derivative, exploitative lamebrains. Uhn-uh. Fuck that and them.*[31]

Mirroring Leary's later observation that the once small and unified scene had splintered ("various ripples off that first wave have become mini–status quos of their own: power pop; buzz-stomp; folk nouveau; art rock mk II"), Wuelfing also despaired how quickly, in his view, that musicians stooped to imitation within a new art form. "Bands emulate rather than initiate," he opined. "Moulding themselves in the image of that which has already proven itself marketable to the mass merchandising concerns."

Few avoided Wuelfing's wrath, whether it was "art-sters" who "elevate it to some holy quest to unchain their oh-so-fascinating personal visions" or the germinating hardcore scene consisting of "Teeny-punks teem[ing] in back rooms retreading Sham [69] licks" or even, conversely, the likes of those who looked down on the young punks, since "at least they're young. This is just getting their feet wet. People of other cliques' age bracket started out aping Mountain[32] for chrissakes!" Building to a crescendo, Wuelfing starts the next paragraph with "The art-rockers . . ." before conspicuously redacting the words that followed, replacing them in a different typeface and larger point size with "this next part was too incendiary—it would have put our asses deep in hot water and most of you grunts wouldn't have understood anyway." His sentiments were clear enough, even for readers who skipped the editorial's conclusion: "Aw, you all make me sick. Grow up and get smart."

In his review of the Slickee Boys' *Separated Vegetables* album elsewhere in the issue, Wuelfing elaborated on his view of the difference between the DC punk's beginnings around 1976 and where things stood by 1980. Despite "a wealth of bad memories" about those earliest days, such as "playing to boogie fiends at The Keg—in an art rock band, no less," Wuelfing defines what was lost in the interim, writing that, in the beginning, "there was a much better sense of community—a better defined sense of us-against-them. The Art-rockers and punkers both got turned on by both the Damned and Pere Ubu, and the music showed that."[33] Howard and Tina Wuelfing's next publication, *Discords*, debuted in March 1981 and focused instead on coverage of regional scenes throughout the United States, though still including a DC scene report by Howard titled somewhat elegiacally "Descenes." During the period between the final issues of *Descenes* and *The Infiltrator* and the debut of *Discords*, a new fanzine stepped to the fore.

Capitol Crisis

Much as *The Infiltrator*'s staff featured alumni of WGTB—the influential radio station operating out of DC's Georgetown University until school administrators shut it down in 1979—another early DC punk fanzine had similar roots. *Capitol Crisis*, launched by the erstwhile WGTB disc jockey Xyra Harper, sought to adapt WGTB's tastemaking magic into print.[34] Harper's view that DC was "such a dead town" inspired the title of the fanzine, which debuted in November 1980. "People were bursting to get out and be creative, and they had to create something because there wasn't anything," she recalled.[35] *Capitol Crisis* was visually striking and critically astute, helping fill the void left by the discontinuation of *The Infiltrator* and *Descenes*. Harper was an experienced interviewer elsewhere—speaking with the Clash for the first issue of *The Infiltrator*, as well as numerous other bands for WGTB broadcasts—but the first issue surprisingly consists almost entirely of reviews and endearingly innocent filler like a quiz ("Who wrote 'Revolt Into

Figure 3.6 Xyra Harper of *Capitol Crisis*, circa 1980. Photo by Lucian Perkins. Used by permission.

Style' and how does it pertain to music today?") and a crossword puzzle (e.g., 47 across: "A 20/20 song").

The first issue positioned *Capitol Crisis* as seemingly another local publication more interested in music from outside DC's new punk community. Local representation was mostly limited to a lukewarm review of a Slickee Boys single, an affectionate—if lightly condescending—live review of the final Teen Idles concert ("I luv the little buggers & am hopeful they'll stick around"[36]), and a handful of news items. The issue concludes with a presentation of three "top 20" lists from the zine's staff. Harper and contributing editors/writers Tim Beard and Steve Gillis touted sixty items, but only one—Nurses' "Hearts"—was local. As with *The Infiltrator*'s top lists, though, most of the choices display a prescient ear for musicians who resonated for decades—the Jam, the Ruts, Bush Tetras, and the Slits, among others. Even better, unjustly forgotten gems from the Pointed Sticks, Rousers, Luxury, and Basement 5 are included, along with choice cuts from other genres like Bootsy Collins' "Mug Push," Sheila and B. Devotion's "Spacer," and Zapp's "More Bounce to the Ounce."

An "extra" supplement to the first issue was subsequently circulated, dominated by references to DC groups like Black Market Baby, Urban Verbs, the Teen Idles, and Tiny Desk Unit, ensuring that the burgeoning local scene was not ignored. "PLEASE NOTE," read a small message pasted in toward the bottom of the layout, "we were anxious to get our 1st issue out, so there were some rough spots. Please bear with us, as putting together a mag with limited time, staff & resources can be taxing. As previously stated, we invite your contributions in way of art, articles & photos."[37]

Capitol Crisis made its mark immediately, combining the aesthetic ambition and creativity of *The Infiltrator* with the handmade energy of *Vintage Violence*. *Capitol Crisis*'s photocopied pages bore a consistent look that, while seemingly rough around the edges, had clearly been produced with thought and skill. Clipped-out reviews and artwork rested on patterned backgrounds shimmering with texture, while the distinctive hand-lettering gives the zine a defining look. Harper credited Beard—an artist and art educator—for much of *Capitol Crisis*'s arresting design: "He used to put pieces of paper on the ground and spray paint them

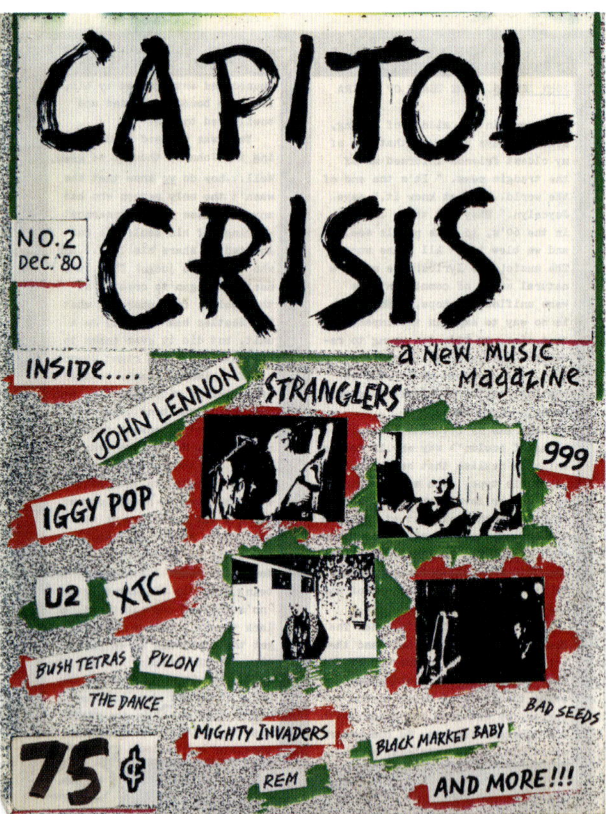

Figure 3.7 Issues 1 and 2 of *Capitol Crisis*, November–December 1980. Published by Xyra Harper. Used by permission.

and then cut them into different shapes and we put them together." *Capitol Crisis*'s logo—designed by Beard—artfully expressed the zine's essence as a crackling, chaotic labor of love.[38]

The second and third issues, published in December 1980 and February 1981, showed increased coverage of local music, which still received minimal attention from most outlets. DC punk coverage grew to include more reviews of recordings and concerts, as well as detailed news on the happenings of Rhoda and the Bad Seeds, Insect Surfers, and others. Nightlife photos of Tommy Keene, Darryl Jenifer of Bad Brains, and a host of other scene participants mingling at various concerts is an anthropological highlight, giving modern readers a vivid look at aspects of the scene then, populated by young people clutching drinks, smiling into cigarettes, and gazing into the lens with their best approximations of cool.

A review in *Sub Pop*—an Olympia, Washington, fanzine that evolved into the successful record label behind music by Nirvana, Mudhoney, the Shins, the Postal Service, Velocity Girl, and hundreds more—complained, however, that *Capitol Crisis* "reviews too much corporate rock to be considered subversive," speaking to a broader issue that might have inhibited *Capitol Crisis*'s appeal to younger members of the scene.[39] Harper's faint praise for the "teeny-punks" indicated her general lack of connection, at least initially, to the new music younger punks were creating. The Unheard Music festival at dc space in December 1980 was a turning point for the scene, as hardcore bands like SOA, Minor Threat, Government Issue, and the Untouchables blended with first-wave groups like Nurses and Martha Hull & the Steady Jobs. Wuelfing later described Minor Threat's performance as "a quantum leap" but, in her review of the event,[40] Harper lamented that DC seemed "a little behind the times" and the new arrivals to the scene made her "happy, but a little bored": "This two-day array of raw expression and talent was an inspiring event, despite the abrasiveness and lack of technical skill that accompanied the 'teeny bands.' Reflective of the last decade's New York and London bands that existed when new wave was punk and new, we are again reminded of how different DC is from cities more on top of what is current and changing

Figure 3.8 "Faces in the Crowd" feature, issue 2, *Capitol Crisis*, December 1980. Published by Xyra Harper. Used by permission.

Figure 3.9 Issue 3 of *Capitol Crisis*, February 1981. Published by Xyra Harper. Used by permission.

in music and lifestyle. We still are reflecting hand-me-down trends."[41]

Extolling innovative music is a righteous mission, but time proved Harper's compass was off here. Historian Kevin Mattson, himself a product of the 1980s DC punk scene, criticized Harper's *"what's-up-with-kids-nowadays* logic" in *We're Not Here to Entertain*, his 2020 book on American punk in the era of President Ronald Reagan.[42] He noted that Harper's usage of the term "teeny-punk" to describe hardcore punks "sounded condescending to those who hated nostalgia and wanted to move ahead and make their own culture."[43]

Indeed, Harper soon heard from several of the new hardcore punks, who were irritated by Harper's muted approval of their music. A group cosigned a letter to her, including Ian and Alec MacKaye, John Stabb of Government Issue and *Critical List* fanzine, Henry Garfield, Nathan Strejcek, Bert Queiroz of No Authority, and Michael Hampton of SOA. Appearing in issue four of *Capitol Crisis*, published in April 1981, the letter assailed Harper for not taking the new hardcore bands seriously, opening with an aphorism the authors borrowed from "News on the Eastern Front," the local scene news round-up that routinely appeared in *Capitol Crisis*: "'The scene you crave should be the one you create' . . . Amen!"

The younger punks wrote of how their initial excitement for *Capitol Crisis* waned in the wake of the zine's approach to covering their music. "A major complaint of ours deals with your treatment (your writers' treatment) of the 'Teeny-Punk' (as you call us) bands," the letter read. "The fact that you refuse to accept us as individual bands shows a great weakness in this aspect of your magazine! We may all be friends, we may share many of the same beliefs and we may have the same energies, . . . but none of us are identical in sound or style."

The previous issue's dismissal of the performances at the Unheard Music festival as reflecting "hand-me-down trends" seemed to particularly grate. "What is happening in Washington now, is different than what happened in London '77 & NY '78," they wrote:

> *We are not running up and down the streets screaming "Anarchy." We are not complaining about how poor and misfortunate we are, and we are not doing it (what we do) because it is such a neat fad. We are using music as a vent of frustration, anger and energy. We've created a scene; The Teen Idles died for it, but hopefully their EP (on Dischord, not Limp) will help in expanding our scene by raising enough proceeds to release other singles from local bands. At the moment we are simply trying to find places to play, supplying a powerful alternative to the types of bands you apparently endorse.*

The letter closed with a combination of slights, asking Harper "if you are so intent on writing about the scene in DC, why don't you try interviewing some of the local bands, to find out what they're about, instead of interviewing bands (irrelevant & out of town) like Tuxedomoon." The coup de grace of the parting line expressed that the group "fear[ed] *Capitol Crisis* is turning into another *Unicorn Times*, which is one magazine we don't need!"[44] Queiroz recalled years later that he and his friends were "definitely a little bit cocky" about their new scene, but that they felt they were "doing something important" that merited more respectful coverage.[45]

Harper felt unfairly attacked by the letter, which arrived on top of earlier criticism from members of the group like Stabb, who had spat out the declaration "this paper is for punks & written by punks, so *Capitol Crisis*, GO DIE!" in the second issue of *Critical List*.[46] She opened the fourth issue of *Capitol Crisis*—which, for the first time, featured a DC punk band on its cover in the form of Black Market Baby—with an editorial defending herself and her fanzine. Harper notes that *Capitol Crisis* "deserves more participation from its readers and fellow music enthusiasts," arguing reasonably that those who do not see their scene represented in her fanzine were free to make their own contributions. Harper admitted to gaps in coverage, urging others in the scene to resolve any oversights: "We are asking for, and including, first-hand opinions . . . straight from the mouths of America's (screaming) Youth!!!!!"[47]

MacKaye later described an unpublished letter Harper initially sent the young punks in response, in which she heatedly responded to the criticisms: "She was so fuckin' mad."[48] Harper later acknowledged that, despite her resentment toward the tone of the "teeny punks" criticism, "we tried to modernize [*Capitol Crisis* and] make it more appropriate to the current scene, their generation."[49]

Harper's openness had an impact, as several of the Georgetown Punks—like MacKaye, Queiroz, and Chris Bald—began contributing to *Capitol Crisis*, writing and assisting with layouts. Queiroz admitted he was initially "taken aback" by Harper's willingness to include their input in her zine, but gladly volunteered record reviews to the final two issues.[50] One of MacKaye's contributions, under the pseudonym "Crackerjack," was a series of brief,

Figure 3.10 Issues 4 and 5 of *Capitol Crisis*, 1981. Published by Xyra Harper. Used by permission.

Figure 3.11 The March, May, July–August, and December 1981 issues of *Discords*. Published by Howard and Tina Wuelfing. Used by permission.

sophomoric interviews he conducted with peers like Bald, Strejcek, Danny Ingram, John Falls, and others, which MacKaye later described as "just bullshit."[51] If the Georgetown Punks were looking to be taken seriously, that particular contribution was a misstep.

"Bullshit" or not, MacKaye's work on the zine had become known enough to lead Harper to include the following disclaimer in the editorial that opened the fifth and final issue of *Capitol Crisis*, published in May 1981: "It is a complete RUMOR that IAN MACKAYE has taken ANY of the editorial responsibility off my shoulders!" MacKaye later confirmed that assertions of that sort were exaggerated, but he also did not want to downplay his efforts and those of his friends. "We'd go over to her house to help put things together," MacKaye described, before adding with a laugh, "you know, taking that editorial pressure off her shoulders."[52]

Packed with electric visuals and impassioned reviews just as previous issues were, there was little indication that issue five would be the final one for *Capitol Crisis*. There was even mention of a classified section planned for the next issue, but a sixth never materialized. A derisive review of *Capitol Crisis*'s final issue in *Touch and Go*—the influential Michigan punk fanzine that was among DC hardcore's most vociferous national boosters—demonstrated the gap between first-wave DC punks and the new American hardcore scene. "If the rumors are true, [*Capitol Crisis*] is dead, which makes no one very sad because this is a shitty DC paper and a disservice to all that pick it up," the review read."[53] The somewhat desultory participation of members of the ascendant DC hardcore scene in the final issues of *Capitol Crisis* fell short of an imprimatur and, seemingly, *Capitol Crisis* no longer fit in. Despite being one of the best fanzines DC had yet produced, another voice from the original wave had moved on without fanfare.

Discords

This left Howard and Tina Wuelfing's *Discords* as the lone holdover from the first wave, yet their output initially seemed stronger than ever. Inspired by their new approach to cover music from scenes throughout the United States, the Wuelfings churned out seven tabloid-sized issues on newsprint from March to December of 1981. Issues overflowed with scene reports, many written by people who went on to significant accomplishments, like Gerard Cosloy (Matador Records, *Conflict* fanzine), Jim Testa (the long running *Jersey Beat* fanzine), Terry Katzman (a colleague of Minneapolis's trailblazing punks Hüsker Dü), Tesco Vee (the Meatmen, *Touch & Go* fanzine) and Calvin Johnson (Beat Happening, K Records). "The idea of this paper is to help re-establish and then maintain the lines of communication in the world of underground music culture," Howard Wuelfing wrote in the first issue's opening editorial. With punk and new wave co-opted by the corporate music industry, in his eyes, "it's obvious that the only way to carry on is as a permanent underground—or at least to maintain one as a lasting fueling station for future assaults on the cultural mainstream. Why not? What do we have to lose? Again."[54]

Interview subjects in *Discords* included national post-punk groups like Pylon, Mission of Burma, and ESG; Southern California hardcore band Circle Jerks; and the DC-adjacent Half Japanese. Perhaps the most notable interview the zine published was in its May 1981 issue. Conducted by Ian MacKaye, this exchange with Black Flag captures everyone involved at crucible points. Within months, Black Flag annexed SOA's Henry Garfield as its new singer, ushering in one of the creatively shape-shifting band's most influential phases. At the time of the *Discords* interview, however, Garfield was present only as a friend of MacKaye's and to offer up the occasional query ("Why don't you have any songs about politics? Most of your songs are personal."[55]). As for MacKaye, with the Teen Idles over, the nineteen-year-old was a few months into his new role as the vocalist for the hardcore band Minor Threat, whose blend of ferocious, breakneck-speed punk was elevated further by MacKaye's lyrics, which unflinchingly expressed his personal standards of discipline and responsibility ("I don't drink! I don't smoke! I don't fuck! At least I can fucking think!"), which were heretofore antithetical to popular youth culture at the turn of the 1980s. For MacKaye, the 1960s counterculture that viewed drugs as a tool of freedom, rebellion, and creativity had "evaporated and the only counterculture I was aware of was one of self-destruction."[56]

MacKaye conducted the interview in his bedroom at

his parents' home, where Black Flag billeted while in town for a concert at the 9:30 Club. Black Flag's bassist, Chuck Dukowski, and the band's then-vocalist, Dez Cadena, discussed everything from their desire to control an environment through intimidation ("Whatever it takes, it's a fear thing") to the unwavering inspiration they derived from their music.[57] When asked if the band ever tired of repeatedly performing its own songs, Dukowski explained that "the emotion in the songs is real and because of that they're not tied to some time limit. It's like I could ski down the same hill a hundred-thousand times and each time I just push harder."[58]

MacKaye, who later described himself as "nervous as hell" talking with the band,[59] fell flat in his attempts to match Dukowski's and Cadena's intensity, flippantly insulting participants in DC's new wave scene as the interview draws to a close.[60] Reflecting on the moment in 2018, MacKaye shook his head, describing it as "so stupid. Yeah, it's unbearable. I was really trying to go toe-to-toe with [Black Flag] . . . trying to be funny and irreverent."[61] Regrettable ending notwithstanding, the interview is a valuable document of several influential figures in American punk coming together as some of their defining moments approached.

Discords progressed throughout 1981, seemingly building momentum with each issue. *Sub Pop*, which acidly dismissed *Capitol Crisis*, conversely declared that reading *Discords* was "your duty as an American citizen." Likewise, New York underground filmmaker Richard Kern's zine, *The Valium Addict*, praised *Discords*, calling it "a very fine tabloid with roots deep and far reaching into the underground American rock-n-roll scene."[62] Even Henry Rollins—having changed his Garfield surname after leaving DC—trusted *Discords* enough to use it as a forum to update his friends on life with Black Flag. The December 1981 issue, with the Boston band Mission of Burma on the cover, features a letter from Rollins where he remarked that "it's really great getting to write this because it's like a letter to all my friends. Sometimes it's hard to get all the letters you want sent out. I miss DC a lot."[63] The unknown, but soon to be critical, DC hardcore band, Scream—later the launching pad for Dave Grohl, who reached the commercial stratosphere in the 1990s with his bands Nirvana and Foo Fighters—introduced themselves on the same page as Rollins' correspondence. "We're Scream from Falls Church," singer Pete Stahl wrote plainly.[64] "We need exposure. We're an original punk quartet that has things to say."[65]

Despite *Discords*' status as a respected part of the local scene, production abruptly and permanently ceased after that December 1981 issue. "My marriage to Tina came to an end," Wuelfing explained. "So, basically, the whole infrastructure went up in smoke."[66] Wuelfing's fanzine publishing days were over and his band, Nurses, concluded earlier that year following the death of the guitarist/vocalist Marc Halpern. Wuelfing went on to play music in Half Japanese and Underheaven, along with writing for other zines and for major publications like the *Washington Post* and *Spin* before launching a long career as a music publicist.

1981: Hardcore Arrives

As the first-wave punks mostly moved on from making fanzines, more new punks took to print. Initially named *Local Noise* and then, as of its second issue, *Critical List*, Stabb's fanzine was one of the first to emerge from DC's hardcore scene in early 1981. Crudely laid out and printed in minuscule runs, each issue was typically a typewritten rundown of concerts that Stabb and his friends had attended, full of his unfiltered opinions on the music around him. "Bad Brains were a sad rack of shit," Stabb declared in one review of a May 1981 concert. "They've gone downhill a long, long way since their fire breathing days in '79. Now it's boring reggae, smoking pot, and having kids. No fucking thank you. Hopefully they'll break up and save everyone the misery."[67] Stabb's writings were hardcore punk reimagined in the form of subcultural criticism.

Visuals generally consisted of collaged covers depicting various scenes of conflict, with inner pages crammed with comics, détourned clip art, and action-packed snapshots from hardcore concerts. These elements were then hastily pasted onto master artwork that was photocopied, collated, and haphazardly stapled together. Everything about *Critical List* spoke to urgency—the plethora of scratched-out and inked-in typo corrections, the unrestrained critical tone, and the defiant elan emanating from the various

page 4 • Discords • December '81

LETTERS

Discords:

We're Scream from Falls Church. We need exposure. We are an original punk quartet that has things to say. We've been together forever playing and this past year we finally got some gigs, our biggest opening for B.M.B. on August 1st at 9:30 Club. We've had problems with clubs for our music is fast-loud. We opened and closed the Stone Hearth Club in Falls Church due to broken violence. Ran into problems at Marble Bar with management. Got cut off from playing by police at Verona Club in Alexandria on September 10 due to broken windows and flying chairs on King Street. With all these happenings you'd think we would get some coverage. I hope you can take the time to give this demo tape a listen and maybe give us some feedback (see review this issue—Ed.). We did get a little airplay from Johnny Walker.

Scream is: Franz—Guitar; Skeeter—Bass; Kent Stax—Drums; Pete—Vocals

Thank you,
Pete

Dear Howard:

In the Bongos' feature (*Discords* Oct. '81) I was quoted as saying "People in America don't want to buy records like those by Throbbing Gristle or Clock DVA." I just wanted to make clear that I was talking about the problems Fetish Records has had in acquiring a decent U.S. distribution deal for these bands; I certainly wasn't trying to voice a negative opinion of these groups who, as well as being personal friends, are two of our favorites.

Also, we *did* tell Paul Morley that we were from Hoboken (even gave him a PATH train route map), although it didn't end up in the finsihed article, probably due to his editor. And we all know how editors can be, right?

Best Wishes,
Richard Barone
(The cover photo of *Discords* Oct. '81 was by Phil Marino.)

Dear Discords! (Howard? Editor?)

As a regular Discords reader and local musician, I'm finally convinced to write and commend you on your obvious dedication to the "new wave" (most notably PUNK) in D.C., and nationwide. Your Circle Jerks interview was chaotic and informative . . . great. We can't afford to buy an ad yet (honestly!). Why don't you acknowledge to everyone that my band exists?

We're *Lunamats*, from Falls Church (Sue D.), Bethesda (Me), Arlington (Drew), and Waldorf, MD (Gerald). Gerry and I used to be Resistors . . . you remember, you saw us and thought Myk, our bassist, was a high-disco kid (he's in BMB now, who'da figured it?) We opened for the Slickee Boys at Psychedelly and despite all our calls and letters (and fans' calls and letters) no one heard we were playing there . . . we did fine anyway. This past weekend Scream opened for us at Johnny Lange's in Arlington, and each band made about $4.50 (we were splitting the door costs and P.A.). We had flyers up everywhere. What's gone wrong? Scream usually draw a good crowd. When we were looking for a bassist (6 *months*) we ran thru a couple geeks and Mike Carr (who was fine but dissatisfied); we sent an ad to *Unicorn Times*, and they LOST it!

Anyway, we have an O.K. 7-song tape (recorded at Innerear and w/Charlie Danbury, ex-Trenchmouth and New Standard, singing 3 of 7 but he's gone to Boston now so I do it all) if anyone wants to hear it—ya gotta let us know 'cuz we're so financially decrepit we can barely afford to have tapes copied. We have a shitload of tunes (listed below, all copyright Lunatoons Music) and if anyone wants us to play, we're CHEAPish. Call us and tell us we're not Just Paranoid . . . love yer magazine, we need STILL MORE PUNK!!!

Real sincerely (as always),
Matt Luna &
Sue D.
Drew
Gerald

P.S. We *have* keyboards but don't hate us 'till you hear us . . . We'll let ya know when we're playing next, Club Verona or Empress Cafe.

Hello again Howard—or should I say 'Dear Editor'?

We here at the Young Pro house were appalled at Discords' lack of journalistic savvy in printing such egotistical dribble as Kim Dubby's Men Without Hats 'interview.' Not only was the article uninformative (we were all devastated to learn that Miss Dubby couldn't speak french) and poorly written (even more devastated that she couldn't pen english), it was also catty and one-sided. Miss Dubby quotes idle dressing room gossip and boring idle dressing room gossip at that (we actually had much more colorful things to say). I thought heresay [sic] was confined to rumor rags like the Washington Post, not one of D.C.'s finer Rock publications.

Moreover, Miss Dubby failed to mention that we (The Young Professionals) showed up at the club promptly at six o'clock only to be treated to a mind-boggling three hour performance by an inept road crew—kind of like the three stooges in slow motion. I mean, french accents are cute but not that cute. We were then told we would get no sound check and although Men Without Hats didn't particularly enjoy sharing their night with anyone else they would condescend and let us play the last two sets. What guys! The Young Pros finally hit that ever elusive stage at 1 a.m.—after a seven hour wait.

Miss Dubby also carefully avoided informing the reader that Men W/out Hats received a decidedly tepid audience response. But then, she didn't seem to interested in their music (about eight words in a half page article touched upon that trivial topic). Instead her main concern seemed to be her initiation into the French-Canadian tongue and a silly fixation with Men W/out Hats equally silly logo—a mock venetian blind atrocity that took the road crew a total time of nearly two hours to set up and take down. Miss Dubby sought great significance in the 'abstract' design—a roadsign style rendering of a man's behatted head with a slash through it— . . . Men Without Hats—Get it? Miss Dubby obviously did. About the only information a reader could garner from her 'interview' was that you can say groupie in any language—n'est-ce pas?

As Always,
Regina
for The Young Professionals

(And she thinks *we're* catty! Just to set the record straight, "Miss Dubby" hasn't succumbed to a single cute French accent since he found out that he was going to become a father—Get it? Ooh la la!—*Discords*)

Discords:

Here we've been playing DC/Balmore more nearly a year and most people in this town think all we do is put out exciting graphix and ads. How about a little mention. We're ACRYLIX and we dont no nobody important in this town, but we are a band. worth listening to. Even if we havent played 9:30 yet. (Is that the definition of making it in this town. Ow ow.) We're Shelly Sienna on drums, Ken Krayola on guitar, Marcus Maroon—bass and James Magenta—keys and synths. We're also in the midst of mixing at Island Studios a bunch of new material for wax release soon. After being together for a year are we still a "new band." Come and hear us sometime. Maybe a mention in descenes. something. anything?

ps we have the best drummer in town. shes recent from NYC.

Yours in truth, justice and the american quay,
Marcus Maroon

Dear Howard:

Comments on October '81 *Discords*: Surprised to see nice Westside Lockers reivew (very well written, I thought), as well as note I scrawled to you, grocery-list style, in Letters page. As for other reviews, I wish I'd read your Norman Salant "Accidents" critique before I'd written mine for *Op* and *D.I.Y.*, then I would have known about the Blondie connection/point-of-departure. Moving along, that Germs' 45 of "Lexicon Devil" did get released to media anyway 'cuz it made it to KAOS-FM (my #3 single of 1978, right after Avengers & R. Stevie Moore) and apparently just got stolen from the station after your mention of it, though I doubt you're the one to blame. And, by the by, do you have an address for Full Moon Records in Port Huron, Michigan?

Best,
John Foster
LMN/OP
Olympia, WA

P.S. Like your contribution to *Sub-Pop* 5 cassette.

P.P.S. Oly music more exciting than ever, but I'm too busy to write about it. Oly cassette in works. *Op* now bi-monthly.

copyright Edward C. Colver '81

Henry Garfield

Dear Howard and Dischord mag:

I hope you are doing O.K. I'm fine thank you. It's been almost three months (well, five now—Ed.) since I've been in BLACK FLAG. We have just finished our album. It's called *Damaged*; it's got 15 songs on it. Being the singer in this band, I got a quick education on a lot of things, there are a lot of scammers trying to waste my time. People seem to like me. I have been christened "the Psycho." Girls don't seem to be too interested in me, I think I scare them a bit.

We work hard on Black Flag practice, phone calls, answering letters. We did a big press conference the other day because all the local radio and TV stations wanted to know why we had lost our MCA distribution deal. We were going to be distributed by the big MCA label, but at the last minute Bergammo, the President, pulled out saying that our material was anti-parent and immoral. We used the press to expose this. Bergammo tried to take us to court to ban the album completely. The case was thrown out of court and Bergammo looks like a jerk.

I've learned that a lot of bands out here are just going for the rock star thing and they are fakes. And the funny thing is, people believe it, go to the shows and buy the records. TSOL is the forefront of this fake band movement. Bands that are happening out here are: Dead Kennedys, Stains, Red Cross, Circle One, Saccharine Trust, Minutemen, the Descendants.

I'm having a good time out here. I'm really working hard. A lot is coming up soon; hopefully we are going on the Tonight Show soon and we are scheduled to go on "Fridays" at some point. We're starting our U.S. tour in November. It's really great getting to write this because it's like a letter to all my friends. Sometimes it's hard to get all the letters you want sent out. I miss D.C. a lot. I haven't changed really, I'm more wild and I can sing a little better I guess. At shows I have a good time, I just lose my mind and I don't remember much about the show. We played a party the other night and I accidentally put my head thru a wall. I wrecked the kitchen we played in. The cops raided and tried to beat me up but all these people grabbed me and ran me out of the house and threw me in a car and I left. It was cool as shit. Anyhow, that's all for now. Please, anybody who wants to be on the B.F. mailing list just send your name and address to SST Records, P. O. Box 1, Lawndale, CA 90260. If you want to write a letter you can reach any of the band at that address. The newsletters are free.

Henry

P.S. Do the creepy crawl
Don't call us we'll crawl you

Figure 3.12 Letters to the editor page of *Discords'* December 1981 issue. Includes letters from Henry Rollins, Scream, John Foster of *OP* magazine, and Richard Barone of the Bongos. Published by Howard and Tina Wuelfing. Used by permission.

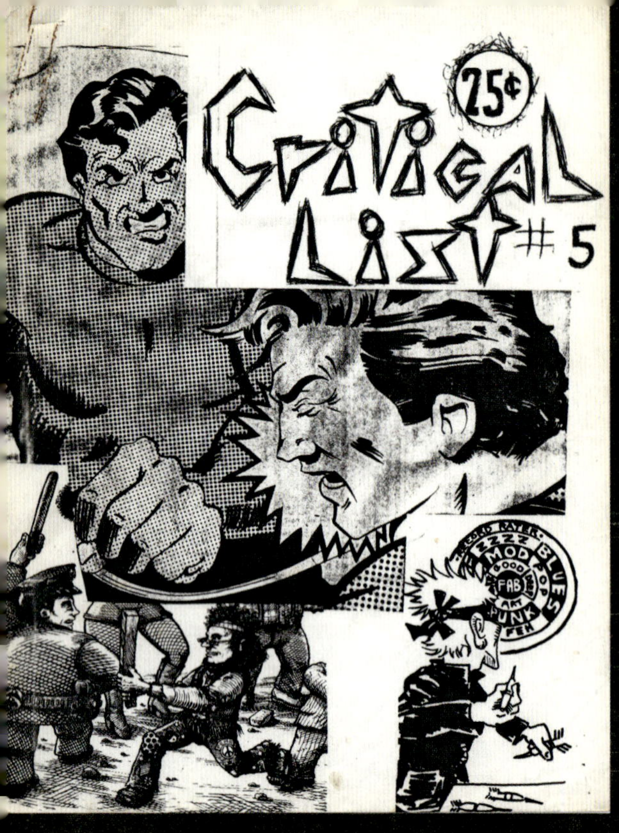

igure 3.13 Issue 5 (with cover variations) and issue 6 of *Critical List*, 1981. Published by John Stabb.

photographs of hardcore punks reveling in their community. Rough-edged and proud, *Critical List* brought a different approach to fanzine creation compared with earlier titles like *Descenes* and *The Infiltrator*.

By design, *Critical List* made no effort to achieve a professional presentation, creating something that *Touch and Go* determined "sure beats the hell out of the competition" in DC.[68] Stabb spelled out his interest in remaining an amateur which, aside from not having the funds to do otherwise, was inspired by not wanting "to be anything like the assholes over at *Unicorn Times*!" He continued: "We want to put this thing out as simple as possible and that, overall, is gonna be our motto. . . . We waited for someone to put something like this paper out, but nobody got off their fucking ass to do it. So, we decided to do it ourselves 'cause we stand by this paper as being honest and writing the facts with opinions about punks."[69]

Stabb's zeal for pushing boundaries with his humor could occasionally veer from satire into toxicity. Some comedic détournements of photos in later issues of *Critical List*, while ostensibly tongue in cheek, did little to differentiate themselves from the racist and sexist notions they purportedly parodied. Stabb presumably intended this as irreverent humor meant to demonstrate fearlessness and a willingness to shock but, then as now, these were patently conventional choices that ultimately upheld mainstream systems of power. *Critical List* usually embodied the electric, galvanizing possibilities of hardcore punk, but its low moments laid the subculture's flaws bare.

After *Critical List*'s final issue later in 1981, Stabb turned his full attention to the ultimately innovative and enduring Government Issue. The band, despite numerous lineup changes revolving around Stabb, helped forge DC punk's evolving sound until splitting in 1989. Along the way, he earned a reputation as a "witty, kind and boundlessly creative" part of the DC scene, within which he would remain active until his death in 2016. As the DC musician and concert promoter Chris Moore remarked upon Stabb's passing, "He had more energy than anyone on this planet, he was funny, wore crazy clothes that only he could pull off, told great stories, he was loving, he was compassionate, he supported young punks, he was extremely creative and just an overall amazing guy."[70]

The best fanzine to come out of the new hardcore scene in 1981 was the aesthetically and intellectually arresting *Now What?* Its editor, Sarah Woodell, only published a single issue that fall, but *Now What?* flaunted the visual flair and critical ear of *Capitol Crisis*, mixed with a heavy dose of local punk coverage on top of interviews with the British postpunk bands Scars and Siouxsie & the Banshees. "I wanted to get involved in the scene somehow, and since I couldn't play an instrument," Woodell said, she ran off two hundred fifty copies of *Now What?* as an alternative to local newspapers that covered punk "in a condescending way."[71]

As Woodell wrote in a brief editorial opening the first issue (labeled on the cover as "Issue 0"), "The DC music scene is getting more and more well-known and respected across the country so it's about time it had a fanzine to help represent it."[72] This negation of zines that came before indicated that, by the end of 1981, the scene centered on the hardcore punks, who already cared far less about what the older punks thought of them than the previous year. "By the time Minor Threat came along, it just didn't matter," MacKaye said of the rift that had once been such a fiery motivator. "It was irrelevant to me."[73]

In addition to interviews with Government Issue and Bad Brains, the lone issue of *Now What?* centers on an illuminating diary of DC hardcore shows from summer 1981, written by Stabb. Minor Threat's climb to the top of the scene's hierarchy was in progress, with the band's debut single released that June and their live performances described by Stabb as "great, never [putting] on a disappointing show."[74] SOA played their final show that June, but new hardcore bands like Youth Brigade, Iron Cross, and Artificial Peace made up for the loss. Stabb's cutting criticism carried over from his work on *Critical List*, amusingly laying into the DC mod/new wave band Count 4, who had the misfortune of sharing a bill with the far grittier Iron Cross and Black Market Baby. "The band played early Who covers and their own originals that had lyrics like "we catch the tubeway & drink our tea," Stabb reported. "Gimme a fucking break."

As Stabb crowed at the end of the feature, "From parties

to clubs, DC has come a long way! By now, DC hardcore has become known & famous all over; especially LA where everyone used to idolize the bands." The sudden expansion of the hardcore scene, which ultimately drove away many of its early participants, was still a point of pride. "The scene has grown from a tiny, underground thing to mass proportions & all the bands are getting famous." Stabb closed out with the observation, garbed in his now-familiar sarcasm: "DC has grown to have quite a reputation of being the home of harDCore. But who wants to be famous, I just want a cult following."

Although Minor Threat later eulogized this era as the community's "Salad Days" in a song written during the band's acrimonious final months in late 1983, MacKaye and his Dischord/Minor Threat partner Jeff Nelson still found fault then within the scene.[75] Now, though, it was apathy within their own peer group riling them, rather than slights from older punks. Their letter to "Jaded Person" in *Now What?* railed against showgoers who socialized instead of watching bands. "It's too bad that these people take the bands so lightly, while the same bands are in such high demand in other cities,"[76] they noted. Later, the duo asks rhetorically, "Is our once-energetic scene coming to an end? I think not, because we still have the young punks who aren't scared to shave their heads or dance or be individuals in mind, not in style."[77]

For all of the DC punk fanzines published in 1980 and 1981, none continued into 1982, a frenetic year when the DC hardcore scene neared its peak. Despite this lack of continuity, thanks to the rapid growth of the scene, more new bands and fanzines soon flooded in to build upon—and strain—the foundations of DC punk.

Notes

1. Tom Carson's review in the May 29, 1980, issue refers to Urban Verbs singer Roddy Frantz as "a pompous shithead" and "the very worst kind of art rock poseur," who "seems to have absorbed all of David Byrne's arrogance and none of his talent" while singing in "the voice of a megalomanic teddy bear." Keyboardist Robin Rose joked about the stunning review in 1985 when the *Washington City Paper* ran a retrospective piece on the band: "I felt like John Kennedy looking for the grassy knoll." Mark Jenkins noted in 2018 that, since Carson had grown up in DC, "I think [he] was proving he was a cool New Yorker by putting down a DC band."
2. Ian MacKaye, interview by the author, audio recording, College Park, MD, September 6, 2018.
3. Mary Levy, "Bad Brains and Teen Idles at Madam's Organ," *Descenes*, June 1980.
4. MacKaye, interview.
5. Mark Jenkins, interview by the author, audio recording, College Park, MD, April 27, 2018.
6. MacKaye, interview.
7. Howard Wuelfing, interview by the author, audio recording, September 11, 2018.
8. Mary Leary, email to the author, September 2, 2018.
9. MacKaye, interview.
10. David Arnson, email to the author, September 10, 2018.
11. Leary, email.
12. *1981* would change its name to *Washington City Paper* the next year, becoming an enduring—if sometimes antagonistic—part of the DC arts scene.
13. From 1979 through 1981, at least thirty murders of children and young adults occurred in Atlanta; these are often referred to as the Atlanta Child Murders. The story was a national concern when the author wrote her letter in June 1981. In defense of the punk mentioned in the letter, the letter's author was about to enter a Dead Kennedys concert when she saw the jacket and, apparently, was unaware that "I Kill Children" was a reference to the satirical song by the San Francisco punk band, not merely a reference to the crimes in Atlanta. This was distasteful attire to wear during a high-profile incident like what was occurring in Atlanta, but the punk subculture, of course, was built on shock and transgression.
14. "The Mail: Punk Bunk," *1981*, June 12, 1981.
15. Skip Groff, "Critic's Poll 1979," *The Infiltrator*, 1980.
16. David Arnson, email to the author, August 20, 2018.
17. Leary, email.
18. Leary.
19. Natalie Hopkinson, *Go-Go Live: The Musical Life and Death of a Chocolate City* (Durham, NC: Duke University Press, 2012), xii.
20. Natalie Hopkinson, "Fluorescent Flags: Black Power, Publicity, and Counternarratives in Go-Go Street Posters in the 1980s." *Communication, Culture and Critique* 13, no. 3 (2020): 275–94, https://doi.org/10.1093/ccc/tcz058.
21. Steve Kiviat and Mike Paarlberg, "What Did DC's punk and Go-Go Scenes Mean to Each Other in the 1980s?" *Washington City Paper*, February 22, 2013.
22. Clone Ranger, "What We Hate!" *The Infiltrator*, issue 6, 1980.
23. Leary, email.
24. Leary.
25. Leary.
26. Leary.
27. Guy Picciotto, email to the author, November 9, 2020.
28. George Pelecanos, email to the author, February 17, 2018.
29. Howard Wuelfing, interview by the author, audio recording, September 11, 2018.
30. Joe Sasfy, "Rockscene: Guest Editorial," *Unicorn Times* 7, no. 6 (March 1980): 10.
31. Howard Wuelfing, "I-And-I editorial: Writing for Spite," *Descenes*, July 1980.
32. Mountain was a protometal rock band from the late 1960s and early 1970s that was best known for its song "Mississippi Queen" and its 1969 appearance at the Woodstock Music and Art Fair.
33. Howard Wuelfing, "Local Wax," *Descenes*, July 1980.
34. As of 2024, her name is now Xyra Harper-Cann.
35. Greta Weber, "Zines Deserve a Bigger Place in Punk History: Here's Why," *Washingtonian*, August 2016, www.washingtonian.com/2016/08/04

/zines-deserve-a-bigger-place-in-dc-punk-history-heres-why/.

36. Xyra Harper, "SVT & Teen Idles," *Capitol Crisis*, November 1980.
37. Xyra Harper, "Supplement to First Issue," *Capitol Crisis*, November 1980.
38. James Schneider, interview with Xyra Harper, August 31, 2013.
39. *Sub Pop*, issue 4, 1981.
40. Mark Andersen and Mark Jenkins, *Dance of Days: Two Decades of Punk in the Nation's Capital*, updated and expanded 4th ed. (Brooklyn: Akashic Books, 2009), 73.
41. Xyra Harper, 'Unheard of Music festival,' *Capitol Crisis*, issue 3, February 1981, 14.
42. Kevin Mattson, *We're Not Here to Entertain: Punk Rock, Ronald Reagan, and the Real Culture War of 1980s America* (New York: Oxford University Press, 2020), 35.
43. Mattson, 35.
44. Ian MacKaye et al., "Letters," *Capitol Crisis*, April 1981.
45. James Schneider, interview with Bert Queiroz, October 16, 2014.
46. John Stabb, *Critical List*, issue 2, 1981.
47. Xyra Harper, "Editorial," *Capitol Crisis*, April 1981.
48. MacKaye, interview.
49. Schneider, interview with Harper.
50. Schneider, interview with Queiroz.
51. MacKaye, interview.
52. MacKaye.
53. Tesco Vee and Dave Stimson, "Publications," *Touch and Go*, issue 15, 1981.
54. Howard Wuelfing, "A Word from the Chief: Don't Expect Anything!" *Discords*, March 1981.
55. Ian MacKaye, "LA's Black Flag Don't Take It Easy," *Discords*, May 1981.
56. Tony Rettman and Anthony Civiorelli, *Straight Edge: A Clear-Headed Hardcore Punk History* (New York: Bazillion Points, 2017), 17.
57. Cadena moved to second guitar when Garfield joined.
58. MacKaye, "LA's Black Flag."
59. MacKaye, interview.
60. MacKaye, "LA's Black Flag."
61. MacKaye, interview.
62. *The Valium Addict*, issue 3, August 1981, 26.
63. Henry Rollins, "Letters," *Discords*, December 1981.
64. Grohl drummed for Scream from 1987 through 1990.
65. Pete Stahl, "Letters," *Discords*, December 1981.
66. Howard Wuelfing, interview by the author, audio recording, September 11, 2018.
67. John Stabb, *Critical List*, issue 5, 1981, 3.
68. Vee and Stimson, "Publications."
69. John Stabb, *Critical List*, issue 3, 1981, 3.
70. Ally Schweitzer, "John Stabb, Vocalist of Government Issue, Dies at 54," *Bandwidth*, May 9, 2016, http://bandwidth.wamu.org/john-stabb-vocalist-of-government-issue-dies-at-age-54/.
71. Laura Outerbridge, "Record Enthusiasts Invade the Ballroom," *The Diamondback*, November 10, 1981, 6.
72. Sarah Woodell, "Editorial," *Now What?* November 1981.
73. MacKaye, interview.
74. John Stabb, "DC Summer 1981," *Now What?* November 1981.
75. Nelson also was the drummer for Minor Threat and, previously, for the Teen Idles. He would go on to drum for the bands Three, Senator Flux, and High-Back Chairs, as well as launch a new label, Adult Swim, in the late 1980s.
76. Ian MacKaye and Jeff Nelson, "Letters," *Now What?* November, 1981.
77. MacKaye and Nelson.

4

Everything Is Right, 1982–1983

HARDCORE PUNK'S RISE in influence throughout 1981 was reflected in both the content and appearance of the DC scene's newest fanzines, which shifted away from the professional elements—halftoned photographs and larger formats, for example—that *Discords* and *The Infiltrator* employed, instead embracing a rougher aesthetic. While no DC punk fanzine published in 1981 continued into 1982, new titles always appeared to replace them. These zines were typically photocopied in smaller runs, employing cut-and-paste layouts mixing hand lettering and typewritten text. Photocopiers often rendered photographs as inky shadows, born from rounded-edge snapshots fresh from the Fotomat, which were then applied onto camera-ready paste-ups of the zine's layout.[1]

Those paste-ups were then duplicated at a commercial copy shop or clandestinely on an employer's photocopier. If a zine editor did not work somewhere with a photocopier, a family member was occasionally drafted to help. "They'd Xerox it at my brother's office," recalled Judy Tinelli, whose son, Mike Ross, edited *Brand New Age*. "He didn't know how many copies they were making. He thought it was just two or three."[2] As author and educator Kate Eichhorn observed, photocopiers were "the Trojan horse of the punk movement—a machine capable of reproducing the most vile, offensive, and controversial materials without the censorship, cost, or delay associated with printed forms of reproduction."[3] Obstacles that undermined DC's earlier underground publications, like *Quicksilver Times*, could now be obviated by the increasingly accessible photocopier.

By 1983, DC punk's vanguard no longer included many of the participants driving its earliest music. Tru Fax & the Insaniacs and the star-crossed Urban Verbs were defunct, leaving the Slickee Boys and Insect Surfers to carry the

Figure 4.1 Flier for Tommy Keene concert at the 9:30 Club in DC, August 26, 1983. Designed by Mark Holmes.

first-wave flag.[4,5] Musical variety within DC punk narrowed with hardcore's dominance, but other musicians still stood out. Captivating postpunk bands like Chalk Circle and Velvet Monkeys made their mark during this period with sounds full of bite and brilliance, while onetime Razz guitarist Tommy Keene embarked on a solo career, progressively refining his melancholic power pop. Meanwhile, Static Disruptors emerged in the early 1980s, blending go-go music (as heard on their 1982 single "DC Groove") with a touch of punk attitude, "[mashing] up go-go and punk power chords years before the [Beastie Boys] or [Red Hot Chili Peppers] threw down a dance groove," band member Kenny Dread asserted in 2016.[6]

Within hardcore, Bad Brains moved to New York City but, in their place, Minor Threat, Government Issue, and the Faith led the scene. *Flex Your Head*, a compilation on Dischord Records showcasing many of the scene's young hardcore bands, was a tangible document of DC punk's growth. Selling out its first pressing of four thousand copies within a week of its release in 1982, *Flex Your Head* swiftly became a definitive American hardcore record. Minor Threat, in particular, had picked up Bad Brains' mantle as DC's premier hardcore band. Although the band temporarily split in fall 1981 when guitarist Lyle Preslar decamped for college, the group's first two EPs—*Minor Threat* and *In My Eyes*[7]—circulated during the interim, establishing Minor Threat as a central part of the American punk scene.

One aspect of Minor Threat's lyrics unexpectedly resonated for many. A clean-living punk movement named after the band's song "Straight Edge" developed, centered on the antidrug and antipromiscuity ideas championed in the song's lyrics.[8] MacKaye insisted those lyrics were only declarations of his own beliefs, rather than a prescriptive set of rules for others to follow, but the idea spread through other punk scenes regardless, particularly those in Boston, Southern California, and New York City.[9] Many who adopted the straight-edge identity adhered to "unyielding, black and white strictures on behavior [which] were similar to fundamentalist religions' rigid, clear-cut beliefs," according to author and educator Ross Haenfler.[10]

Minor Threat's reunion in spring 1982, after Preslar's return to the fold, signaled DC hardcore's ascent to a new level of innovation and popularity. Simultaneously, however, the scene's rapid growth and the dominance of bands associated with Dischord led many original participants to feel estranged, fueling a common perception that the subculture's musical output was not adventurous enough. The increase of violence at concerts compounded the feeling that hardcore's center might not hold. "With the growth of the scene came large helpings of good and bad," Henry Rollins later wrote. "The shows were great but with more people came fights, division, and the ritualistic behavior that sometimes lessened the fun and put a clampdown on spontaneity."[11] John Stabb of Government Issue and *Critical List* fanzine lamented that "once it became too popular, it became tainted."[12] Some of the punks who so recently disrupted the scene's first wave in 1980 and 1981 were now uneasy about the arrival of new participants in 1982 and 1983.

Fanzines played a key part in the navigation of this period, offering a tool to critique the scene for those in both the inner and outer circles of the subculture. As popular as DC punk was becoming, discontentment reverberated throughout local zines. Also, punk and mainstream society were more homologous than advertised, with racism, sexism, and homophobia found as readily in the pages of some DC punk zines as they were in corporate media. Worse, these sentiments were presented as rebellion, despite subverting nothing about oppressive mainstream hierarchies. Conversely, the purpose and joy most zine editors derived from punk was a reminder of what drew people to the subculture. Cynicism lurked, but most DC zines of this period still demonstrated an earnest commitment to punk's possibilities.

If This Goes On

Sharon Cheslow, whom activist and author Mark Andersen called "a very significant fanzine creator and creative force, in general, in the scene,"[13] later described DC's punk subculture as having become "more macho and less about a tight-knit group of friends" once hardcore dominated. "We always thought of punk as having no rules, but when hardcore became more popular, there developed a code to which Chalk Circle didn't adhere," she noted of the band in which

Figure 4.2 Left: Sharon Cheslow, circa fall 1982. Photo by Hal Schmulowitz of *Argus Weekly*. Right: Colin Sears, circa 1984. Photo by Sharon Cheslow. Used by permission.

she sang and played guitar. Despite the increasingly violent climate, "Anne [Bonafede of Chalk Circle] and I still loved hardcore and went to all the shows."[14] Cheslow's steady presence in the scene throughout the previous few years—through her band, as a disc jockey on the University of Maryland's WMUC campus radio station, and a job at Skip Groff's Yesterday & Today Records—was encapsulated by her statement in a 1982 interview: "Music's My Life."[15]

Chalk Circle was notable, not just for its music, but also for being the first band composed solely of women to perform in DC's punk scene. Additionally, according to musician and archivist Don Fleming, Chalk Circle was even the first "well-known, DC-based, all-female band" since the International Sweethearts of Rhythm,[16] an integrated jazz band active in the early 1940s.[17] Sab Grey's review in *Critical List* of Chalk Circle's first concert on July 24, 1981, displayed how threatened some men in DC's punk scene were by women performing at punk shows. "Oh no, what am I doing here?" he asked of the event that also featured the Velvet Monkeys and REM, both local bands including women.[18] "It's bimbo nite at dc space,"[19] he wrote, before dismissing Chalk Circle as a "boring all-girl band" and adding an incongruous "(sorry Sharon)" afterward. Decades later, Grey expressed regret over the insult, calling it "cringeworthy" and noting that "the worst bit is I really liked Chalk Circle. They were a good band! But no, 'look at me I'm so edgy, ooooooo!'" he said, mocking his earlier behavior.[20]

Having contributed to *Now What?* the previous year, a collaboration Cheslow called "a great experience," she soon teamed up with fellow musician Colin Sears to start a new fanzine, *If This Goes On*.[21] Cheslow was inspired by punk zines she picked up from Yesterday & Today—like *Slash*, *Search & Destroy*, and *Sniffin' Glue*—as well as local zines like *Discords*, *Descenes*, and *The Infiltrator*. The new zine's title was gleaned from Robert Heinlein's science fiction novella *If This Goes On—*. "It felt like we were living in dystopian times under Reagan," Cheslow recalled. "Creative community was a form of resistance to that."[22]

Over three issues, Cheslow, Sears, and their cast of contributors—including Bonafede, photographer Leslie Clague, and musicians like Kevin Mattson, Roger Marbury, Chris Niblack, and Geoff Turner[23]—created a publication of honest music journalism filled equally with love for the music and concern over the subculture's direction. Zine production centered in Bethesda, Maryland, a DC border suburb where most of the zine's contributors lived or hung out. Cheslow later noted that, although she and Sears "were definitely interested in creating a homegrown Bethesda ('B-town') scene, and we worked on the zine in Bethesda (the address for the zine was Colin's dad's house), we never considered what we did with the zine or BMO[24] as separate from DC punk/hardcore."[25]

Text was usually typewritten onto paper, then cut out and laid on top of photocopied images from old films Cheslow and Sears had found in books. The preponderance of horror and science fiction stills, along with other dark absurdities skulking behind the text, gives the zine a beguiling mix of ominousness and bubblegum kitsch. Interviews conducted throughout the zine's run are with a mix of bands from DC and elsewhere, like the Raincoats and Sort Sol. Most absorbing are the discussions with DC bands, capturing a scene seemingly both inspired and troubled by its increasing popularity.

Figure 4.3 *If This Goes On*, issues 1 and 2, 1982. Published by Sharon Cheslow and Colin Sears. Used by permission.

"I've noticed that these people who've been around for a longer time think these new people are breaking up the scene by thinking in their own way," observed Eric Lagdameo, vocalist for Double-O.[26] "But the fact is the old people aren't even trying to get to know the new people. . . . There's a clique attitude to everything. . . . That's why people feel the scene's falling apart." Lagdameo's assertions attest to the breakneck pace of punk's development, as the hardcore scene was barely three years old when he made his comments in the summer of 1982. The band's drummer, Rich Moore, complained about the amount of criticism peers in Minor Threat and Iron Cross received, but also explained some of punk's appeal. "The thing that got me into this music was that it had something to say," he said. "What made me wanna start a band was that I wanted to do something and say something."[27]

Scene discontent was also a theme in the Iron Cross interview appearing in issue two. Their inclusion was a rather magnanimous act from Cheslow, considering less than a year had passed since Iron Cross vocalist Sab Grey's disrespectful review of Chalk Circle in *Critical List*, although the issue was never broached in this discussion. Since first appearing on the scene in 1981, Iron Cross had been controversial. As author, concert promoter, and filmmaker Steven Blush wrote, despite breaking ground as one of the first American bands to employ the Oi! style of punk popular in the United Kingdom,[28] "many in DC laughed off Iron Cross as quasi-Nazi buffoons,"[29] due to the band's name,[30] and to its violent and homophobic lyrics.[31] Grey quickly disavowed "Psycho Skin," a song from the band's first EP, *Skinhead Glory,* which included lyrics about its protagonist beating up gay men—"I just beat up my third queer"—among other crimes. In addition to insisting that the song was a fictional, cautionary tale about a person who was out of control, Grey insisted he had not written the song and never liked it.[32] These explanations aside, the song enhanced the band's negative reputation.[33]

Grey, bassist Wendel Blow, and drummer Dante Ferrando argued in the *If This Goes On* interview that their sense of humor was frequently misunderstood as racism,[34] which Cheslow called out explicitly. After Ferrando noted that the band gets "shit on" despite trying to support others in the scene, Cheslow countered that the band gets "shit on because of your image and instances like at the Wilson Center when you were sieg heiling Government Issue." Grey rationalized that it was "a personal joke between us" and Government Issue vocalist John Stabb. "We were going '[Stabb] is a homo'" while *sieg heil*ing, he explained. Despite this behavior, Grey insisted that "we have never been Nazis. We may joke about it, but everybody else does, too." Reflecting on this period decades later, Grey observed that "part of being young, of course, is reveling in seeing your elders squirm, so taking delight in being extreme can become the norm and sort of a badge of honor. The word they use now would be 'edgelord,' but a better description would be 'loudmouth prick.'"[35]

Two other notable interviews from *If Those Goes On* complemented each other, with one expressing the bitterness of local punks who felt alienated by the Dischord scene and the other relaying MacKaye's dismay at the community's fraying bonds. Hate From Ignorance, a Bethesda band that debuted in spring 1982, criticized Minor Threat in an interview with Sears that ran in the zine's first issue, published that summer. "I don't like them," the bassist Eugene Bogan flatly declared, while vocalist Clark Chapin mixed praise for Minor Threat's music with disgust toward their reunion: "I mean, why? It's like they're trying to create a movement when it just can't be made."

That same issue, Cheslow also questioned the wisdom of Minor Threat's return in a review of an April 30 concert at the Wilson Center. "They used to be the best band in DC, but now that they are back together it's not the same," she wrote:

Figure 4.4 *If This Goes On*, issue 3, 1983. Published by Sharon Cheslow and Colin Sears. Used by permission.

> *Not only is most of the music sounding stale (they seem to be bored with it) but what about Ian's statements not even 5 months ago that it's good to start a new band with new songs so that you remain humble and underground? Playing old songs just to please an audience and using the name Minor Threat to attract an instant audience seems far away from Ian's original attitudes. If Minor Threat had just thought up a new name, discarded some of the old songs, and created a whole new set, they definitely would've been DC's best hardcore band.*

Cheslow and Sears interviewed Minor Threat for the third and final issue of *If This Goes On*, published in June 1983. MacKaye admitted that his friend Cheslow's criticisms from the first issue "tore me up. . . . Imagine me coming home and reading your magazine. It's like, what?!" Hate From Ignorance's barbs equally hit their mark. "I mean, goddamn, these were my friends from Bethesda," he lamented. "I was always like . . . 'B-Town!' And it was just a slap in the face. I'm really sensitive about that kind of stuff. I'm really, really, really sensitive." The interview demonstrated the power of fanzines within the hardcore scene. While the occasional article in mainstream outlets like the *Washington Post* typically offered a sensationalized take on the scene, slights or inaccuracies from those sources were to be expected. When a respected voice from within the scene like Cheslow's questioned a band's intentions, however, MacKaye's response made it clear that it cut deep.

More Musicians Creating Fanzines: *Skin Flint*, *The Alexandra Father Fucker*, *DOD*, and *Insurrection*

The scene's growth throughout 1982 was visible through more new fanzines hitting record store racks or being distributed at concerts, schools, and anywhere punks gathered. As with *If This Goes On* from Sharon Cheslow and Colin Sears (who also collaborated in the band Bloody Mannequin Orchestra), several of those new titles were created by musicians in the scene. Within DC punk, performers like Howard Wuelfing and John Stabb had already created fanzines leading up to 1982. Members of Iron Cross, Psychodrama, Deadline, and Insurrection soon joined them with zines of their own, however minute their circulations might have been.

Sab Grey's fanzine *Skin Flint* picked up where he left off with his contributions to Stabb's *Critical List* zine. "Made with skinheads, punks, and hardcores in mind," *Skin Flint* ran for three issues in 1982.[36] Never exceeding a print run of more than twenty-five copies—"We had to use Kinkos to get them printed and it got expensive," Grey explained—publishing *Skin Flint* proved to be more work than he initially expected.[37] "Being young is all about trying different coats to see what fits, so I probably thought I'd give it a go," he said of creating his own zine. "I'm sure it seemed sort of glamorous or, at least, like a punky Kolchak, intrepid reporter bringing punk to the masses.[38] It's not, by the way. It's a lot of hard work and rather dull. I discovered I preferred playing in a band rather quickly."[39]

Aside from an interview with Black Market Baby in issue three, the contents are mostly record and concert reviews, short editorials on the ills of the scene, and photos of British skinhead culture. Comics appear in each issue, including an ugly one that closed the first issue, bearing racial epithets couched in humor. "The opinions in this fanzine are mine and those of the contributing writers and cartoonists," Grey writes in the zine's introductory editorial. "If you don't like them—fuck off." That straddling of the fine line between proud confidence in your ethics and a defensive lack of interest in self-examination was common in the often-inelastic world of punk zines. Grey did, however, add a thoughtful closing line: "Or better yet, start your own fanzine."

Like other DC punk zines of this period, Grey aired his concerns over the direction of the scene. "So, what's the matter with DC lately?" he asked. "No dancing, no band support, just sideline soap operas and complaining about 'the dancing being too rough' from the snotty brats who came through with punk over the summer." As with tensions that arose when the first wave was shoved aside by hardcore's new arrivals, 1982's neophytes expanded the scene and rankled gatekeepers. Seemingly for Grey, violence came from an urgent need to preserve both safety and the shared ethics of otherness that fueled punk. "Sad, sad times are in store for DC if these children do not grow up quickly and stop trying to force their pre-pubescent daydreams upon the rest of the DC hardcore," he wrote:

> *Dreams of Anarchy, peace and love are very nice (God knows I wish they were true) but if you walk into the real world thinking like that, well, we'll be reading about you in the obituary column very soon. Now, I'm not saying we should all be muscle bound goons who fight everyone in sight, but if you wish to "prove your individuality" you MUST be prepared to fight for it! If someone comes out on our dance floor with the wrong attitude, they must be cleared off—with violence if necessary!*[40]

Black Market Baby's 1981 single on Limp Records—"Potential Suicide," backed with "Youth Crimes"— and their two outstanding songs on Limp's *Connected* compilation,[41] demonstrated that hardcore's breakneck speed was not a necessity for bands wanting to knock listeners flat with energy and ferocity. The band's vocalist, Boyd Farrell, had been involved in the scene since the late 1970s and was familiar with punk's alternating currents. For him, a primary problem within the creative community was not violence but apathy. "I would just like to see everyone getting involved in things," he said when Grey interviewed him for *Skin Flint*. After crediting Grey, the "DC Skins," and other loyal fans for their support, Farrell warned that more effort within the scene was necessary to keep it thriving.[42] "There's some certain cliques that you should tell 'em to get off their ass and start supporting these people before they lose 'em," he said,[43] citing Trenchmouth and the Penetrators as area bands that "have gone down the tubes 'cause they don't give 'em support."[44]

The racist cartoon and some homophobic material in *Skin Flint*—a review of Wasted Youth in issue one ends with "buy it or be a fag," while an editorial smirks that those who disliked the first issue of *Skin Flint* would find gay-focused magazines like *Blueboy* and *Out* "much more to your liking"—are all the more disappointing in light of

FREE FREE FREE FREE FREE FREE FREE

THE ALEXANDRIA FATHER-F*CKER

(THE PUNISHMENT TIMES) APRIL '82, ISSUE #1

THIS IS A NEW FANZINE BECAUSE D.C. REALLY NEEDS IT.

NATIONWIDE MUSIC SCENE CHECK-UP:

BOSTON: SUCKS

NY: SUCKS. DAVID BYRNE AND LAURIE ANDERSON BRUISE MY MIND WITH BOREDOM. THE BUSH TETRAS ARE SO SHITTY, THEY SHOULD PLAY THE CAPITAL CENTRE THE NEXT TIME THEY COME TO WASHINGTON.

LA: SUCKS.

SAN FRAN: SUCKS. FLIPPER ARE MORE LETHARGIC AND DULL THAN D.C. NOW THAT'S QUITE A FEAT.

CHICAGO: SUCKS.

PHILA: SUCKS.

D.C.: SUCKS LIKE ALWAYS.

CLUB NEWS:
DOODOO BOWERS SUCKS. BILL WARRELL IS A COCKSUCKING PHILISTINE. OH YEAH, d.c. SPACE IS BEING "AVANT-GARDE" W/THE DINNER THEATRE. YAY! WE'RE SO LUCKY.

NEW D.C. GROUPS:
VELVET MONKEYS SUCK SHIT. SIGMUND AND THE PENIS ENVY ARE AMERICAN U. ASSHOLE JOCKS AND POSEURS. NANCY REAGAN WOULD LIKE THEM. DJ BAND, SPEED RACER'S BROTHER RACER X, DOES A COVER VERSION OF "LOUIE, LOUIE."

OLD D.C. GROUPS:
SUCK, NATURALLY. WHEN ARE SUSAN MUMFORD AND RODDY FRANTZ GOING TO O.D. ALREADY?

NEW RECORD REVIEWS:
THEY ALL SUCK, ESPECIALLY SINCE THE GROUPS WHO PUT THEM OUT SUCK.

HARDCORE PUNK SCENE:
SUCKS. ALL THESE DYED HAIR ANTI-NAZI PUNKS ARE ENOUGH TO MAKE ME JOIN THE NAZI PARTY AND I'M JEWISH.

ART SCENE:
AS FOR THOSE D.C. DUMPSITES KNOWN AS THE WPA, THE LANSBURGH BUILDING, AND THE OLSHONSKY, THEY ALL SUCK.

RECORD STORES:
RTX SUCKS. PENGUIN FEATHER SUCKS.

FASHION:
SUCKS. WHO NEEDS IT EXCEPT ALL THOSE WORTHLESS PEOPLE WHO LIVE IN AND AROUND DUPONT CIRCLE.

RADIO:
SUCKS. BUT THEN AGAIN WHO CARES ANYMORE?

FREE-FREE-FREE
FREE-FREE-FREE
FREE-FREE-FREE

IF YOU LIKE TO SCREAM, AND MAKE NOISE, AND BE SICKENING, AND EXPOSE YOUR TITS LIKE I DO THEN COME SEE

PSYCODRAMA

THE CHANCERY
704 NEW JERSEY AVE
BETWEEN 1st + 2nd ST. N.W.
DOWN BY UNION STATION

FRI. APRIL 23rd + SAT APR. 17th

©1982 THE PUNISHMENT TIMES. FOR AD RATES CALL 783-0360

Figure 4.5 *The Alexandria Father Fucker / The Punishment Times*, issue 1, April 1982. Published by Leslie Singer. Used by permission.

Grey's sincere passion for music and community. "Punk is the greatest thing to happen to rock music," he writes, a disarmingly earnest statement that is easy to lose track of among *Skin Flint*'s flaws. Grey repeatedly denied that he and his band genuinely held racist and homophobic views. Towards the end of Iron Cross's initial run—the band broke up in 1985, but reunited periodically in the years since—Grey denounced some of the newer, openly racist skinheads in the DC scene from the stage at a September 1984 concert, angered that his band was viewed as an inspiration for people he thought of as "fascists." Grey recalled a separate incident where "I seen one kid who had [Iron Cross] on his arm and there was a swastika in the middle and I said, 'you take that off, 'cause if I see that on you tonight, I'm gonna beat you up.'"[45] Likewise, by the end of 1983, he rejected homophobic and misogynistic violence in an interview with *Maximum Rocknroll*, asserting if "you abuse someone for being who they are, be it gay, woman, punk, or redneck, then you've lost your rights as a human being."[46]

Another divisive DC band with its own zine was Psychodrama. Fairly described by *OP* as "disturbing,"[47] Psychodrama's music and its performances realized punk's purported powers to shock and disgust more effectively than any other DC band to that point, if ever. A cacophony of shrieks, clangs, and howls, there is much to admire about Psychodrama's assault on punk, even if most would find it unlistenable. The group's vocalist, Leslie Singer, recalled that at Psychodrama's first concert in February 1982, at Saint Stephen and the Incarnation Church in Washington, "all ten people in the audience hate[d] us and walk[ed] out during the show."[48]

Little changed, in terms of audience response from the DC punk scene, with the group earning bans from several venues and even, supposedly, "intervention and persecution of the group" from "vice squad detectives."[49] It was no wonder, then, that the "fanzine" Psychodrama debuted in April 1982 had nary a drop of fandom within. *The Alexandria Father Fucker*, subtitled *The Punishment Times*, only lasted for two issues, but the band's scabrous personality was on full, often-humorous, display. "I think that Brett [Kerby, also of Psychodrama] and I were frustrated that our work wasn't getting a better reception in DC and that this zine was a maladaptive response to that," Singer recalled. "We were blowing off steam and trying to be 'transgressive.'"[50] The first issue of *The Alexandria Father Fucker* featured a "nationwide music scene check-up" that ran through major American punk scenes like New York, Los Angeles, Chicago, and Boston, most dismissed with a one-word assessment: "Sucks."

DC gets skewered, as well. The Velvet Monkeys, a recent transplant from Charlottesville, Virginia, "suck shit." The older DC bands "suck, naturally. When are Susan Mumford and Roddy Frantz going to OD already?" As for the hardcore scene, it sucked, too: "All these dyed-hair, anti-Nazi punks are enough to make me join the Nazi party and I'm Jewish." Singer later admitted that "the zine does come off as being very bitter." Reflecting on the hostile tone of *The Alexandria Father Fucker*, she wondered "if Brett and I were also adopting the pose and mouthing the story line that other bands in DC had at that time: DC sucks, it's so conservative, blah, blah, blah."[51]

Singer compiled the zine primarily alone, "with some input and giggles of encouragement from Brett."[52] Distribution occurred at Psychodrama's shows, and the print run never exceeded fifty copies. Regarding the zine's brackish name, Singer declared that "Brett and I were saying 'Fuck the Patriarchy.' The title is an inversion of 'motherfucker.' I guess that is more of a political statement than a taboo breaker."[53] The second issue, dated May 1982, maintains the slam book atmosphere, which had already earned the band criticism. "Well, goddamn, it's not our fault that everything sucks the way it does," issue two's bristly introduction read. "We are trying to improve things with this fanzine," Singer wrote, "so, if all you're doing is hanging out down at 9:30 and buying records in Georgetown and at RTX,[54] don't say a fucking word to us, 'cause you're not doing jack shit." Singer and Kerby moved to San Francisco later in 1982, bringing to mind the musician Damon Edge's quote about that singular city: "People who don't fit in anywhere else come here. . . . There is no place else to go in America."[55]

A more optimistic approach to DC's punk community came from a group of teenagers informally calling themselves DOD. Emanating exuberance and awe for the music scene they were a part of, the DOD crew included members of the hardcore band Deadline, which appeared on *Flex Your Head,* along with friends like Guy Picciotto, John Falls, and Mike Fellows. DOD stood for "Dance of Death," a maneuver that members of the group humorously employed at concerts, poking at macho elements of the hardcore scene by irritatingly crawling on the floor and between the legs of slamdancers in front of the stage. "It was one of those little things that has an esoteric non-meaning that just happens to mean everything," Picciotto later said of the DOD moniker.[56]

Inspired by DC bands whose members created their own fanzines—Picciotto cited *Skin Flint* and *Critical List* as examples—the DOD crew published an eponymous zine in spring 1982.[57] Packed into nine, single-sided, photocopied pages are a flurry of record and concert reviews—mostly written by Deadline's vocalist, Ray Hare, and its bassist, Terry Scanlon—along with a capsule rundown of bands in the DC hardcore scene written by Picciotto, Fellows, and Falls. Tiffany Pruitt's concert photography transcends the murky shroud of the photocopier, vividly expressing the energy of DC bands like Government Issue and the Faith,

Figure 4.6 *DOD,* issue 1, 1982. Used by permission.

or those from elsewhere like the Misfits and SS Decontrol. Upon reading *DOD* decades later, Picciotto expressed that he was "struck by how positive the vibe is. It is full on unapologetically boosterish of the local scene with no concern for having a critical point of view. That, to my mind, is to its credit."[58]

The cover image of a broken arm in a cast derived from an incident that occurred when Deadline opened for the pointedly hostile San Francisco punk band Flipper at the 9:30 Club on March 14, 1982. Hare "dove into the nonexistent crowd" during Deadline's performance and broke his wrist. After a set by Flipper that "annoyed many with [its] pro-drug, anti-DC banter [and] forced many people to leave the club," Deadline returned for a second set to "a rockin' four person crowd."[59] Hare gritted his way through the concert before going to the hospital. "The cast was signed by all us punks and, obviously, it was xeroxed to make the cover," Picciotto explained. Few ever read *DOD,* however, due to its minuscule circulation. "I am almost certain it wasn't distributed anywhere to speak of, possibly at a show but I have no memory of that," Picciotto said. "I think there were very few made and never a second issue."[60]

As thriving as American hardcore punk was in the early 1980s, British punk still resonated with the DOD crew. Picciotto later described himself as "struck by how many of [*DOD*'s] record reviews are focused on the British bands of the time that we were into. It reminded me of the zeitgeist/mindset that we were all in that led to Insurrection, the band that came out of Deadline." Hare and Deadline's guitarist, Christian Caron, departed for college after the band's last recording in August 1982,[61] so Scanlon and drummer Brendan Canty (the former switching to vocals) founded Insurrection with Picciotto and Fellows. Insurrection only lasted from fall 1982 through summer 1983 but is notable for, essentially, evolving into Rites of Spring—Picciotto, Fellows, Canty, and guitarist Eddie Janney—one of DC punk's most innovative bands.

Insurrection never released any recordings, but the band did leave behind—to the apparent future mortification of its members—a zine of its own. Far more ironic in presentation than *DOD,* the *Insurrection* zine "was not a legit fanzine in any sense of the word," Picciotto later insisted. "It was an inside-joke style parody of *Tiger Beat*,[62] done for our own juvenile amusement."[63] Over ten photocopied pages, *Insurrection* chortled its way through a series of "pin-ups" of the band, displaying a picture of the band member and a variety of absurd and clearly fictional details about them. "With Guy's swift and raw movements, one can get a bad and empty feeling in the bowels," one section warned.[64] Shared only with the band's friends at the time, Picciotto later seemed chagrined that the cheeky *Insurrection* zine did not disappear into the mists of time, ultimately turning up instead in multiple DC punk archival collections in the 2010s: "The idea that it is in an archive for scholarly perusal is baffling to me, obviously."[65]

Touch and Go and the Hardcore Sense of Humor

Humor—or attempts at it—was a key element in DC punk fanzines of this period. In addition to aforementioned titles that used humor as a tool to express difference, creativity, anger, bigotry, or any number of goals, other zines centering on a sense of humor came and went quickly. *Punk Is No Hobby*, appearing in 1983, satirized self-righteous hypocrisy in the scene. Presumably-pseudonymous editor Hovis Clayburg asked: "Firstly, who do all these new punkers think they are, anyway? I've been a punk for six years and I think that these new kids all suck. Secondly, let's try to get some unity in this scene. Everyone should stand strong and proud together and stop fighting punk against punk. We should fight against real problems like Reagan and Nuclear war instead of each other."[66]

Based on the handwriting seen on the cover of *Recorded Matter*, another short-lived zine appearing in 1983, Clayburg—or whoever they actually were—was behind that title, too. *Punk Is No Hobby* had its fair share of reviews poking fun at bands in the DC scene—Minor Threat gets called out for its "straight edge crap" and "dogma"—but *Recorded Matter* really leaned into a dyspeptic stance toward most punk bands. Hardcore favorites like SS Decontrol and Necros go through the wringer, while punk pioneers like the Sex Pistols and the Damned are maliciously dismissed. Yet again, Minor Threat received specific derision, this time through a rant against their *Out of Step* EP so overheated, you can practically hear the author snickering over the clacking typewriter:

Figure 4.7 *Punk Is No Hobby*, issue 1, circa 1983. Published by Hovis Clayburg.

> *UUUUUUGH! SPIT! This is definetly [sic] the year's absolute worst release. Eight infantile Mickey Mouse tunes rehashing that god damn "Straight Edge" horse manure does not a fine album make. . . . DO NOT UNDER ANY CIRCUMSTANCES BUY THIS ALBUM INTENTIONALLY OR BY MISTAKE, UNLESS YOU WISH SUPPORT THE END OF HARDCORE MUSIC AS WE KNOW IT, AND POSSIBLY JEOPARDIZE NATIONAL SECURITY AT THE SAME TIME BY SUPPORTING A COMMUNIST PLOT TO INFILTRATE THE AMERICAN PUNKER, KNOWN TO THE KGB AS "DISCHORD RECORDS."*

Whether or not *Recorded Matter* and *Punk Is No Hobby* were unintentional self-parodies or sardonic spoofs—presumably the latter—was not the point. They were more proof that fanzines—even the microdistributed titles that saw just a few photocopies passed around to friends—were an essential part of punk, giving their creators a forum to vent, joke, critique the scene, and add their voices to the mix, no matter how small the audience. Whether they liked it or not, Minor Threat's success put the band on a pedestal and zines like *Recorded Matter* queued up with their slingshots before retreating into the shadows. Perhaps "negazine" would be a better category title for zines like these but, in their own cantankerous way, they said as much about the passion of fandom as any of their more panegyrical counterparts did.

Irreverent humor was a stock punk attribute, but no one in the DC scene brandished their sense of humor with as much abandon as Tesco Vee. Vee founded *Touch and Go* fanzine with Dave Stimson in 1979 while living in Michigan, creating a prime example of the new wave of American punk zines appearing in the early 1980s. Influenced by titles like *Slash* and *Search and Destroy*, *Touch and Go* presented the next step forward from those publications, even if their production standards were more rough-hewn. Mixing the fervor and aesthetics of those earlier California zines with the teenage delinquent attitude of the New York scene, then channeling it all through an acerbic Midwestern lens, Vee and Stimson forged a distinct voice in American punk fanzines. "*Slash* was what really inspired [Stimson] and me to turn into gonzo guerilla scribes, banging out our diatribes on IBM Selectrics into the wee morning hours,[67] ashtrays piled high with Lucky Strike heaters in our respective hovels," Vee later wrote.[68] "In its ugliness, [*Touch and Go*] was the perfect vehicle to announce what was wrong with the tepid music that was heralded as good by such once-esteemed publications like *Rolling Stone*," author and punk musician Steve Miller observed.[69] "And in its parallel beauty, *Touch and Go* magazine, with its mimeographed aesthetic and its reliance on the profane, the obscene, and the unheard, was truly what it took for the times."[70]

In early 1981, MacKaye found a copy of *Touch and Go*'s eleventh issue at the Record and Tape Exchange in Arlington, Virginia. Penelope Houston of the Avengers, a San Francisco punk band, stared back from the zine's cover. "I remember thinking, 'Whoa! Who the fuck knows who the Avengers are outside of DC and West Coast,'" he wrote. MacKaye mailed *Touch and Go* a copy of Teen Idles' *Minor Disturbance* EP, but the record shattered during the shipping process. Undeterred, Vee and Stimson responded they had "taped it together and what we can hear, because the needle jumps all over the fuckin' place, sounds cool!" MacKaye noted "it was really one of the first times that anyone outside of Washington really paid us any mind."[71] Rollins, too, felt the gravity of the new connection. "It was as if we were sending out a signal to see if there was life on other planets and one day we got a response," he wrote.[72]

The lasting impact of the connection had not seemed to register with Stimson yet when he sent a copy of *Touch and Go* to *Discords*, including a letter the latter published in their May 1981 issue. Stimson's note groused about the DC scene's lack of interest in his zine. "I guess people aren't all that enthused on reading about how shitty it is out here"

Figure 4.8 *Touch and Go*, issue 22, 1983. Published by Tesco Vee. Used by permission.

in Michigan, he grumbled. Having sent a copy of *Touch and Go* to *The Infiltrator* for review without receiving a response, Stimson speculated that "their metropolitan egos probably got the best of them and [they] decided to snub these 'hicks' from the corn belt." Setting his feelings aside, Stimson began contributing Michigan scene reports to *Discords*. Vee—also a *Discords* contributor—remembered Howard Wuelfing and his zine fondly, noting he "always dug"[73] Wuelfing's writing.

Their prospects dimming in Michigan, Stimson and Vee moved to the DC area. "Meeting Ian, Jeff [Nelson], and the gang was really exciting and the scene had a serious energy and cast of characters," Vee remembered. "I was getting ready to lose my teaching job due to declining enrollments in Michigan and [DC] seemed like a cool place to move to."[74] Stimson had moved out to DC ahead of Vee but, despite a thriving new scene to cover, he lost interest in publishing a fanzine and dropped out. Vee persevered, publishing several more issues of *Touch and Go*. "It was a small scene and I think they accepted me alright," he recalled. "It was a target rich environment for new bands to interview and I dove right in!"[75]

Touch and Go's coverage of DC punk was exceptional, capturing many of the short-lived hardcore bands blooming during 1982 and 1983. Barely documented groups like Red C and Insurrection are interviewed alongside more prominent names like Minor Threat, Iron Cross, and Void. The zine's influence is obvious on *Critical List* and *Skin Flint*. Offensive humor and imagery—the gory art by Pushead appearing in the zine was often somehow not the most shocking content within[76]—was even more pervasive in *Touch and Go* than in its DC followers.

"Vee shoots nearly every story he writes full of grotesque and graphic references to anything remotely obscene," one contemporary review reported. *Touch and Go* "manages to offer something offensive for just about everyone: It's been called racist, sexist, anti-homosexual; it's even been accused of ridiculing the punk music it supports."[77] Vee relished his shock reputation, though he asserted it was born of a desire to point out hypocrisy in the scene and slay sacred cows. "To offend a punk is the ultimate," he remarked. "Punk has become so staid and sterile in a lot of ways." Despite the contents of his zine, Vee insisted he was not sexist, declaring that "in my dealings with women, I treat them with ultimate respect."[78]

Provocation was at the core of Vee's identity, whether through his zine or his band, the Meatmen. "I purposely say things that are way out just to see if people will challenge me," he claimed at the time, "and nine times out of ten they don't."[79] When asked, decades later, if he learned anything from the occasions someone *did* challenge him, he replied: "Not really. I had a bit of a swagger, I guess you could say, and it was my mag, so I shot from the hip. But I always looked forward to dissenting opinions. I'm sure I published their opinion and then piled on. I didn't mind laying the wood to someone if I didn't like 'em, be it a band or a hater, much like *Creem*."[80]

Touch and Go ended in September 1983 with its twenty-second issue which, like the previous few issues of the zine, had seen its print run climb to around two thousand offset printed copies. "1983 felt like the end of something to me," Vee observed. "The first wave of [hardcore] bands was giving way to new bands and I can't really say definitively why I stopped. Doing the zine solo was a lot of work and I guess I just felt it had run its course." Vee has positive memories of working with Stimson, noting they "played off each other well," each working on their own portions of a new issue before reconvening to "read each other's pages, drink beer, listen to the first Suicide album over and over, and then it was off to the print shop!"[81]

Touch and Go Records, a label spun off from the fanzine in 1981, outlasted its counterpart by decades. Vee and Stimson originally collaborated on the label with Corey Rusk of Necros, but the pair dropped out when they moved to DC. Rusk moved label operations to Chicago in 1983 and helped Touch and Go Records become a pivotal American punk label, issuing influential music from Big Black, Butthole Surfers, Jesus Lizard, Slint, Yeah Yeah Yeahs, TV On The Radio, and many more. With the zine gone, Vee continued making music with the Meatmen and other projects like Tesco Vee's Hate Police, all generally similar in crudely comedic tone to his zine. *Touch and Go*'s impact on American punk was profound.[82] Reflecting on it decades later, Vee acknowledged he was "really glad we did it, in retrospect. . . . The zine gave me a creative outlet for my writings. I called it a divine calling, to sing it to the heavens to anyone who would listen about all this new music!"[83]

Brand New Age and DC Riot

John Kelly's[84] 2015 article in the *Washington Post* illustrated the bittersweet story of Arlington's Malcolm "Mike" Ross and *Brand New Age* fanzine, which ran for two issues in 1983. In October 1987, while residing in New York City to attend New York University's Tisch School of the Arts, twenty-one-year-old Ross died when he fell while climbing with friends on the Williamsburg Bridge. His words and passion for music live on, however, through the remaining print copies of *Brand New Age*, archived at both the University of Maryland and the DC Public Library. There, as Kelly wistfully wrote, researchers can "go back in time, back to what promised to be a *Brand New Age*, an age that Mike Ross lives in forever."[85]

Some of *Brand New Age*'s initial readers were actually drawn in thanks to *DC Riot*, a short-lived fanzine which published two issues in March and August of 1982. Despite each issue's limited space—issue one consisted of a single, double-sided photocopy, while issue two was a stapled pair of double-sided photocopies—*DC Riot* presented a highly opinionated, incisive appraisal of DC's punk scene. Mostly approving in its fandom, editor Pete M's writings displayed a willingness to criticize, when necessary. One critique of the 9:30 Club asked "why do the bouncers get so uptight out of the least bit of rowdiness in the back when the dancers are killing each other up front? One time this guy told our table to behave in between sets at a Black Flag gig. I mean, come on."[86]

Pete M appeared to have placed an advertisement in *Flipside* around this time, offering a copy of his fanzine to anyone in exchange for a stamp. A number of requests came in, including one from a little-known New York City musician and editor of *Killer* fanzine. Thurston Moore, guitarist for the ultimately canonical Sonic Youth and ever searching for new music to explore, wrote elliptically, "Here's a stamp. Please send me a *DC Riot*." However, as Kelly described, the

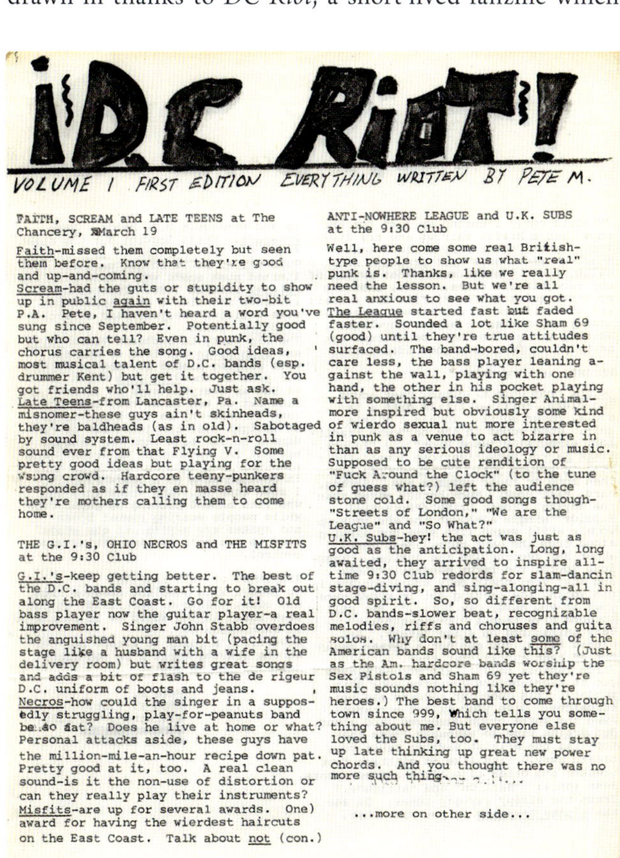

¡D.C. RIOT!

VOLUME 1 FIRST EDITION EVERYTHING WRITTEN BY PETE M.

FAITH, SCREAM and LATE TEENS at The Chancery, March 19

Faith-missed them completely but seen them before. Know that they're good and up-and-coming.
Scream-had the guts or stupidity to show up in public again with their two-bit P.A. Pete, I haven't heard a word you've sung since September. Potentially good but who can tell? Even in punk, the chorus carries the song. Good ideas, most musical talent of D.C. bands (esp. drummer Kent) but get it together. You got friends who'll help. Just ask.
Late Teens-from Lancaster, Pa. Name a misnomer-these guys ain't skinheads, they're baldheads (as in old). Sabotaged by sound system. Least rock-n-roll sound ever from that Flying V. Some pretty good ideas but playing for the wrong crowd. Hardcore teeny-punkers responded as if they en masse heard they're mothers calling them to come home.

THE G.I.'s, OHIO NECROS and THE MISFITS at the 9:30 Club

G.I.'s-keep getting better. The best of the D.C. bands and starting to break out along the East Coast. Go for it! Old bass player now the guitar player-a real improvement. Singer John Stabb overdoes the anguished young man bit (pacing the stage like a husband with a wife in the delivery room) but writes great songs and adds a bit of flash to the de rigeur D.C. uniform of boots and jeans.
Necros-how could the singer in a supposedly struggling, play-for-peanuts band be so fat? Does he live at home or what? Personal attacks aside, these guys have the million-mile-an-hour recipe down pat. Pretty good at it, too. A real clean sound-is it the non-use of distortion or can they really play their instruments?
Misfits-are up for several awards. One) award for having the wierdest haircuts on the East Coast. Talk about not (con.)

ANTI-NOWHERE LEAGUE and U.K. SUBS at the 9:30 Club

Well, here come some real British-type people to show us what "real" punk is. Thanks, like we really need the lesson. But we're all real anxious to see what you got.
The League started fast but faded faster. Sounded a lot like Sham 69 (good) until they're true attitudes surfaced. The band-bored, couldn't care less, the bass player leaning against the wall, playing with one hand, the other in his pocket playing with something else. Singer Animal-more inspired but obviously some kind of wierdo sexual nut more interested in punk as a venue to act bizarre in than as any serious ideology or music. Supposed to be cute rendition of "Fuck Around the Clock" (to the tune of guess what?) left the audience stone cold. Some good songs though-"Streets of London," "We are the League" and "So What?"
U.K. Subs-hey! the act was just as good as the anticipation. Long, long awaited, they arrived to inspire all-time 9:30 Club redords for slam-dancin stage-diving, and sing-alonging-all in good spirit. So, so different from D.C. bands-slower beat, recognizable melodies, riffs and choruses and guita solos. Why don't at least some of the American bands sound like this? (Just as the Am. hardcore bands worship the Sex Pistols and Sham 69 yet they're music sounds nothing like they're heroes.) The best band to come through town since 999, which tells you something about me. But everyone else loved the Subs, too. They must stay up late thinking up great new power chords. And you thought there was no more such thing...

...more on other side...

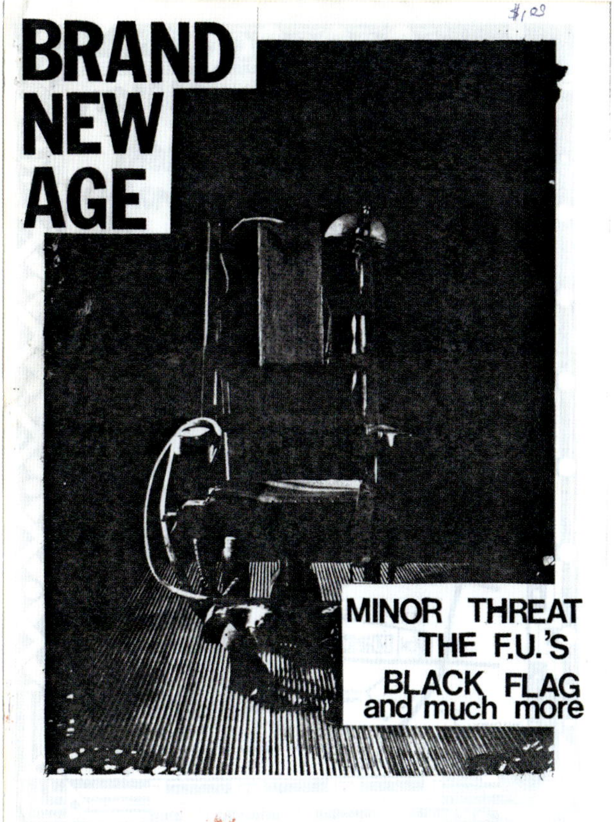

Figure 4.9 Left: *DC Riot*, issue 1, March 1982, published by Pete M. Right: *Brand New Age*, issue 1, 1983, published by Mike Ross.

DC Riot,
HERE'S A STAMP
PLEASE SEND ME A DC RIOT
THANKS
THURSTON MOORE
SONIC YOUTH
84 ELDRIDGE ST. #5
NYC 10002

Figure 4.10 Note by Thurston Moore requesting an issue of *DC Riot*, circa 1982. From the DC Punk archive, The People's Archive, Martin Luther King, Jr. Memorial Library. Used by permission.

letters requesting copies of *DC Riot* ultimately wound up in Ross's hands, presumably passed off by Pete M when he realized a new issue of his own zine was not going to materialize. What truly happened is likely lost to time, but it seems plausible that Ross inherited the requests and used them to spread the word on his new fanzine, *Brand New Age*.

Ross—a student at Arlington's H-B Woodlawn High School when he started *Brand New Age*[87]—and the friends he collaborated with on the fanzine reported on the scene's concerts and recordings with an eager, but not unjaundiced, perspective. “We were just high school kids who were really into the music and the zine kinda came about because we really were into seeing shows every weekend at 9:30 or dc space,” recalled contributor Stafford Mather. “We would drag a big boombox to shows at 9:30 and talk our way into the dressing room to chat with the bands, most of whom were very cool to us.”[88] That a zine as unheralded as *Brand New Age* included interviews with prominent hardcore bands like Black Flag, Minor Threat, Circle Jerks, and Hüsker Dü speaks to the democratic aspect of punk that valorizes accessibility. “We got to interview Minor Threat at their practice space because I met [drummer] Jeff Nelson while he was working at my local 7-Eleven,” Mather remembered.[89]

Despite the access that Ross, Mather, and their friends obtained, the group still considered themselves outsiders. “The ‘scene’ was considered mostly cliquish at that point,” Mather said. “Again, we were very young and didn't make a lot of friends in the ‘scene’ until after high school when I started playing in bands and meeting more people from other local bands.”[90] Nevertheless, the quality of the interviews in *Brand New Age* demonstrated that Ross and his friends knew enough to get their subjects talking beyond the rote exchanges clogging many fanzines.

Passive-aggressive tension among members of Minor Threat led to one bit of badinage that, while partially in jest, spotlighted widening cracks in the band's foundation. “Our fights will become physical one day,” Nelson warned, as the others banter about the times they have all nearly come to blows. After MacKaye claimed to have previously “asked some of them out for a quick round,” a skeptical Nelson asked, “When? You never asked me.” MacKaye declared he had kicked down Nelson's door before, to which Nelson responded “Yeah, but you never touched me.” MacKaye's retort of “Well, you're lucky. YOU WANT TO FIND OUT RIGHT NOW” is delivered with a teasing mock belligerence, but the jockeying within the group is awkward to witness. “The band will break up when Ian is no longer big enough to beat us up,” guitarist Brian Baker added sarcastically.[91]

As for what brought *Brand New Age* to an end after only two issues, Mather could not recall a specific reason, simply noting that “I think we lost interest as we headed into post–high school life.”[92] Mather remembered Ross fondly as the original driver of the zine, noting that “he was always into something.” Speaking with Kelly, Ross's mother, Judy Tinelli, remembered her son as a handsome redhead whose grades did not always match his keen intelligence. “Ninety-ninth percentile in SATs [but a] 2.2 [grade point average],” she recalled with a laugh.[93] That promising new era that Ross, essentially, named the zine after was a flawed but exciting reality as 1983 unfolded. The two issues of *Brand New Age* left behind remain proof of both the subculture's growth in the hardcore era and of the too-brief, incandescent life of Mike Ross.

Thrillseeker

In College Park, the home of the University of Maryland, another group of young outsiders started a fanzine of their own. Steve Kiviat and Tony Lombardi both fell for punk rock as teenagers in suburban Bowie, Maryland, about 12 miles northeast of the DC line. Like so many other zine creators in the DC scene, the pair was influenced by *Creem* magazine, as well as local radio station WGTB and disc jockey Steve Lorber.

Lorber's show on WGTB inspired the teenagers to drive to the College Park Record & Tape Exchange to hunt for the new music they heard. From there, Kiviat recalled "starting to then get interested in seeing bands and seeing local bands. Seeing Razz . . . and then the Slickee Boys. And soon sort of hearing about the Georgetown punk bands and things."[94] In addition to the Razz and the Slickee Boys, Lombardi cited DC's punk-friendly rockabilly singer Tex Rubinowitz as another early inspiration.[95] "We went to see [those bands] play every chance we got and purchased their records on small local labels like Dacoit, Limp, and O'Rourke," he remembered. "I still have and treasure those records."[96]

Kiviat and Lombardi matriculated at the University of Maryland in the fall of 1979, gravitating toward WMUC, the campus radio station, to find like-minded people and play the music they loved. Although WMUC was still more of a training ground for people interested in working at commercial radio stations than a musically eccentric, free-form environment, a new group soon made a difference at the station. Kiviat, Lombardi, and others like Josh Friedman, Sharon Cheslow, and future *Heavy Metal Parking Lot* codirector Jeff Krulik broadened the types of sounds heard on WMUC. For Kiviat, "the radio station then became this additional sort of mind-opening thing," in addition to publications like *New York Rocker* and *Trouser Press*.[97]

Figure 4.11 Left: Tony Lombardi and Steve Kiviat of *Thrillseeker*, fall 1982. Photo by Hal Schmulowitz. Right: *Thrillseeker*, issue 2, 1983. Used by permission.

Another galvanizing moment was a Bad Brains concert at dc space on September 1, 1979. "After seeing the Bad Brains, I don't think any of us slept that night," Lombardi said. "I came to the realization that night that the music being made in DC was as good, as vital, and as important as the music being made anywhere else in the world." Earlier DC fanzines like *Vintage Violence* and *Capitol Crisis*, too, were in the mix of influences setting Kiviat and Lombardi toward making their own zine. Lombardi and Brian Kiviat, Steve's younger brother, had interviewed Black Flag for *Capitol Crisis*, which ran in the May 1981 issue. Steve Kiviat also contributed reviews to *Capitol Crisis*, as well as DC scene reports to *OP* magazine from Olympia, Washington, gradually honing his music writing chops in the buildup to launching a fanzine.

Elliot Klayman and Sue German, part of the WMUC cohort, traveled to California in summer 1982, returning with several band interviews they wanted to publish in print, rather than air on WMUC. "The rest of us readily agreed and since we were already heavily promoting local music and doing interviews with both local and national bands, it seemed like a natural progression to put it all in print ourselves," Lombardi remembered. "Steve and I volunteered to put it all together. The contributions mostly came from WMUC DJs [, and we] did not put any restrictions at all on content."[98]

Needing a name for their fanzine, Kiviat recalled an *LA Weekly* article on the Gun Club, an innovative Los Angeles postpunk band in which the vocalist/guitarist Jeffrey Lee Pierce dismissed some showgoers from outside their punk scene's inner circles as "thrill seekers." The idea of adopting "thrill seeker" as a badge of honor immediately appealed to Kiviat and his friends. Kiviat said his group identified with those "not cool enough kids" because they "weren't high school age or whatever, and hanging out in Georgetown with . . . that core group of hardcore Dischord folks," nor were they part of what they perceived as "a bigger group [of] people that were in Bethesda."[99] Seeing themselves as outsiders among the outsiders, they christened their fanzine, *Thrillseeker*. Lombardi added that, for him, "it was an acknowledgment that the music we loved was a bit dangerous but also lots of fun."[100] Thanks to Klayman and German's contributions, the first issue of *Thrillseeker* is filled with California bands like Black Flag, Dead Kennedys, X, and Fear. Despite that, the cover of the first issue boldly declares it is a "DC ZINE" alongside a photo of Government Issue.

Thrillseeker's cover logo employed a reenvisioning of the DC flag, substituting Xs for the three stars at the top, a motif also appearing on concert fliers in 1981 for the short-lived DC hardcore band Youth Brigade. This new DC hardcore logo was additionally found on a poster created by graphic designer Bob Raiter to promote a Government Issue concert organized by Malcolm Riviera at the Wilson Center on June 25, 1982. Raiter introduced a striking red spot color for the Xs and bars, as well as a bold, sans-serif typeface that read "HARDCORE" along the base. Later that summer, for a Black Flag concert on September 17—with openers Double-O, Iron Cross, and the Faith from DC and the Effigies from Chicago—Raiter blanketed his poster design with miniature DC flag hardcore logos, emphasizing the scene's new role as an influential force in American punk rock.[101]

Perhaps the most widely seen example of the DC hardcore logo was found on Dischord's *Flex Your Head* compilation, which intriguingly used four different covers throughout its many pressings. The first two designs, from 1982, were amusingly incongruous images culled from the record-pressing plant's stock photo options. One featured grain waving peacefully against partly cloudy skies, while the other showed a violin surrounded by roses and sheet music. A fourth design would appear in 1985 bearing a blurred photograph of a person looking off into the distance but, first, a third variation debuted on a British pressing in early 1983. This one dynamically used an austere black-and-white graphic centering the bars and Xs of the DC hardcore logo beneath the compilation's title to convey the no-frills focus and intensity of the music within.

Thrillseeker's use of the DC hardcore emblem saw the fanzine's name wedged between the Xs and bars, laying claim to its place in the scene. An opening editorial acknowledged the glut of national coverage in the first issue, writing "we know fanzines are supposed to be regional and we tried to have as much DC stuff as possible, but there's still too much out of town shit. Next issue should be focused more on the local scene."

That first issue, for September 1982, captured the scene's transition from a tight-knit community to a broader subculture containing various segments. Lombardi's review of a concert by the Dead Kennedys, Government Issue, Double-O, and the Faith on July 22 at George Washington University's Marvin Center expressed amazement at the turnout. "Where did all these people come from?" Lombardi asked. "All types: hardcores, hippies, nu-wavers, curiosity-seekers, Marines (boo!), intellectuals, technos, airheads, blonds, brunettes, etc., etc." A review of a Minor Threat concert from earlier that summer dispensed with any hand-wringing about the band's success. "Minor Threat transcends rock and roll and creates something which can't be labeled," Lombardi enthused. "They're consistently one of the best live bands I've ever seen."

The hardcore scene's struggles with establishing a reliable concert venue during this period were illustrated by a news item recapping a meeting at the 9:30 Club. Members of Minor Threat and the Faith, along with WMUC staff and other punks, met with 9:30 Club representatives. "Over Cokes, everyone discussed how to have hardcore shows at 9:30 and keep everyone happy," the item read. Club co-owner Dodie Bowers relayed her concerns, primarily consisting of violence at shows, and loitering and graffiti outside the club. The meeting disbanded with a tentative agreement to host Sunday hardcore shows at the club twice a month: "Everyone there suggested to Dodie the idea that 'hardcore regularity' would help resolve some of the problems the 9:30 worries about." Indeed, it did, as the 9:30 Club remained one of DC punk's primary venues for years.[102]

As promised, *Thrillseeker*'s second issue focused more on DC. That issue, published in March 1983, had a heretofore unusual two-color cover, mixing red and black and further evoking the vivid look of Raiter's designs. Brian Kiviat's cover photo of the Faith's Alec MacKaye helps cement the notion that the Faith was, at least locally, gaining in stature

Figure 4.12 Posters designed by Bob Raiter for concerts promoted by Malcolm Riviera at the Wilson Center in 1982.

to creatively and politically spin its wheels as the mid-1980s approached.

Figure 4.13 Ian MacKaye of Minor Threat, circa 1983. Photo by Jim Saah. Used by permission.

on Minor Threat and Government Issue as the premier DC hardcore band. Lombardi's review of a "chaotic and thrilling as ever" set by the Faith ends with a sentiment capturing everything vital and immediate that punk could provide: "It's fucking great to be alive."

Thrillseeker intrigued further by including culture from outside punk's immediate terrain, bringing to mind some of *The Infiltrator*'s diverse sensibilities. The second issue—alongside interviews with local punks the Faith and Scream, as well as national groups like Hüsker Dü, Big Boys, and the Bangles—included an interview with DC go-go band Trouble Funk and underground New York City filmmaker Beth B. "The vision of *Thrillseeker*, of course, was as a music zine first and foremost but I never wanted it to be strictly focused on the punk scene, or even music for that matter, although music makes up a large majority of the content," Lombardi said. "Steve and I made a good pair of editors. He could obsess about the latest world music from some remote part of the world and I could obsess about, well, the Obsessed."[103] *Thrillseeker*'s first two issues established it as a forceful second wave DC punk voice that thrived outside the better-known core of scene participants. Aside from the depth and detail of the writing, its broad musical palate presented a path forward for a punk subculture beginning

Zone V

Punk's dissolution of old barriers between fans and musicians is impeccably illustrated in a Minor Threat photograph by Jim Saah, taken in 1983. A shouting, perspiring Ian MacKaye is pictured surrounded by a crush of fans enveloping him like a wave cresting a retaining wall. Saah closely documented the hardcore scene, forging numerous indelible images of the leaping, contorting bodies traversing the stages and floors of venues like the 9:30 Club and the Wilson Center. Starting in summer 1983, Saah published *Zone V*, a fanzine where he could share the images he captured.[104]

A midnight screening in DC of *The Rocky Horror Picture Show* piqued Saah's interest in punk. Before the film started, audience members danced down in front of the screen while punk rock played over the sound system, introducing Saah to the music that shaped his life. Saah became fascinated by British punk, trolling for new records amid the bins at Joe's Record Paradise, another long-running DC area shop. An attentive employee advised him that, if he liked punk, there were great local bands to investigate. "So, then I went to a show," Saah recalled. "[Government Issue] and Minor Threat at University of Maryland, in 1982, and [I] was just hooked."[105]

Saah had already explored photography starting in high school, but punk presented him with an opportunity to use that artform for further creativity and connection. New York photographer Glen E. Friedman published his *My Rules* photozine in 1982, which Saah acknowledged as a likely inspiration for *Zone V*, along with other punk fanzines like *Flipside*, *Touch & Go*, and *Maximum Rocknroll*.[106] Already contemplating a career in photography, Saah said he "got permission through punk rock to, instead of waiting

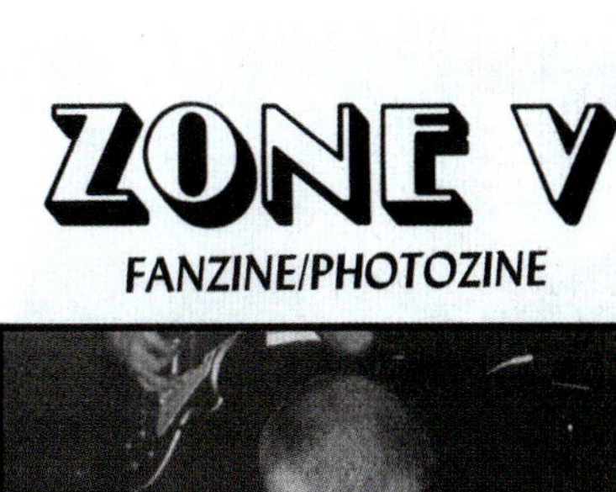

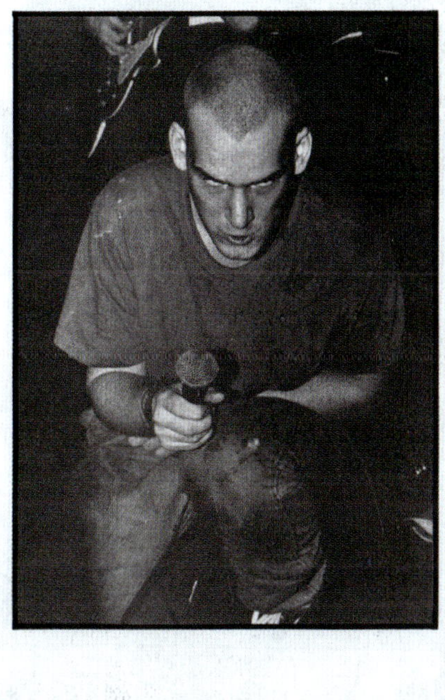

Figure 4.14 *Zone V*, issues 1 and 2, 1983. Published by Jim Saah. Used by permission.

for someone to want to publish me, just do it myself."[107]

Zone V, named after a photographic technique, presented dozens of Saah's concert photographs, with locals like Minor Threat and Hate From Ignorance alongside national bands like Naked Raygun, Suicidal Tendencies, Necros, and Flipper. The energy radiating from the DC bands—particularly Void and the Faith—in Saah's photos eclipses nearly anything generated from the bands from elsewhere. The photograph of Void's John Weiffenbach pinwheeling over the front row of fans and audio monitors epitomizes the catawampus ferocity of the band's live shows. Likewise, Saah's shot of a leaping Chris Bald from the Faith juxtaposes memorably with the bottom of the image, where a grimacing woman in the front row appears stricken by the cathartic scene before her. Only Saah's picture of a feral-looking Henry Rollins—fists clenched at his side and the microphone lodged inside his mouth—surpasses the intensity of the DC bands, showing that Black Flag remained a pacesetter in hardcore punk performance.

Zone V also included interviews with the bands Big Boys and X, as well as a lengthy talk with Henry Rollins about his first two years in Black Flag. A nod to the Pete Frame–style "family tree" drawings *Descenes* once employed to map out the city's punk roots is tucked away at the end of *Zone V*'s first issue. The diagram detailed Minor Threat's lineups and origins, bearing references to short-lived bands like the Slinkees and Skewbald while illustrating the band members' journey from high school garage bands to American punk's forefront. "Back to the original lineup and as explosive as ever," the graphic states approvingly of Minor

Figure 4.15 The Faith perform as the photographer Jim Saah looks on, 1983. Photo by Ellie Moran. Used by permission.

Threat's recent deconfiguration from a quintet to a quartet.

Saah's DC scene reports are thorough and concise, demonstrating that the area's hardcore community had grown, with newer bands like United Mutation and Media Disease favorably mentioned. Thurston Moore of Sonic Youth provides a New York City scene report, outdoing even Saah's granularity. Moore's passion for his city and scene are palpable in his writing, as was his yearning to transcend what came before. Describing the attitude of the new crop of bands, including his own, Moore writes: "New York is not the Bush Tetras, ESG, Liquid Liquid, Konk, Lounge Lizards, The Raybeats, or Polyrock. We do not look up to their success. We are part of the new American underground. This is nothing personal against those bands or their music. It is just their position on the so-called new wave scene here. Let it die."

Minor Threat's breakup toward the end of 1983 and the ebbing of the hardcore scene, as well as Saah's increasing interest in other types of music, led him to end *Zone V* after the second issue that autumn. Saah returned to zine publishing in the 1990s with *Uno Mas*, a standout DC punk zine offering a cerebral lens on punk and the emerging alternative and indie rock scenes. A higher-profile project appeared in 2014, when Saah collaborated with writer-director and fellow DC punk zine editor Scott Crawford on *Salad Days*, a documentary film on DC punk in the 1980s.

Truly Needy

No fanzine from DC had more impact on the scene than *Truly Needy*, debuting in 1982. Due to the quality of its writing, variety of coverage, hefty page count, and relatively long run of almost four years, *Truly Needy* is often cited by participants in the DC scene of this era as the definitive DC punk zine, with *Thrillseeker* running a close second. "Oh, my God, maybe one day I can be like these guys," Scott Crawford remembered thinking when he started his own zine later in 1984. Later issues of *Truly Needy* were "really thick" and "like *Vanity Fair*," he recalled.[108] Mark Robinson, of Teen-Beat Records and the band Unrest, voiced a similar comparison, stating that *Truly Needy* was "like *Time* magazine or *Newsweek*" to him.[109]

Over the course of a ten-issue run ending with its December 1985 issue, *Truly Needy* was published by Barbara Rice and Bill Wort, a married couple who, like the creators of *Thrillseeker* and *Brand New Age*, did not especially fit in with the hardcore scene's inner circle. In Rice and Wort's case, the pair were older than most in the scene and generally eschewed punk attire.[110] "Basically, I don't dress up," Rice noted. "It was hard at first, being a woman and being a little bit older than everybody else.... People were suspicious."[111]

Any suspicions were likely allayed by *Truly Needy*'s obvious dedication to punk. Its name was a sarcastic reference to a speech Ronald Reagan made shortly after taking office, promising he would not cut the social safety net for the "truly needy."[112] Rice and Wort were "totally disgusted with Washington," both politically and in the pretentiousness they perceived was rampant in DC's underground music scene. "We started *Truly Needy* because we were getting tired of elitism in the music scene—you know, 'rock star' attitudes in the name of art," Rice explained.[113] Mike Heath of *Vintage Violence* recalled that Rice had told him a sentiment he expressed in his fanzine—"Nobody who writes for this has anything you don't"—was another inspiration for starting her own. Heath, who later contributed to *Truly Needy*, admitted with a laugh that he "totally ripped off" that message from *Creem*.[114]

Truly Needy's first issue appeared in February 1982, with one hundred twenty-five copies photocopied at a friend's office.[115] Issues tended to appear quarterly in the first two years, but gaps between publication widened as the zine went on. Like *Thrillseeker*, *Truly Needy* carried on the tradition of the earliest DC zines in their variety of coverage, a trait netting both fanzines praise from *Sub Pop*, which called them "outstanding" and "more open-minded than 90 percent of the competition."[116] Punk was at *Truly Needy*'s core, but it broad-mindedly covered music outside that realm, such as an interview with jazz pianist Gil Evans. Contributor Michael Salkind, also a member of the DC bands United Mutation and No Trend, said of Rice and Wort that "we shared strong feelings for wanting to express ourselves, and a passion for the groundswell of all types of music."[117]

Page counts eventually swelled to eighty by later issues, lending the fanzine an authoritative heft complementary to its edifying content. James Schneider—director of *Punk the Capital*, a documentary covering the DC punk scene's early years—described *Truly Needy* as "almost like a catalog, practically. I mean, it smacks of DC bureaucracy, in a way. But inside, it's obviously got a lot of love in there."[118] Crawford discovered *Truly Needy* as an adolescent just getting involved in the scene. To him, the generous page count was a seemingly endless fountain of information to absorb about DC punk. "I just wanted to sink my teeth into this new world that I had discovered," he said.[119] *Washington Waves* publisher and Record & Tape Exchange owner Bill Asp commented that *Truly Needy*'s first issue was "stunning" and "already surpasses any other local publication (music wise) in terms of general objectivity, openness and scrutiny."[120]

Although DC bands were rarely interviewed in early issues of *Truly Needy*—Alan Vega, Jello Biafra, and Fear were some of the national musicians spoken to—local coverage was still excellent due to copious concert and record reviews. Ironically, one of the few DC bands to merit an interview in *Truly Needy* was the oft-neglected Psychodrama, appearing in issue three. This opened up more by issue four, which included conversations with locals Nuclear Crayons and Velvet Monkeys. That same issue includes a downbeat exit interview with Roddy Frantz and Danny Frankel of the recently defunct Urban Verbs. The conversation includes abundant venting—the 9:30 Club, Egoslavia, and Howard Wuelfing all come in for criticism—and the sadness is palpable when Frantz and Frankel reminisce with Rice about Urban Verbs' brief moment on the edge of success. "People, I think now especially, expect us to sort of resent Washington, but I don't think any of us at all have that feeling," Frantz said, sounding like someone speaking in the aftermath of a romantic breakup. "I really don't know if any other city would have welcomed us as enthusiastically as Washington has."[121]

Rice was present throughout punk's development in DC, positioning her to be yet

Figure 4.16 Barbara Rice (left) and the staff of *Truly Needy*, circa fall 1982. Photo by Paul Souders. Used by permission.

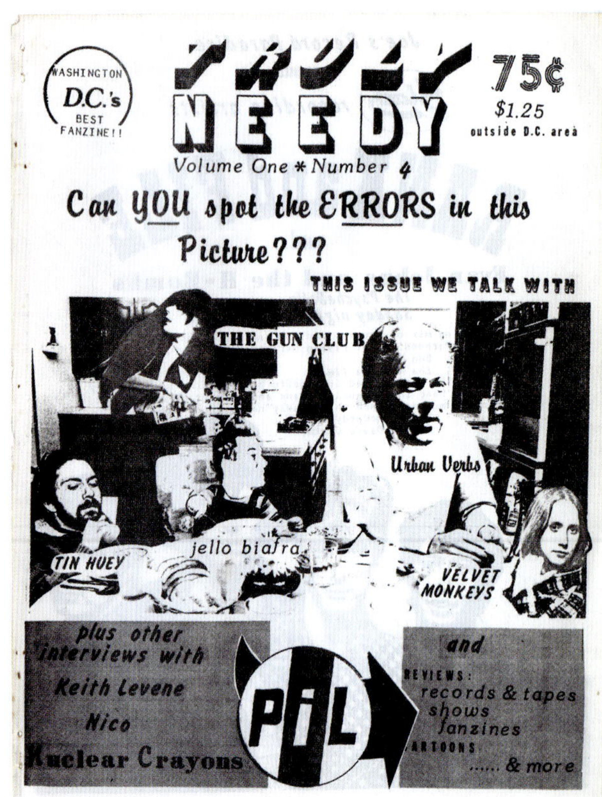

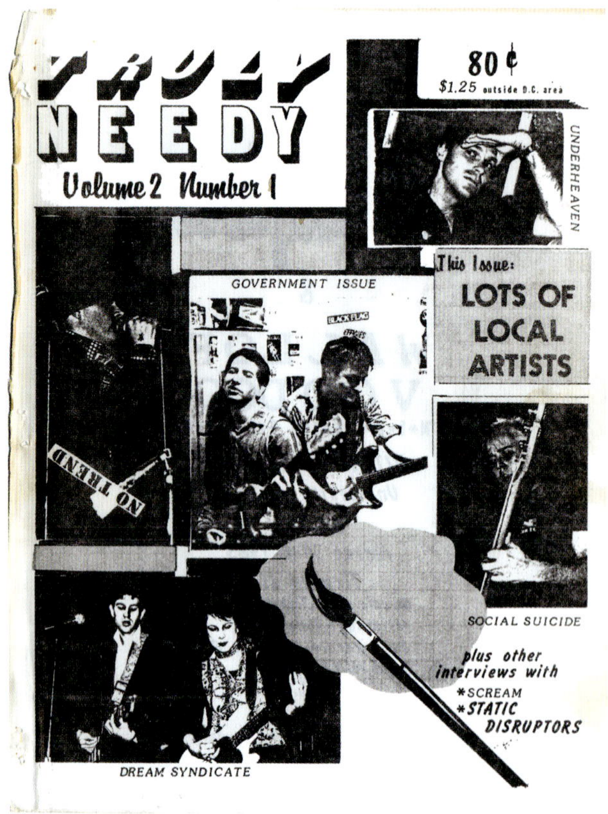

Figure 4.17 Issues 2 through 5 (also known as volume 2, issue 1) of *Truly Needy*, 1982–83. Published by Barbara Rice and Bill Wort.

another voice complaining about how the scene was not what it was. However, her respect for hardcore bands was clear. "DC hardcore is breaking its own ground and maintaining a vital rock tradition: musical democracy," she wrote after attending a concert by the band Social Suicide. She continued: "No need for hero worship 'cause there's very little difference between performers and spectators. It's the purest form of rock n' roll, simple self-expression among people. That night I sensed the same sincere spirit I experienced at the Keg in '76–'77 and at the Atlantis in the beginning of '78. And, for the first time in a while, I was glad I was in DC."[122]

Truly Needy and *Thrillseeker* continued into 1984, covering a scene splintering despite its successes. Vee's observation that 1983 "felt like the end of something" was borne out by the breakups of Minor Threat and the Faith and the increasing violence at shows. Something new for the scene was already germinating, however, and would flower fully in 1985 through bands like Rites of Spring, Embrace, and Gray Matter, as well as the emergence of the activist group Positive Force DC. First, though, 1984 loomed, and the scene approached a flash point.

Notes

1. Fotomat was a ubiquitous American business from the 1960s through the 1980s that specialized in overnight photography development and printing. Fotomat was known, as well, for its distinctive drive-through kiosks.
2. John Kelly, "A Surprising Legacy of DC's Punk Rock History, *Washington Post*, September 16, 2015.
3. Kate Eichhorn, *Adjusted Margin: Xerography, Art, and Activism in the Late Twentieth Century* (Cambridge, MA: MIT Press, 2016), 105.
4. Howard Wuelfing, "Notes," *Washington Tribune*, October 8–21, 1982.
5. Tru Fax & the Insaniacs and Urban Verbs would each occasionally reunite in later years.
6. Alona Wartofsky, "Static Disruptors Reissue Its Go-Go Classic 'DC Groove,'" *Washington City Paper*, March 17, 2016, https://washington citypaper.com/article/398527/static-disruptors-reissue-its-go-go-classic-d-c-groove/.
7. The two EPs were later combined into a single, eponymous LP release in 1984.
8. From 1981's *Minor Threat* EP.
9. Tony Rettman, *Straight Edge: A Clear-Headed Hardcore Punk History* (New York: Bazillion Points, 2017), 36–41, 95.
10. Ross Haenfler, *Straight Edge: Clean-Living Youth, Hardcore Punk, and Social Change* (New Brunswick, NJ: Rutgers University Press, 2006), 10.
11. Susie J. Horgan and Henry Rollins, *Punk Love* (New York: Universe, 2007), 8.
12. Scott Crawford, Jim Saah, and Cynthia Connolly, *Spoke: Images and Stories from the 1980s Washington, DC, Punk Scene* (Brooklyn: Akashic Books, 2017), 34.
13. Mark Andersen, interview with the author, September 20, 2019.
14. Don Fleming, *Reflections* (Chalk Circle, Mississippi Records, and Post-Present Records), PPM-040, MR-069, 2011, LP record; liner notes.
15. Eduardo Dalere, "Fanzines: Underground Journalism Put to Music," *Argus Weekly*, 1:13, December 3, 1982.
16. Fleming, *Reflections*.
17. Fleming goes on to note that the DC area boasted several "excellent local 'girl groups'" in the interim, like the Delights and the Fawns, but all were "groups of singing women who were backed with a male band."
18. The DC band named REM soon changed its name to Egoslavia, due to the emergence of the Athens, Georgia, band REM. The Georgia band went on to become one of the most commercially and critically successful rock bands ever, with the albums *Murmur*, *Document*, *Green*, *Out of Time*, *Automatic for the People*, and many others.
19. Sab Grey, "Local Noise," *Critical List*, issue 5, 1981, 2.
20. Sab Grey, email to the author, February 13, 2021.
21. Sears would later drum for the band Dag Nasty, as well as an embryonic version of Fugazi.
22. Sharon Cheslow, email to the author, January 10, 2019.
23. Turner, later of bands Gray Matter and Three, spelled his first name Jeff during this earlier period.
24. Bloody Mannequin Orchestra, or BMO, was a band that formed during this period and included Cheslow, Sears, Marbury, Charles Bennington, and Alex Mahoney.
25. Cheslow, 2019.
26. Double-O was a short-lived band that featured former members of Red C, Youth Brigade, and the Untouchables. The band issued a single EP on R&B and Dischord Records, although songs from their various demo tapes crop up on a few compilations.
27. *If This Goes On*, issue 2, December 1982, 6–7.
28. Oi! is a subgenre of punk that scholar Matthew Worley described as "aggressive stripped-down (punk) rock [that] brought punk's class rhetoric to the fore [and] claimed to engage with aspects of young working-class life from authentic experience. Theirs were songs of youth cultural antagonisms, work (or the lack of it), football violence, petty crime, police harassment and a suspicion of authority in all its forms." Worley also notes that Oi! was frequently "accused of flirting with the language and imagery of National Socialism to provide a conduit for 'violent-racist-sexist-fascist' attitudes to feed their way into popular music."
29. Steven Blush, *American Hardcore: A Tribal History*, edited by George Petros (Los Angeles: Feral House, 2001), 148.
30. The Iron Cross was a German military decoration with a long history, but was closely associated by many with Nazi Germany.
31. Mark Andersen and Mark Jenkins, *Dance of Days: Two Decades of Punk in the Nation's Capital*, updated and expanded 4th ed. (Brooklyn: Akashic Books, 2009), 126.
32. Bassist Wendel Blow was the song's composer. He would later acknowledge the impact of his actions during this period, telling filmmaker Scott Crawford that "I pray that having made the many changes in how I deal with things in life and realizing how I affected people from every angle I can imagine, I hope there is some way to see that time in my life with an objective sense of well-deserved scrutiny, if not outright condemnation."
33. Tony Rettman, "We Interviewed Sab Grey from Iron Cross," *Vice*, October 12, 2012, https://web.archive.org/web/20201118021622/https://www.vice.com/en/article/ppqvjm/we-interviewed-sab-grey-from-iron-cross.
34. Ferrando was later a member of the bands Gray Matter and Ignition, as well as an entrepreneur who founded the Black Cat, a long-running DC

punk and indie music venue. He described in Andersen and Jenkins' *Dance of Days* how, among his group of friends, fighting for self-defense soon devolved into harassment and abuse of innocent people. He recalled witnessing fellow members of the "Rat Patrol" gang attack a gay man, a crime so grievous that Ferrando declared he "knew [his] days in the Rat Patrol were over."

35. Grey, email.
36. Sab Grey, "Introduction," *Skin Flint*, issue 1, 1982.
37. Grey, email.
38. Ever dauntless, slightly rumpled, and ready with a quip, Carl Kolchak was a character from two television horror movies (*The Night Stalker* and *The Night Strangler*) and a television series (*Kolchak: The Night Stalker*) in the 1970s. Described by John Kenneth Muir in his book *Terror Television* as "one of the terror TV greats," *Kolchak: The Night Stalker* featured the titular journalist investigating paranormal crimes, providing a "gutsy, go-for-the-throat horror excursion with heart to match its horror."
39. Grey, email.
40. Grey, "Introduction."
41. Also released in 1981, *Connected* featured songs by Tommy Keene, Bad Brains, Slickee Boys, Velvet Monkeys, Nurses, and others.
42. The DC Skins were not a gang, Grey later said: "It was just a bunch of friends who happened to be skinheads. Then, all of a sudden it went sour. Some people who had shaved heads were beating up people [so] we decided to bag it. We grew our hair out and went back to being punks, which is what we were in the first place."
43. Another forgotten band of DC's early punk years due to having never released a record. Active from June 1979 to March 1980, Trenchmouth was formed by the vocalist Charlie Danbury, who sought to assemble "the most vile and disgusting band of all time." High points like "Preacher Boy" and "Don't Know Why" show a band that would have fit in nicely on a bill with the Saints or the Vibrators. Unlike many prehardcore bands in DC's punk history, there was no mistaking if Trenchmouth sounded like a punk band or not. Members went on to Black Market Baby and Crippled Pilgrims.
44. Sab Grey, "Interview with Black Market Baby," *Skin Flint*, issue 3, 1982.
45. *WDC Period*, issue 6, December 1984, 8.
46. *Maximum Rocknroll*, issue 11, January–February 1984, 42.
47. Graham Ingles, "Castanets," *OP*, September–October 1982.
48. Leslie Singer, "Psychodrama Timeline," *Unsound* 2, no. 1, 1985.
49. Singer.
50. "Psychodrama," no date; and HalTapes, no date; http://www.haltapes.com/psychodrama.html.
51. HalTapes.
52. HalTapes.
53. HalTapes.
54. Bill Asp's Record and Tape Exchange.
55. Simon Reynolds, *Rip It Up and Start Again: Postpunk 1978–1984* (New York: Penguin Books, 2006), 197.
56. Andersen and Jenkins, *Dance of Days*, 97.
57. Guy Picciotto, email interview with the author, November 9, 2020.
58. Picciotto.
59. Guy Picciotto, "Flipper/Deadline at 9:30," *DOD*, issue 1, 1982, 8.
60. Picciotto, email interview.
61. This was eventually released in 1989 as the *8/2/82* LP on Picciotto's Peterbilt Records. It was reissued by Peterbilt and Dischord on compact disc in 1997.
62. This was a fan magazine, founded in 1965, that was aimed at teenagers and was known for its fawning coverage of pop music, film, and television celebrities.
63. Picciotto, email interview.
64. *Insurrection*, issue 1, 1983, 3.
65. Picciotto, email interview. *Insurrection* can be found in the DC Public Library's DC Punk Archive and in the University of Maryland's DC punk and indie fanzine collection at Special Collections in Performing Arts.
66. Hovis Clayburg, *Punk Is No Hobby*, issue 1, 1983, 2.
67. The IBM Selectric was a popular electric typewriter of the period.
68. Tesco Vee, Dave Stimson, and Steve Miller. *Touch and Go: The Complete Hardcore Punk Zine '79–'83* (Brooklyn: Bazillion Points, 2010), xi.
69. Miller was vocalist for the Fix, an early Midwestern hardcore band. Their single, "Vengeance," was the second release on Touch & Go Records.
70. Vee, Stimson, and Miller, *Touch and Go*, xvi.
71. Vee, Stimson, and Miller, xvii.
72. Vee, Stimson, and Miller, xxv.
73. Tesco Vee, email interview with the author, November 8, 2020.
74. Vee, email interview.
75. Vee.
76. Brian "Pushead" Schroeder is an artist and musician who has collaborated with numerous metal and punk bands, creating iconic artwork for Metallica and the Misfits, among others.
77. Laura Outerbridge, "Fanzines: Underground Journalism Put to Music," *Argus Weekly* 1, issue 13 (December 3, 1982).
78. Jim Saah, "Talking Back to TV," *Zone V*, issue 1, 1983, 14.
79. Outerbridge, "Fanzines."
80. Vee, email interview.
81. Vee.
82. Michael H. Carriere, "Touch and Go Records and the Rise of Hardcore Punk in Late Twentieth-Century Detroit," *Cultural History* 4, no. 1 (2015): 19–41.
83. Vee, email interview.
84. John Kelly, is a native Washingtonian, a longtime columnist for the *Washington Post*, an advocate of the DC area's cultural arcana, and the drummer in the power pop band the Airport 77s.
85. John Kelly, "A Surprising Legacy of DC's Punk Rock History," *Washington Post*, September 16, 2015.
86. Pete M., "Records and Otherwise," *DC Riot*, issue 1, 1982, 2.
87. H-B Woodlawn is a high school in Arlington that was developed out of the "alternative education movement" in the 1970s. It hosted several hardcore shows in the early 1980s, featuring bands like Minor Threat, SOA, Youth Brigade, SS Decontrol, Iron Cross, DOA, and the Faith.
88. Stafford Mather, email interview with the author, November 14, 2020.
89. Mather.
90. Mather.
91. Mike Ross and Stafford Mather, "Minor Threat Interview," *Brand New Age*, issue 1, 1983, 5.
92. Mather, email interview.
93. Kelly, "Surprising Legacy."
94. Steve Kiviat, interview with the author, December 21, 2017.
95. Rubinowitz shared stages with the Teen Idles, the Razz, DCeats, the Cramps, and other punk-connected bands in the late 1970s and early 1980s.
96. Tony Lombardi, email interview with the author, November 17, 2020.
97. Kiviat, interview.
98. Lombardi, interview.
99. Kiviat, interview.
100. Lombardi, email interview.
101. Between 1982 and 1984, Raiter, who died in 2007, designed posters to promote hardcore concerts organized by the musician and promoter Malcolm Riviera (who passed away in 2023); several of these posters became

iconic within the punk demimonde.

102. The 9:30 Club is still a thriving venue and a cultural institution in Washington, DC, but DC punk bands constitute a small percentage of the performing artists at the club in the twenty-first century, migrating instead toward the Black Cat and other, smaller, venues.
103. The Obsessed is an influential metal band from the DC area with numerous ties to the DC punk scene.
104. The V in the zine's name is pronounced "five."
105. Jim Saah, interview with the author, June 11, 2018.
106. Friedman is a highly accomplished photographer, responsible for numerous iconic photos of punk bands like Black Flag, Minor Threat, and Fugazi, as well as hip-hop artists like Public Enemy, Ice-T, and the Beastie Boys. His documentation of American skateboard culture in the 1970s and early 1980s was equally powerful. A photozine is a type of zine consisting almost exclusively of photography.
107. Saah, interview.
108. Scott Crawford, "Flash in Time: Discussing D.C. Punk Fanzines," panel discussion, University of Maryland, College Park, April 7, 2016.
109. Mark Robinson, interview with the author, December 27, 2018.
110. Rice often wrote under the name Barbaranne Rice throughout the zine's run.
111. Jeff Zeldman, "Truly Barbara," *Washington City Paper*, July 29, 1983, 14.
112. Howell Raines, "Reagan Won't Cut 7 Social Programs That Aid 80 Million," *New York Times*, February 11, 1981.
113. Zeldman, "Truly Barbara."
114. Michael Layne Heath, interview with the author, January 6, 2019.
115. Barbara Rice, radio interview with Steve Kiviat on WMUC, March 4, 2013.
116. Bruce Pavitt, *Sub Pop USA: The Subterranean Pop Music Anthology, 1980–1988* (Brooklyn: Bazillion Points, 2014), 215.
117. Michael Salkind, email to the author, November 15, 2020.
118. James Schneider, interview with the author, May 24, 2019.
119. Scott Crawford, interview with the author, December 19, 2017.
120. "Letters," *Truly Needy*, issue 2, 1982, 3.
121. Barbara Rice, Bill Wort, and David Berman, "An Interview with the Urban Verbs," *Truly Needy*, issue 4, 1982, 54.
122. Barbara Rice, "Social Suicide / Secret Mammals Chancery June 19," *Truly Needy*, issue 3, 1982, 21.

5

Fallen Pieces, 1984

GEORGE ORWELL'S NOVEL *1984* has unsettled most who have read it since its publication in 1949. The dystopian classic was as prescient as it was flexible in its ability to convince readers across the political spectrum that the protagonist, Winston Smith, was *their* avatar. *1984* particularly resonated with numerous authority-averse punks, who often seemed to view it as a prophecy, rather than just a work of fiction. Standard-bearing bands like the Clash, the Jam, Subhumans, and Dead Kennedys referred to the book in their lyrics, triggering a knowing dread in listeners. Within DC's punk subculture, *Capitol Crisis* editor Xyra Harper claimed to have predicted in the aftermath of WGTB's unceremonious silencing in 1979 "that the United States will become a combination of *1984* and *Brave New World*,"[1] Aldous Huxley's equally plutonian masterwork from 1932.

When the year 1984 finally arrived, the cover of the San Francisco punk fanzine *Maximum Rocknroll*'s January–February issue shouted "Welcome to 1984!!! It's always been here!" Beneath that banner read Orwell's memorable line from *1984*—"If you want a picture of the future, imagine a boot stamping on a human face—forever"—laid out in the style of Jamie Reid, with "ransom note" letters haloing a graphic visualization of the quote. Regarding the Orwellian nightmare many feared, *Maximum Rocknroll* columnist Gerry Hannah[2] wrote in the March issue that "I certainly don't think I'm being paranoid when I say that if it's not here now in some form or another, then it's just around the corner."[3]

Others in the punk community scoffed at the idea of Orwell's book possessing soothsaying powers. Dead Kennedys vocalist Jello Biafra quipped: "It doesn't matter if Big Brother *is* watching us, 'cuz most people spend all their time watching him, glued to the boob tube."[4] Jack Rabid, editor of the New York punk fanzine *The Big Takeover*,[5] also dismissed the scene's concerns, dryly predicting that "1984 will be the year that will go down in history as the year that preceded 1985 and came after 1983."[6] All this tense chatter about 1984 complemented the misgivings and disillusionment settling in throughout punk that year. The cover of *Maximum Rocknroll*'s April–May issue asked what many were thinking: "Does Punk Suck???"

That issue gathered essays from more than thirty zine editors and musicians throughout punk, among whom were Barbara Rice of *Truly Needy* and Steve Kiviat of *Thrillseeker*. An indicator of their new status as respected voices from DC's scene, the two expanded on the complaints routinely lodged against punk in 1984. "Much of the criticism about hardcore being boring is absolutely correct," Rice wrote. "The main problem with the current scene is its conformity. Often, any band that tries a new approach is shut out of the scene." This supported lamentations commonly heard from more abstruse DC bands like Nuclear Crayons, No Trend, and 9353, who argued that deviating from DC's typical "thrash" hardcore sound had rendered them outsiders in the scene.[7]

"There's still lots of powerful, emotional, and exciting punk/hardcore out there," Kiviat argued, "but,

Figure 5.1 Barbara Rice of *Truly Needy*. Photo by Lucian Perkins. Used by permission.

unfortunately, hardcore on many levels is now merely a set of cliches put out by people trapped in their own little thrash world." In her essay, Rice acknowledged that punk's low barrier for entry was among its most meaningful traits but, conversely, many punks' "rudimentary knowledge of music" hindered innovation. This was a conundrum, because if punk's mission allowed for anyone to participate—and the mission for punk fanzines was to propagate that notion[8]—asking people to wait to do it themselves until they got more proficient at their instrument or when they broadened their musical interests rebuilt the barriers whose razing made the subculture special.

"What has hurt punk most is a paucity of new ideas," Rice posited. "I support cultural anarchy." Her call for punks to branch out and incorporate new genres of music into their sound, an idea echoed by Kiviat, was understandable, but punk already had an extensive history of genre cross-pollination. Punk and postpunk groups like the Clash, Pop Group, the Slits, Public Image Limited, the Contortions, Gang of Four, and the Ruts had long since integrated elements of dub reggae, jazz, and funk into their punk with dynamic creative results. Even within hardcore, Bad Brains and Big Boys expanded the parameters of what hardcore bands could play by incorporating reggae and funk. Those bands, though, were indeed exceptions among a broader scene increasingly choked with groups that unimaginatively followed the hardcore template, lacking the unique and aberrant elements that the scene's pioneers had displayed.

Conversely, 1984 was a year when popular music was in full flower. Musicians like Prince, Michael Jackson, Madonna, and numerous others handily innovated the form in ways that felt inclusive and life-affirming. Punk positioned itself as a fearless alternative to the mainstream but, by 1984, noticeably trailed pop when it came to infusing music with energy and fresh ideas. Ultimately, hardcore seemed hamstrung less by a dearth of musical skill than by a lack of daring and creativity. Change came by year's end, as groups from around the United States like Hüsker Dü, Meat Puppets, the Replacements, and Minutemen released new music in 1984 retaining hardcore's emotional intensity while incorporating more melodic and experimental sounds.

Another source of frustration within punk was the violence that felt inextricable from its culture. Rather than Orwell's *1984*, punk increasingly resembled *Class of 1984*, the cult classic exploitation movie released in 1982, which depicted its punk antagonists as deranged, nihilistic criminals.[9] By 1984, punk's violent state seemed as inspired by imitation of lurid depictions of punks on television and in films as it did by genuine countercultural urges. Violence was an undeniable element of the punk subculture,[10] but sensational depictions of punks in mainstream television shows like *CHiPs* and *Quincy, ME*,[11] seemed as laughably clueless to most punks at the time as they do today.[12] How many unwitting teenagers, though, were introduced to punk through these sources, drawn in by a warped representation of the subculture, which they subsequently mimicked? "It was do or die then," Henry Rollins said of the time before hardcore's second wave swelled its ranks: "Now, it's a casual attitude—casual youth casually shitting where they live because there's always some kind of Mom to clean up for them. In those days, there was no 'Mom.' We did it." Rollins' frustrated reflections on this shift came in the context of a wild Black Flag concert at Pierce Hall in DC's All Souls

Church on April 6, 1984. The concert was plagued with violence and property damage, leading a church employee to tell Rollins that he had played his last show there.[13] "There were always bad eggs in punk but now the ratio of jerks has gone up to where there are forty jerks at a show breaking bathrooms," he explained. "And All Souls had this beautiful marble bathroom—it took some breaking!"[14]

Within DC punk, violence rose further, and what had once seemed to some—though, certainly, not all—like a harmless bonding ritual or a justified act of self-defense was often becoming thoughtless barbarity.[15] The growing numbers of racist skinheads mingling with the subculture cast an ominous shadow, as well. Shortly after moving to DC from Montana in September 1984, activist and author Mark Andersen recalled coming across graffiti that read "Nazi punks rule! Oi oi oi!" written on a payphone,[16] an encounter he described as "wrenching" for someone who deeply believed in punk's uplifting powers.[17] Monica Richards, vocalist for Madhouse—one of the newer bands working to expand DC punk's creative boundaries beyond hardcore—and onetime cartoonist for *Skin Flint*, came face-to-face with what she labeled "the new generation of skinheads." She added: "We were playing and they were throwing lit cigarettes at me and saying things like 'take off your shirt.' I'd written an anti-rape song ["Cut"], and I said 'This next song is about rape, which I've been through.' These stupid boys, who'd just discovered their penises, all said 'fuck you!' Man, I was so angry. That made me never want to play or go to a hardcore show again."[18]

Dischord and the first wave of DC hardcore might have "put DC on the map,"[19] but—along with media coverage playing up punk's salacious traits—increased exposure inched their scene further out of the underground, opening it to variables that could either send the community into an exhilarating future or render it a forgotten footnote. The DC scene that photographer and author Cynthia Connolly described as having once been "a small community" and "like one big family" was changing.[20] The rise in violence,

Figure 5.2 *Metrozine*, issues 2 and 3, 1984. Published by Scott Crawford. Used by permission.

sexism, and homophobia; the creative stagnation; and the loss of the flagship bands Minor Threat and the Faith had put the DC punk scene of 1984 in a precarious place. Punk was a positive space to find identity, create art, and express views that conformist mainstream culture stifled, but its recalcitrant nature and antielitist, democratic aspirations served, ironically, as some of its greatest obstacles. Increasingly so for some participants, the toxic behavior found in punk—often cloaked in humor or irreverence—could easily drift from momentary frisson to central purpose.

The new DC punk fanzines debuting in 1984, however, represented the best parts of punk's accessible nature, bringing an enthusiasm and perspective that seemed sapped from the more experienced participants who were so recently neophytes themselves. Punk was such a transformative world that zines like *WDC Period* and *Metrozine* were created by fans with only weeks of exposure to the subculture. Likewise, established fanzines—*Truly Needy* and *Thrillseeker*—proved that DC's punk scene was too active and inspiring to be limited to an occasional scene report in *Maximum Rocknroll* or *Flipside*. DC punk's first two waves built a community that, despite its flaws, was still lively and brimming with promise. The year 1984 strained the scene yet, simultaneously, seeded the soil for some of its finest moments to come.

Metrozine

Punk fanzines typically exuded a youthful energy and, indeed, most DC zine creators so far had been in their late teens to mid-twenties. One punk zine debuting in 1984 took juvenile origins to an even greater extreme. "I wanted people to know who I am and I was sick of seeing no monthly DC zine," Scott Crawford, twelve-year-old editor of *Metrozine*, said at the time, when asked why he started publishing.[21] Like *Zone V*'s Jim Saah, Crawford was introduced to DC punk through a visit to Joe's Record Paradise. On July 13, 1984, after buying a Dead Kennedys record, Crawford asked an employee where punk shows occurred in the DC area. Upon learning that Void and Dove[22] were performing that night at the Newton Theatre,[23] Crawford made his way to the venue and saw his first punk concert.[24]

Crawford was already familiar with *Flipside* and *Maximum Rocknroll*, but a Joe's Record Paradise employee advised him not to overlook DC's punk zines. He was subsequently impressed with the heft of *Truly Needy* and *Thrillseeker*, immersing himself in page after page of writings on DC punk. "I just was an obsessive kid," Crawford recalled, "so once I found this world that I somehow seemed like I felt some type of connection to, . . . I remember just spending hours in my room reading about this stuff. And then I just started buying records every weekend and educating myself."[25] Almost immediately, Crawford decided to create his own zine, lavishing attention on the DC scene while still unaware of the scene's internal frictions. "I just did it myself," he said. He continued: "I was like 'OK, so you Xerox pages, and you staple them together. That's pretty simple. I can do that.' So, I just started to do paste-up, and I used my grandmother's typewriter that I swear was from the 1920s. Some of the keys didn't work, so I would just write in the letters for missing keys."[26]

Metrozine began a run that summer that extended in fits and starts into 1987. Crawford laid out new issues at home in Silver Spring, Maryland, and all were as sloppy and enthusiastic, as you might expect a twelve-year-old's punk fanzine to look. Another record store visit for Crawford—this time to Yesterday & Today—led to the zine's first interview. Crawford recalled that store owner Skip Groff sold him a Minor Threat record and then spoke the words no Led Zeppelin or Pink Floyd fan likely ever heard after buying a record by one of those bands: "You know, the singer works here on Wednesdays and Sundays and you should come talk to him."[27] Crawford returned to the store and secured an interview with Ian MacKaye, but the discussion captured the latter at a low ebb. Minor Threat was defunct, and the band's final recording from December 1983, later heard as 1985's *Salad Days* EP, were still unreleased. MacKaye's state of mind regarding the scene was evident in the lyrics to "Salad Days," which he composed in September 1983 as the band disintegrated: "But I stay on, I stay on, where do I get off? On to greener pastures, the core has gotten soft."

MacKaye gamely answered the youthful zine editor's queries, which Crawford later recalled "were so asinine and stupid, but I'm sure it wasn't the first time he'd been asked such questions."[28] When Crawford asked for his thoughts on the DC hardcore scene at that point in the summer of 1984, MacKaye described it candidly as a "very disorganized, confused, and unfortunate scene at the moment." When it came to the scene's future, MacKaye was pessimistic, yet defiant. "I think you basically have a group of people who are so half-assed that they'll be gone in a year anyway," he said. "A long time ago, H. R. from the Bad Brains told me, he quoted Bob Marley, he said that when the smoke clears, only the true rebels will stand."[29]

An interview with John Stabb of Government Issue that ran in *Metrozine*'s eight-page second issue—published in September—revealed that he shared MacKaye's concerns for the scene's health. After citing newer bands like Marginal Man and Malefice as positive additions, Stabb grumbled that "there hasn't been as many shows" and that many in the scene "come to shows just to make fun of the groups and trash the places just for the hell of it." When Crawford noted that Stabb and his band had "changed a lot" since the previous year's *Boycott Stabb* record, Stabb concurred. "Yeah, it was a lot more fun then. Our songs were more relaxed than [they are] now."

Crawford's enthusiastic coverage of the scene contrasted with the downhearted countenances of veterans like MacKaye and Stabb. It is almost as if Crawford was born too late to enjoy the hardcore scene's peak, but was still so enraptured by the power of punk that the community's foibles were nearly irrelevant. *Metrozine*'s record review rating system charmingly consisted of the Xs and bars making up the DC flag détournement seen earlier on Bob Raiter's Wilson Center concert poster and *Thrillseeker*'s cover. Here, the highest rating was a full three Xs and two bars, shedding bars and Xs to match the reviewer's disapproval. A negative critique from Crawford was rare, however, as his enthusiasm generated plaudits for most punk records. "At that point, for me, every record was amazing," Crawford recalled with amusement. "I didn't know what the fuck I was doing."[30] One ecstatic review of Minor Threat's *Out of Step* record—already more than a year old, by then—has "Read This IAN!" typed in large letters above it, with an arrow pointing to the praise like a garish highway hotel sign.

Crawford's guileless fandom, which flagged slightly by the time *Metrozine* eventually wound down later in the decade, was something fanzines created by older, increasingly jaded members of the scene were losing touch with. If other local zines often felt like forums for hashing out ills of the scene, Crawford's innocent boosterism was a reminder that fanzines are almost always at their best elucidating the joys of their subject.

Figure 5.3 Entrance to the 9:30 Club at 930 F Street NW in DC, during the 1980s.

DCene

Stuart Hill and Bobby Jones, two music-loving teenagers from DC's Glover Park neighborhood, had heard that the 9:30 Club often held punk concerts on Sunday afternoons. Neither was familiar with the local punk scene, and what few punk groups they had heard of, like the Sex Pistols, struck Hill as "whacked-out" and "untouchable" music at the time, too deviant to engage with.[31] Despite their qualms, the pair caught a Metrobus down to the club at 930 F Street NW for a Sunday matinee gig. Hill and Jones passed beneath the club's large transom window, proceeding down the long entrance hall, which was fragrant with the peculiar ambrosia that imbued the place.[32] Each step immersed them further in one of DC punk's baptismal sites.

Hill's and Jones' neighbor Alec MacKaye—only slightly older than them—took the stage that day with his band, the Faith. "It just blew me away that . . . this is a guy that I know, and he's on stage playing," Hill remembered. Stunned by the power of the group's performance—as well as an elbow to Hill's forehead landing seconds after he joined the slam dancing—the young duo immediately fell for hardcore punk. "*That's* what I want to do," Hill remembered thinking after the show. The pair attended as many concerts as they could and, toward the end of 1983, Jones proposed creating their own fanzine. Hill concurred and *DCene* was born. "We just wanted to be involved, and learn more, and do something," Hill said. "So, that's what we did."[33]

DCene debuted as 1983 turned into 1984, its first issue featuring an illustration by Jones—"definitely the more artistic one," Hill noted—on its cover. The drawing of a bald-headed punk with a fist in the air looked less like a ferocious skinhead and more like a punk Silver Surfer, but the adolescent, comic book element of the zine factored into its charm. Pretentiousness and affectation were absent, withheld by the innocence and admiration for the scene that Hill and Jones brought. Like *Metrozine*, record and concert reviews were almost exclusively positive. It seemed to pain them to admit that a record's production quality was substandard or that a concert was uninspiring. "It was all new to us," Hill recalled. "We had a lot of energy about it."[34]

Figure 5.4 *DCene*, issue 1, 1984. Published by Bobby Jones and Stuart Hill. Used by permission.

Crammed with Hill's concert photography, Jones' illustrations, and the occasional interview—conversations with Madhouse and Underground Soldier were highlights—*DCene* ran for four issues until later in 1985. "I have to use air quotes," Hill joked when discussing the zine's editing process, which, though clearly avocational, still effectively conveyed the teenagers' thoughts. As for the cut-and-paste layouts, they were "rudimentary," he noted, with text pecked out on a typewriter and slotted in amid the visual elements of the zine. As with so many other zines, the photocopier at a relative's work came in handy to duplicate issues for free. In this case, Hill's mother was the benefactor. "She would pay for the paper," Hill added sheepishly.[35] With zines in hand—a print run for *DCene* never exceeded one hundred copies—Hill and Jones circulated through the crowd at concerts, doling out their creation to anyone interested.

The pair's engagement in *DCene* waned by late 1985, exemplified by the zine's final issue that fall, which consists of just a double-sided photocopy. A full-page photo of Scream's Pete Stahl occupies one side, leaving the verso for a smattering of comics; a trivia quiz; a piece of absurdist flash fiction; and a picture of Scream's bassist, Skeeter Thompson. Jones and Hill did include a humorous explanation for that issue's brevity—"We don't feel like doing any stapling this year, so you can have it all on one page"—before signing off with a clue that *DCene* was coming to an end. "We're not going to promise when you'll see us again," they wrote. "Bye."

"It just faded out," Hill said of *DCene*'s production. "We got busy doing other stuff, I guess." Aside from the zine and their schoolwork, Hill and Jones manufactured and sold Government Issue T-shirts and Minor Threat stickers, which earned them mention in a *Washington Post Magazine* article about entrepreneurial teenagers. "It was just hysterical," Hill remembered. "All the other kids were doing this really cool stuff, making money and we were like 'Uh, we don't really make any money. We're just doing this for fun.'"[36] Additionally, Hill and Jones collaborated in the band, Stuge, which (without Jones) evolved into Shudder to Think, one of the DC punk scene's unique and most highly acclaimed bands.

WDC Period Begins

Comics and punk fanzines were cohorts since punk's earliest days. John Holmstrom's *Punk* remained the sine qua non, but other notable artists like Raymond Pettibon and Gary Panter published comics bristling with the dark humor and bleak worldview that swiftly became inextricable with punk. As hardcore punk zines flourished, comics with punk themes and attitudes were ubiquitous, none more so than John Crawford's *Baboon Dooley* comic strip. *Baboon Dooley* mocked "the aesthetes and corporate tastemakers who constantly intrude upon punks," appearing in countless fanzines throughout the national scene thanks to Crawford's willingness to let his work run in any zine that wanted it.[37]

DC punk zines employed comics and illustrations from its beginnings, too. Katie Puchrik's comics in *Capitol Crisis* were often framed in a calendar format, while *Vintage Violence* included illustrations and comics from Caki Kallas, Robin Walden, Adrienne Crombie, and the Insect Surfers' David Arnson. Later DC zines like *If This Goes On* and *DCene* employed comics to express humor and rage, or to criticize both the mainstream and the punk subculture. *The Boogins*, a comics collection from DC, debuted in 1984 and described itself as "exclusively [featuring] a theme of graphic horror / senseless violence, and fun. . . . Because we fucking love it and you do too!"[38] Assembled by Rene Farkass, the zine evinced a distinct punk essence and included grotesque, often highly skilled, artwork bearing the influence of midcentury publisher EC Comics. At one point, a copy of the zine was declared "indecent or obscene" by England's Commissioners of Customs & Excise and seized due to "material depicting excessive violence" and "overemphasis on mutilation and cannibalism."[39] One serial strip running through several issues of *The Boogins*, Ken Taylor's *Punk Death Cult*, unrolled a cheeky narrative about an underground punk cult targeting freethinking music critics, while Farkass's *9:30 Bouncer* parodied heavy-handed club security staff, undoubtedly influenced by Farkass's gig as "the greatest bouncer in the world" at the 9:30 Club, as *Truly Needy* dubbed him.[40]

June saw the publication of *WDC Period*, a new fanzine blending comics, collage, twisted humor, and a tight embrace of the unusual. It persisted through the end of the decade and, ultimately, stands as one of the definitive DC punk fanzines. Gordon Ornelas moved to DC from Michigan in the early 1980s, but had not yet connected with the city's punk scene when inspiration struck to create his

Figure 5.5 *The Boogins*, issue 1, 1984. Published by Rene Farkass; cover artwork by Linda Tobin. Used by permission.

own zine. One of his roommates possessed a zine titled *Fly By Night,* which Ornelas remembered "was just a bunch of newspaper cutout articles, jokes and collages, but [it] reminded me of what I thought an underground newspaper might have been like." Having created "a few hand-drawn one pagers of my own in the past," Ornelas thought that producing his own, more substantial, fanzine was "something that I could do and it looked fun."[41]

WDC Period's debut issue, which Ornelas described as "very rude and crude," did not portend the influence the zine ultimately wielded locally.[42] Comix-inspired illustrations by Ornelas—under the pseudonym Gordon Gordon—abound, as does his coarse, deliberately offensive sense of humor. Substantive music coverage is nearly nonexistent in issue one, its aggressive waggery aiming for prurience but landing as sophomoric. Still, amid the puerile drawings of genitalia and references to bodily functions lay something more interesting. Ornelas's intelligence and desire to connect are undeniable, particularly when he admits to the zine's editorial shortcomings from the start. Ornelas included a handwritten "disclaimer" early in the issue, where he noted that the zine is "not intentionally trying to be an anti-feminist mag, but due to ignorance and lack of female participation, I've been told that it appears as such. I'm going to be honest and admit that I needed this to be pointed out to me. Normally, I wouldn't care who thinks what, but I don't want to appear to be discriminating toward anyone according to sex, race, creed, etc. We must correct this at once! Ladies write!!"[43]

That level of self-awareness was rare in the DC punk zine world Ornelas was about to join. Along with Ornelas's declaration later in the issue that *WDC Period* serves the "non-conformist/gay-bi-straight/hardcore/rock-n-roll/anarchist community of DC,"[44] it showed that *WDC Period* was already as inclusive as any zine the scene had produced yet. That first issue consisted of eleven single-sided, photocopied pages stapled together—Ornelas later admitted that "double sided copies didn't occur to me until issue two and I'm pretty sure that someone who I met at a show suggested it to me"—and it gave him a reason to venture out into the local punk scene.[45] With fifty copies to distribute, Ornelas attended a concert at the Newton Theatre, and "I found that people were friendly and interested in what I was doing," he said. "They may not have actually liked the zine's content—and some people told me later that they hated it—but I liked the music and the people I met so I kept going back."[46]

Figure 5.6 *WDC Period,* issue 2, July 1984; cover art by Gordon Ornelas. Published by Gordon Ornelas. Used by permission.

Ornelas brought a copy of *WDC Period* to Orpheus Records in Georgetown—then a primary record store in the local punk ecosystem—and was advised by a clerk to check out *Flipside* and *Truly Needy,* neither of which the new zine editor had previously come across. Both fanzines notably influenced the second issue of *WDC Period,* which followed in July. *High Times,* the monthly, marijuana-centric magazine, was a less likely, but still potent, influence on early *WDC Period,* which, Ornelas recalled, "would later cause some confusion amongst the locals because they thought I was making fun of the local straight-edge scene." It took a brief talking-to from John Stabb to enlighten Ornelas on the dynamics of DC's hardcore scene. "I had never heard of any kind of 'youth philosophy' that *didn't* encourage drug use, let alone discourage it," Ornelas said.[47]

By *WDC Period*'s third issue in August, it more closely resembled other punk fanzines, with extensive reviews of concerts and recordings, as well as the zine's first band interview. Consisting of only two questions with a member—"I'm not sure which one," Ornelas wrote in the interview's introduction—of Arizona avant-rock band Sun City Girls, the conversation came to an abrupt end when the band member's uncle showed up. "Blood is thicker than journalism," Ornelas quipped. This issue's full-page "DC Area Drug Update"—filled with detailed information on the types of drugs available on DC streets and what they cost—still made the zine an outlier in a scene where straight-edge held putative sway. Any irreverent charm the drug report might have had at the time has dissipated with age, considering the damage drugs wrought on DC, particularly its Black residents. "By the end of 1985, Washington surpassed all other US cities in per capita drug arrests," historians Chris Myers Asch and George Derek Musgrove noted in their book *Chocolate City: A History of Race and Democracy in the Nation's Capital*. "The next year, as cocaine spread down the income scale to poor and working-class African American addicts, it topped heroin as DC users' drug of choice."[48] At the start of issue four of *WDC Period*, Ornelas relented. "Enough! No more drug update anymore," he wrote. "It was meant to be a pun about *High Times* but people were taking it much too seriously. So, stop asking me where to get your drugs, cuz I don't know!"

A roundup of DC punk zines in that September issue

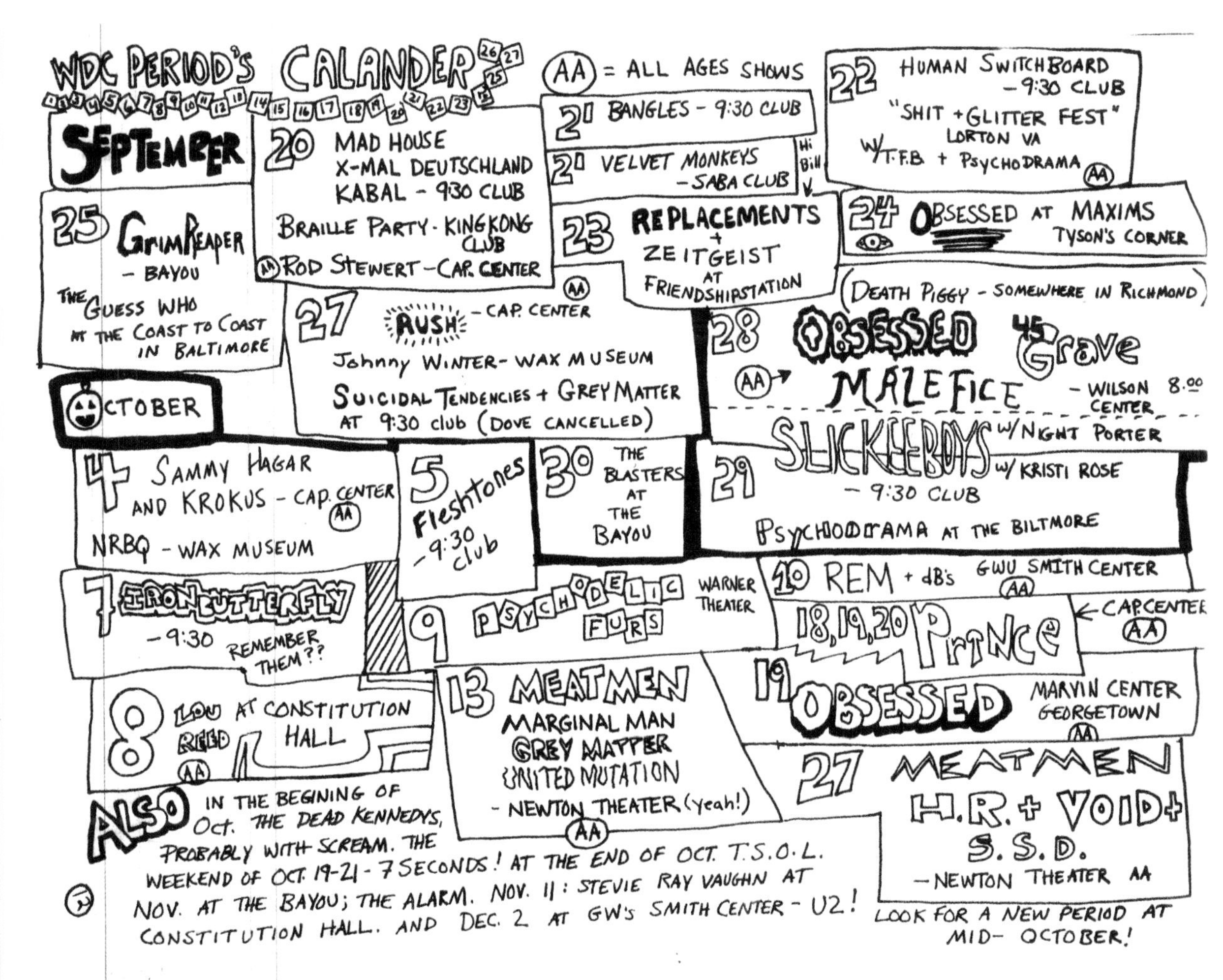

Figure 5.7 *WDC Period* concert calendar from issue 4, September 1984. Drawn by Gordon Ornelas. Used by permission.

captures a thriving community, featuring reviews of *Thrillseeker, DCene, Zone V, Truly Needy,* and *Metrozine* ("Heard some laughs about its large print, but so fucking what? What have you done??"). While callow jokes continued to dot the page of *WDC Period* ("Q: Why does the Gipper during sex have to be on the bottom? A: 'Cause he can only 'fuck up,'" went one about President Ronald Reagan[49]), its fourth issue saw the zine develop further into the publication that ultimately inherited *Truly Needy* and *Thrillseeker*'s role as DC punks' source for incisive reviews, unsparing critical assessment, and exhaustive coverage of scene news. *WDC Period,* though, boasted a far more idiomatic voice than either of its inspirations, despite its numerous contributors. Ornelas's sense of humor and genuine eccentricity helped to differentiate it from any other fanzine in the scene. The comics, odd jokes, and irrepressible passion for music and culture outside of the mainstream combined to eventually create something indelible.

The fourth issue also marked the debut of the elaborate concert calendars Ornelas illustrated, soon to become his signature. The drawings were an extension of Ornelas's cleanly handwritten record and concert reviews, featuring his picks for the show he was most interested in on a certain date. That first calendar for September 1984 included concerts featuring locals like Marginal Man, Gray Matter, Void, Malefice, and Madhouse, along with out-of-towners like the Replacements, the Bangles, and REM. Admittedly, the quality of bands in the DC scene had flagged slightly as compared with earlier years, but this was still an exceptional slate of shows.

A review in that issue of a September 29 concert at Food for Thought—a health food restaurant owned by the father of Gray Matter's Dante Ferrando, which occasionally hosted punk shows and employed numerous punks—gave a preview of three of the bands at the heart of the renaissance soon to grip the scene. Rites of Spring, Beefeater, and Gray Matter were all central to the upcoming period in 1985 known as "Revolution Summer"—when members of the scene creatively and politically pushed back against the violent behavior and repetitive hardcore sounds taking over—but this review from fall 1984 catches them at the beginning of their respective ascents. "This was the first time I've seen Rites of Spring," Ornelas writes. "Shit, they've got lots of energy and power to spare. . . . I can't wait to hear them with working microphones."[50]

By the fifth issue, in October, Ornelas was joined in the zine's production by Dan Snoke, *WDC Period*'s new coeditor. "He had published a few zines of his own and was a contributor to *Truly Needy* so his experience was a big influence on me," Ornelas recalled.[51] The zine's rapid production schedule already necessitated delegating tasks, so "there were always a lot of contributors helping with the zine in a variety of ways," Ornelas said. Contributors like Dave McDuff, Razor, and Robbie White were important parts of the operation,[52] "writing poetry, drawing comics, typing the reviews, [providing] miscellaneous production help, collating and stapling—and of course writing about music."[53] Issue five incorporated more band interviews than earlier efforts had, featuring one with the California punks, Dr. Know, and another with the Obsessed, a Maryland band straddling the line between metal and punk, a distinction that grew fuzzier as the 1980s progressed. Despite the Obsessed's crossover acceptance within DC's punk community, the band's guitarist, Scott "Wino" Weinrich, offered only tepid enthusiasm when asked about the scene. "I don't know man, it's kind of dubious," Weinrich said, before citing 9353 and Iron Cross as exceptions.[54]

Although Ornelas had only been involved in DC hardcore since earlier in the year, he already began airing his frustrations with the scene's atmosphere. Upset that some punks inflicted "mindless violence" upon gays in DC, Ornelas called out those that "go around beating up and oppressing other people just because of how they look or act," noting that their behavior was in lockstep with "governments (like ours) and mainstream folks (like rednecks) and fascists (like the KKK)." This was some of the most outspoken internal criticism from within DC's scene to be found in a fanzine yet, holding punks accountable for actions with much higher stakes than merely whether they were paying attention at concerts or if a band's music was derivative. It was clear that lives were at stake.

The last issue of *WDC Period* published in 1984 appeared that December, featuring twenty-four pages printed on newsprint for the first time. This issue included an interview with Iron Cross's Sab Grey, a conversation Grey fondly remembered decades later as "a very pleasant evening chatting over a bottle of vodka," adding that Ornelas was "a good guy."[55] In the interview, Grey seemed as concerned as Ornelas was about where the scene had gone. "It's so fucking stupid," Grey said, describing the violent punks that populated the scene. He continued: "It's like all they do. They go out and they drink and they're like "I'm a man, I can fight' and if there's nobody else to fight, they beat each other up. . . . Why can't you just go out and drink and have a good time instead of hanging around beating people up for no reason? I mean, if you have a reason to fight, that's one thing, but I don't see the point of beating somebody up because you don't like the way he looks or where he sticks his dick or whatever."[56]

Ornelas pivoted into questions about Iron Cross songs that used violent imagery, including "Psycho Skin" and "Fight 'Em All," wondering how Grey's criticism of violence in the DC scene jibed with some of his band's songs. Grey explained that "Fight 'Em All" was a retort to newer punks critical of the violence that Grey and his friends engaged in at shows, which he insisted was only done in self-defense. "We used to fight a lot at gigs, . . . because you used to get Marines and rednecks and, you know, other people that were coming and picking on the punks and thinking they're gonna get away with it," Grey said, noting that punks like himself, Ian MacKaye, and Dante Ferrando did not seek violence but were always willing to defend each other. Grey continued: "If I saw Ian or any of the old crew in a fight, you didn't have to know who started it or why because they didn't go to gigs looking for trouble. They went to enjoy themselves and to have a good time. This was our scene, these were our friends on stage, and this was our private little party, and these fuckers—used to be big ones, too—they used to come in to pick fights. What are you supposed to do?"[57]

In six issues over the second half of 1984, *WDC Period* evolved considerably from an aimless collection of comics and ribald humor into a zine integrating those elements with detailed coverage of the music scene, a newcomer's ardor, and a willingness to bluntly call out the scene's flaws. That Ornelas so quickly reached his goal of making the *WDC Period* "a community zine,"[58] incorporating numerous voices from the scene, is all the more impressive considering he accomplished that feat while maintaining his own singular timbre just above the choir of contributors. *WDC Period* was clearly Ornelas's zine, but it was equally apparent that ripples from its impact extended further out, reaching more people and giving them a voice in the scene.

Thrillseeker Ends; *Truly Needy* Continues

For as many new zines appeared in 1984, the two most influential local titles that year remained *Thrillseeker* and *Truly Needy*. Michael Salkind, a *Truly Needy* contributor, recalled that "we were in some friendly competition" with *Thrillseeker*, but the two zines shared a sometimes-icy relationship.[59] When *Thrillseeker* excluded *Truly Needy* from its zine review section, the latter's coeditor, Barbara Rice, wrote "[coeditor] Bill [Wort] said I shouldn't even mention these guys since they didn't even mention our little selves

Figure 5.8 *Thrillseeker*, issue 3, 1984. Published by Steve Kiviat. Used by permission.

in their zine roundup. [Another *Truly Needy* contributor] said if I didn't review 'em, I'd be playing the same game. My bleeding-heart sense of fairness won out. . . . Their 'punker than thou' attitude seems to have diminished, which makes this a more enjoyable read."[60] *Thrillseeker* editor Steve Kiviat recalled eventually meeting Rice and Wort, which helped dissolve some tension, leading them to coexist on "a more friendly basis."[61] Rice opted for a rapprochement in the next issue of *Truly Needy*, noting that she was "sorry I said nasty things about *Thrillseeker*."[62] As indicated by Kiviat and Rice's inclusion in that town hall issue of *Maximum Rocknroll*, the two zines were the preeminent sources for DC punk news going into 1984 but, like so many local zines before it, *Thrillseeker* was reaching its end.

Kiviat graduated from the University of Maryland in spring 1983 and started law school that fall, while Lombardi continued working toward his undergraduate degree at the university. The duo's increasingly incongruous schedules reduced the attention they could give to *Thrillseeker*. Plans to finish a third issue over their respective winter breaks in early 1984 sputtered, and Kiviat felt that Lombardi was losing interest.[63] "By that time, I felt that I had less to contribute and less time to devote to it," Lombardi concurred. Despite maintaining his radio show on WMUC, Lombardi's focus shifted more toward his studies and somewhat away from the rapidly changing DC music scene. "So, I decided not to be heavily involved, but was happy that Steve decided to continue with it," Lombardi recalled of the period when Kiviat pressed ahead with a third issue.[64]

With much of the third issue's material prepared, Kiviat considered changing the zine's title since Lombardi was no longer coediting. New titles like *Cheap Thrills*, *Son of Thrillseeker*, "and a million other names" were bandied about,[65] likely with varied degrees of seriousness, but changing the title would erase much of the reputation and name recognition *Thrillseeker* established over its first two issues. Factoring in Lombardi's continued—albeit diminished—presence in the new issue via various record reviews he had written, Kiviat decided to retain the *Thrillseeker* name.

New assistant editors Rachel Sengers and Paul Bushmiller—along with numerous contributors like David Nichols, Thurston Moore, Jeff Krulik, Hal Schmulowitz, and Kiviat's brother, Brian—helped Kiviat assemble an issue that held up to previous efforts.[66] Kiviat recalled Sengers' contributions to the zine's aesthetics as being a highlight of that third issue. Despite layout constraints imposed by *Thrillseeker*'s printer, "a fair amount of [Sengers'] fairly ambitious artwork" appeared in the third issue, Kiviat said, adding, "so, I sort of enjoyed that touch."[67]

Published in the latter half of 1984, *Thrillseeker*'s third issue teemed, as ever, with reviews and interviews covering musicians from diverse musical styles. Like earlier issues, the lineup of interviews—Marginal Man, Minutemen, Black Market Baby, Motorhead, Outrage, Michael Enkrumah, Reptile House, Wailing Souls, DOA, Immaculate Consumptive, and Barrence Whitfield & the Savages—weaved through punk, funk, reggae, metal, and soul, illuminating the overlap between genres, rather than heedlessly stratifying them further.

Lombardi felt the third issue was "a very entertaining and informative read and a great continuation of what we did in the first two issues. I am definitely proud of what Steve and company put together."[68] Indeed, the quality of that third issue validated Kiviat's decision to keep the name alive, but plans to assemble a fourth issue fizzled. New interviews with the Athens, Georgia, postpunk band Pylon and the Cleveland new wave band Human Switchboard were recorded, but Kiviat's law school schedule led him to eventually determine publishing another issue "was too much."[69] Kiviat remained in the DC area, and his law career grew, and he continued writing about music in the years ahead, contributing to zines like *OP* and, eventually, larger titles like *Option*, *Washington City Paper*, and the *Washington Post*. Lombardi, too, stayed local, but retired from music writing to serve as a government contractor in information technology.

"We're all still proud of what we did with these [zines] and documenting that time period," Kiviat said, reflecting on *Thrillseeker*'s existence. "I love the DC metropolitan area and am proud that we were able to document on paper some of what was happening during a very exciting time," Lombardi added. He continued:

> *I also think all of it—*Thrillseeker*, WMUC, the group of creative and inspiring people at the*

University of Maryland—[contributed] to who I am today. I married one of our extended group at the University of Maryland and we're still married 33 years later. I took my six-year-old son to see Fugazi at the 2000 Smithsonian Folklife Festival. I don't know that it made any impression on him but, ten years later, I was happy to hear him blasting X-Ray Spex from his bedroom and to find out that he was buying Bad Brains albums on vinyl. I would like to think that some of the musical and cultural exploration that his parents did at the University of Maryland in the early 1980s has been a positive influence on him and his younger brother.[70]

With *Thrillseeker* concluded, *Truly Needy* had no other competition yet as the DC scene's primary fanzine in 1984. It held that unofficial status despite producing only one issue that year, a period Rice later referred to as "an extremely hard time for us," without further explanation.[71] That publication gap provided space for new, more frequent publications like *Metrozine* and *WDC Period* to make a stronger impression on the local subculture. Although planned for release in December 1983, the eighth issue of *Truly Needy* did not appear until the spring. Having secured national distribution by this point, income from advertising and zine sales helped Rice and Wort break even, but assembling a new issue was an arduous task.

Figure 5.9 *Truly Needy*, issue 8, 1984. Published by Barbara Rice and Bill Wort.

Abandoning the photocopied approach used to duplicate previous issues, the new issue was offset printed on newsprint, then folded and saddle stapled along its narrow spine. All these elements combined to make a more magazine-like reading experience, rather than the heavy, side-stapled stack of paper used for previous issues. The acquisition of an Osborne personal computer,[72] along with Wort's increasing design proficiency, helped Rice and Wort attain the "cleaner, more original look" they sought for *Truly Needy*. "Perhaps this emphasis on packaging may seem phony," Rice said, "but I believe graphics say a lot about the mag, nearly as much as its content."[73] Issue eight, with the California punk band the Dickies on its cover, came in at a weighty eighty pages, which was an accomplishment of its own. Few, if any, punk zines—including standard-bearers *Maximum Rocknroll* and *Flipside* or increasingly important national zines like *Ink Disease* and *Leading Edge*—had surpassed that page count yet. "Wow, what a monster," the musician and writer Calvin Johnson later wrote approvingly,[74] "a very entertaining monster."[75]

In this issue, erstwhile *Vintage Violence* editor Mike Heath interviewed Al Bum, the vocalist for the Southern California punk band White Flag. Within the conversation with Heath, Bum referred to Wort's back cover illustration from issue six of *Truly Needy*, which satirized someone dabbling in the punk subculture—eventually fronting a band and leading a crowd of lookalikes in a chant of "Fuck Conformity!"—before heading to Harvard at the end of the summer to begin "my career as a brilliant lawyer, thank God." The cartoon resonated with Bum, who remarked "now this is exactly what White Flag are all about. Obviously, you've been to shows, you see these people talk about how everyone should be unique and different. Then here are all these people with the same T-shirts on, the same haircut . . . remember when it was really unique to be a punk?"

Issue eight appealingly pinballs around topics, featuring interviews—Sisters of Mercy, Your Food, Cabaret Voltaire, Proletariat and others—and reviews from the punk milieu, but also a column on DC sports discussing the Washington football team's recent Super Bowl defeat, in which we also learn that H. R. from Bad Brains and Zion Train is a Dallas Cowboys fan. A rundown of local radio stations presents a bleak slate for fans of adventurous music, other than Heath praising WMUC as "fine listening" for those who could capture its faint ten-watt signal. Anne Dropoff—presumably a pseudonym poking fun at the Soviet leader Yuri Andropov, who died in February 1984—took a more whimsical ride along the AM band, a survey providing "a sick sort of pleasure." Delightedly skewering local religious radio stations, Dropoff mockingly noted "you can almost see the long stringy hair and pizza faces of the DJs as their mellowing voices drift through the airwaves." Regarding the "incredibly wimpy music about loving Jesus" the stations aired, Dropoff suggested that "punks should listen to this horrific stuff to remind themselves of why punk rock exists."

Despite the prevalence of bearish opinions on the state of the DC punk scene in 1984, *Truly Needy*'s local news roundup offered a mostly upbeat assessment of where things stood that spring. "After a winter in hibernation, the DC scene is warming up again," the section read. "Nearly everyone of note plans to release a record." The amount of activity condensed into three columns spread over half a page is impressive. Readers are updated on stalwarts like Government Issue, Scream, Ian MacKaye, Void, and Velvet Monkeys, while emerging bands like No Trend, Outrage, Crippled Pilgrims, Malefice, and Nuclear Crayons are also included. Even the evergreen Slickee Boys earned congratulations for the "international attention" their latest album, *Cybernetic Dreams of Pi*, received.

Sharon Cheslow's post–Chalk Circle band, Bloody Mannequin Orchestra, is listed in the "upcoming groovy releases" and interviewed elsewhere in the issue. In the interview with Cheslow and her bandmates (former *If This Goes On* coeditor Colin Sears among them), she discussed sexism's role in the response the all-female Chalk Circle received compared with Bloody Mannequin Orchestra, whose other members were male. "It's a lot different being in a band where you're the only girl," she observed. "Sometimes I don't like it, sometimes I do. I like being in BMO because people take me seriously. With Chalk Circle, it was like 'well, you're all girls, you can't do anything.'"[76] Later in the interview, she noted how the respect accorded to male musicians who utilize humor and other "fun" elements in their bands was not granted to Chalk Circle. "We had to be real serious and really intense for us to get our message across," Cheslow recalled. "It was hard for me to say 'you don't have to be like that. You can be fun and still get something across.'"[77]

Rice would later share her own experiences with sexist double standards in the scene when she was interviewed by *Flipside* in 1986. "My situation as a female fanzine writer is a double-edged sword," she explained. "Sometimes men in bands are more receptive to women. Mark E. Smith, Bob Mould,

Figure 5.10 Government Issue and the 400 concert flier, University of Maryland, College Park. December 6, 1984. Designer unknown.

Mike Watt, Nick Cave, and Jello Biafra seemed to be more at ease with me than they would have otherwise.[78] Dunno if this has anything to do with my gender, though. Then again, there were the bands who dismissed me as a groupie, who ignored me, but I think these were more in the minority." Rice added that musicians were not the only culprits. She continued:

> *I do wish there were more female rock critics. I've found critics to be more sexist than the bands. If I didn't work on* Truly Needy, *I'd probably remain unpublished. In rock criticism, it's been the fashion recently to ruminate on what certain music does to your pud, an option not open to me. Around the scene, I've noticed cold shoulders from some local musicians. It's funny when band members communicate messages to me through Bill. Perhaps they feel uneasy with me. Who knows?*[79]

DC Punk at the End of 1984

One definition of punk from 1978 described the music and its subculture as "an attitude of threat. It is a threatening look which says that the status quo is something that can be changed."[80] In 1984, the DC punk scene sometimes reflected poisonous norms of mainstream society—sexism, racism, homophobia, and violence—leading one to wonder just how much punk culture truly was a rejection of the mainstream. DC punk's rising renown was a positive sign, even if it corresponded to the increased troubles besetting the community. DC punk fanzines deftly balanced the boundary between fandom and criticism, serving as forums to starkly challenge the scene while still, almost always, validating its attributes.

The emergence of new voices in the DC punk fanzine community—*Metrozine*'s Scott Crawford; Stuart Hill

Figure 5.11 Gray Matter and Rites of Spring concert flier, Food for Thought, DC, November 29, 1984. Designed by Steve Niles. Used by permission.

and Bobby Jones of *DCene*; and *WDC Period*'s Gordon Ornelas—demonstrated that punk's appeal endured, continuing to draw positive new participants into its orbit. Likewise, although several of DC hardcore's premier bands broke up, established groups like Government Issue and Scream grew in popularity while expanding creatively. Newer bands connected with the Dischord Records community—Marginal Man, Beefeater, Gray Matter, and Rites of Spring—displayed early signs of that scene's forthcoming direction, maintaining the intensity of hardcore while exploring more melodic and lyrically vulnerable territory. Meanwhile, Promethean outliers like No Trend, Grand Mal, 9353, Peach of Immortality, and United Mutation were generally overshadowed by bands related to Dischord, yet made a bigger impact than they might have realized. No Trend and United Mutation,[81] in particular, eventually saw their critical legacies grow in stature into the twenty-first century. The aggression and oppositional nature of these bands' music and performances was an innovation in itself, precluding extensive homogeneity or complacency from setting in.

DC punk's conflicted state in 1984 compelled some of its participants to analyze the scene more rigorously. Few were satisfied with what they saw. In *WDC Period*, Ornelas implored more experienced punks to resist burnout and continue vocally participating in the scene: "If people with common sense don't give in to these 'others,' and keep stating what they think, sooner or later some of these kids are gonna start catching on."[82] Between perceptions of stagnating musical development and the prevalence of violence and drugs, there was plenty of negativity in the air. In the early months of 1985, however, a group of DC punks endeavored to improve their scene with one word in mind: Revolution.

Notes

1. James Schneider, interview with Xyra Harper, August 31, 2013.
2. Hannah, a former member of the Vancouver punk band the Subhumans, was serving a ten-year sentence in prison when he wrote his column. Hannah was jailed for crimes committed while a member of the Direct Action activist / "urban guerilla" group.
3. Gerry Hannah, "Smile! Big Brother Is Watching You," *Maximum Rocknroll*, issue 12, April–May 1984, 13.
4. Al Flipside, "Jello Biafra Talks Yak Yak," *Flipside*, issue 41, February 1984, 56.
5. Named after a Bad Brains song, *The Big Takeover* is still publishing as of 2024.
6. Jack Rabid, "1984: The Year That Preceded 1985, and Came After 1983 . . . ," *Flipside*, issue 41, February 1984, 57.
7. Lara Lynch of Nuclear Crayons founded a record label, Outside Records, whose name was a testament to the sentiment. Outside released the "Mixed Nuts Don't Crack" compilation, featuring several of the best non-Dischord bands in the punk scene, like Chalk Circle, Media Disease, and United Mutation.
8. Stephen Duncombe, *Notes from Underground: Zines and the Politics of Alternative Culture*, Haymarket Series (London: Verso, 1997), 118–19.
9. *Destroy All Movies* coauthor Zack Carlson described *Class of 1984* as "a perfect exploitation movie; . . . it's relentlessly seedy, overflowing with assault, suicide, racism, grimy sex, drug use, and crime crime crime, all of which is perpetrated by minors!"
10. Heath Mattioli and David Spacone's harrowing *Disco's Out, Murder's In* book describes some of the nightmarish acts of violence that punk gangs perpetrated in early-1980s Southern California. See Heath Mattioli and David Spacone, *Disco's Out, Murder's In: The True Story of Frank the Shank and LA's Deadliest Punk Rock Gang* (Port Townsend, WA: Feral House, 2015).
11. Both programs aired punk-themed episodes in 1982, with punks serving as the ostensibly frightening villains in each. Quincy, played by Jack Klugman, lambastes one impertinent punk with tales of noble elders. "You know, not so many years ago, there was a generation of people who were as mad as you are about the world," Quincy scolds, his basset hound face grave. "Only they worked their tails off to change it. Trying to end a war they didn't believe in. Trying to correct injustices that they saw. All you do is gripe." This revisionist mainstream support of 1960s counterculture activity must have been cold comfort to those who were actively oppressed trying to "work their tails off," such as the staff at underground papers like *Quicksilver Times*. This moment in *Quincy* is also a symptom of the Baby Boomer generation's ascent into positions of power—in this case, a Hollywood screenwriter—enabling them to venerate *their* end of *their* generation—former hippies—while dismissing its pole—the punks. This episode is worth watching for one moment alone, when a ludicrously garbed punk turns the rhetorical tables on Quincy—scouring the punk demimonde to find a murderer—melodramatically informing him that "you're the killers! Your whole sick society! That's who's guilty, man!" The episode aired on December 1, 1982. By 1983, the Philadelphia punk fanzine *Savage Pink* was already lampooning the "Quincy Punks" coming to shows only for the violence.
12. *Savage Pink* 2, issue 10.5, 1983.
13. Despite the violence and property damage at the concert, Howard Wuelfing wrote a positive review of it for the April 9, 1984, edition of the *Washington Post*. "Black Flag's performance . . . was nothing short of astonishing," he exclaimed, noting that the band mostly played then-unreleased material "to a wildly appreciative house." The crowd greeted Henry Rollins with "tumultuous applause when he loped on stage, presenting an intimidating presence with his unfashionably long hair, tight blue jeans, and bare, heavily muscled chest." Punk concerts did eventually return to the space later in the decade, including a concert on September 22, 1989, featuring Fugazi, Shudder to Think, and Jawbox.
14. Mark Andersen and Mark Jenkins, *Dance of Days: Two Decades of Punk in the Nation's Capital*, updated and expanded 4th ed. (Brooklyn: Akashic Books, 2009), 153.
15. Andersen and Jenkins, 152–53.
16. Cynthia Connolly, Leslie Clague, Sharon Cheslow, and Lydia Ely, *Banned in DC: Photos and Anecdotes from the DC Punk Underground ('79–'85)*, 7th

ed. (Arlington, VA: Sun Dog Propaganda, 2015), 150.

17. Andersen and Jenkins, *Dance of Days*, 159.
18. Connolly et al, *Banned in DC*, 148.
19. Alan Keenan, "Angry Young Men," *Washington Tribune*, October 8–21, 1982.
20. Sharon M. Hannon, *Punks: A Guide to an American Subculture* (Santa Barbara, CA: Greenwood Press, 2010), 63.
21. *Metrozine*, issue 4, circa November 1984, 2.
22. Dove was an intriguing DC hardcore band, featuring members of Double-O and Red C, that seemed to fall between the cracks in the scene's punk history. "Dove really wants you to get worked up," Crawford wrote in his review of that first concert he attended. "Definitely thrash."
23. This was an art deco theater in DC's Brookland neighborhood that opened in 1937 and briefly hosted punk concerts in 1984, including some organized by Rice and *Truly Needy*. As of 2025, the building was a CVS pharmacy.
24. Connolly et al., *Banned in DC*, 144.
25. Scott Crawford, interview with the author, December 19, 2017.
26. Crawford.
27. Crawford.
28. Crawford.
29. Scott Crawford, "A Minor at Heart: An Interview with Ian MacKaye," *Metrozine*, issue 1, August 1984.
30. Crawford, interview.
31. Stuart Hill, interview with the author, January 15, 2021.
32. *Washington City Paper* once described the 9:30 Club scent as "a mephitic perfume, . . . a certain combination of keg slop, butts, cloves, puke, and sweat-sopped polyester that stays with you—literally."
33. Hill, interview.
34. Hill.
35. Hill.
36. Hill.
37. Kevin Mattson, *We're Not Here to Entertain: Punk Rock, Ronald Reagan, and the Real Culture War of 1980s America* (New York: Oxford University Press, 2020), 117.
38. *The Boogins*, promotional preview issue, circa 1983, 3.
39. M. J. Whitson, "Letters to God," *WDC Period*, issue 16, 1987, 5.
40. "Fanzine Round Up," *Truly Needy*, issue 8, 1984, 13.
41. Gordon Ornelas, email to the author, January 24, 2021.
42. Ornelas.
43. *WDC Period*, issue 1, June 1984, 3.
44. *WDC Period*, 11.
45. Ornelas, email.
46. Ornelas.
47. Connolly et al., *Banned in DC*, 151.
48. Chris Myers Asch and George Derek Musgrove, *Chocolate City: A History of Race and Democracy in the Nation's Capital* (Chapel Hill: University of North Carolina Press, 2017), 402.
49. Reagan was making his own bad jokes in 1984, but his bore potential consequences of cataclysmic magnitude. While performing a sound check for a radio address, Reagan jokingly said "My fellow Americans, I am pleased to tell you today that I've signed legislation that will outlaw Russia forever. We begin bombing in five minutes." Guffaws all around until a tape of the sound check was leaked, its context unclear, ramping up tensions with the Soviet Union. The *Los Angeles Times* reported that the Soviet government referred to the joke as "unprecedentedly hostile" and that Reagan's "secret dream has burst forth."
50. *WDC Period*, issue 5, October 1984, 10.
51. Ornelas, email.
52. White also did a stint as manager for the Slickee Boys and copublished their fanzine/newsletter, *Slickzine*, with Bill Hanrahan.
53. Ornelas, email.
54. *WDC Period*, issue 5, October 1984, 8.
55. Sab Grey, email to the author, February 13, 2021.
56. *WDC Period*, issue 6, December 1984, 6.
57. *WDC Period*, 6–7.
58. Ornelas, email.
59. Michael Salkind, email to the author, November 15, 2020.
60. Barbara Rice, "Fanzine Round-Up," *Truly Needy*, issue 7, 1983, 49.
61. Steve Kiviat, interview with the author, December 21, 2017.
62. Barbara Rice, "Fanzine Round-Up," *Truly Needy*, issue 8, 1984, 15.
63. Kiviat, interview.
64. Tony Lombardi, email to the author, November 17, 2020.
65. *Thrillseeker*, issue 3, 1984, 3.
66. Nichols went on to be an academic and an author, with the notable *Dig: Australian Rock and Pop Music 1960–1985* among his works. Krulik gained renown for codirecting the 1986 cult classic documentary short *Heavy Metal Parking Lot*.
67. Kiviat, interview.
68. Lombardi, email.
69. Kiviat, interview.
70. Lombardi, email.
71. "Fanzine of the Month: *Truly Needy*," *Flipside*, issue 49, Summer 1986.
72. Osborne created a portable microcomputer that was briefly popular in the early 1980s. As Paul Ceruzzi wrote in *A History of Modern Computing*, "Just as revolutionary as its small size was the fact that the computer came with the CP/M operating system and applications software, all for less than $2,000."
73. "Fanzine of the Month," *Flipside*.
74. Johnson contributed to *OP*, an Olympia, Washington–based music zine that was one of the few at the time able to exceed *Truly Needy* in heft and variety of coverage. *OP* featured punk, postpunk, and hardcore, but also covered jazz, avant-garde music, folk, country, and more. One issue featured Hawaiian guitarist Gabby Pahinui, postpunk band the Pop Group, composers Larry Polansky and Harry Partch, jazz saxophonist Art Pepper, garage band the Chesterfield Kings, and other fascinating tangents.
75. Calvin Johnson, "Death Threats," *Truly Needy*, issue 9, 1985, 4.
76. Barbara Rice and Dak Finch, "Bloody Mannequin Orchestra," *Truly Needy*, issue 8, 1984, 27.
77. Rice and Finch, 29. Bloody Mannequin Orchestra split up later in 1984, its members eventually going on to Dag Nasty, Blood Bats, Suture, Senator Flux, and Red Eye.
78. These were prominent male musicians from, respectively, the bands the Fall, Hüsker Dü, Minutemen, Nick Cave & the Bad Seeds, and Dead Kennedys.
79. *Flipside*, issue 49, Summer 1986.
80. Isabelle Anscombe, Roberta Bayley, and Dike Blair, *Punk* (New York: Urizen Books, 1978).
81. Chris Richards, "In 1983, No Trend Prophesied America's Ruin to Anyone Who Could Bear to Listen," *Washington Post*, May 21, 2020.
82. Gordon Ornelas, "Letters," *WDC Period*, issue 6, December 1984, 3.

6

Take It Back, 1985–1986

BY 1985, HARDCORE REMAINED popular, but its hold on the punk subculture gradually loosened due to pervasive violence, drug abuse, and creative stagnation. Punk's inability to effect significant practical change in wider society, too, led to cynicism and burnout. Years of railing against President Ronald Reagan and the oppressive banality of suburban life through punk music and artwork ran into the reality of his resounding reelection in November 1984. Despite Rock Against Reagan, Reagan Youth, and the rest of punk's anti-Reagan fusillades, "the Enemy Father" had won.[1] It was all the more demoralizing that 61 percent of voters age eighteen to twenty-four years—the punk peer group—chose Reagan, a share surpassed only by voters sixty-five and older.[2]

As early as 1982, members of Minor Threat expressed fatigue with punk's declamatory political elements. Commenting on the vacuity of mainstream rock lyrics in an interview with *Flipside*, the band's guitarist, Lyle Preslar, added that he was also "becoming immune to the 'Reagan sucks / WWIII' thing, too, unfortunately." Preslar urged readers to stay politically aware, while also recommending a Stoic philosophy toward life: "Everybody should exert influence on things they have control over. In other words, if you see John Doe walking down the street, you deal with John Doe."

Protest through punk music might have felt like an exercise in futility in 1985, with Reagan re-upped and American popular culture drenched in jingoistic films like *Red Dawn* and *Rambo: First Blood, Part II*, but some voices still urged activism. *WDC Period* editor Gordon Ornelas attended a speech at American University by televangelist and Moral Majority cofounder Jerry Falwell, whose right-wing dictums elicited a mix of cheers and boos from the students in attendance. "Personally, I could rag on quite a bit about how I consider the Moral Majority to be, perhaps, the most dangerous group in the world today, . . . but I won't," Ornelas wrote. Instead, he urged his readers to realize conservative influence was spreading. "Take a good look at the world around you, remember thinking that Reagan would never get re-elected, and listen to Jerry Falwell preach to his cattle of holy followers 'Bush in '88.'"

By 1985, hardcore's stasis had cracked. A growing number of bands, nationally and locally, abandoned the strictures of tempo and vocal delivery that had grown stale to many. Building from the intensity, anger, and alienation synonymous with hardcore, groups like Hüsker Dü and Rites of Spring married some of hardcore's traits with gifted songwriting and a willingness to explore sonically. Notably, the lyrics were vulnerable and nuanced, rendering the repetitive political bromides of preceding years mostly insufficient in comparison. Other divergent hardcore bands evolved differently, moving toward varied strains of heavy metal, such as the sludgy miasma common in Black Flag's later efforts and the crossover thrash of Corrosion of Conformity and Suicidal Tendencies. As hardcore splintered, punk entered an imperative period of renewal.

Stylistically, DC punk expanded into 1985. More experimental groups like 9353, Madhouse, and Peach of Immortality mingled on bills with hardcore bands, stretching the scene's creative parameters. In lyrics and activism, DC punk had mostly avoided serious political thought so far—"No DC bands are overtly political at all," Minor Threat's vocalist Ian MacKaye stated in that 1982 *Flipside* interview—but this changed before 1985 ended. Perhaps having learned from the first four years of punk's response to Reagan, some DC punks realized that "dealing with John Doe," as Preslar put it, consisted of direct action on the streets, rather than only shouting slogans in a song or, worse, giving in to apathy. The years 1985 and 1986 brought a political awareness to the scene, revitalizing it and opening up new artistic possibilities. Revolution was a byword among some DC punks during this period and, if a bit grandiose, the earnestness and intensity behind that idea propelled DC into a rangier phase, with room for the invention and collaboration that the fanzine editors Barbara Rice and Steve Kiviat called for in their 1984 *Maximum Rocknroll* essays.

The earliest days of 1985, however, did not portend renaissance. A broken collarbone for drummer Brendan Canty transmogrified the normally explosive Rites of Spring when they opened for Minutemen at the 9:30 Club on January 3. Canty gamely banged on a snare with one arm while his bandmates donned acoustic guitars, leading to a set tethered by its temporary limitations. "Crosby, Stills, and Nash meets Minor Threat?" chortled *WDC Period* before adding, tartly: "They played too long and people seemed to get bored."[3] The group's guitarist/vocalist Guy Picciotto was chastened by the ordeal. "If you think you're a crazy live band, see how crazy you are when you're acoustic," he said. "You lose your total wall that you hide behind . . . . That was definitely an experience in humility."[4]

Just over a week later, MacKaye joined Henry Rollins for part of the latter's spoken word performance at dc space. On that cold January night, the pair "went through what seemed like improvised comic dialogues about jobs they used to have and strange things they did together," per *WDC Period*'s review, which flayed Rollins' poetry while offering muted praise for MacKaye's presence: "MacKaye played the piano nicely and said some funny things that were also sad in a way I can't define." The melancholy suffusing *Metrozine*'s interview with MacKaye from 1984 might have lingered but was soon to dissipate.

The year 1985's opening fortnight found some of the scene's strongest voices struggling publicly as they tried to perform with a hand tied behind their creative backs, whether it was due to Canty's injury or MacKaye's struggle to get a new band off the ground. Later in 1985, MacKaye reemerged with Embrace, a group that—along with Beefeater, Gray Matter, and a restored Rites of Spring—helped move DC forward in giant steps. The period of 1985 and 1986 likewise saw several new DC punk fanzines debut, while *WDC Period* bloomed and *Truly Needy* unexpectedly concluded.

Yet Another Unslanted Opinion

One of those new fanzines, *Yet Another Unslanted Opinion*, appeared in late spring 1985. Assembled by three teenagers—Brian Gathy, Sean Lesher, and Frank Charron—from suburban Burke, Virginia, the first issue crackled with reports on events laying the groundwork for the imminent Revolution Summer. Mark Andersen, cofounder of the activist group Positive Force DC, contributed an essay titled "Change: It Comes from the Inside," capturing much of the scene's burgeoning political ethos. He urged punks to shake off their languor and look within to incite progress. "If we want the outside world to change," Andersen wrote, "we've got to be working on ourselves first and foremost, trying to make ourselves more aware, active and caring. We've got to be respectful of others and their views even as we insist on respect for ourselves. Sure, 'Middle America' is a dead-end street, but have you been to a show recently? It's not exactly 'heaven' there either."[5]

An interview with MacKaye in that same issue—conducted at Dischord House in Arlington, Virginia—included similar thoughts on methods for achieving real change. "I'm twenty-three now, but when I was eighteen, I didn't give a fuck about politics," MacKaye explained:

> *But, after a while, you get to see just how sick everything is. I don't think I can overthrow the*

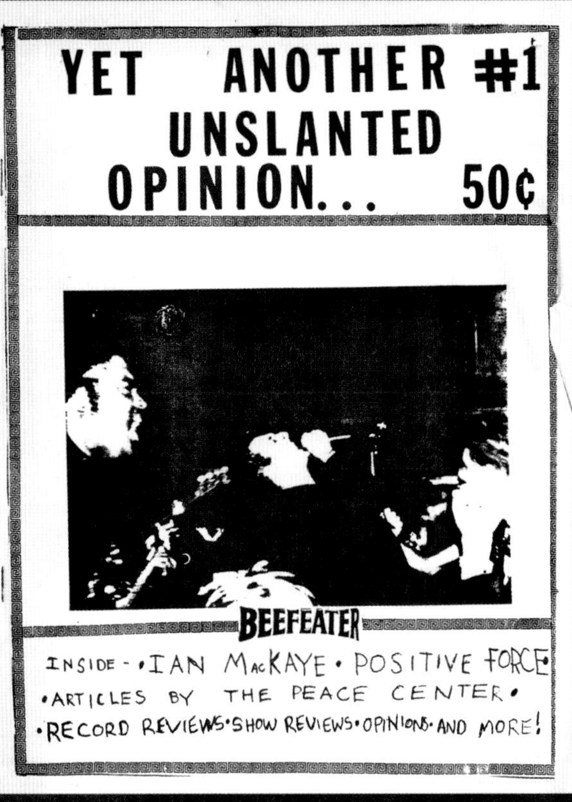

Figure 6.1 *Yet Another Unslanted Opinion*, issues 1 through 4. Published by Sean Lesher and Brian Gathy, circa 1985–86. Used by permission.

government. . . . I can just improve myself the best I can to make myself as caring and compassionate [a] human being as possible. And try to help other people and stuff like that. . . . Maybe by doing that, I can influence others to do the same and maybe if they can do that, we can sort of put on a different sort of general mood.[6]

Embrace was in its earliest days and the boost in MacKaye's spirits was evident, as was his wariness of expressing too much hope. "If the band's good, if it works well, we'll put out some records," he offered. "We'll just sort of play it by ear." It was particularly clear that MacKaye was bursting with creative energy. "If it doesn't work out, I'll try to find something else. I'm gonna try to make more music, singing, playing guitar, bass, whatever. I don't give a fuck, you know? I just wanna play."[7] For MacKaye, infused with purpose and inspiration, it appeared that 1984's dark clouds finally scattered.

When interviewed in 2020, Gathy happily recalled the palpable positivity at Dischord House during the 1985 conversation, with MacKaye raving about the forthcoming Rites of Spring album and proudly displaying the guitarist Eddie Janney's cover artwork. "He couldn't stop talking about them," Gathy remembered. MacKaye left an indelible impression on Gathy. "I was a little, scrawny kid," he said with a laugh. "That [MacKaye and his roommates] would have serious conversations with me, not condescending in any way; . . . it meant a lot to me." When Gathy mentioned that he would be taking public transportation home once the interview was over, MacKaye insisted on giving him a ride back to Burke. "It just shows what kind of person he is," Gathy declared. "It was a really cool experience, a good learning lesson about integrity and authenticity."[8]

Gathy and Lesher published five issues of *Yet Another Unslanted Opinion* through 1985 and 1986, offering readers a compendium of the scene as it developed into a more politically active punk community. An interview with Scream in the third, fall 1985, issue featured band members ruminating on apartheid in South Africa, war in Nicaragua, communism in Ethiopia, and the disquieting prevalence of segregation in the DC area, manifesting in its housing and

Figure 6.2 *Yet Another Unslanted Opinion*, issue 5, circa 1986. Published by Sean Lesher. Used by permission.

public services. "We all need to pull together to stop that over there and also stop it here," the band's bassist, Skeeter Thompson, observed. A political urgency had surfaced in the scene, highlighting how much had changed since MacKaye's comment to *Flipside* in 1982 about DC bands not being "overtly political."

"I'm just eternally grateful to have had the opportunity to have some small part in that scene, that time period, because it really did shape everything about how I view life," Gathy said, observing how the DC scene empowered him. "You don't have to wait for someone else to articulate something in your name. [You] can do it. And there's this whole network of people that are always doing something to make the world a better place."[9]

Turn Around

As a student at the University of Texas in Austin, Jenn Thomas (known today as Jennifer Fox-Thomas) grew disillusioned with the town's party atmosphere, which, to her, "was just not what I was about or anything." Catching wind of Minor Threat, however, brought her attention northward to DC. "When I realized that there was this whole part of punk rock that was about straight edge," she recalled, "it was like 'I found my people.'" Thomas took a bus to DC, found MacKaye's contact information in the phone book, and introduced herself. "At that point, I drank the Kool-Aid," Thomas joked. "I was in." DC's punk scene was exactly what she was looking for: "It wasn't about punk and destruction. It was about punk rethinking and building."[10]

Thomas dove into the scene, attending concerts by DC bands like Rites of Spring, Scream, Beefeater, and Embrace, as well as out-of-towners like the Minutemen and the Red Hot Chili Peppers. She observed that the thriving community was about more than just the musicians. The people organizing the shows, creating the zines, designing the fliers, and, especially, the fans who imbued concerts with energy, were equally important pieces of the ecosystem. Thomas eagerly read other zines from DC, absorbing various perspectives on the scene. "The biggest thing about it was seeing how other people were viewing the same thing that you were viewing," she recalled. "That was always the piece that connected me, you know? Just this common experience. But even though it was a common experience, we were all kind of seeing it in different ways. And when you were able to pull together all those different perspectives, then you finally had the closest approximation of truth that you could get to."[11]

Thomas was an avid reader of *WDC Period* and *Metrozine*, but she was as interested in the people behind the fanzines as much as the zines themselves. Regarding *Metrozine*'s Scott Crawford, she admiringly recalled that "he was intent on doing things and bringing energy and documenting," attributes that inspired her to eventually start her own fanzine. For that, Thomas specifically centered the *fans* in her zine. "It was really about the people in the scene. It wasn't so much about the music."[12]

Figure 6.3 *Turn Around*, issue 1, 1985; and issue 2, 1986. Published by Jennifer Fox-Thomas. Used by permission.

Turn Around published three issues between 1985 and 1988, its title a "directive," according to Thomas, albeit a "completely corny" one.[13] While fans at concerts were used to keeping their gazes fixed on the stage while musicians performed, Thomas urged her readers to, literally, look at the people around them and understand that the punk subculture was about *all* its participants. The first issue consisted almost entirely of Thomas's photography, with a few lyrics and short essays sprinkled throughout the twelve pages. The photographs—often somewhat unflattering and mystique-puncturing—include bands like Dag Nasty, Marginal Man, and Brief Weeds,[14] but nearly as many focus on audience members, who appear everything from rapt to bored, singing along or staring at the ground. It makes for a unique document of punk showgoing in the mid-1980s.

The second issue, published toward the end of 1986, is in a similar cast, but its content is expanded by an essay by Mark Andersen titled "From the Heart" and an interview with Beefeater, then rapidly redefining DC punk with their politically charged blend of punk and funk. The band's vocalist, Tomas Squip (who later changed his name to Onam Emmet), and its bassist, Dug E. Bird, conversed earnestly with Thomas about topics—animal rights, spirituality—that are hard to imagine reading about in the DC punk zines leading up to this period. Squip questioned just how subversive it really was to be a punk in 1985, opining that punk had been recuperated to the point that its threat had dulled. "It's been around for a long time and it's much safer to be a punk," he said. "Much easier. And if you go to a punk concert and look at the values of the kids who are punks now, their values differ very, very little from regular teenagers. I mean, they like sports, and bad food, and loud music. Their clothes might be a little bit different and their hairstyle might be a little shorter or something but, apart from that, they live very normal lifestyles for kids their age."[15]

Decades later, Thomas described the interview, along with subsequent conversations she had with Squip around that time, as "so pivotal to who I would become today, working in nonprofits, working with kids in DC for 35 years since 1985. [It] all comes from that . . . talking about our impact on each other." After Thomas moved on from *Turn Around*, she embarked on a career as an advocate for

Figure 6.4 Marginal Man concert photomontage from *Turn Around*, issue 1, 1985. Published by Jennifer Fox-Thomas. Used by permission.

children and their families, as well as drumming in bands like Sweetie and Cry Baby Cry. *Turn Around*'s documentation of the start of her longtime participation in the DC punk scene, however, remains significant to her, as does the period itself. "I think that's one thing about the DC punk scene is that so many of us have gone on to do things that are really meaningful and impact people's lives," she said. "Not necessarily leaders, but participants and connectors and facilitators. . . . I love that about the DC scene."[16]

Metrozine

Crawford was an occasional contributor to *Turn Around*, but his attention primarily remained on *Metrozine* during this period, branching out into releasing music under the *Metrozine* banner. *Can it Be?* compiled DC bands from 1984's new crop, like Gray Matter and Mission Impossible, along with stalwarts Government Issue, United Mutation, and Velvet Monkeys. *Maximum Rocknroll*'s Tim Yohannan gave the cassette compilation a critical pat on the head, dubbing it a "tunefully varied musical earful" and a "solid effort."[17] Such was *MRR*'s power in the national punk scene that even such temperate praise buoyed Crawford to the point that he included it in advertisements for *Metrozine*'s wares. Another compilation followed later in 1985, this one a collaboration with WGNS, a Bethesda punk label and recording studio. *Alive and Kicking* brought back Gray Matter, Mission Impossible, and United Mutation, while adding Marginal Man, Beefeater, and Cereal Killer, offering a snapshot of a scene evolving beyond hardcore.

On top of this, Crawford released new issues of *Metrozine* nearly every month as 1985 advanced. Issue seven emerged in early spring, its cover spoofing the video for USA For Africa's then-ubiquitous anthem "We Are the World." The mawkish, if well-intentioned, video assembled dozens of pop stars in an earnest fundraising effort to combat famine in Africa, and was easy grist for cover illustrator Brian Walsby. Rather than choral risers lined with the likes of Michael Jackson, Bruce Springsteen, and Diana Ross, *Metrozine*'s cover jokingly features a panoply of punks like MacKaye, Rollins, the Misfits' Glenn Danzig, and Suicidal Tendencies' Mike Muir singing "we are the world / we are the future."

Crawford's prolific publication clip ran into reality when school resumed at the end of the summer of 1985. Issue eleven, published in September, prominently featured the words "now bi-monthly" beneath the zine's name on the cover, a concession to Crawford's youthful responsibilities. Indeed, he admitted a need to "concentrate on hitting the books more" in a brief introductory editorial. Crawford's age and prolificity were a narrative that was never far from the surface. When *Washington City Paper* profiled Crawford in August 1986, it noted that "he still has trouble getting people to concentrate on his products, not his age," but not without first cracking that that cherubic teenager looked like "a Boy Scout who took a very wrong turn on his way to the troop meeting."[18]

As high school progressed, Crawford's ardor for the scene persisted, yet his devotion to publishing *Metrozine* dimmed. "If I remember correctly," Crawford recalled of what drew his attention away from zine creation, "it was

Figure 6.5 *Metrozine*, issue 7, 1985. Published by Scott Crawford. Used by permission.

basically girls." Following a break-up, he resumed production of *Metrozine* for one last issue in 1987 but, from there, his social life and a new band, Darkness at Noon, took priority. However, the draw of chronicling punk in print and, eventually, through documentary film, drew Crawford back often in the years to come.

Truly Needy, Revolution Summer, and Positive Force

Another central fanzine winding down during this busy 1985–86 period was, perhaps, the scene's primary source for information: Barbara Rice and Bill Wort's *Truly Needy*. Issues nine and ten were published in 1985, although a long gap preceded issue nine's release. One reader grew so impatient that they posted a classified ad in the *Washington City Paper*, asking plaintively "Does anyone know where *Truly Needy* Magazine is? What happened? Please answer."[19]

Issue nine finally appeared in early 1985, the abundance of content justifying the wait. Its eighty pages were packed with waves of brief record and zine reviews, as well as interviews with Hüsker Dü, Meat Puppets, Clay Allison (soon to change their name to Opal), Einstürzende Neubauten, Nick Cave, and former Psychodrama artist/provocateur and now DC expatriate Leslie Singer. Singer's distaste for the DC "art rock" scene persisted despite her departure for San Francisco. "They drove me out," she contended. "They banned me everywhere." Compared with what she felt was a more "encouraging" creative atmosphere in San Francisco, Singer felt that DC's creative community lacked conviction:

> *What bugged me about it was, [in DC], all these artists derived so much from Dadaism and expressionism movements that brought art to the masses, trying to bring art off its pedestal. They're bourgeois*

Figure 6.6 *Truly Needy*, issues 9 and 10, 1985. Published by Barbara Rice and Bill Wort.

elitists. They use the aesthetics of it, they don't get into the art of it. In Nazi Germany, the pioneers were persecuted for their art. Would these people continue making art if they knew it was going to be burned or they would be put into prison?[20]

Due to the long gap between issues, the concert review section becomes the most transportive section of issue nine, serving almost like a DC punk concertgoer's yearbook, in this case for concerts that occurred between February and September of 1984. Reviewers like Hugh Byers, Haiti Ho, Michael Salkind, and Marc Sterling—the last also published *Final Update*, an absurdist DC-area zine full of kitschy clip art and dark-humored ramblings—reported back on night after night of concerts from the musical underground, most of which occurred at the usual spots like the 9:30 Club and dc space. Unlike *Truly Needy*'s sometimes perfunctory fanzine reviews, the concert reviews were usually detailed accounts.

Kathleen Connell's review of a June 1984 H. R. and McRad concert at the Newton Theatre preserves the moment that the short-lived DC venue hosted its first punk show, an event that saw many of the venue owners' fears about punks realized. Aside from the sparse attendance, "the owner's son was laughing hysterically while watching people slam in the pit while the mother ran down the stage with a worried look and then threw her hands up in the air and walked away!" This humorous anecdote spoke to just how difficult it was for punks to find a reliable place to book concerts. Intrepid restaurant and club owners sometimes gave punk shows a chance but, nearly without fail, they begged off future engagements. This climate made venues like the 9:30 Club and dc space all the more necessary, and deserving of gratitude, as they persevered as punk concert sites throughout the 1980s.

Other concert reviews in issue nine of *Truly Needy* comment on the luxurious air conditioning at Saba Club or describe the impact that the Wilson Center's concrete floors have on the sound mix, all adding a welcome level of filigree to a form that frequently lapsed into incurious recitations of setlists or concluded with torpid summaries like "overall, it was a good show." The concert reviews in this issue of *Truly Needy* that resonate are those with a holistic approach to the event's description, evoking *Turn Around*'s philosophy that a punk scene's heart is not found solely on the stage.

Issue ten gave no warning that it would be *Truly Needy*'s last, its page count robust-as-ever, at eighty pages. San Pedro, California, punks Minutemen were on the cover, just weeks after front man D. Boon died in an automobile accident. Aside from including a now-poignant interview she had conducted with the band, Rice also wrote an essay mourning Boon's passing. She closed the essay with an anecdote from her recent interview with the band where, after working up the nerve to ask if the band would allow *Truly Needy* staff to take photographs of the band, Boon replied with characteristic bonhomie, "sure, we're populists."

An interview with Rites of Spring was a standout moment in issue ten. It captures the band at the start of Revolution Summer, an artistic and political movement within the DC punk community that rebuked apathy and ruinous behavior. Musician and longtime Dischord Records employee Amy Pickering coined the phrase "Revolution Summer," when she included it in a series of "corny and cheesy" anonymous notes she wrote between tasks at her part-time job at a DC Neighborhood Planning Council office.[21] Pickering circulated the missives to friends in the local punk subculture, including her critiques of violence in the scene and the need for DC punks to connect more with wider political issues around the globe.[22] This was the inspiration that so many within the scene needed to steer the community's direction away from self-destruction and nihilism. A mission for the upcoming summer months had come together.

Revolution Summer was expressed partially through activism, such as the "Punk Percussion Protests" organized outside the South African Embassy on March 14, June 21, and September 6, protesting that government's racist policies and American complicity in the system. The Reagan administration had been conspicuously soft on the South African government and, as the flier for the September 6 protest asked, "Does Ronald Reagan speak for you? If not, then let the world know!" Sparked by Tomas Squip and Embrace's Chris Bald and Ian MacKaye,[23] who were themselves motivated by Pickering's agitations, the protests served as a dividing line between DC punk's more apolitical beginnings and its activist future. Protesters were asked on the September 6 flier to "bring any drums and cans and noisemakers," which generated a clangor reportedly loud enough to be heard in Georgetown, more than a mile away.[24]

The year 1985's burst in political activity was fortified by the emergence of Positive Force DC, a punk activist group cofounded by Mark Andersen and former Hate From Ignorance guitarist Kevin Mattson. Andersen had only recently relocated from Montana, a place he understatedly recalled had "a lot of dislike of punk," whereas Mattson was from Bethesda, Maryland, and had grown skeptical of punk's ability to create significant change in the world. "So, that's my inspiration for Positive Force," Andersen recalled. "It's heading *to* the punk scene initially to try to bring a positive force within that. For Kevin, he was kind of interested in *leaving* the punk scene and building something more. Kind of a general youth activist umbrella."[25]

Andersen and Mattson had each seen an article in *Maximum Rocknroll* in March 1985 written by a Las Vegas activist group called Positive Force. The Las Vegas group had broken off from an eponymous group in Reno centered on 7 Seconds, a DC-allied hardcore band.[26] "Initially, [Positive Force Las Vegas] was kind of an affinity group," Andersen explained, using

> *non-violent, disruptive, blockade kinds of demonstrations. And the idea was you create these affinity groups of a small group of people who work together in this and support each other. I think that's what the original idea was, that they would be this group of kids from the punk scene and go do this thing. But then it kind of expanded. They put on shows, including benefit shows. They would work together at a homeless shelter or a soup kitchen or something. And the idea was to turn the rhetoric of punk into action.*[27]

Galvanized by the Las Vegas branch of Positive Force, the DC chapter came together in the summer of 1985, creating another facet of the push within the scene to cast off the pall of the previous few years. The first event Positive Force DC organized was a screening of the punk documentary *Another State of Mind* at DC's John F. Kennedy Center for the Performing Arts on June 7 and 8, 1985. Andersen distributed a booklet there that, amid the political information, asked attendees: "DC, what does punk mean to you?" The slogan, "Don't just be different, make a difference," appeared, as well. "Both of which one could accuse of being *extraordinarily* corny, but they were heartfelt," he later said of his handiwork. Positive Force DC even launched its own zine in 1985, *Off Center*, which published intermittently

Figure 6.7 *Off Center*, issue 1, circa 1985. Published by Positive Force DC and the Student Union to Promote Awareness. Used by permission.

throughout the latter half of the 1980s. *Off Center* gathered essays, poetry, and comics into a simple bulletin that helped establish the group's identity—serious, urgent, and committed to art as a tool of change and justice.

Those same characteristics applied to Revolution Summer writ large. In later years, Pickering and Andersen each self-effacingly referred to some of their early efforts to rouse punk's activist spirit as "corny," but their initial words spoke to a willingness to drop punk's increasingly cynical pose in favor of sincerity and hope. Along with activism, the movement's ethos particularly manifested through unabashed introspection in song lyrics. Earlier DC bands like Minor Threat, SOA, and Iron Cross sang about their willingness to fight, ostensibly in self-defense, but Embrace proposed a different sort of combat. "If you have to fight, then fight the violence that rules your life," MacKaye urged in "Said Gun." Gray Matter's Geoff Turner, meanwhile, graduated from cheeky rhymes about anxiety in the band's earlier songs—for example, "I'm afraid of pimps and whores, I'm afraid of Roger Moore"—to more unguarded, earnest offerings like his lyrics in "4 AM" on the *Take It Back* EP: "Now's the time to pull things close, but to lose what's close can hurt the most. Can this really be the end or could we maybe start again?"

Guy Picciotto's lyrics on Rites of Spring's "Theme" offered a level of vulnerability and emotional intelligence yet to be broached within the DC punk scene. "Cruelty is the better part of your honesty," he sang. "And when you're so direct, it's just for yourself to protect. And if I started crying, would you start crying?" A new artistic standard was forming, repudiating pessimism and ennui. "[Picciotto's] lyrics were always amazing and his delivery was always something to rally behind," drummer Brendan Canty said later. "His vision as a lyricist was just heads above everyone else at the time, especially considering he was eighteen years old."[28] As scholar Shayna Maskell observed: "Picciotto is often cited as the patriarch of emo singing, not because he reinvented an innovative melodic singing style, but because he merged the traditional hardcore vocal delivery of inflamed shouting with an authentic-feeling outpouring of varied emotion. Yelling became a vehicle for Picciotto's feelings, rather than merely an end in and of itself; volume and timbre articulated the intensity with which he felt."[29]

Figure 6.8 Rites of Spring concert flier for a June 21, 1985, performance at the 9:30 Club in DC. Designed by Cristina Martinez. Used by permission.

Truly Needy's interview with Rites of Spring was conducted on June 21, 1985, just hours after band members participated in a percussion protest at the South African Embassy—"We screamed 'Freedom, yes! Apartheid, no!'" Picciotto enthused—and shortly before their performance at the 9:30 Club that night. When Rice asked the band if they were arrested at the demonstration, the group collapsed into seemingly sheepish laughter. "No, we had to play tonight," Picciotto acknowledged. Rites of Spring was Revolution Summer's flagship band and one could not more closely document the movement's peak than *Truly Needy* had. Picciotto spoke of how the band's principles dovetailed with that of Revolution Summer's, as personified by the group's name. "We were trying to create a rebirth of what's going on here," he explained. "It seemed to be stagnating for a long time and we just

Figure 6.9 *WDC Period*, issues 7 and 8, 1985, cover art by Dan Snoke (7) and Dave McDuff (8). Published by Gordon Ornelas. Used by permission.

thought the name kind of fit the way we felt, a springtime type thing."

The DC scene appeared to be entering a period of renewal, but *Truly Needy* had surprisingly reached its unheralded end. When *Flipside* interviewed Rice for its "Fanzine of the Month" section in early 1986, the future held promise. "We want 1986 to see at least three" new issues of *Truly Needy*, she stated. No follow up to issue ten ever emerged, however. The interview in *Flipside* served as a final editorial of sorts for Rice, who signed off the exchange with words capturing the unpretentious insight, prescience, and passion for art her zine exuded from its beginnings:

> *I'll simply add that it's very important to keep the underground network thriving and open-minded in these politically, socially, and culturally conservative times. I don't mean just overtly political organs either. The similarly conservative 1950s had Burroughs, Kerouac, Ginsberg, as well as the jazz giants. We have not worked hard enough to challenge "conventional wisdom." Perhaps cultural historians will rate Minutemen, Minor Threat, and Black Flag with Coltrane and Charlie Parker. I dunno. But we've got to have more artistic ammunition to challenge these static, often repressive times (not that this is enough).*[30]

WDC Period, Chow Chow Times, and Enola Gay

WDC Period developed throughout 1984, but was not quite ready to replace the recently folded *Thrillseeker* as *Truly Needy*'s friendly foil. The years 1985 and 1986, however, marked the emergence of *WDC Period* as a zine that mattered, ably filling the void left by *Thrillseeker* and building a collegial relationship with *Truly Needy* benefiting both publications. Barbara Rice viewed *WDC Period* as a positive inspiration, stating that "much

YEP IT'S BACK

go ahead and take one......... IT'S FREE!

The Chow Chow Times

FEBRUARY 1985 NO. 2

A STARTLING ANNOUNCEMENT! GASP

R.I.P.
WILSON CENTER
NEWTON THEATHER
LANSBURG
HALL OF NATIONS
PIERCE HALL
SPACE II ARCADE
GLENMONT RECREATIONAL

HARDCORE

WELL, WELL, WELL, AS YOU MAY HAVE HEARD THERE'S A NEW (DIFFERENT) HALL IN TOWN THAT'S WILLING TO HAVE HARDCORE SHOWS! yippee!! THATS GREAT TO HEAR, IN FACT YOU MAY BE READING THIS AT THAT VERY HALL (SANCUTARY HALL 1459 Columbia rd. NW). Considering ALL THE PLACES THAT ARE NOW CLOSED TO HARDCORE (SEE ABOVE), THIS NEW PLACE IS ALMOST A SIGH OF RELIEF. OTHER THAN INDEPENDENTLY BOOKED HALLS, THE ONLY OTHER PLACES WHICH WILL EVEN CONSIDER HARDCORE ARE: THE UNIVERSITY OF MARYLAND; KING KONG CLUB; 9:30 club; and maybe D.C. SPACE. 9:30 aside these places are very infrequently used, and even the 9:30 club only will have shows once or twice a month and never on weekends. "So what", you may be thinking, "there's nothing going on anyways". Which is perhaps half true-G.I.'s this weekend and Social Distortion next month-not alot of bands can tour during the school year-but what about this coming summer? Without any of the big halls allowing HARDCORE there won't be a hell of alot of places to play around here. The reasons why the other halls have closed are really quite petty and easy to resolve if you treat other peoples property with respect (and that includes their neighbors!). WE ARE THEIR GUEST AFTERALL, AND EVEN THOUGH THEY'RE MAKING MONEY OFF US, THEY'RE STILL DOING US A FAVOR, SO PLEASE TRY TO REMEMBER THIS BEFORE DOING ANYTHING THAT MIGHT ADD THE "SANCUTARY" TO THE TOMBSTONE. XXXX

Hi There, its me again. Remember in the last Chow-Chow Times I said that if it got a favorable response that I'd do another one? Well as you can see, I was encouarged to keep it up, in fact I got quite a bit of support for this, both verbally and in the form letters and orders for the new Period. What can I say? While I don't feel as if I'm an egomaniac (or nothing like it), I still appreciate a verbal pat on the back once in a while, so THANKS to everyone who commented one way or the other. Of course I wouldn't be able to afford to dothi very often-(I've never even broke even with the zine yet)- WITH OUT SOME SORT OF SPONSER OR ADVERTISOR HELPING OUT. BUT MY GUARDIAN ANGEL WAS WATCHING OUT FOR ME, OR AT LEAST THE EDITORS OF "THE DUCKBERG TIMES" WERE, CUZ THEY HAV OFFERED TO GIVE THE CHOW CHOW TIMES SPACE IN THEI NEXT ISSUE (#3 due out in mid-MARCH) SO IT LOOK AS IF THATS WHERE THE NEXT CHOWCHOW WILL SHOW UP. YOU CAN FIND THE DUCKBE TIMES IN BASICALLY THE SAME PLACES YOU'LL FIND ANY OTHER FREE PAPER IN D.C. HOPEFULLY THIS WILL WORK OUT NICELY FOR EVERYBODY-LEMME KNOW WHAT YA THINK-OK? UNTIL NEXT TIME, "I'll SEE YA IN THE DUCKBERG"-GORDON GORDON

CHOWCHOWCALANDER

FEB 22 Government Issue, NIKE CHIX, MALEFICE, COOL AND THE CLONES - SANCUTARY HALL

23 9353 w/Specimen, fred - D.C. SPACE

MARCH 2 GRAND MAL, TROUBLED GARDENS - NATHAN B. CHAMPIONS

PLEASE NOTE: GUN CLUB CANCELLED THEIR 9:30 CLUB SHOW

7 9353 + CEREAL KILLER - 9:30 CLUB

8 DEATH PIGGY AND CEREAL KILLER - D.C SPACE 10pm

ALSO ON MARCH 8 Social Distortion, GOVERNMENT ISSUE, REPTILE HOUSE, PHLEGM - SANCUTARY HALL. TICKETS ARE 5.00 IN ADVANCE 6.00 day of the show. OK?

PLEASE NOTE: THE RUDE BUDA, GREY MARCH SHOW AT NATHAN'S HAS BEEN RE-SCHEDULED TO THE 16th

12 RICHARD THOMPSON - 9:30 CLUB

16 RUDE BUDA, GREY MARCH - NATHAN B. CHAMPIONS

AND MAYBE ON THE 31st THE FALL AT THE 9:30 CLUB

14 BLACK MARKET BABY - 930 CLUB

29 RONALD SHANNON JACKSON OUTRAGE - 9:30 CLUB

PHONE NUMBERS YOU'LL find useful
NATHAN B. CHAMPIONS # 347-4333
D.C. SPACE # 347-4960
9:30 Club # 393-0930
THE LORD JESUS CHRIST # HPQ-5081
also WMUC keeps a good concert calander call (301)-454-FM88

PERIOD #7 ON SALE NOW. #8 ON SALE MID-MARCH - SEND 1.00 POSTPAID TO: CHOWCHOW PRODUCTIONS P.O. BOX #43311-9-311 WASHINGTON D.C. 20010

BE SURE TO CHECK OUT: THE BOOGINS #2, METROZINE #6, DCene #3, DUCKBERG TIMES #2, A FREE UNICORN TIMES?

Figure 6.10 *Chow Chow Times*, issue 2, February 1985. Published by Gordon Ornelas. Used by permission.

cross-fertilization" had occurred between the two zines in 1985. She singled out *WDC Period* heads Gordon Ornelas, Dan Snoke, and Dave McDuff for their influence on *Truly Needy*, proudly noting that "some of us write for the *Period*," too.[31]

WDC Period maintained a steady publication schedule, turning out nine new issues throughout 1985 and 1986, while Ornelas's ambitions led him to also publish two additional zines during this period—*Chow Chow Times* and *Enola Gay*—and wade into the world of concert promotion at a short-lived venue called the Complex in Summer 1986. *WDC Period* grew increasingly polished throughout this time, relatively speaking, improving in its music writing and layout while inching toward becoming the semiprofessional production it became by the late 1980s.

The year 1985 started, however, with an unwelcome obstacle. Contacted by a student who offered to print copies of *WDC Period* at cost using the high school's vocational print shop, Ornelas gladly agreed to publish issue seven this way, as the expense was lower than the newsprint printing used for issue six, never mind the superior paper quality. Weeks passed without word on the print job's status until, eventually, Ornelas learned that the school's principal had discovered the project and destroyed the copies, presumably piqued by the contents.[32]

Ornelas found a new printer before long, but he still used the downtime to launch *Chow Chow Times*, a one-page zine he distributed separately from *WDC Period*. The first two issues of *Chow Chow Times* were published in January and February, respectively, of 1985. Each broadside packed in information on upcoming shows, band news, venue details, and other scene happenings written in Ornelas's clear, distinctive handwriting and supplemented with illustrations. Reportage on the crowded single page ranged from debunkings of harrowing hearsay—"Now, about the kid who got hurt on New Year's Eve. No, he wasn't stabbed and, no, he didn't die. Ok?"—to mundane briefings on studio sessions and band lineup changes.

Issues three through six of *Chow Chow Times* migrated onto the pages of the *Duckberg Times*, a DC-area alternative newspaper loaded with comics and a few nuggets of music news that Ronald Baker began publishing in January 1985. Within a few issues, the *Duckberg Times* covered underground music as much as it did comics, thanks to the influence of new editor Lisa White, who later booked the 9:30 Club from 1991 to 2013. It evolved into something of an underground DC culture newspaper before changing its name to *Washington Media EAR* in March 1988, lasting a few more issues before petering out.[33] The *Duckberg Times'* first few issues in 1985, however, focused mostly on comics, with *Chow Chow Times* and its font of local scene information living at the locus of punk and comics. The milieus were natural bedfellows as each were low-cost spaces of unfettered creativity offering outlets for ideas and imagery considered too distasteful for the mainstream.

Other punk and comics crossovers existed within DC alongside *Chow Chow Times*, *WDC Period*, and *Duckberg Times*. *The Boogins* turned out several more issues during this period. "If you care to dig and analyze, there is a message," the editor and contributor Rene Farkass insisted about his publication, an ethos that dovetailed with punk's. "We just can't be like television comics, which will entertain

Figure 6.11 *Crawl or Die*, issue 1, 1986, Published by Scott D. Miller.

but won't stimulate thought. It makes you a couch potato."[34] Even zines where comics were secondary to the publication's identity, like *Metrozine* or newer titles from the scene like *Most Things Suck* and *Binary Load Lifter,* interspersed doodles and comics amid their reviews and scene news.

Crawl or Die, published by Scott D. Miller of Rockville, Maryland, in early 1986, repurposed an image from EC Comics' 1950s horror comic *Shock SuspenStories* for the cover of its first issue. The hand-drawn headers Miller applied throughout the issue were clearly indebted to EC's evocative, macabre style. EC's illustrations and storylines had once shocked mainstream America so deeply with its gore and depravity—and, most egregiously, its honesty about humanity's baser instincts—that EC publisher William Gaines was brought before the US Senate Subcommittee on Juvenile Delinquency in 1954 for a grilling on the content of the comics he published.[35] His spirit lived on in *Crawl or Die,* which gleefully described itself as "the zine dedicate to subverting the morals of middle amerika !"

issue number one, fall 1985. for further info mail a S.A.S.E.. to ENOLA GAY, po box 7062, Silver Spring MD. 20907.

Welcome to the first "attempt" of this publication. You'll notice that this looks a little amateurish but what can I say? A gay-hardcore fanzine is something that I felt this town has needed for a long time (maybe I should say this <u>nation</u> because I've never heard of any other gay "zines" before). What with all the other "straight zines" around like the Period, and Yet Another Unslanted Opinion and all the "main stream" gay publications available such as the Blade (etc.), there doesn't seem to be any middle ground available. (I.T. does have its moments though.....) What I hope to acheive with ENOLA GAY is give us non- mainstream gay youth (punks?) a place to speak out and voice our views and perceptions of the world around us (such as the "hardcore scene" or the gay bar scene..). Since gay news is aptly handled by many other publications, there's very little need for this publication to repeat it (in fact there's very little I know about that I haven't read in the Blade first) instead I'd like to focus more on recreation and entertainment- things that may not be as "important" as our "rights", but most certainly affect us on a more day to-day level- especially if you don't hang around in the established "gay areas" of town (like dupont circle). I don't want to knock the Blade too hard because i believe it to be an important publication, it informs us of many political and social events which have the capability of directly and/or indirectly affecting our lives(and civil rights)..But when it comes to the forms of entertainment that they cover, in my opinion, it bites the big one. By reading what shows, books,and concerts they cover you'd think that all of us (gays) were such high "class", high "cultured" . "lets go check out the ballet" type of people.A real reinforcement of the gay stereotype if you ask me.Admittedly D.C. is a real "snobbish" place to live, with so many people in the upper class (both gay & straight) looking down on everyone in the working class, why should the cities main gay publication be any different? Just because you're gay doesn't mean you have an open mind, but fuck man doesn't every gay man just love henry rollins? wadda bod. But do you think the Blade would even whisper the name Black Flag? Fuck no! It's the little things like this that I'd like to see written about in my ideal "gay" publication. Other things that need to be mentioned are not as funny or pleasent, such as the hateful bullshit that this asshole to the right has a habit of uttering. The exerpts were taken from a recent interview HR did in the WDC Period. Kids today have enough prejudices already without having to read this guys sexist/homophobic views.(the worst of it being that since the Bad Brains have got back together, HR is getting even more attention and misguided respect than usual). <u>It's really fucked up</u> because "punk" <u>is suppose</u> to be a thinking form of music and punks claim to be so opened minded, yet once sex or even worse homosexuality is mentioned, that open mindedness gives way to conditioned beliefs of manhood, masculinity, and whats right and wrong in the bedroom. —Dee Wayne

what a studd right?

HR

boycott this man..

"Faggots can't have babies!

"When a woman is disobedient to her man, and is consisten in the disobedience, it is t man's responsibility to administer justice to protect her from herself."

hopefully #2 will be larger.

Figure 6.12 *Enola Gay,* issue 1, fall 1985. Published by Gordon Ornelas. Used by permission.

Daring as many of the punk and comics crossover zines published throughout 1985 and 1986 could be, none were as genuinely subversive within the punk scene as *Enola Gay,* Ornelas's one-off zine from fall 1985. Presented entirely from the perspective of a gay punk, *Enola Gay* was bluntly critical of homophobia in the punk scene and outspoken in its desire to belie gay stereotypes. Writing under the pseudonym of Dee Wayne, Ornelas acknowledged the positive activist work done by the *Blade,* DC's long-running gay newspaper, but bemoaned the stuffiness of its arts coverage. "By reading what shows, books, and concerts they cover, you'd think that all of us (gays) were such high 'class,' high 'cultured,' 'let's go check out the ballet' type of people," he wrote. "A real reinforcement of the gay stereotype, if you ask me."

After joking about his perception that Henry Rollins held universal appeal for gay men—"wadda bod"—Ornelas turned serious, aiming his ire at Bad Brains vocalist H. R. The extraordinarily gifted musician and performer who inspired so many with his positive lyrics had developed a penchant for open homophobia. This notably reared its head when Bad Brains verbally skirmished with members of the punk bands MDC and Big Boys during a fateful visit to Austin in 1982. Allegations that H. R. made homophobic statements during the argument circulated throughout the national punk scene quickly, damaging Bad Brains' reputation.[36] In 2007, Bad Brains bassist Darryl Jenifer defended his bandmate, citing youth, overzealousness—band members were relatively early into their embrace of the Rastafari religion—and antagonistic behavior from the other bands:

> *And now you got one incident in our struggle within ourselves and the struggle within the band's self that stuck with us. I'm telling you: This is all simple, stupid shit, and that to me is racist, because if the Dead Kennedys would have came and done the same thing, that shit would not have stuck on and stigmatized them. If Black Flag would have came through there and called them dudes "fags" and took their weed, [Black Flag roadie] Mugger or somebody, that shit would not stigmatize them as homophobes and carry on throughout their careers.*[37]

Jenifer's observations about race are legitimate, as Bad Brains' legacy includes arguably more persistent discussion of their homophobia than white peers in punk who used slurs in their lyrics.[38] The homophobia described in the Austin incident, however, was not isolated. An April 1982 interview with Bad Brains in *Flipside* opened with H. R. complaining that San Francisco had "too many faggots." Even more disturbingly, he mused "if they just act sensible they wouldn't be so bad. Most of them act so crazy even out in public, it disturbs me, makes me want to go and shoot one of them."[39]

This was the prelude to a troubling interview with H. R., going by the name Joseph I., in issue ten of *WDC Period*. Jimi, a graphic designer and *WDC Period* contributor, probed H. R. on rumors related to his sexism and homophobia. H. R. rebuked the notion that he thought women should be "barefoot in the kitchen making babies," insisting that "every woman belongs to JAH and they are soldiers. They must take their place on the battlefield alongside the mon, so that doesn't involve the kitchen." When asked about "physical violence towards your women," however, he responds: "When a woman is disobedient to her man, and is consistent in the disobedience, it is the man's responsibility to administer justice to protect her from herself." Jimi then asks H. R.'s reasoning for his "virulently vocal . . . anti-homosexual rhetoric":

> *H. R.: Faggots can't have babies!*
> WDC Period*: But doesn't it say in the Bible, "Judge not, lest ye be judged" and the "Golden Rule"?*
> *H. R.: But it also says "Blessed are those who execute the judgement before his namesake."*
> WDC Period*: Where is that?*
> *H. R.: Everywhere.*
> WDC Period*: I mean in the Bible.*
> *H. R. Psalms.*
> WDC Period*: Where?*
> *H. R. If I tell you, it would only take the fun out of it.*[40]

Ornelas found his side project *Enola Gay* a more suitable outlet to vent his anger with "the hateful bullshit that this asshole . . . has a habit of uttering," he seethed. Reusing the photo of H. R. from the *WDC Period* interview, Ornelas pastes "boycott this man" over the musician's head, cutting out the offending quotes from the interview and applying them directly onto the image. "Kids today have enough prejudices already without having to read this guy's sexist/homophobic views," Ornelas wrote. "It's really fucked up because 'punk' is supposed to be a thinking form of music and punks claim to be so open-minded, yet once sex or, even worse, homosexuality is mentioned, that open-mindedness gives way to conditioned beliefs of manhood, masculinity, and what's right and wrong in the bedroom."

H. R. later distanced himself from his earlier comments. "At that time, it was very much about Rasta, hardcore Rasta, and what I understood from becoming a member of the 12 Tribes," he said:

> *It was basically very strict Christianity, but we called it Rasta. Today, I am much more live-and-let-live. I would not say those things today. I think*

age and experience changed me. We went from teen adults or juveniles to authentic adults, so our music changed. Our ideas changed along with our philosophy, and responding to things in a more responsible, mature, and adult way. And what we thought at the time when we were young was just old-fashioned, old ideas. But now, through experience, I've learned that it's better to use those laws and those teachings to make one's efforts more reasonable.[41]

The homophobia H. R. expressed in the 1980s was painfully common at the time, contributing to the atmosphere leading Ornelas to adopt a pseudonym for *Enola Gay*, eschewing his signature handwriting in favor of a typewriter when laying out the zine. He even used a different mailing address for *Enola Gay*, cloaking his identity further. "I wanted to keep it on the down low and bought a different PO box from the one I was using for *WDC Period*, mostly because I didn't want the skinheads to know that I was gay," Ornelas explained.[42] The first issue included a note that "hopefully #2 will be larger," but a second issue did not materialize. "I never received any mail about it and since I was busy with *WDC Period*, I never followed through with other issues," he said.[43] Though overlooked due to its limited circulation, *Enola Gay* was at the front end of the wider queercore scene building through the 1980s, which included the influential Toronto zine *JDs* and the San Francisco zine *Homocore*. Ornelas revisited the theme of a gay zine in the 1990s with a new publication, *Teen Fag*, which he started after moving to Seattle.

Greed

Among the cluster of new fanzines debuting in 1985 and 1986, none were more visually polished and innovative than Kurt Sayenga's *Greed*. After graduating from the University of Michigan, Sayenga returned home to the DC area as the first wave of hardcore wound down. "Basically, I got there when Minor Threat broke up," he recalled with a laugh. "Which is like the one band who was clearly the standout band of the bunch. The Faith, I got to see, and [they] were great. Then they broke up, of course."[44] The brief lifespan of most DC punk bands frustrated many in the scene, although Government Issue and Marginal Man were two thriving exceptions. Even the Slickee Boys carried on, reaching their tenth anniversary in 1986, although their fusion of new wave and garage rock led them to operate mostly parallel to younger punk bands by then. Their fanbase remained strong enough, however, to generate numerous issues of *Slickzine*, a newsletter/fanzine hybrid that published regularly throughout the eighties, winding down, as the band itself did, in the early 1990s.

The ascent of Rites of Spring and their peers throughout 1985 was "a fresh breeze," Sayenga recalled. "So much of that probably has to do with Guy [Picciotto] also bringing in his very literate sensibility to everything, and that kind of made everybody else up their game." He continued: "There

Figure 6.13 *Greed*, issue 1, winter 1986. Published by Kurt Sayenga. Used by permission.

was a real sea change in DC and what people were listening to, and more of a willingness to embrace the fact that they were artists interested in art. Whereas before that, that was considered suspect and possibly; . . . there was a lot of homophobia also in [punk] culture early on too."[45]

Much as Sayenga was motivated by the energy of the musical community, comics were also a passion. He drew his own, which *WDC Period* published in 1985, and was particularly inspired by *Love and Rockets*, a punk-inspired underground comic series created by the Hernandez Brothers from Oxnard, California. "When that came out, that's another thing that changed everything for me," Sayenga said. "Just the first issue, just seeing the promos for Jaime [Hernandez]'s first cover of that, was just like, 'This looks so great.' And that was something you did not see at all. Nobody had approached punk in anything like that way in comics. When this first came out, it was just like, oh, these guys are actually living it. It's not like some outsider perspective on it. It's super insider."[46]

Sayenga figured that an interview would be a way to engage in a discussion with the Hernandez Brothers, so he tracked down their contact information and set up a conversation. The interview went well, but Sayenga was wary of turning over the copy to *WDC Period* for publication. "I looked at [an issue of] *WDC Period* and I thought, 'I don't want this to look like that,'" he said with a laugh. "Because, as much as I love Gordon, I wanted it to look nice." Thanks to his day job writing for and editing a newspaper published by the DC based political cable news channel, C-SPAN, Sayenga was able to lay out the article with professional equipment and submit the article already designed for issue twelve of *WDC Period*. "It really stuck out like a sore thumb," he recalled.[47]

The experience pushed him to start his own zine. Originally titled *Uptight*, Sayenga reconsidered due to fears that another zine might have shared the name. "And then I just stumbled upon *Greed* because it seemed just very representative of the times, which again is laughable compared to where we are today," Sayenga said in 2017. "This was, like, full-bore Reagan administration. It came out of that. . . . It's just designed to attract attention."[48]

Greed's first issue took clean typesetting and layouts like those found in Howard and Tina Wuelfing's *Descenes* and *Discords* zines from the turn of the 1980s and polished them further. Bearing a surreal illustration by DC musician Peter Hayes on its cover, issue one's contents ranged from interviews with Rites of Spring, the Replacements, and Velvet Monkeys to columns, reviews, and comics. Other DC zines in 1985–86 had taken steps to use cleaner layouts that were easier to read, moving away from cut-and -paste layout and handwritten text. *Greed* was even more in line with the professional layout of national alternative music magazines like *Matter* and *Option*, indicating that Sayenga's aspirations went beyond distributing copies of his zine by hand at a few local record shops and venues.

Much as *Truly Needy*'s interview with Rites of Spring found them at a turning point, Sayenga's interview with the group in *Greed* caught them at another important transition: Breaking up. Following a final show in December 1985 and a recording session in January 1986—released on Dischord Records in 1987 as the *All Through a Life* EP—internal dissension splintered the quartet, with bassist Mike Fellows departing. "It feels like everything you've done is destroyed, but it's not true," Picciotto said, his grief palpable. "The shows existed, the people came out to the shows, I played the shows, the record came out—it's just changed my whole life."[49]

Greed's editorial tone was clever and sardonic and its layout was slick, but it was all unmistakably the product of fandom. Sayenga and his friends' love of punk and underground culture emanates from the page, no matter how orderly the presentation was. "Write us if you like this magazine," Sayenga urged in the introduction, before employing parting words that evoked those of earlier DC hardcore zines. "If you don't like it, fuck off." As impressive as *Greed*'s debut was, the rest of the 1980s saw the zine explore even more dynamic meridians of writing, graphic design, and comic art.

"But When One Wave Stops, Another Begins"

Rites of Spring was not the only Revolution Summer group to disband before 1986 was through. Embrace played their final show on March 13, 1986, and Gray Matter split at the end of the summer. "Embrace played a few shows, . . . but there was always a sense that things just weren't jelling the way they should," the group's guitarist, Michael Hampton, recalled. "It was not the band that I think Ian wanted to be in. It eventually became the band that none of us wanted to be in. Everything was just too hard in Embrace."[50] Hampton and former Rites of Spring members Picciotto, Janney, and Canty briefly collaborated as One Last Wish, but that group, too, broke up after a handful of concerts later in 1986.

Seeds of discontent and dedication planted in 1984 and into early 1985 fomented this period that transformed DC's punk scene and, soon, punk around the world. Amy Pickering remarked later, however, that contrary to Revolution Summer's reputation as a rebirth of the scene, "Revolution Summer was the climax, it was the end of something."[51] This is true in the sense that the bands who blossomed in and around 1985 flamed out quickly, but the short-lived season of creative and political renaissance launched a new wave of purposeful, inventive punk in DC as the decade waned and a new one approached. "Do your own thing," Picciotto urged in that final interview with *Greed*. "Get it going and get creative. When we first started playing there weren't many bands, and now there are a lot of bands. Everyone has something to do, and everyone has a part to play. Fill our gap, if we've left one at all."[52]

Notes

1. Nicholas Rombes, *A Cultural Dictionary of Punk: 1974–1982* (New York: Continuum, 2009), 230.
2. "How Groups Voted in 1984," Roper Center for Public Opinion Research, https://ropercenter.cornell.edu/how-groups-voted-1984.
3. Doug, "Live in DC: Minutemen, Rites of Spring, Braille Party," *WDC Period*, issue 8, February 1985, 17.
4. Kurt Sayenga, "Winter Kills," *Greed*, issue 1, Winter 1986, 8.
5. Mark Andersen, "Change: It Comes from the Inside," *Yet Another Unslanted Opinion*, issue 1, 1985, 6.
6. Sean Lesher, "Ian MacKaye," *Yet Another Unslanted Opinion*, issue 1, 1985, 10–14.
7. Lesher.
8. Brian Gathy, interview with the author, March 25, 2020.
9. Gathy.
10. Jennifer Fox-Thomas, interview with the author, May 25, 2021.
11. Fox-Thomas.
12. Fox-Thomas.
13. Fox-Thomas.
14. Brief Weeds was an intriguing alter ego of One Last Wish, the collaboration between Michael Hampton of Embrace and Guy Picciotto, Eddie Janney, and Brendan Canty of Rites of Spring. Brief Weeds veered away from the intense punk of the members' other groups, opting instead for a whimsical, psychedelic-influenced folk sound. The short-lived project's 1980s recordings remained unissued until a pair of EPs appeared via K Records in 1991 and 1993.
15. Jenn Thomas, "Dug and Tomas," *Turn Around*, issue 2, December 1986, 12.
16. Fox-Thomas, interview.
17. *Maximum Rocknroll*, issue 23, March 1985.
18. Kathi Whalen, "Punktrepreneur," *Washington City Paper*, August 15, 1986, 7.
19. *Washington City Paper*, October 19, 1984, 32.
20. Barbara Rice, "Two White Chicks Sitting Around Talking About Art," *Truly Needy*, issue 9, 1985, 32–33.
21. Mark Andersen and Mark Jenkins, *Dance of Days: Two Decades of Punk in the Nation's Capital*, updated and expanded 4th ed. (Brooklyn: Akashic Books, 2009), 173.
22. Andersen and Jenkins.
23. Barbara Rice, "From Insurrection to Resurrection," *Truly Needy*, issue 10, 22.
24. Cynthia Connolly, Leslie Clague, Sharon Cheslow, and Lydia Ely, *Banned in DC: Photos and Anecdotes from the DC Punk Underground ('79–'85)* (Arlington, VA: Sun Dog Propaganda, 2015), 166.
25. Mark Andersen, interview with the author, September 20, 2019.
26. Ian MacKaye coproduced 7 Seconds' *Walk Together Rock Together* (1985) and *New Wind* (1986).
27. Andersen, interview.
28. Alexandros Anesiadis, *We Can Be the New Wind: The Interaction of Punk, Hardcore Punk, Power Pop and Neo-Garage with Alternative Rock in the 1980s* (Ticehurst, UK: Earth Island Books, 2022), 206.
29. Shayna L. Maskell, *Politics As Sound: The Washington, DC, Hardcore Scene, 1978–1983* (Urbana: University of Illinois Press, 2021), 216–17.
30. *Flipside*, issue 49, Summer 1986, 9.
31. *Flipside*, 8.
32. *WDC Period*, issue 7, 3.
33. Lisa Miller, email interview with the author, February 14, 2021.
34. Leslie Bates, "DC Comics: Underground Cartoon Mag *The Boogins* Is Born," *Washington City Paper*, October 12, 1984.
35. Amy Kiste Nyberg, *Seal of Approval: The History of the Comics Code* (Jackson: University Press of Mississippi, 1998).
36. Andersen and Jenkins, *Dance of Days*, 106–9.
37. Dave Maher, "Bad Brains," *Pitchfork*, August 7, 2007, https://pitchfork.com/features/interview/6663-bad-brains/.
38. Evan Rapport, *Damaged: Musicality and Race in Early American Punk* (Jackson: University Press of Mississippi, 2020), 229–30.
39. *Flipside*, issue 31, April 1982.
40. *WDC Period*, issue 10, 1985.
41. Howie Abrams, James Lathos, and D. Randall Blythe, *Finding Joseph I: An Oral History of H. R. from Bad Brains* (New York: Post Hill Press, 2019), 119–20.
42. Gordon Ornelas, email interview with the author, January 28, 2021.
43. Ornelas.
44. Kurt Sayenga, interview with the author, June 13, 2017.
45. Sayenga.
46. Sayenga.
47. Sayenga.
48. Sayenga.
49. Sayenga, "Winter Kills," 4.
50. Scott Crawford, *Spoke: Images and Stories from the 1980s Washington, DC, Punk Scene* (Brooklyn: Akashic Books, 2017), 89.
51. Connolly et al., *Banned in DC*, 162.
52. Sayenga, "Winter Kills," 8.

7

Let It Ring, 1987–1989

REVOLUTION SUMMER'S PROMISE was immense but, a mere eighteen months later, the bands leading the resurgence were defunct. Most musicians at the core of the movement remained in DC, however, reconfiguring into new bands—Fugazi, Ignition, Three, Happy Go Licky, and Fidelity Jones—refining and expanding upon what the music members had previously made, propelling the scene through the rest of the 1980s. As intense as hardcore, yet steeped in melody and adventurous rhythms, a flood of other new groups emerged during this time, as well, like Fire Party, Soulside, Geek, Edsel, Thee Evolution Revolution, Vile Cherubs, MFD, Thorns, Broken Siren, and Holy Rollers. Some were short-lived, but a few newer groups—particularly Shudder to Think, Unrest, Jawbox, and Nation of Ulysses (initially known as Ulysses)—were at the scene's vanguard by the early 1990s.

Fugazi was a collaboration between bassist Joe Lally, Embrace's Ian MacKaye (now singing and playing guitar), and both Rites of Spring's drummer Brendan Canty and guitarist/vocalist Guy Picciotto. Their distinctive integration of dub reggae cadences, postpunk guitar textures, and anthemic songwriting proved profoundly influential on punk, building from the melodic hardcore foundation that the Faith established and Marginal Man, Rites of Spring, and others expanded upon. By the end of the 1980s, that melodic, earnest "DC sound" was broadly acknowledged within punk, although it only represented a portion of DC punk's actual musical characteristics.

Equally tied to Fugazi's public image was their disinterest in the machinations of the music business. Band members' commitment to low concert admission and retail recording prices, their dedication to DIY touring practices, and an outspoken repudiation of violence at shows all loomed large, helping define a conception of punk that some criticized as self-righteous and controlling. Despite the brickbats, Fugazi transformed punk on their own terms. "Fugazi, they changed *everything*," fanzine editor and musician Todd Ransick later declared, citing the group as a model of "what you can do after hardcore."[1] Fugazi worked closely with Positive Force DC, collaborating on the production of many of the band's local concerts, which uniformly raised funds for DC-area charities.

Although DC punk's nascent activism in the 1985–86 period tended to look, with occasional exceptions, outward internationally at crises in South Africa, El Salvador, Chile, and elsewhere, the devastating impact of drugs, violence, and racism in DC was unignorable by the late 1980s. In 1988 alone, DC endured 372 murders, a record at the time, earning the city the unwelcome sobriquet of "murder capital." Marion Barry, DC's mayor since January 1979, insisted that "Washington is not Dodge City," but he seemed powerless to stop the crime surge.

The murder rate continued rising, disproportionately affecting Black communities already reeling from systemic forces working against them.[2] Urban policy scholar Derek S. Hyra noted that "the decisions of white-controlled city councils, planning commissions, and public housing authorities to concentrate high-rise public housing in certain neighborhoods, the decisions of white-controlled banks to redline and deny credit to African Americans; and the decisions of white-operated companies to leave inner-city areas were critical to the downward spiral of these neighborhoods into concentrated poverty pockets."[3] DC had changed since punk appeared in 1976, and a city in crisis demanded more. Seeing this, much of the punk scene worked earnestly throughout the late 1980s to make an impact on the larger community around them. This manifested, for example, through an increase in support for local causes through benefit shows and protests, as well as a highly visible postering campaign seeking to shame US attorney general Edwin Meese into resignation over allegations of unethical behavior.

From 1987 to 1989, *WDC Period* and *Greed* were the leading DC punk fanzines, in circulation, editorial acumen, and design prowess. Both moved away from the cut-and-paste, handmade elements common to punk fanzines toward clean lines, orderly layouts, and colorful covers. Much as a fresh group of bands repopulated the scene, new zines proliferated at the end of the 1980s. A second wave of hardcore arose in DC, documented in fanzines like *Hands Up!* and *No Scene*. Likewise, indie rock—a more tuneful spinoff of punk, still imbued with its DIY ethics—developed steadily, its burgeoning influence visible in the humorous, eccentric zines *Sweet Portable You* and *The Straight Line*. Revolution Summer might not have lasted long, but its vestiges fueled late-1980s DC punk, making good on the movement's artistic and social promise, while drawing more participants to the community.

Action Time and DC Spotlight

Erik Grotz, a teenager from suburban Dumfries, Virginia—about 30 miles south of DC—learned of punk through his interest in skateboarding culture. After seeing Government Issue and the Slickee Boys perform as part of a "Rock Against Apartheid" concert at George Washington University's Lisner Auditorium in May 1986, Grotz was hooked.[4] Grotz avidly read the national punk fanzines closely covering DC bands, such as *Flipside*, *Maximum Rocknroll*, and the Los Angeles–based *Ink Disease*. Grotz was soon motivated to publish his own zine, publishing ten issues of *Action Time* through the turn of the decade.

When Grotz interviewed Fugazi for *Action Time* in spring 1988, the group was six months removed from its debut at Wilson Center. MacKaye reported that the group had played about twenty shows to that point, a modest figure for most active bands, but one that already exceeded Rites of Spring and Embrace's limited output. "It's pretty crazy," Picciotto said. "In other bands I've been in, you may get a show a month if you're lucky and you put everything into that show. And it was so great and it would tide you over for a long time while, with this band, you get that every week or so."[5] Fugazi performed more than one thousand concerts before going on indefinite hiatus in 2003,[6] but Grotz captured them in a raw phase for the interview, which appeared in *Action Time*'s sixth issue from November 1988. "I'm just having a hard time keeping up because when we go on tour, playing three shows in a row, it is something I'm totally not used to," Picciotto admitted. "I have to get into better shape."[7]

For Grotz, the interview was a galvanic experience. "I went to Dischord House and I got to actually watch Fugazi practice in the basement, which was just phenomenal to think about," he recalled:

> *And then I interviewed them and they were just so down to earth. So nice, so kind. And I was all of like 17, 18 years old. . . . I went away with such a warm feeling from all of that and I felt like I was getting properly grounded and schooled, as well. But not in a bad way. It's just, you look up to those people for so long when they're on stage and, regardless of how punk rock everything is, they're still heroes to you, you know? So, it was nice and wonderfully humbling to be able to ask them questions and get valid answers.*[8]

An earlier issue of *Action Time* featured another of Grotz's memorable interactions, as well as another documentation of a significant musical development's beginnings. Grotz met with DC punk stalwarts Scream at their rehearsal space

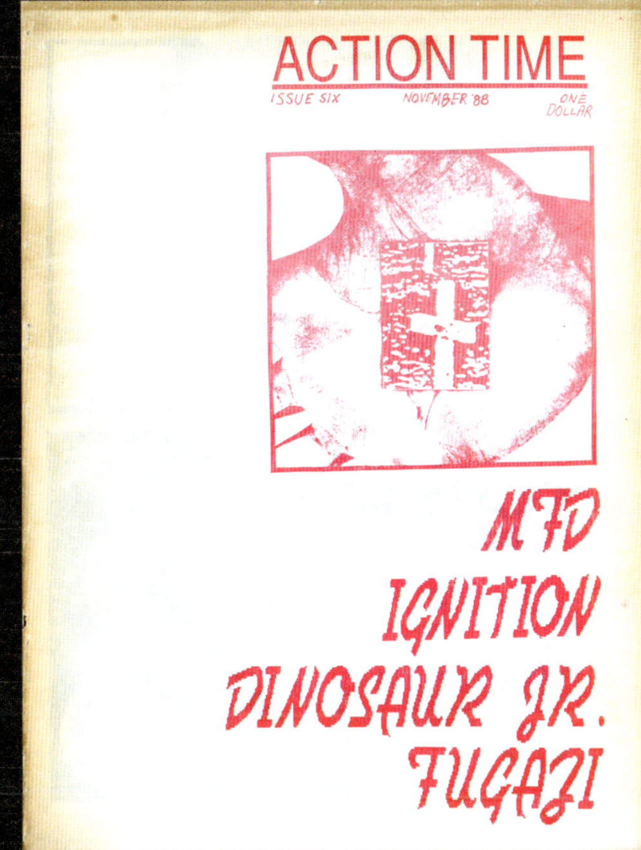

Figure 7.1 *Action Time*, issues 6 and 7, 1988–89. Published by Erik Grotz. Used by permission.

in Baileys Crossroads, Virginia, about 9 miles outside DC. The interview, spaced out over issues four and five in fall 1987 and spring 1988, occurred shortly after Dave Grohl replaced Kent Stax as the band's drummer. Grohl held the role until Scream split in 1990, where he was then snapped up by the soon-to-be staggeringly popular alternative rock band Nirvana, whose members learned of Grohl on one of Scream's tours. When Nirvana disbanded following the death of the vocalist/guitarist Kurt Cobain in April 1994, Grohl formed another massively successful band, Foo Fighters.

When Grotz met Grohl in 1987, however, their discourse began with the former asking "what's your name? I didn't get your name." Grohl identifies himself as "Dave from Dain Bramage," citing the short-lived band he had departed to join Scream.[9] Vocalist Pete Stahl did his best to steer the conversation into serious topics like the African National Congress in South Africa or a recent benefit concert the group performed for Amnesty International, but his efforts could not withstand the bonhomie in the room. Various band members punctured the earnestness with off-color jokes and the group repeatedly fell into laughter. "It was a good, comfortable scene," Grotz recalled fondly.[10]

Scream's inclusive behavior satisfied Grotz's desire to be a part of the DC punk community, which he otherwise perceived as "cliquish." Grotz later felt that Dischord's informal policy of only releasing DC bands made it easier for the DC scene to be negatively perceived as exclusive.[11] "A lot of the blame for that [perception] could legitimately fall at Dischord's feet because they're kind of our kingmakers, at the time," he said in 2021. "They were viewed that way and I think they still, in a way, are. Granted, Ian [and] Jeff [Nelson] are fantastic guys. I mean, absolutely amazing at what they were able to create and what they were able to continuously do. . . . So, it was weird that, as much as I loved the DC scene, it did at some point become too much of an insular thing."[12]

Picciotto addressed the perception of the Dischord scene being elitist in a 1989 interview with *Scratch*, a fanzine from Takoma Park, Maryland. "For Dischord, it's a group of people that are interested in their music and their friendships," he explained:

> *Dischord is like that because it doesn't use contracts. It doesn't want to be a label for all bands or all cities. For Dischord to do what Dischord does, it needs to work with that certain group of people, or whatever. And it's not to say that, from day one, it's been the same group of people, because lots of different bands have come on from different groups. There's no formula to it. A lot of people say DC is elitist but, I mean, what city isn't? That's my reply. If you have a group of friends, are you elitist?*[13]

Grotz viewed *Action Time* as an instrument to extol the DC scene beyond Dischord, with the Dunn Loring, Virginia, label DSI Records serving as another favorite, although "they had their own kind of somewhat cliquish thing going, as well," he observed.[14] DSI specialized in harsh punk and hardcore mining a darker vein than most of their peers in the DC scene. DSI bands like United Mutation, MFD, and Malefice were less popular than most Dischord bands, but their presence crucially added aesthetic and musical diversity to DC punk. Several integrated elements of metal and goth, helping DSI forge a distinct identity in a broader scene that revolved so much around Dischord.

After moving to Richmond to attend college, Grotz lost the free time required to publish another issue. "Yeah, it was school [and] it was going out every night to see bands," he said. "Continuously thinking, 'yeah, I'll put it out next month. I'll put it out next month.' And, then, it just never happened." The experience of creating *Action Time* resonated for Grotz, however, in the decades ahead:

> *I'm still in many ways the same punk rock kid, you know? [I] DIY most everything around this house. I still make music with friends. . . . I still love going to see bands. I still love reading about bands and hearing about bands and listening to music. . . . It's very much still who I am, in terms of not only personality but politically. I definitely think that I haven't outgrown that kid yet.*[15]

Like Grotz, another young punk fan in the Northern Virginia suburbs was pulled further into the scene through Scream. Chris Henderson was excited by punk stalwarts like the Sex Pistols or Black Flag and DC bands 9353 and Government Issue. The latter group disbanded during this period, performing their farewell in 1989 after a long run. Another of the handful of bands remaining from DC hardcore's first wave, Marginal Man, broke up in March 1988, leaving Scream to reach its own finish line in 1990.

Henderson had a fortuitous, if unexpected, encounter while walking home from high school when a punk-informed groundskeeper spied the Government Issue logo stenciled on Henderson's jacket. They discussed DC punk and the man mentioned he knew Scream's then-drummer Stax and connected Henderson with him. Henderson had already "fallen instantly in love" with Scream's *This Side Up* album when he had recently heard it, so he asked Stax about getting together to play music.[16] The jam session never materialized, but Stax invited Henderson to a Scream practice in early 1987, which he happily attended.

Photographs from the rehearsal spawned a new zine Henderson assembled called *DC Spotlight*, debuting later in 1987. Focused on Scream—aside from a few reviews and a DC scene report cribbed from *Maximum Rocknroll*—*DC Spotlight*'s first issue is a loving dispatch from his early months in their orbit. Henderson interviewed band members throughout the year, including one of Grohl's earliest as a member of Scream, interspersing them with snapshots from their concerts throughout 1987.

Over four issues from 1987 to 1989, Henderson employed cut-and-paste layouts, black marker, and typewritten text to craft an unpretentious encomium to the scene. *DC Spotlight* showcased his concert photography, the images fighting through the photocopier's obscuring effects to effectively impart nuance and motion. "I always just wanted to try and convey in a visual image what I felt inside when I heard this music," he recalled. "Because this music was touching me in a way that [did not happen] from music that I heard on the fucking radio."

The zine peaked with issue three, accompanied by *DC Metro Mayhem*, a cassette compilation Henderson assembled of DC area punk bands. Like previous issues, issue three's circulation was one hundred copies and the contents were essentially the compilation's liner notes. The roster is deceptively heavy hitting for such an obscure compilation, with Dischord bands (Government Issue, Scream, Shudder to Think) and DSI bands (United Mutation, Thorns, MFD) mingling with younger groups like Darkness at Noon,[17] Indian Summer, and Unrest.[18] The inclusion of Moss Icon, slowly carving an influential niche of their own in Annapolis, Maryland—30 miles east of DC on the Chesapeake Bay—highlights Henderson's ear for music that mattered, even if it fell outside obvious scene parameters.

DC Spotlight's fourth issue upped its circulation to two hundred fifty copies, which Henderson later assessed as a fatal blunder. "I don't even think I sold 100 issues," he said. "For some reason, it just didn't sell and, to this day, I've got a box somewhere where I'm stuck [with] probably one hundred [copies]." Citing lack of reader interest, as well as his own, Henderson ended *DC Spotlight*. Despite the disappointing conclusion, Henderson recalled that his zine "gave me an invaluable skill to be able to see the world differently."[19]

Figure 7.2 Top: Chris Henderson poses with his fanzine for an article in his high school newspaper, circa 1988. Bottom: *DC Spotlight*, issue 1, 1987. Published by Chris Henderson. Used by permission.

Hardcore's Second Wave Begins: *No Scene*

Running almost parallel to the Dischord scene led by Fugazi during this period, a second wave of hardcore punk developed in late-1980s DC, heavily influenced by metal and the "youth crew" style of hardcore coming out of New York City. DC's new hardcore scene centered on a series of Sunday afternoon concerts at 925 5th Street NW, "a square, one-story windowless joint, where bands loaded in through an upward-rolling metal grate in the front," as the authors Shawna Kenney and Rich Dolinger described it.[20]

That adaptable building, the Safari Club, was a bar serving Ethiopian food on weekdays, an Eritrean dance club on weeknights, and a venue for go-go concerts on weekend nights. This left a sliver of the schedule open for Kenney and Pam Gendell, two teenage friends from Southern Maryland, to book punk shows, most of which featured bands playing the new strain of hardcore, although not exclusively. "Pam and I didn't just like hardcore," Kenney recalled. "We loved punk rock in all of its forms. . . . We were known for putting together weird bills, so we would have King Face play with a New York band like Supertouch, or Government Issue with someone from Boston. We liked that kind of mash-up."[21]

Many of the concerts the pair promoted were billed as "*No Scene* Presents," a nod to the fanzine they published. Kenney started *No Scene* as a high school student in 1986. Its name referred to the isolation Kenney felt in exurban California, Maryland, over 60 miles south of DC. "Basically, all that was there was a Navy base and Amish farms," she said. "So, it wasn't a big happening city like DC."[22]

No Scene was an endearing blend of handwritten and typed text, shadowy photographs, playful doodles, and sincere punk fandom. "We were going to copy shops and blowing up text, and shrinking text in order to fit better on the page, and just kind of doing our own little mish-mash layouts, with tape and glue," Kenney remembered with a laugh. "We also used those rub-on letters . . . when we wanted a really straight-looking font. Magic markers. It just had a really rough punk aesthetic, especially for the first few issues."[23]

Kenney coedited various issues of *No Scene* with her friends Mike Ely and Mary Alice Woodburn, but Gendell joined for the final few issues and the zine hit its stride. Kenney's high school friend, Toby Morse—later known as the vocalist for the New York hardcore band H20 and a successful podcaster—introduced Kenney and Gendell. Morse "met [Gendell] first and could not wait to introduce us to one another, because there were so few girls that I knew that were into shows and punk as much as I was," Kenney said. "Pam and I clicked right away. Shared our love of music with each other. Became roommates. Started doing the zine together, started booking shows together. Kind of became inseparable for the next few years."[24]

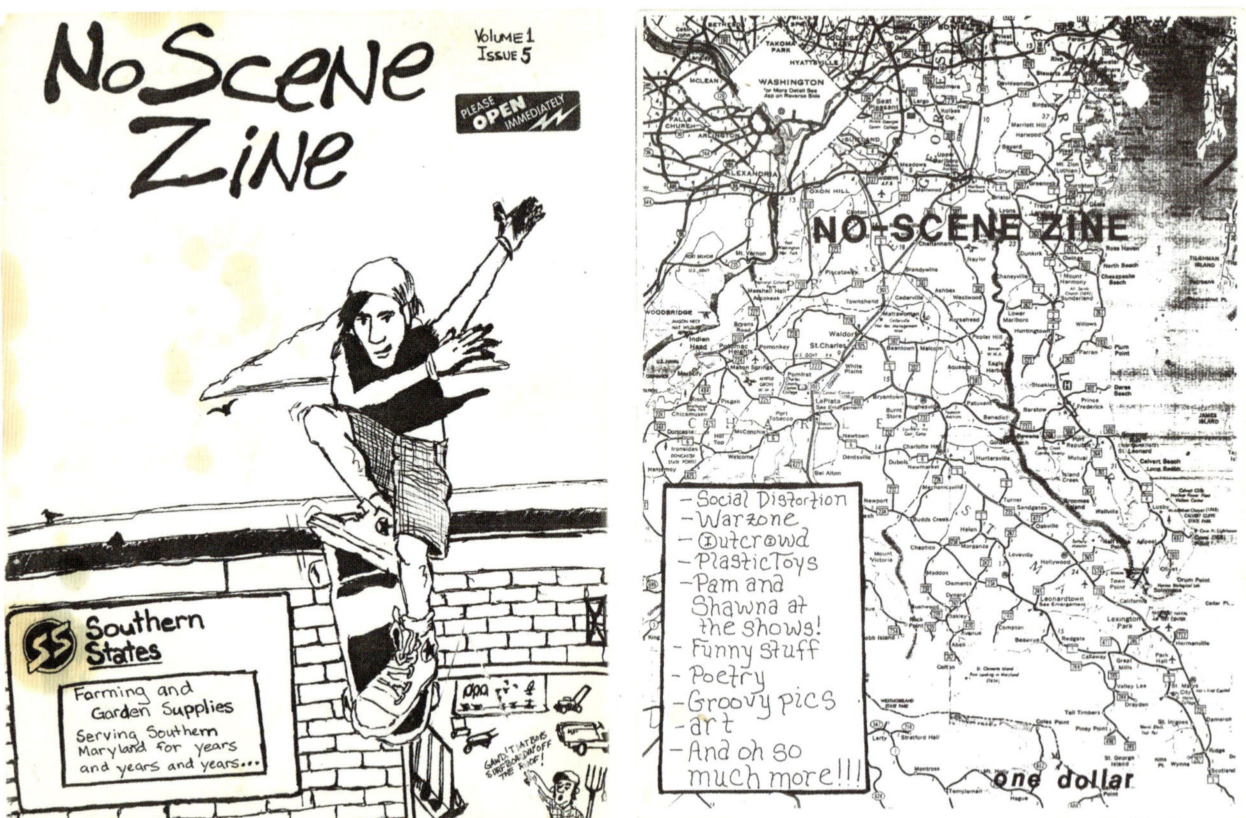

Figure 7.3 *No Scene*, issues 5 and 8, 1987–88. Published by Shawna Kenney and Pam Gendell. Used by permission.

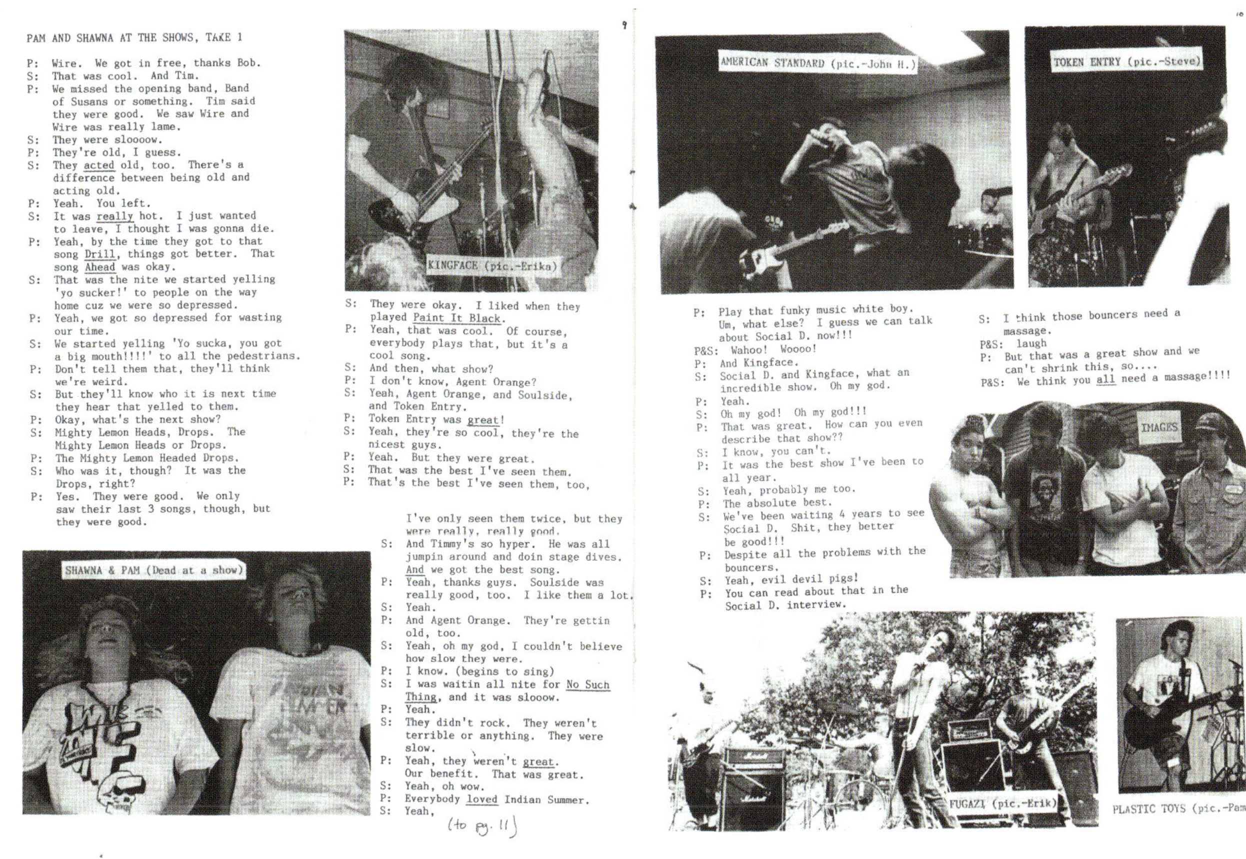

PAM AND SHAWNA AT THE SHOWS, TAKE 1

P: Wire. We got in free, thanks Bob.
S: That was cool. And Tim.
P: We missed the opening band, Band of Susans or something. Tim said they were good. We saw Wire and Wire was really lame.
S: They were sloooow.
P: They're old, I guess.
S: They acted old, too. There's a difference between being old and acting old.
P: Yeah. You left.
S: It was really hot. I just wanted to leave, I thought I was gonna die.
P: Yeah, by the time they got to that song Drill, things got better. That song Ahead was okay.
S: That was the nite we started yelling 'yo sucker!' to people on the way home cuz we were so depressed.
P: Yeah, we got so depressed for wasting our time.
S: We started yelling 'Yo sucka, you got a big mouth!!!!' to all the pedestrians.
P: Don't tell them that, they'll think we're weird.
S: But they'll know who it is next time they hear that yelled to them.
P: Okay, what's the next show?
S: Mighty Lemon Heads, Drops. The Mighty Lemon Heads or Drops.
P: The Mighty Lemon Headed Drops.
S: Who was it, though? It was the Drops, right?
P: Yes. They were good. We only saw their last 3 songs, though, but they were good.

SHAWNA & PAM (Dead at a show)

9

KINGFACE (pic.-Erika)

S: They were okay. I liked when they played Paint It Black.
P: Yeah, that was cool. Of course, everybody plays that, but it's a cool song.
S: And then, what show?
P: I don't know, Agent Orange?
S: Yeah, Agent Orange, and Soulside, and Token Entry.
P: Token Entry was great!
S: Yeah, they're so cool, they're the nicest guys.
P: Yeah. But they were great.
S: That was the best I've seen them.
P: That's the best I've seen them, too, I've only seen them twice, but they were really, really good.
S: And Timmy's so hyper. He was all jumpin around and doin stage dives. And we got the best song.
P: Yeah, thanks guys. Soulside was really good, too. I like them a lot.
S: Yeah.
P: And Agent Orange. They're gettin old, too.
S: Yeah, oh my god, I couldn't believe how slow they were.
P: I know. (begins to sing)
S: I was waitin all nite for No Such Thing, and it was slooow.
P: Yeah.
S: They didn't rock. They weren't terrible or anything. They were slow.
P: Yeah, they weren't great. Our benefit. That was great.
S: Yeah, oh wow.
P: Everybody loved Indian Summer.
S: Yeah,

(to pg. 11)

10

AMERICAN STANDARD (pic.-John H.)

TOKEN ENTRY (pic.-Steve)

P: Play that funky music white boy. Um, what else? I guess we can talk about Social D. now!!!
P&S: Wahoo! Woooo!
P: And Kingface.
S: Social D. and Kingface, what an incredible show. Oh my god.
P: Yeah.
S: Oh my god! Oh my god!!!
P: That was great. How can you even describe that show??
S: I know, you can't.
P: It was the best show I've been to all year.
S: Yeah, probably me too.
P: The absolute best.
S: We've been waiting 4 years to see Social D. Shit, they better be good!!!
P: Despite all the problems with the bouncers.
S: Yeah, evil devil pigs!
P: You can read about that in the Social D. interview.
S: I think those bouncers need a massage.
P&S: laugh
P: But that was a great show and we can't shrink this, so....
P&S: We think you all need a massage!!!!

IMAGES

FUGAZI (pic.-Erik)

PLASTIC TOYS (pic.-Pam)

Figure 7.4 "Pam and Shawna at the Shows" section from issue 8 of *No Scene*, 1988. Published by Shawna Kenney and Pam Gendell. Used by permission.

No Scene's most charming feature in those final issues from 1988 and 1989 is "Pam and Shawna at the Shows," a lengthy transcript of Kenney and Gendell extemporaneously talking about concerts they had recently attended. Unlike typical show review sections, filled with discrete capsule rundowns, Kenney and Gendell effervescently trade opinions about the shows. Their dialogue crystallizes a vital gift within fandom—the deep reservoir of happiness, bonding, and inspiration awaiting friends who partake in the sincere repartee it sparks.

No Scene's eighth issue, published in August 1988, was its finale, as Kenney and Gendell's responsibilities with bookings at the Safari Club gave them little time and money to spare for a ninth issue. Issues with Safari Club management also drained their verve for continuing concert promotion. "Our shows kind of fizzled in 1989. We were having problems with the club, and we just kind of went our separate ways," Kenney said. "[Gendell and I] were no longer roommates. We both got boyfriends. She went into college. Different things were happening. So, the zine kind of just fell by the wayside and wasn't a priority anymore. I think we didn't have the money to print it, and kind of just forgot about it."[25]

The impact that they had through their "*No Scene* Presents" productions at the Safari Club was lasting. "Safari was almost the first steady matinee situation, which was perfect for that crowd," the musician and record producer Ken Olden recalled. "You could tell that kids had almost been waiting for that—kids like us, who were out in the suburbs knowing each other and hanging out with each other but the only other thing you had was the 9:30 Club."[26] Other than local quartet Swiz, DC hardcore's late-1980s wave mostly centered on out-of-town bands coming through to perform. Soon, however, a new batch of homegrown hardcore punks incubated in the scene, such as Olden's groups Battery and Worlds Collide, and DC hardcore's second wave grew larger in the early 1990s.

For Kenney, *No Scene* opened new possibilities. "My zines were just a way for me to connect with other people," she said. "I was a shy kid and I wasn't going to play in a band on stage. I'm not going to just go up to people at a show and talk to them for no reason. But the zine gave me a reason to go up and introduce myself and feel like I could have a conversation with a stranger."[27] Kenney became an author and writing coach, issuing her memoir *I Was a Teenage Dominatrix* in 1999 and, with her husband Dolinger, the 2017 oral history, *Live at the Safari Club: A History of harDCore Punk in the Nation's Capital, 1988–1998*. As for her and Gendell, the young friends who blazed a path for a new type of DC hardcore: "I'm the godmother to her daughter," Kenney laughed. "We've remained friends all of these years."[28]

Axtion-Packed, *Hands Up!*, and *Take a Stand*

The community that Kenney and Gendell helped build in DC attracted other young punks from the DC area. Tim Owen, a high school student in Bethesda, Maryland, was introduced to hardcore through his classmate Chris Toliver, soon a notable photographer. Toliver took Owen to a Dag Nasty and Swiz double bill at the 9:30 Club on November 18, 1987, and, from there, "growing up in the DC suburbs made it easy to get into the DC/Dischord bands as well as [New York] and [California] bands," Owen recalled. "I went to a lot of shows put on by Shawna Kenney at the Safari Club, BBQ Iguana, etcetera, besides [the] Positive Force, 9:30 Club, [and] WUST Hall shows."[29]

The hardcore concerts at Safari Club especially caught Owen's interest and he was quickly immersed in the growing subscene of DC's punk community. While learning the craft from school photography classes, Owen took action when he noticed few photographers documenting shows at Safari Club. "I would get on stage, go behind the drum set, in front of the stage to take photos from all the angles I could," he said:

> *I was drawn in by being able to be a part of it all and captured what I could. . . . Since photography was the one thing I was interested [by] in high school—and music and skateboarding were my other interests—I took as many pictures as I could. I didn't really know what I was doing but I learned. I didn't have a grand plan or thought about it, I just did it.*[30]

Inspired by *Maximum Rocknroll*, *Flipside* and, particularly, the New Jersey hardcore punk zine *Boiling Point*, Owen thought starting his own fanzine would provide an apt forum for his concert photography. "The layouts, graphics, type, photos, [and] style of *Boiling Point* fanzine, to me, was so cutting edge and looked so good," he recalled.[31] Owen channeled those influences into *Axtion-Packed*. Only a single issue was published in 1988, but its clean layout, Owen's sharp concert photography, and proud representation of the new school of straight-edge hardcore made it memorable.

Bands featured in issue one—Wide Awake, Insted, Supertouch, and Bold—all hailed from outside DC, underscoring the fact that this new wave of hardcore's epicenter pulsed elsewhere. Owen's photographs of fans pressed to the edge of the stage, immersed in the communal joy of

Figure 7.5 *Axtion-Packed*, issue 1, 1988. Published by Tim Owen.

the group singalong, are quintessential evidence of punk's inclusive power. Unlike most photocopied zines that saw their photos obscured by the blunt contrasts of the reproduction process, *Axtion-Packed*'s photographs are remarkably clear. This is likely due to the print shop Owen chose having a copier with Xerox's then–cutting edge DocuTech technology, which was advanced enough to provide crisp photographs surrounded by dark black text. "The photos were, of course, important to me, but I understood that the layout, type, [and] graphics were also important," Owen said. "I learned how to cut and paste and try to figure out laying out the fanzine with Xerox copies, glue sticks, etc."[32]

Owen printed 100 copies of *Axtion-Packed*, distributing them at concerts, as well as record stores like Yesterday & Today, Smash, and Vinyl Ink. "I don't think [*Axtion-Packed*] was groundbreaking," he said. "I just focused on interviewing and taking pictures of some bands I liked that I saw and found out about primarily by going to shows at the Safari Club."[33] The zine morphed into a record label of the same name, issuing recordings by a few hardcore bands, most notably the Richmond group Four Walls Falling, before *Axtion-Packed* was retired by the end of 1990. Owen then launched a new label, Jade Tree, out of Wilmington, Delaware, achieving notable success within the punk world during its run from 1990 to 2016. Jade Tree released music by Promise Ring, Jets to Brazil, Lifetime, and a slew of others that deeply influenced indie music in the late 1990s and early 2000s.[34]

Several of Jade Tree's earliest releases featured a young musician from Potomac, Maryland, one town over from Owen's residence in Bethesda. Todd Ransick and his family moved to the quiet, affluent suburb from Connecticut, where he obsessed over skateboarding and, soon, straight-edge DC hardcore bands like Minor Threat. Thrilled to be living in the region that birthed so many of his favorite bands, Ransick looked for connections through area record stores. Still in early teens, Ransick felt his youth and fandom erected barriers between him and older punks from the Dischord community he admired. "That scene was kind of insular," he remembered. "*Super* great guys and we worshipped everything they did but, when we would go into Yesterday & Today and Skip [Groff] was there and Ian [MacKaye] would walk in; . . . we were more starstruck, really, as little . . . skater kids. [MacKaye] was super friendly, but the [Dischord] scene wasn't a scene that we felt we were really a part of."[35]

Ransick and his friends were motivated by achievements of the older punks, yet determined to build their own scene, one more focused on the other type of punk they loved. "[It was] largely influenced by what was going on around the country [in] New York [and], specifically, Los Angeles with Uniform Choice and those guys," he said. "The new uprising of our interpretation of what straight edge was."[36] Ransick employed a two-pronged DIY approach to legitimize his younger peer group: Start bands and publish fanzines. He was in a variety of hardcore groups during this period, like On Edge, Far Cry, and Touchdown. Crackling with inspiration and energy, Ransick also worked on two fanzines: *Pathedy of Manners* and *Hands Up!*

Pathedy of Manners was coedited with J. J. Wilcoxon, whom Ransick credited with the idea for the zine and for emphasizing that the pair "lean into that, [that] this is our scene. It's not Dischord. It's ours. It's the younger generation's." The duo published two issues of *Pathedy of Manners*, interviewing hardcore groups like Youth of Today, while still keeping tabs on Dischord through coverage of Beefeater and Soulside. Each issue's print run generally topped out around one hundred copies, "basically until we ran out of toner," Ransick said. The first issue "was done at J. J.'s Dad's . . . company, . . . and we would sneak in there after hours and do it. [J. J.] got in big trouble for that one." A second issue came together when Ransick "got a job at a Hallmark store specifically to steal photocopies."[37]

Differences in ambition and musical taste, however, led to Ransick breaking off to start his own fanzine. *Hands Up!* plunged further into straight-edge hardcore, interviewing Underdog, Four Walls Falling, Uniform Choice, and like-minded groups. Swiz, whom Ransick referred to as "the only 'hard' band left in DC," appeared in issue three in fall 1988. The guitarist Jason Farrell praised Kenney and Gendell in the interview for their work at the Safari Club, declaring "they are like gods for doing that. I mean, I don't even think anyone knows who they are. They are not getting as much respect as they should."[38] Ransick joined the choir in that

Figure 7.6 Top left: *Pathedy of Manners*, issue 2, 1987. Published by Todd Ransick and J. J. Wilcoxon. Top right: *Hands Up!*, issue 2, 1988. Published by Todd Ransick. Used by permission. Bottom: Todd Ransick, circa 1989. Photo by Tim Owen.

same issue's opening editorial. "In recent years, I remember when the only place to see good shows was the 9:30 Club, who only allows bands to play that have a record out and are popular," he wrote. "I am grateful to Pam, Shawna, and the Safari Club for putting smaller bands on the bill."[39]

Hands Up!'s fourth issue was plagued with issues recalling *WDC Period*'s earlier misadventures with a high school printing press. Ransick enrolled in a printmaking class at Walt Whitman High School in Bethesda, using it to print one thousand copies of *Hands Up!*'s new issue. "I paid for the paper and everything," Ransick recalled, but the school principal confiscated every copy. Ransick pleaded his case, ultimately learning that an earlier group of punks at Whitman once circulated a fanzine that ran afoul of school authorities. As Ransick remembered it, the principal was "scarred from it. All they wanted to do was talk about, like, 'oh, we know about punk rock stuff.'"[40] Most of the seized copies were eventually returned and issue four appeared, covering more national hardcore bands like Verbal Assault, Token Entry, and Gorilla Biscuits.

Ransick's broader love of music was clear throughout most of the zine's run, evidenced by opinionated reviews of melodic musicians like REM, the Go-Betweens, and Morrissey. By the time Ransick left the DC area in 1990 to attend college in Boston—where *Hands Up!*'s fifth issue was created—his increasingly varied musical enthusiasms became more prominent within the zine. "I moved to Boston and took a really big pivot in terms of my music taste," Ransick said. Interviews in issue five with the college rock stalwart Camper Van Beethoven and the new DC indie rock band Edsel are a testament to the change.

The slicker graphic design for issue five was another step in the zine's evolution, as well as an indicator of the increasing access that some young punks had to desktop publishing software. After getting his first computer and some graphic design training in 1990, Ransick became "obsessed with the Mac and with PageMaker [and] early-on Photoshop." Through a sixth and final issue of *Hands Up!*, as well as the numerous 7-inch single layouts he did for his own bands, Ransick's improving graphic design skills led to his first professional job. "Somebody gave me a job in an architecture firm in Boston to try to help the architects make the desktop computing leap because they were all doing stuff by hand," Ransick recalled. "And then it just kept going and the desktop publishing thing got me my first job at an ad agency [as] a graphic designer and [I've been] doing it ever since."

DC hardcore's growing popularity in the late 1980s—particularly with suburban teenagers—led to a small surge in zines. Aside from *No Scene*, *Axtion-Packed*, and *Hands Up!*, new titles from the DC area like *Truth or Justice*, *Bombshell* and *Take a Stand* helped establish hardcore as an undeniable part of the local punk ecosystem during this period. The visual identity of these fanzines was steeped in hardcore iconography, style, and slogans, many of which—aside from the black "X" markings that DC's earliest straight-edge punks drew on their hands in 1980–81, becoming an enduring symbol worldwide of a drug-free lifestyle—grew out of the New York City area hardcore scene during this time. While the early-1980s hardcore style often involved leather jackets, chains, and engineer boots, clothing signifiers shifted by decade's end toward athletic wear (e.g., hooded sweatshirts, baseball caps, and basketball shoes) and hardcore's visual aesthetics were markedly influenced by hip-hop graffiti culture.

Punk and graffiti had a history together—Black Flag's logo was notoriously spray painted on public surfaces throughout Southern California in the late 1970s and early 1980s[41]—but the infusion of hip-hop culture into punk iconography was new in the latter half of the 1980s. The sinuous, bubbly flow of hip-hop graffiti was apparent in hardcore band logos populating *Hands Up!* and other zines, fliers, and artwork from this period. Logos for *Truth or Justice* and *Take a Stand* would have fit in seamlessly on the city walls that served as a linear canvas for graffiti artists, rushing past as riders on the Red Line of DC's Metro subway system gazed out at the urban panorama.

Take a Stand and its short-lived predecessor, *Morbid Cactus*, were the work of a Takoma Park, Maryland, teenager named Dave Brown. Already intrigued by hardcore records he dredged up at local mainstream record chain Waxie Maxie's, Brown began shopping at a new Silver Spring, Maryland, indie record store, Vinyl Ink. While there in early 1989, he came across a copy of the

Take A Stand Fanzine
·ISSUE 1·NO.2 · DECEMBER 89 · $1.50·
In This Issue:
Token Entry
Release
Fall Brawl
Battered Citizens
Strength In Numbers
Interviews, Reviews, and Tons More

Figure 7.7 Dave Brown, circa 1989. *Take a Stand*, issue 1, number 2. Published by Dave Brown. Used by permission.

Manassas, Virginia, hardcore zine *Truth or Justice* and was electrified by the combination of punk, hardcore, and skateboarding coverage. "I had seen skateboarding zines, but I had never seen punk zines," Brown recalled of that moment. Duly inspired, he found a way to attend punk shows, most of which occurred in neighborhoods grappling with crime. "I didn't have anybody to go to shows with [and] my mom was not gonna let me go to the worst parts of DC—that I wouldn't be able to afford to live in now [in 2022]—by myself in my early teens," Brown later said. "So, I had to basically trick my friends into getting into punk rock."[42]

Skateboarding and American punk had been linked since the late 1970s.[43] Hardcore's explosion in the early 1980s furthered the bond, seen in photographer Glen E. Friedman's images of Minor Threat mingling with skateboard pioneer Rodney Mullen. "By the time Minor Threat was playing in the early 1980s, punk and skateboarding had really begun to knit together and the radicalness of both worlds combined to make something unpredictable and explosive," Ian MacKaye observed:

> *The fact that hardcore punk bands were so off of the cultural map in the United States meant that it was often left to the kids to set up the shows in unorthodox spaces. This created situations that existed outside of the law. These are circumstances very familiar to any person who, in the dead of winter, has dug under or jumped over a fence to skate an empty pool. It was in these moments that the absence of authority figures (or any authority, for that matter) allowed for innovation and creativity to be the guides.*[44]

Brown regularly photographed skateboarders he came across at clandestine meeting points for skating around the

DC area. This soon expanded to shooting bands he saw at the Safari Club and elsewhere. Like punk zines around the United States, DC titles like *Aggro Pig*, *Zero Gravity*, and *Truth or Justice* mixed photographs of their friends skateboarding with punk coverage.[45] Brown added to this, creating a zine incorporating his love of the two rebellious forms. "I want to start showing my friends what I'm seeing and then I'll trick them into going to shows, too," Brown remembered of his thought process at the time.

The new zine found its name stochastically, with Brown asking two friends to blurt out a random word, which he then combined into *Morbid Cactus*. Brown typed, laid out, and—with an unknowing assist from his mother's employer—photocopied thirty copies of the zine, then numbering ("I already understood [to] make things seem rare"), and distributing them almost entirely through Vinyl Ink, where he soon became a longtime employee. Much like working at the record store, publishing a fanzine opened up Brown's social world, with showgoers approaching him to remark they had seen themselves in photos within *Morbid Cactus*. "I ended up becoming friends with so many people because of that one issue that there were only thirty copies of," he said.

When it came time for a second issue, Brown renamed his zine *Take a Stand*, a slogan more aligned with the righteousness of contemporary straight-edge hardcore. Brown published two issues, which were bold, spare platforms for his photography and interviews with hardcore bands like DC's Strength in Numbers and New York's Gorilla Biscuits. Brown's deep knowledge of the hardcore scene gives his interviews an elastic, unpretentious quality. Default interview questions about musical influences or how bands had formed are in the mix, but they transcend pablum when paired with Brown's informed conversational style and his evident love of hardcore punk and its power to connect.

The Straight Line and *Sweet Portable You*

Northern Virginia cultivated strains of punk and indie rock in the late 1980s that, while significantly different musically, shared commonalities with the new DC hardcore in their distinctness from the Dischord bands. DSI Records had its own unique hallmarks, but a label from Arlington, Virginia—Teen-Beat Records—was a thoroughly uncommon entity of its own. Led by Mark Robinson of the band Unrest, Teen-Beat's 1980s output mostly centered on bands and projects he or his bandmates were involved in.[46] Those early recordings generally had a low-fi, humorous, and experimental bent recalling the "B-Town" scene in Bethesda that offered irreverent alternatives during DC hardcore's first wave.

Robinson also published a fanzine intermittently from 1983 to 1989 called *The Straight Line*. The zine's title was derived from a 1982 exhibition on the Dutch art movement De Stijl called "Visions of Utopia" that Robinson attended at DC's Hirshhorn Museum and Sculpture Garden. The teenager was awed by the bold primary colors and geometric forms. "And the De Stijl movement is named after . . . a periodical called *De Stijl*, which means 'the style,'" Robinson said. "And the original name of that periodical was *The Straight Line*."[47]

Robinson was equally inspired by the punk fanzine *Maximum Rocknroll*. "I never missed an issue of that," he recalled. "That was even bigger than *Time* and *Newsweek*." Appropriating the title of his zine from the De Stijl movement and the spirit from punk zines, Robinson released the first issue in 1983, with a second appearing later in 1985. The first two issues were relatively basic affairs, although hints of Robinson's burgeoning visual aesthetic crop up by the second issue, and his anarchic sense of humor romps throughout.

By issue three of *The Straight Line*, Unrest's profile rose in the American indie rock scene and Teen-Beat's demands on Robinson's time had increased, as well. After a long gap, he churned out one more issue in early 1989 before the zine went defunct. In one of the more amusing interviews ever printed in a DC punk fanzine, Robinson (under the pseudonym of "jk. Vandelly"—"Vandelly was the name of our senior year government teacher," he later explained) interrogates Calvin Johnson of Beat Happening and K Records. When laying out the interview, Robinson replaced the questions he actually asked Johnson with unrelated queries[48]

Figure 7.8 *The Straight Line*, issue 3, 1989. Published by Mark Robinson. Used by permission.

leading to comic absurdity, perfectly conveying the humor at the heart of both Teen-Beat and K Records:

> The Straight Line*: Where were you 10/31/83?*
>
> *Calvin Johnson: We've been playing together for five years.*
>
> The Straight Line*: Do you sleep with your clothes on?*
>
> *Calvin Johnson: Heather moved to Seattle, so Bret and I would play a lot in the practice room of some friends of ours.*

"The whole thing with the fanzine and the record label was [that] we are just entertaining ourselves," Robinson said through bursts of laughter. "We are not trying to do anything else. That's all [laugh] we're trying to accomplish. [laugh] It's all one big inside joke, and if someone else wants to read it or listen to it, then that's fine."

No fanzine in the DC scene took absurd humor and a Dadaist approach to fandom and music criticism further than Patrick Foster's *Sweet Portable You*. From its first issue in 1989 through more than one hundred issues leading up to its finale in spring 2000, *Sweet Portable You* reinvigorated music criticism through its fantastical, often-bizarre editorial tone. While many of the zine's reviews hewed more toward traditional assessments and observations of concert performance or the way a record sounded, other reviews are abstract to the point of impenetrability, critiquing music journalism itself as much as it did the music it covered. Like a museum patron gazing quizzically at the Theo van Doesburg artworks that fired Robinson's imagination at the Hirshhorn, Foster's zine often prodded readers to project their own meanings onto the writing.

In 1989, Foster was a Sam Goody record store employee who had recently left college. "I found out academics and the self-discipline it required being away from home wasn't exactly for me, so I came back home and was kind of at a loose end," Foster said.[49] Uninspired by school and chilled by the career path his older coworkers had taken, Foster searched for purpose during this "rudderless" time. "I didn't necessarily want to go back to school, because I didn't really have any particular passion for a subject or anything I really wanted to study," he recalled. "But what I did like to do was write."

An admirer of two opinionated, idiosyncratic zines from Massachusetts—*Forced Exposure* and *Conflict*—Foster decided to create his own. "I had seen some [zines], but out in the suburbs of Northern Virginia, it was just more about making your own kind of expression, and that's really kind of why I started to do it," Foster said. "I wanted to give myself something to do, some direction that I enjoyed." In 1989, Foster published more than twenty issues of *Sweet Portable You*, often working at a weekly clip. Issues were usually one or two legal-sized sheets of papers printed on both sides, though some issues slightly expanded beyond that. A misheard Fleetwood Mac lyric was one inspiration for the zine's name, but the ephemeral nature of zines was even more at the title's core. "The fact that it was portable and disposable, . . . I really believed that's what it should be," Foster said of his zine:

> *I loved being at a show, picking something up and reading it, and then kind of being done with it*

before like the next band would come on. . . . I didn't necessarily ever think it would be preserved. A lot of the discussions I would have with my friends, these passionate discussions—the next day, you might have changed your mind, or the next week, you might have changed your mind about your opinion, because you learned something else, and I kind of wanted it to reflect that.

Foster brought several friends in—A. J. Dubuc, Ford M, and Will Croxton were contributors during this period—to review concerts and recordings. Issue fifteen from July 19, 1989 offers five different reviews of Fugazi's *Margin Walker* EP on Dischord. Foster's page-length review gestures toward traditional critical analysis and Croxton's dabbles in the profane irreverence associated with *Forced Exposure*, but the remaining reviews seemingly ignore the details of the music completely, churning like fever dreams. Easy as it is to view *Sweet Portable You*'s abstract qualities as a sort of cynicism via opacity—in step with the smug pessimism often threaded through Generation X culture in the late 1980s and early 1990s—the zine's playfulness and enthusiasm for music actually clarifies its intent. "Within our little circle of friends, there was nothing more exciting than going to a show or getting a new record and then discussing it in that little intellectual circle that fueled *Sweet Portable You*," Foster recalled. "So, in some ways, it was like our official mouthpiece for what we were into and who we thought was cool."

VOLUME ONE NUMBER TEN MAY 27, 1989 GRATIS.BRÖ.

The Land of Significant Gestures and Events

I think this is naked. I think this is going to be about Happy Go Licky. Potted head.

$$$$$$$$$$$$$$$

The first time I saw Happy Go Licky perform, a Sunday, I had gone with Dave and Steve to a matinee Naked Raygun gig at the now-defunct Hung Jury Pub. Reptile House and one other band were on the bill as well, but I mostly recall the Raygun set being pretty stale, lots of 1981-

ish behaving doing absolutely nada to boost the ambiance. I remember eating a cheesburger there, and listening to a guy in a Jim Carrol Band t-shirt talking to a girl. I made stuff up about them. I saw them leave together. I remember seeing a girl I hadn't run into in about two years. She had gotten some breasts. I didnt talk to her, but I drew a picture of her a few days later that excited me in the sexual way tremendously.

The important thing going on that day was Sonic Youth's doing the 930. I can recall going in and finding the atmosphere to be highly unusual. That is to say I felt comfortable. Real-dark seeming and room to elbow. Happy Go strutted up and discoed right along with the 'tween sets tuneage, We're all friends here, right? Guy was dressed down, brown windbreaker all the way up. Edward was shirtless and had "Nasty Bob" emblazoned across his chest in what looked like charcol. I couldn't really figure out what they were doing for the first few tunes (fancy that— I've got SCARECROW on the turnatble as I'm writing this). Was something wrong with the PA? Were the guitars on? Was the bass supposed to sound like a blowtorch? They exit to a lot of yelling. Ian had to pick up a mike and inform the assembled that there would be no encore. And that even Sonic Youth, I say Sonic Youth was gonna have a hard time topping <u>that</u>.

$$$$$$$$$$$$$$$

Famous money. All spent in famous places. Suggesting the rhythm by playing everything except it.

$$$$$$$$$$$$$$$

"Ansol" was/is a burst of unprecedented newness. Jenkins said it was coiled tension. At one point Guy sounds like Lydia Lunch, of all people. The guitar sounds like parts of an airplane rubbing into each other after a hole was ripped in the side and ten or so folks were sucked out. Maybe it is over Hawaii or somewhere.

$$$$$$$$$$$$$$$

I think there is a little truth in the generally held idea among folk who saw HGL in the flesh that they record they put out is okay, but nothing in comparison to what they were if you were in the same room with them. I think it's closer to the truth to say that the disk is great, but with footnotes. It unravels itself to this day, a long time after it came out. It sounds better very loud (given), it's naked, and it has a pretty awful song ("Boca Raton") on it. The important thing, the thing that makes it great, is the sheer force of possibility that exsists somewhere within it. Not only in what it suggests that they could have done in the studio (ever heard ALL THROUGH A LIFE?) but what you or I could imagine going on somewhere down the line. The what-if inside makes it both awful depressing and stunning.

$$$$$$$$$$$$$$$

Sometimes I see Guy with a bag of records. I sometimes wonder where he bought them, but I always wonder what they are.

$$$$$$$$$$$$$$$

It may be pointless to go on praising dead musics, but discharge of feelings, problems, is a very healthly activity. Makes things smaller. Happy Go Licky's music was a discharge, a throttle, an inspiration, a black hole. And real hard to write about. [illegible] singing about God. –Patrick Foste

INSIDE: BUCKETS-O-LIBEL

SWEET PORTABLE YOU

REVERSE MODE

NUMBER EIGHTEEN AUGUST THIRTY NINETEEN 89 HEY! HOLD ON...

The Contents, or Masking the Relevant Beast

He was now beyond bare-bodied cataclysms, beyond the possibility of incorporating bright objects, wax fruit, glassy slivers, into his scheme, beyond the seeing what there was to be seen. It was hard to be visible in a tepid flood because the enigma saw nothing but the contents, the contents being of the same realm, the crusted trinkets of the dead, a few stray beads, a tiny grey-fringed mirror which reflected the lower regions, the ones swelling with color, arriving at a kind of sneer from the dislocation. All this seemed superfluous now: he had two rough stones for eyes, a small rain having communed over ages.

The foreshadowing of ruins had been the smell of wavering soldiers with immaculate bouquets, the metamorphosis perfuming the confines. Earlier, dragging a flushed sky across the floor, he dragged himself along with it. He chronicled this thoughtfully, but his pages had a fear.

"Let this meek rain slicken my walls," he confided, "so the fear is like my clocks, the explanation inundating like my only dream lurking." He did not understand the difference. A cloud was different.

Later, he was atop with a resilient fish, making alterations on the weather vane. The windows feasted like intercourse: footsteps in the corridor. However, assessed as overly meticulous, the windows were carted away towards the supreme gala. No one was invited and again: footsteps in the corridor.

"If the saliva of my clocks exsisted in my dry palms, then how can we prolong this relationship? I'm suggesting the difference between needles and nails, not swords." Tumultuous was the afternoon. His slow ink scrutinized to bolster memoirs as in the time of the rigorous quiet.

The incipient war was banal talk. It urged no dreams to slacken from the fingertip air. Nor astonish. He buried the contents under a mound and a city heaved forth there. Its bony structures were impressed. He smoothed his bedspread for the last time, skirted through concrete spaces to where steam ascends from the long grates of the streets, but there were no beasts pacing underneath. A breath was a shape.

"Quiet," he mouthed, "the chamber of my hands."

— Stephen Healey

"Rectal Thermometers Please"

Pussy Galore/Honeymoon Killers/Unsane
cbgb's, new york city, 8-6-89

There once was a band, they lived in DC, and they made music that sounded like live chainsaws being dropped down a giant metal chasm— a chaotic, sputtering, grueling, clanking buisness. They thought of themselves as truly great avant-garde geniusses of some sort, and in 1985 they were considered 'radical' and 'hip.' Soon enough, the band said to themselves, 'Obviously, we're much too cool to stay in this parochial village called "da District." We've got to be in a real city where there are real art ists who don't spend so much time worrying about society and politics and all that naiive tripe.' So, they packed their chainsaws in the trunk of their Buick, and they rambled off for the Big Apple.

Now something really strange started to happen. It must have been the intensity of all those great artists all around them, because they actually started to make some good fucking albums. Bob Bert could be heard bragging about it in a pizza parlour to some Japanese chick he was trying to scam: 'Our new EP blows away Sonic Youth's, you know.' She coyly nods. 'You saw us in Tokyo, right? We thrashed Sonic Youth's show didn't we?' More nods, more self-gratification, etc... (yes, I really heard this. I almost threw up on him.)

So, off to CBGB's on a Saturday night, headline gig goes the Pussys, sans Julia Cafritz. (How can a band reap chicks with a girl in it?) Two opening acts play: Unsane, a trio of Big Black-influnced power-thrashing like you were watching it in the garage, the door just ripped open, and 'pow' they were playing CBGBs. And the HOneymoon Killers were pretty good and nasty (yeah, like herion, dude)...now, PUSSY GALORE! Huh? Where are they? It sounds great, like "Dial M" on fire, man. I fuck, I can't see 'em, straining my eyes. Oh Shit! Wrong sensory mode. My nose is overcome by the stench of overblown egos sprouting forth spoodge and shit. I'm forced to leave.

—Eric Forst

Figure 7.9 *Sweet Portable You*, issues 10 and 18, 1989. Published by Patrick Foster. Used by permission.

Interrobang?!

It had been six years since Sharon Cheslow and Colin Sears' fanzine, *If This Goes On*, published its final issue, but both remained busy. Sears went on to drum for Dag Nasty, a band emerging from the Revolution Summer period that grew into one of DC's most consequential bands. Cheslow, meanwhile, collaborated with the photographers Cynthia Connolly and Leslie Clague on *Banned in DC: Photos and Anecdotes from the DC Punk Underground ('79–'85)*, among the first photo books on American punk and the first comprehensive book on DC punk.[50] Its publication in late 1988 was a watershed moment for the scene, putting the explosion of the hardcore and Revolution Summer eras into context, vividly letting participants bask in the community they had created together. The author and zine editor Osa Atoe acknowledged *Banned in DC* for its inclusion of so many of the women and people of color active in that period of the scene, writing appreciatively in 2015 that it told "the story of a truly unique and diverse scene that stood apart, by leaps and bounds, from any other punk or hardcore scene in the country."[51]

By the end of 1989, Cheslow returned to making fanzines with *Interrobang?!*'s debut issue, opening with an editorial challenging the scene to improve. "It's occurred to me as we approach 1990, we need to reinject ourselves with a shot of vigor," Cheslow wrote:

> *There's plenty of people doing stuff here in DC, but it always seems to be the same bunch of people I've known for the past million years. We need fresh blood, we need more involvement, we need thinking individuals, we need new ideas. I know you're out there. So, come out of your shells and contribute in some way to this community, this "scene." If we want something to change, we've got to make it happen ourselves.*[52]

Cheslow called out *Washington City Paper* in her review of a Jawbox concert for its sexist treatment of bassist Kim Coletta. Deborah Lewis's article on Jawbox—a new arrival to the DC scene led by the former Government Issue bassist, now-guitarist/vocalist J. Robbins—in the December 8 issue of *City Paper* referred to the band members as "Robbins, his sweetie/band bassist Kim Coletta, and drummer Adam Wade." Robbins and Coletta were dating at that stage of the band but, as Cheslow rightly asked, "What the hell? She's the fucking bass player. Whether or not she's involved with [J.] has nothing to do with the band. Would anyone ever refer to [J.] as Kim's sweetie? I doubt it."[53] The casual sexism embedded in the *City Paper* article illustrated that the hurdles Cheslow and her peers faced during Chalk Circle's tenure in the early 1980s endured.

Figure 7.10 *Interrobang?!*, issue 1, 1989. Published by Sharon Cheslow. Used by permission.

Much as *No Scene* recast live reviews, Cheslow also reimagined how to convey what happened at a concert. There are a few traditional concert reviews in *Interrobang?!*, but an overview of a Holy Rollers and Fidelity Jones concert on December 1 at BBQ Iguana served as a forum for audience members to provide the analysis. Cheslow asked attendees for their thoughts and, through their responses—ranging from praise to criticism, rapture to ennui—you can feel the warmth and buzz of the packed room.

Nomadic Underground

Among the DC scene's strengths was drawing in the "new blood" Cheslow called for, allowing for the regeneration necessary to maintain a long-term community. Throughout the 1980s, DC proved itself to be a vital forum for creative and, increasingly, political expression. While most DC punks during this period came from DC and its suburbs, a growing number came from outside the immediate area. Brad Sigal, a teenager from Atlanta, had already published six issues of his fanzine *Nomadic Underground* there before relocating to DC for its final two issues in 1988–89. Sigal ostensibly made the move to attend George Washington University but he "purposely decided that I wanted to go to DC more than anywhere else because of the punk scene."[54] The combination of political activism Positive Force engaged in and the ferocious creativity of DC musicians were "a holy grail" for Sigal.[55]

Issues seven and eight of *Nomadic Underground* saw Sigal diving into the scene, interviewing bands like Shudder to Think, Darkness at Noon, and Fugazi. The answers given in the Fugazi interview, however, challenged Sigal's expectations, as he found the band "elusive" when he sought more concrete definitions of song meanings or band intentions. "I was, at that point in my life, trying to go towards more definition of my politics and a course of action and being more defined in those things," he said:

> *And it felt like they were kind of pulling in the opposite direction. Going from, you know, especially Ian earlier on had been very explicit and straightforward, hitting you over the head with what he thought. And [he] was moving away from that towards more interpretable meanings for things. I really was super thankful they did an interview and I loved doing that.*[56]

Nomadic Underground folded after the eighth issue in winter 1989, but Sigal remained involved with the scene

Figure 7.11 *Nomadic Underground*, issues 7 and 8, 1988–89. Published by Brad Sigal. Used by permission.

through the early 1990s via his participation in Positive Force DC and, later, the short-lived Beehive collective.[57] As scholar and fanzine editor Sara Marcus described him, Sigal "had marched against the Gulf War, organized in support of campus cafeteria workers at George Washington University, and traveled to El Salvador to meet with the Marxist guerillas of the FMLN. All the while, he delved into political theory and revolutionary history, trying to divine the best way to transform the world."[58]

Sigal craved "radical change" through his activism, and he soon questioned whether punk was the best framework to work in. "The reality is it's not gonna be just people who listen to one style of music who are needed to make that change," he said:

> *Just organizing within the punk scene felt really limiting to me, . . . especially in a city like DC, in terms of racially. It's like a predominantly white [punk] scene in the middle of a Black city. If I want to make political change, how does it make sense to stay? Keep my activism just within this scene of people who aren't reflective of the broader city? If you wanna change the city, you know, this isn't gonna cut it. Not that it's bad, it's just not enough. And so, yeah, I kind of felt pulled away from the punk scene, in general, and punk activism, specifically.*[59]

Despite this shift, the writing and design skills Sigal learned during his time publishing *Nomadic Underground* persisted through the years ahead: "And that actually has been a thread of something that I've done pretty consistently ever since then. Pretty much every political project I've been involved with I've either written for publications or started my own publications."

Greed and *WDC Period*

The two publications at the front of DC punk's fanzine scene during the late 1980s were *WDC Period* and *Greed*. Evolving quickly during this period, the zines' design and circulation became increasingly professional. *WDC Period* switched to a newsprint tabloid format for its fourteenth issue in spring 1986, but was laid out in a way, both for that issue and its follow-up in the fall of 1986, to be folded in half for easier retail sale. "I was always intrigued by early issues of the *Rolling Stone* magazine which were on newsprint and folded into a standard magazine size, so the next couple of issues were done like this," *WDC Period*'s editor, Gordon Ornelas, explained.[60] That approach changed with issue 16, which employed a clean, spare, full-size tabloid design and a striking, abstract cover by the designer Daryl Wakeley that was miles away from the crude bricolage of *WDC Period*'s earliest issues.

Issue sixteen's slicker appearance presaged a larger step in *WDC's Period*'s evolution during this time. Dennis Sobin, whom the *Washington City Paper* referred to as a "smut king,"[61] published an adult newspaper in the 1980s called *The Free Spirit* that could be purchased from newspaper boxes on the street. Sobin learned of *WDC Period* and offered to fund Ornelas's zine if the back cover featured an advertisement for one of Sobin's ventures, along with a few other requirements—issues would be monthly, free, and every cover would include at least one spot color.

Ornelas agreed and embarked on volume two of *WDC Period*, generating thirteen issues from June 1987 to July 1988. As promised, the back cover of *WDC Period* featured advertisements including sex work recruitment, "976" phone numbers providing sexual titillation to callers for a fee, and "assertiveness training" at a place called the King Kastle Dungeon ("reservations are a must"). The zine's page count dropped dramatically by more than half for volume two, although the larger, cleaner layouts were easier to read, if a bit sterile.

Ornelas's article—"Is Meese a Pig?"—in the March 1988 issue, imparts the frisson that spread throughout the District when posters emblazoned with the words "Meese Is A Pig" mysteriously appeared around town in late 1987 and early 1988. The poster assailed Edwin Meese, US attorney general in President Ronald Reagan's administration, noting that Meese was under investigation by special prosecutors related to two scandals, Wedtech and Iran-Contra. "Meese's personal conduct and muddled testimony before Congress suggest that he is either a chronic liar or a confused man with a sloppy sense of ethics," the small print at

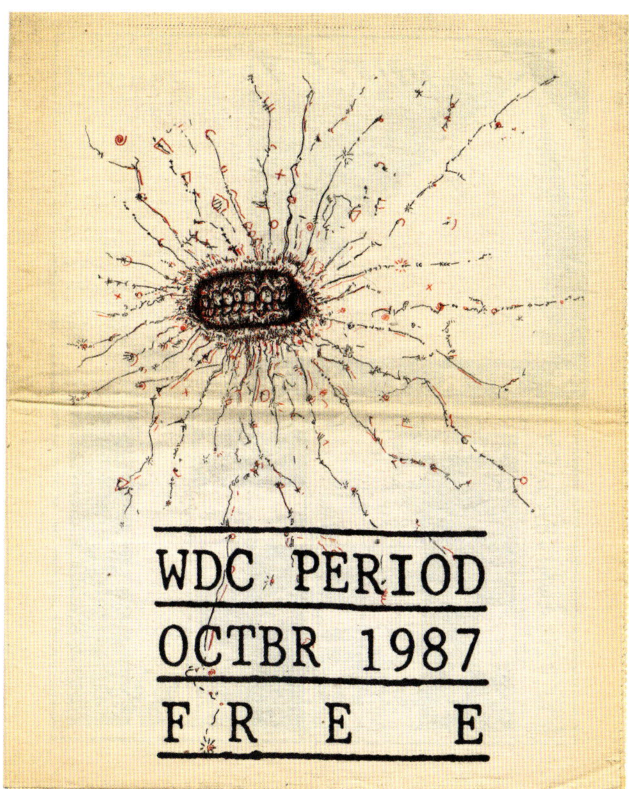

Figure 7.12 *WDC Period*, volume 1, issue 16; and volume 2, issue 4, 1987, cover art by Daryl Wakeley (16) and Scott Larson (4). Published by Gordon Ornelas. Used by permission.

the bottom of the poster read. The poster urged Americans to contact their representatives and "make this odious little weasel resign right now."[62]

"As anyone who lives near DC knows already, whether or not Meese is a pig isn't *that* big of a mystery," Ornelas wrote. "The question is: Where the heck did all those 'Meese is a Pig' posters come from?" The answer was Dischord Records cofounder Jeff Nelson. "I was very, very, angry at the Reagan-Bush administration for all sorts of things," Nelson explained. "I was frustrated with feeling powerless to stop these tyrants and the only way I could think of to get my message out was to print up a big poster."[63] The campaign eventually gained national media attention, embarrassing Reagan's administration and, arguably, playing a role in the climate leading to Meese's resignation in August 1988. The memorable campaign—an original print resides in the Smithsonian National Museum of American History—was a tangible example of DC punks moving protest off the lyric sheet and onto the street.

As for *WDC Period*, the end was near. "Once it began not being fun for me and the core staff, I ended the relationship with Sobin and went back to the sporadic tabloid format with a cover price," Ornelas recalled. *WDC Period* published three more issues before Ornelas, overworked after the departure of coeditor Tim Wincinski and fatigued with the increasingly professional indie music business, shuttered the long-running zine at the decade's close. "It was actually quite liberating because I liked not having any other responsibilities other than having fun, hanging out with my friends, traveling for no particular reason," recalled Ornelas, who subsequently left DC for Seattle in 1992. "*WDC Period* was an important part of my life, not only because I met a lot of people who are still my friends but because it also helped me discover an artistic outlet that I enjoy and feel like I'm good at."

Kurt Sayenga's *Greed* also expanded during this period, following up on the debut issue from 1986. *Greed*'s cover images morphed from the skillful, nightmarish black-and-white illustrations contributed by DC artist and musician Peter Hayes for issues one through three to full color explosions by notable illustrators Charles Burns, the Hernandez Brothers, and Bob Burden for the final three issues. The overlap of comics and punk culture never looked better in a DC zine than it did in the cleanly laid-out pages of *Greed*.

Early issues of *Greed* saw Sayenga use the design equipment at his day job to give the layout a professional look, but his acquisition of a personal computer halfway through the zine's run allowed him a new level of freedom. Longtime scene participant and critic Mark Jenkins noted in his 1988 *Washington City Paper* article on *Greed* that "in some ways, the desktop publishing software has cheapened the magazine's expertly designed look" but, for Sayenga, access to Apple Macintosh design software like Aldus PageMaker[64] brought "some power of communication to the people."[65]

Greed's fifth issue, published in August 1988, included an interview with Dag Nasty, early in their attempts at leaving DC's scene in their rearview mirror. The quartet, led by former Minor Threat bassist/guitarist Brian Baker, adroitly merged pop and hardcore on a pair of albums for Dischord—1986's *Can I Say* and 1987's *Wig Out at Denkos*. The band's drummer, Colin Sears, departed in 1987, just before the group moved to Los Angeles. Dag Nasty seemingly lost the plot with the move west, releasing the substandard, slickly produced *All Ages Show* EP in 1987 and *Field Day* LP in 1988 on Giant Records.[66]

Yet Sayenga dismissed Dag Nasty's Dischord output in the interview's introduction as a "successful attempt to sell hardcore hamburger to the steak-craving masses," and he referred to the band's DC iteration as "the one that sucked." Vocalist Peter Cortner, who joined the band before *Wig Out at Denkos*, is more circumspect in his assessment of *Field*

Figure 7.13 Two versions of the poster designed by the musician Jeff Nelson criticizing then–US attorney general Edwin Meese, 1988. From the collection of Jeff Nelson, used by permission.

Figure 7.14 Kurt Sayenga, circa 1987. Photo by Ann Chervinsky. *Greed*, issue 2, spring 1987. Published by Kurt Sayenga. Used by permission.

Day, describing it as "a complete mystery to us. It was not really what we expected, but we are happy with it." Dag Nasty had transformed into a very different band, and the interview finds Cortner processing fan expectations and creative freedom. Intriguingly, he asserts that *Field Day* is Dag Nasty's most genuine record. "As far as the 'meaning' and 'truth' that most of the punk scene gets out of it, I think that's really funny, because if ever there was a case of people trying to cater to the tastes of a certain audience in order to get their record sold, that's it," Cortner said of *Can I Say*. "You have your ex–Minor Threat guy, you have your ex-DYS, you have your hardcore tunes, [and] you have vague lyrics that basically point to being angry with society and parents."[67]

A sixth and final issue of *Greed* appeared in January 1989, but the zine's success ultimately led to its demise. "It was getting away from what I set out to do," Sayenga said. "Essentially, it got too big too fast, which is a nice problem to have in that world. But at the same time, there's certain trade-offs that come when, all of a sudden, in order to pay for the color covers and stuff like that, I had to sell advertising." As bigger record labels paid for more advertising, they urged Sayenga to cover their bands. "Most of the time I said 'no,'" he recalled with a laugh. "But then, sometimes, it would be like, 'Oh, OK. Full-page ad? *Color* full-page ad?' I'd say, 'Hmmm.'"[68]

Sayenga planned a seventh issue centered completely on Fugazi but, despite having started production, shelved it and ended *Greed*.[69] "I just felt like, well, they're my friends, and I don't want to be perceived as or feel like I'm making money off of them or something," he said. "Just the fact that I felt conflicted by it was enough, basically. Because then I said 'OK, wait a minute, why am I doing this?'" Soured on the magazine business, Sayenga delved into graphic design for Dischord Records, handling Fugazi's releases through 1991's *Steady Diet of Nothing*. Sayenga eventually relocated

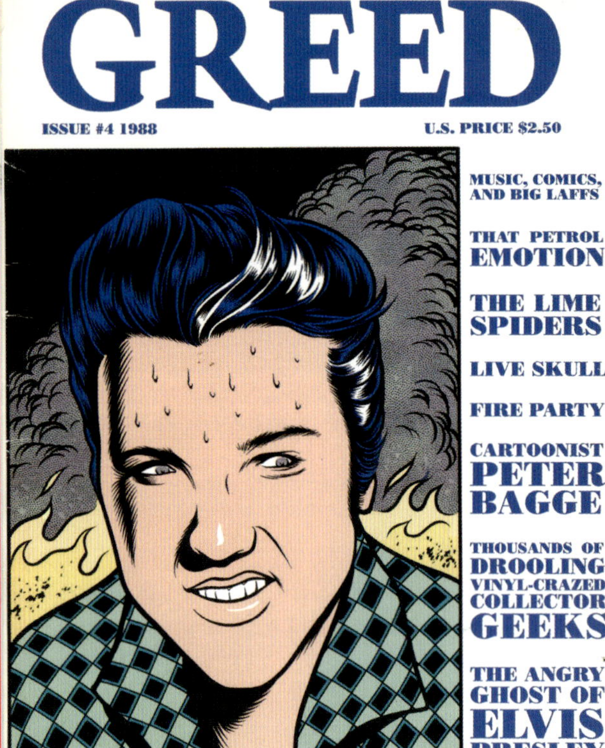

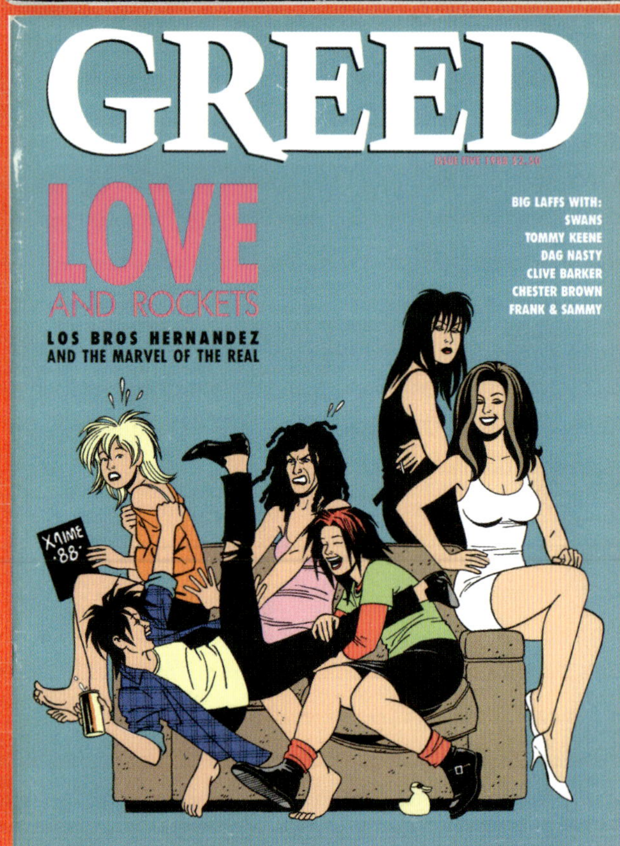

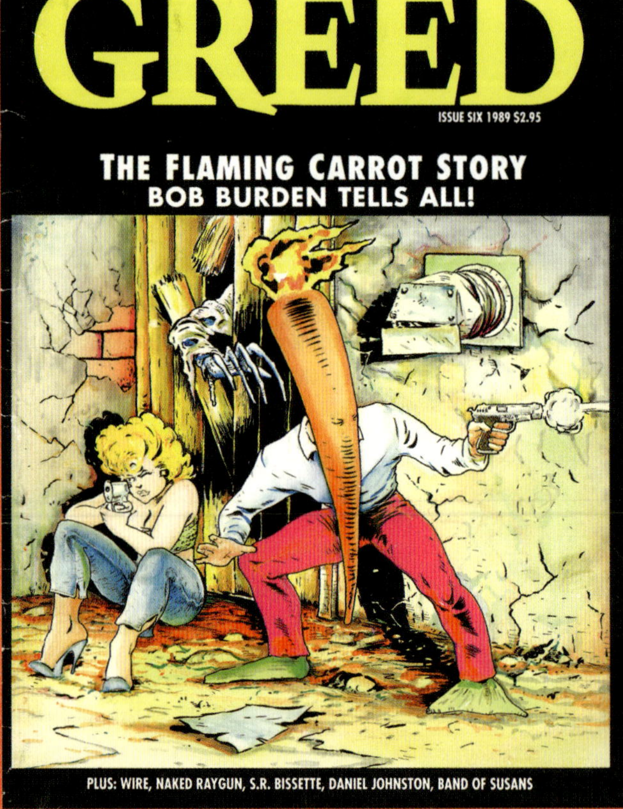

Figure 7.15 *Greed*, issues 3 through 6, 1987–88. Published by Kurt Sayenga. Used by permission.

to Los Angeles and forged a successful career as a documentary producer and director for television networks like Discovery, National Geographic, and Shudder. "I think the core of what I do still ties back to my belief in the essential principles of the punk rock movement and manifesto, at least as I interpreted it," he said.

Moving into a New Decade

The 1980s were a defining decade for DC's punk scene. Hardcore's rise and resurgence, straight edge, Revolution Summer, emo, and punk activism all occurred during this period. Like the local publications that came before, DC punk fanzines in the late 1980s reliably gave voice to people furthering the scene, urging scene participants to make their community and planet a better place. "The world is not our facility," Ian MacKaye sang on "Burning Too," on Fugazi's 1989 EP, *Margin Walker*. "We have a responsibility to use our abilities to keep this place alive." That drive to create something better is at punk's core, evincing an optimism belying the nihilist tropes routinely trotted out when addressing punk.

As the 1990s beckoned, that inherent bullishness was on display when *Interrobang?!* interviewed the Nation of Ulysses. "I hate to define a decade as being anything, because I know the 1980s will go down as this sordid decade, and I don't believe it was altogether," the vocalist Ian Svenonius declared. "I've seen the gems of goodness that existed. I don't like how history has a glaze over things. The 1990s, man, righteousness will prevail."[70]

Notes

1. Todd Ransick, interview with the author, October 31, 2022.
2. Harry Jaffe and Tom Sherwood, *Dream City: Race, Power, and the Decline of Washington, DC* (New York: Simon & Schuster, 1994), 223.
3. Derek S. Hyra, *Race, Class, and Politics in the Cappuccino City* (Chicago: University of Chicago Press, 2017), 6–7.
4. Erik Grotz, interview with the author, February 5, 2021.
5. Erik Grotz, "Fugazi: I Don't Like What I See . . . ," *Action Time*, issue 6, November 1988, 17–20.
6. "Fugazi Live Series: A to Z," no date, www.dischord.com/fugazi_live_series.
7. Grotz, "Fugazi."
8. Grotz, interview.
9. Erik Grotz, "Scream," *Action Time*, issue 4, Fall 1987, 6–7.
10. Grotz, interview.
11. Aside from a few exceptions where Dischord collaborated with another record label to co-release a recording of a band from outside DC—Boston's SS Decontrol or Maumee, Ohio's Necros are early examples—Baltimore band Lungfish was the only group from outside the immediate DC area to routinely issue full-length, non-split-label records on Dischord. Lungfish's first album, 1990's *Necklace of Heads*, was a co-release with Simple Machines, but subsequent albums issued from the early 1990s to the early 2010s were full-label releases. Void, from the distant suburb of Columbia, Maryland, was on the fringes of being an exception—Columbia was slightly closer to Baltimore than it was to downtown DC—but was undeniably a key part of the early 1980s DC hardcore scene.
12. Grotz, interview.
13. "A conversation with Guy Picciotto of Fugazi," *Scratch*, issue 2, 1989, 5–6.
14. Grotz, interview.
15. Grotz, interview.
16. Chris Henderson, interview with author, November 10, 2022. Other quotes from Henderson are also from this interview.
17. Scott Crawford from *Metrozine*'s short-lived band.
18. Indian Summer was the future Chisel drummer John Dugan's first band of note.
19. Henderson, interview.
20. Shawna Kenney and Rich Dolinger, *Live at the Safari Club: A History of harDCore Punk in the Nation's Capital, 1988–1998* (Los Angeles: Rare Bird Books, 2017).
21. Shawna Kenney, interview with the author, June 14, 2017.
22. Kenney.
23. Kenney.
24. Kenney.
25. Kenney.
26. Kenney and Dolinger, *Live at the Safari Club*, 27–28.
27. Kenney, interview.
28. Kenney.
29. Tim Owen, email to the author, October 31, 2022.
30. Owen.
31. Owen.
32. Owen.
33. Owen.
34. Andy Greenwald, *Nothing Feels Good: Punk Rock, Teenagers, and Emo* (New York: St. Martin's Griffin, 2003), 120.
35. Ransick, interview.
36. Ransick.
37. Ransick.
38. Todd Ransick, "Swiz," *Hands Up!* issue 3, 1988, 10.
39. Todd Ransick, "Editorial," *Hands Up!* issue 3, 1988, 2.
40. Ransick, interview.
41. David A. Ensminger, *Visual Vitriol: The Street Art and Subcultures of the Punk and Hardcore Generation* (Jackson: University Press of Mississippi, 2011), 72.
42. Dave Brown, interview with the author, October 31, 2022. Other quotes from Brown in this chapter are also sourced from this interview.
43. Konstantin Butz, *Grinding California: Culture and Corporeality in American Skate Punk* (Bielefeld: transcript, 2012), 99–101.
44. Ian MacKaye, untitled essay, in *Glen E. Friedman: My Rules* (New York: Rizzoli, 2014), no page numbering.
45. *Aggro Pig* and *Zero Gravity* were copublished in the late 1980s by James Schneider, who later directed the DC punk documentary *Punk the Capital*.
46. Teen-Beat is still in business as of 2025.

47. Mark Robinson, interview with the author, December 27, 2018. Other quotes from Robinson in this chapter are also sourced from this interview.
48. Kurt Sayenga also employed this trick to humorous effect in the third issue of *Greed*, published in fall 1987. For the published transcript of his interview with the band Three, Sayenga substituted questions posed to Oliver North during congressional hearings in summer 1987 related to the Iran-Contra affair for the ones he actually asked the band.
49. Patrick Foster, interview with the author, July 18, 2018. Other quotes from Foster in this chapter are also sourced from this interview.
50. *Hardcore California* and *Loud 3D* were among *Banned in DC*'s American punk precursors.
51. Osa Atoe, "Cynthia Connolly: Photographing DC Punk's Salad Days," October 2015, https://antigravitymagazine.com/feature/cynthia-connolly-photographing-d-c-punks-salad-days/.
52. Sharon Cheslow, "Editorial," *Interrobang?!* issue 1, December 1989, 2.
53. Cheslow, 3.
54. Brad Sigal, interview with the author, January 20, 2021.
55. Sigal.
56. Sigal.
57. As Sigal detailed in "Demise of the Beehive Collective: Infoshops Ain't the Revolution," his 1995 article for the Love and Rage Revolutionary Anarchist Federation, the Beehive Collective began meeting in July 1993 and opened an infoshop at 925 U Street NW in October 1993. The group sold records, organized concerts, and—central to its mission—planned political and community activism. By April 1995, the Beehive was defunct, riven by internal tensions and disagreements on how to operate. It defined itself as "an all-volunteer collective promoting communication through books, records, 'zines, performance, meetings, and social/political networking. In our attempt to break the cycle of an historically classist, sexist, racist, heterosexist and authoritarian social system, we feel it is imperative to oppose capitalist oppression. It has denied us self-realization and free association. Beehive intends to bridge the ever-increasing gap between privilege and underdevelopment by providing access to space and information at low cost or free. We will: be organic, radical, wild, and revolutionary; creative and critical locally and internationally." As Sigal later wrote about that statement of purpose: "When you take away what we are abstractly for and against, that leaves only promoting communication and providing a space for other people to 'do their own thing.' While this is a good thing to do, it does not differ fundamentally from the mission of a public library, for example. And I would argue in the current context, at least in DC, it is not the most valuable use of our energies in building a revolutionary anti-authoritarian movement."
58. Sara Marcus, *Girls to the Front: The True Story of the Riot Grrrl Revolution* (New York: HarperPerennial, 2010), 298.
59. Sigal, interview.
60. Gordon Ornelas, email to the author, January 24, 2021. Other quotes from Ornelas in this chapter come from this source.
61. Will Sommer, "DC's Oldest Living Smut Kingpin Tells All," *Washington City Paper*, September 17, 2010, https://washingtoncitypaper.com/article/222804/dcs-oldest-living-smut-kingpin-dennis-sobin-tells-all/.
62. Jeff Nelson, "Meese Is a Pig," poster, 1987, National Museum of American History, https://americanhistory.si.edu/collections/search/object/nmah_1053365.
63. Fat Rich Warwick, "Jeff Nelson: Do It Yourself," in *Pump Me Up: DC Subculture of the 80s*, edited by Roger Gastman (Los Angeles: R. Rock Enterprises, 2013), 166–71.
64. PageMaker was later bought by the Adobe company and rebranded as Adobe Pagemaker.
65. Mark Jenkins, "Money, Power, *Greed*," *Washington City Paper*, May 27, 1988.
66. Giant Records was a New York independent label that also released late-era music from Marginal Man, Government Issue, and the Slickee Boys.
67. *Can I Say*–era vocalist Dave Smalley was previously with the Boston hardcore band DYS.
68. Kurt Sayenga, interview with the author, June 13, 2017. Remaining Sayenga quotes in this chapter are sourced from this, as well.
69. The Fugazi interviews were eventually published in 2024, when Sayenga relaunched *Greed* on Substack, an online newsletter platform.
70. Sharon Cheslow, "(The Nation of) Ulysses," *Interrobang?!* issue 1, 1989, 14.

8

This Is Not a Test, 1990–1992

DC PUNK CRESTED AGAIN in the early 1990s, akin to earlier peaks like hardcore's first wave or the creative and political renaissance of Revolution Summer. The local ecosystem of bands, fanzines, venues, record stores, and more gained momentum through the late 1980s, setting the stage for a period of dramatic expansion in the first half of the 1990s. This occurred against the backdrop of a new reality for underground culture, where punk bands and aesthetics became mainstream, threatening punk's contrarian soul as it simultaneously swelled its ranks.

Several factors enabled the exploding popularity of zines in the early 1990s: increasingly accessible home computers and desktop publishing software, more outlets for national distribution, affordable postage rates for mailing zines within the United States to connect with other fans,[1] and greater awareness of the zine medium through coverage in mainstream publications like *Sassy* magazine or the *Washington Post*. As the journalist and zine editor Jennifer Bleyer later wrote, new zines "sprouted up like resilient weeds inside the cracks of the mainstream media concrete."[2] Whereas zine creators once were limited to distributing their works by hand at shows or local record stores, national chains like Tower Records and Borders Books now had magazine buyers disseminating zines throughout their network of stores. For fanzine creators looking to reach a broader audience, this was a powerful tool.

The propagation of commercial copy shops throughout North America—particularly the ubiquitous 24-hour chain Kinko's—was another critical development in the growth of zines. "At its height of popularity between the late 1980s and mid-1990s," scholar Kate Eichhorn observed, "Kinko's outlets in urban center across North America were catch basins for writers, artists, anarchists, punks, insomniacs, graduate students, DIY bookmakers, zinesters, obsessive-compulsive hobbyists, scam artists, people living on the street, and people just living on the edge. Whether you were promoting a new band or publishing a pamphlet on DIY gynecology or making a fake ID for an underage friend, Kinko's was the place to be."[3]

The mainstreaming of punk culture following the punk-rooted Seattle band Nirvana's unexpected commercial success beginning in late 1991 was another key piece of the zine boom. Their 1989 debut album, *Bleach*, was released on Sub Pop, an indie label that started as a fanzine in the Pacific Northwest punk scene of the early 1980s. The label helped spawn grunge, a weighty branch of underground rock fusing punk with metal's sludgier elements. Grunge was improbably at the core of mainstream rock music in the first half of the 1990s, headlined begrudgingly by Nirvana and other Seattle groups like Pearl Jam, Soundgarden, and Alice in Chains.[4] "Grunge wasn't suburban metal, despite what Alice in Chains and Pearl Jam would have us believe," the music journalist Everett True wrote in 2011. "It was stripped-back primeval rock music, no artifice, just SWEAT and BEER and heads banging in bass speakers."[5]

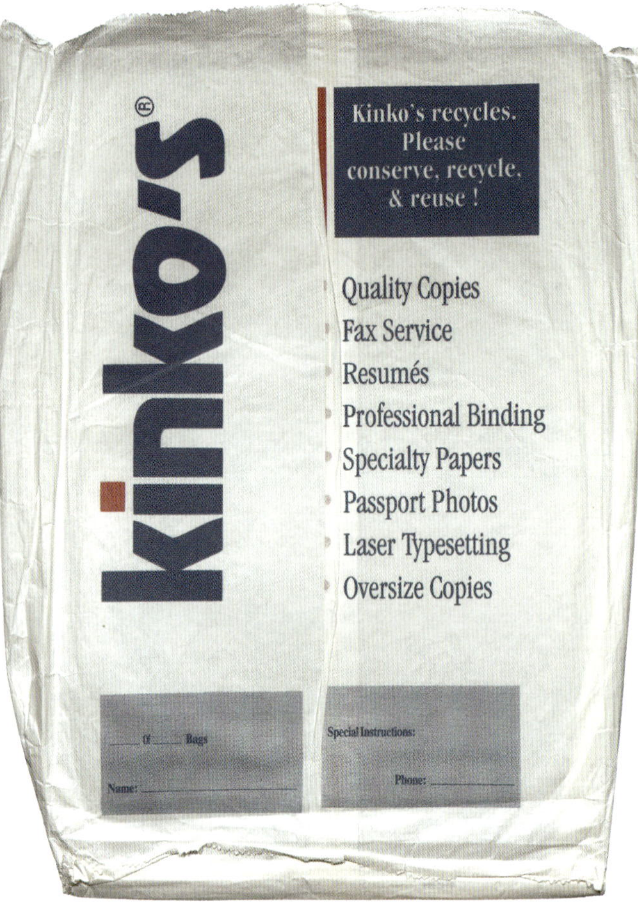

Figure 8.1 Left: The self-service section of a Kinko's location, 1998. Photo by Mark Murrmann. Used by permission. Right: Paper bag from Kinko's, circa 1991, from the Daisy Rooks collection at the University of Maryland.

Nirvana departed Sub Pop for DGC, a major label founded by the longtime industry figure David Geffen. DGC's roster at the turn of the 1990s was still a peculiar mingling of bands like noise-punk innovators Sonic Youth; power pop quartet the Posies; flaxen-haired, chart-topping twins Nelson; and sundry hirsute rock groups thrown against the wall to see what stuck. Few foresaw that Nirvana's September 1991 debut for DGC, *Nevermind*, would unseat popular music titan Michael Jackson at the top of *Billboard* magazine's album charts over two nonconsecutive weeks in January and February 1992.[6] Suddenly, punk culture was a driving force in mainstream popular culture. Punk's attendant aura of authenticity had emerged as an essence to be drained by commercial forces seeking their latest source of vitality.

Corporate America swooped in to co-opt Nirvana's air of authenticity and irreverence, which Generation X[7] highly prized. Fashion designer Marc Jacobs' incorporation of grunge style into his runway show for Perry Ellis in 1992 was a stunning move, though more shocking was the price tag on his wool ski caps ($175 in 1992) and rayon, faux-flannel shirts ($275), which emulated thrift store clothing usually found for pocket change. "Grunge has run its course," *New York* magazine sighed afterward, beneath the headline "Grunge: 1992–1993, RIP."[8] The nadir of grunge appropriation occurred in a 1992 commercial for Subaru, where the automobile manufacturer hired young actor Jeremy Davies to sell their Impreza model. Davies paced around a parking lot—grasping for the oddball charm of then-recent independent films like Richard Linklater's *Slacker*—anxiously spitting out lines with studied eccentricity:

> *This car is like punk rock! Now, just trust me, this is relevant. Do you remember when rock 'n' roll was*

really boring and corporate? Well, punk challenged all this and said "hey, excuse me, but here's what's cool about music, remember?" Now, Subaru, with this Impreza, is challenging some car thinking here. This car is all about reminding you and me what's great about a car, and moving forward, and making cars better, and less disappointing. Just like punk, 'cept it's cars.

More than ever, authenticity was paramount within punk, leading to a heightened sense of gatekeeping and frequent accusations of selling out levied toward any band gesturing toward the mainstream. Seattle's high profile inspired major labels to scope out other regional scenes in search of "the next Seattle." From metropolises like Chicago to college towns like Chapel Hill, North Carolina, and Halifax, Nova Scotia, major label scouts scoured North American punk scenes "far enough away from New York City and Los Angeles to consider themselves cool, and noncorporate enough to make room for the strikingly unconventional," as *Time* magazine then wrote.[9]

DC's vibrant scene was an appealing target. When Nirvana hit, Fugazi's record sales were already in six figures, high for an independent punk band. Major labels tried to pry them away from Dischord, but were rebuffed. "This is an incredibly fertile scene, but DC remains independent of the traditional rock 'n' roll/entertainment industry," Positive Force's Mark Andersen told Joe Brown of the *Washington Post* in 1992. "The difference in this city is that the leading voice is Fugazi, and they set a very different tone. . . . New bands like Bikini Kill and Nation of Ulysses are pursuing a really underground, creative and truly alternative and subversive way of creating music." Brown's article reeled off a list of DC bands likely to attract major labels, including Unrest, Bratmobile, Jawbox, and Shudder to Think, in addition to the aforementioned Nation of Ulysses and Bikini Kill. Andersen's hopeful assertion about DC punk bands' disinterest in mainstream culture proved somewhat true, yet many—all lacking Fugazi's concert draw and record sales—wavered openly about whether or not to jump to major labels in the pages of new DC punk zines like *Who Cares?* and *Noise Works*.

A variety of print additions to the DC scene debuted from 1990 through 1992, with diverse aesthetics and motivations. *Uno Mas'* extraordinary photography and professional production style coexisted harmoniously with *Riot Grrrl*, a rough-hewn photocopied zine meant to be ephemeral, but with a cultural impact that proved far from temporary. DC was flush with remarkable zines, from the good-natured fandom of *Action Teen* and *Teenage Gang Debs* to the ideologically dense sloganeering of *Ulysses Speaks*, which helped the Nation of Ulysses—charismatic and antigrunge, with their sharp clothing and pomaded hair—solidify their identity. No other period in DC punk's zine history was as compelling and varied as the early 1990s.

Uno Mas, Noise Works, and *Whack*

Greed folded in 1989, but its influence persisted in the early 1990s through a trio of new DC punk titles—*Uno Mas, Noise Works*, and *Whack*. The grimy textures of most 1980s punk fanzines, which Jim Saah and Scott Crawford had each memorably created then, were almost completely worn away within these new publications. Like *Greed*, they were professionally printed, laid out with desktop publishing software, and aimed for a larger audience. Broadening the scope of their coverage beyond punk and hardcore—Saah's *Uno Mas*, in particular, could feel as much like a literary magazine as a music one—these titles each attempted to reshape the notion of the punk fanzine in the 1990s, offering up intelligent, artistic content that was more accessible than most of their predecessors' work in the scene.

Following the two issues of *Zone V* fanzine Saah published in the early 1980s, his concert photography enlivened the liner notes of releases throughout the decade by Minor Threat, Marginal Man, and Fugazi. He returned to making zines in 1990 with *Uno Mas* and the first issue, coedited with Gregory S. Pierce, appeared that fall.[10] Aside from Saah's interview with Thurston Moore and Lee Ranaldo of the New York City band Sonic Youth, issue one mostly eschewed punk coverage. Poetry, photography, essays, and art dominated, signaling *Uno Mas* was something different.

The follow-up issue in spring 1991 continued this

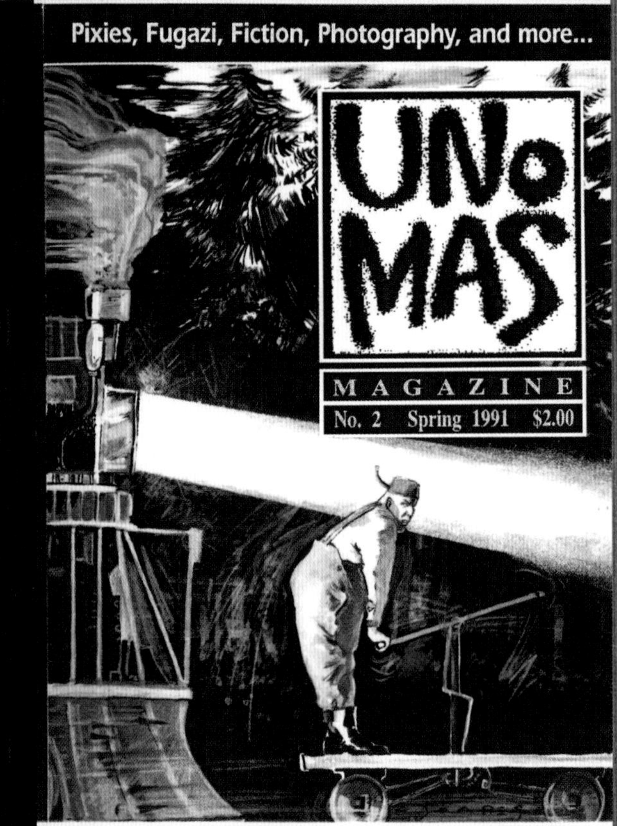

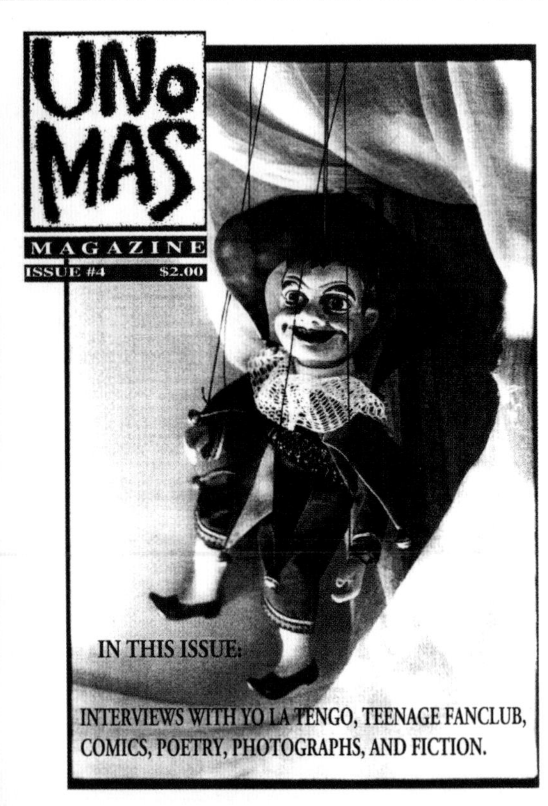

Figure 8.2 *Uno Mas*, issues 1–4, 1990–92. Published by Jim Saah. Used by permission.

approach, mingling fiction with comics, poetry, a book review, and interviews with *On Our Backs'* Susie Bright and the Massachusetts band, Pixies, who were near the end of their brilliant run as one of alternative rock's most influential groups.[11] Saah and Kurt Sayenga conducted the Pixies interview together with the intention of the conversation running in a new issue of *Greed*, which Sayenga never completed, "partially because of interviews like this one," he and Saah wrote in the interview's introduction. "[Sayenga] got tired of meeting hot bands and discovering that vast open spaces often exist where one would hope to find the lumps of tissue and fiber that constitute a fully-functioning brain," they continued. Sayenga later described the interview as "just one of those disappointing things, where it's like, you go and meet the band, and I just wasn't used to that—the band being assholes, except for [bassist] Kim Deal, who was super cool. But the rest of them were just like—oh my god."[12]

Later issues during this period shared their predecessors' broad creativity. Saah's ability to seamlessly weave revelatory photo essays on Mexico, Czechoslovakia, Egypt, and other locales in with poetry, fiction, illustrations, and smart coverage of alternative rock music created a new kind of zine for DC. Nuanced views on art, sexuality, and cultures outside of the United States might have drawn awkward titters from earlier DC punks, but *Uno Mas'* perspective was open, respectful, and curious. The critical eye and mistrust of authority Generation X held as fundamentals of its identity were present in *Uno Mas*, yet it was free of the cynicism those traits curdled into elsewhere.

The major label debate was in full swing within *Uno Mas'* pages. Interviews with Dischord bands Shudder to Think and High Back Chairs delved into the possibility of departing for something bigger. "The only reason we would leave Dischord would be for better distribution," High Back Chairs drummer and Dischord cofounder Jeff Nelson explained. "If a label offered us everything we wanted and could get us out there, we might think about it. But that's all very hypothetical, we'd have to look at everything."[13] Stuart Hill, bassist for Shudder to Think and onetime coeditor of *DCene* fanzine in the mid-1980s, declared he did not see the band leaving for a major label anytime soon. "It's pretty hard to really take the A&R people that have come to our shows very seriously," he said. "Dischord is the perfect label for us to be on. Now that Fugazi is so successful, it's much more of a business than a couple of years ago. It really works out because they pay for the recording and now we actually get royalties off the records."[14] Shudder to Think would, however, depart for Epic Records—home of Michael Jackson, Pearl Jam, and other cultural heavyweights—by 1994.

Aside from Sayenga, the impressive list of contributors to *Uno Mas* included musicians like Damon Locks (Trenchmouth), Steve Raskin (Edsel), John Pamer (Tsunami), Jack Hornady (Tuscadero), and J. Robbins and Zach Barocas (both of Jawbox), who all added artwork or writing. Steve Kiviat went from coediting *Thrillseeker* fanzine in the first half of the 1980s to a career as a government attorney, but he never stopped writing about music in larger publications like the *Washington Post* and *Washington City Paper*. Kiviat regularly contributed to *Uno Mas*, as well, interviewing the stylistically diverse Globestyle Records, influential music critic Greg Tate, and rising alternative bands Stereolab, Sugar, and Yo La Tengo.

Scott Crawford, another zine editor from hardcore's first wave, was only a few years removed from publishing *Metrozine*. An *Uno Mas* contributor in the early 1990s, he returned to zine publishing during this period with *Noise Works*. This new publication mirrored *Uno Mas'* clean, professional layouts, but stripped away much else outside of band interviews and music criticism. Crawford aimed to carve out a living through *Noise Works*, bringing in more advertisers and boosting circulation beyond the limited ambitions of *Metrozine*. *Noise Works* published bimonthly throughout 1991 and 1992, with cover subjects like Henry Rollins, Helmet, L7, and Mudhoney reflecting the zine's focus on heavy alternative rock from around the United States.

Fugazi's appearance on the cover of issue three coincided with the release of its second full-length album, *Steady Diet of Nothing*, in late summer 1991. The band was so popular that larger music magazines like *Rolling Stone* and *Spin* clamored to cover them, yet Fugazi generally refused interviews outside of fanzines. "We just didn't want to deal with them," guitarist/vocalist Guy Picciotto explained to *Noise Works*. "To me, what we're doing is fragile. The minute it becomes

Figure 8.3 *Noise Works*, issue 3, September–October 1991. Published by Scott Crawford. Used by permission.

overexposed it loses some of its power." The group's antipathy for corporate magazines sniffing around the punk subculture was evident. "I don't read those magazines or like them anyway," Picciotto said. "I certainly don't need a mag that puts 'for men' on the cover like *Details*," he added.

Picciotto touched on the issues of authenticity and connection at the heart of the tension within punk, noting he would rather trust "a fanzine or a mag done in the spirit of fanzines, where the impetus is the spirit of the music [and] the agenda is different than *Spin* or *Details*, which are basically ad sheets that are targeted to capitalize on a certain movement or whatever."[15] *Rolling Stone*'s incorporation of a promilitary yellow ribbon into its logo for the front cover of the March 21, 1991, issue, supporting the recently launched "Operation Desert Storm" phase of the Persian Gulf War, was further proof to Fugazi that, as MacKaye insisted to *Noise Works*, "*Rolling Stone* has *nothing* to do with Fugazi."

Noise Works offered a smart, unpretentious overview of the alternative rock landscape as it claimed significant space in the pop culture mainstream. However, just as the zine gained momentum, Crawford decided to move on. He served briefly as the guitarist in the new DC-area band Clutch, which potently merged metal, punk, and alternative ingredients into a unique sound earning the group an enduring cult following. Crawford's lead guitar work appears on portions of Clutch's 1991 debut EP, *Pitchfork*, but he bowed out of the group almost as quickly as he had joined it. "[Clutch] was never my thing, but I did it because they asked me to, and I thought it might be kind of fun," Crawford recalled.[16] Still, the band proved enough of a distraction to derail *Noise Works*.

Crawford returned to print publications in the years ahead, however, launching *Bent*—a slickly designed alternative rock magazine with full-color covers—in the mid-1990s and, later in the 2000s, *Harp* and *Blurt*, two glossy music magazines that were thoughtful American counterparts to British rock magazines like *Mojo* and *Uncut*. Crawford ultimately settled into filmmaking, the medium where he had his broadest impact, directing the 2014 documentary, *Salad Days: A Decade of Punk in Washington, DC (1980–90)*, in collaboration with Saah. "It's about storytelling, for me," Crawford reflected, acknowledging the thread running through his work from the mid-1980s to the present. "I think that, at the end of the day, that's what I most enjoy, and that's what I'm doing."[17]

Whack was another DC publication with big goals, residing somewhere between punk fanzines and alternative newspapers. The blend of tabloid size and larger circulation—more than twenty-thousand copies per issue—recalled earlier DC zine/newspaper hybrids like *Duckberg Times* and, particularly, the later issues of *WDC Period*. While the glut of advertising, downtown vending box distribution, and clean layout evoked the *Washington City Paper*, there was plenty of fanzine-style coverage within *Whack* of DCs thriving punk, indie rock, and alternative scenes. Edited by musician and graphic designer Rob Myers—later to make his most significant mark as part of the successful electronic music group Thievery Corporation—*Whack* published monthly for thirteen issues before ending in summer 1992.

Whack was funded by owners of the 15 Minutes Club,

an aspiring competitor to the 9:30 Club—already an institution by the early 1990s. Publication launched in June 1991 under the dubious title *CrackDC*, which it maintained through its first four issues. Considering the epidemic of crack cocaine usage and drug-related violence haunting DC throughout the late 1980s and early 1990s, the name's attempted irreverence struck many as vulgar and thoughtless. "Some people really hate it," 15 Minutes owner Joe Englert said.[18] "It is a provocative, attention-getting name and that was intentional. But we're not advocating taking drugs or anything. We mean it as a crack in your face to get going and do something."[19] Shaky explanation or not, *CrackDC*'s mission echoed sentiments heard from the earliest days of punk fanzines: Something exciting is going on here, and we want people to know about it.

Sloughing off the bad vibes with a name change to *Whack*, Myers assembled an efficient read that, throughout its remaining issues, weaved through DC's subcultures to document a city rich with activity. Local music was covered closely, with dozens of band blurbs crawling along the bottom third of several pages, succinctly defining the blend of punk, go-go, rock, indie, garage, and bar bands populating the city's stages nightly. Pithy, two-to-three sentence band descriptions gave readers a helpful digest for navigating show listings, anticipating the clever brevity later found on Twitter (now X), the influential twenty-first-century microblogging site. "Loose music-like pop from Virginia that's stacked with good ideas," the contributor Ian Christe wrote in a characteristic blurb on Wingtip Sloat, a new band including *Sweet Portable You*'s Patrick Foster.[20] "A messy sandbox."

CrackDC/Whack was among the earliest supporters of Cool "Disco" Dan, a graffiti artist whose distinctive tag dotted DC surfaces—and *CrackDC*'s first cover—during this period. Cool "Disco" Dan's true identity was initially unknown—later revealed to be DC resident Dan Hogg, who died in 2017—lending an air of mystery to the art, which *CrackDC/Whack* frequently championed. "We just felt he was symbolic of something uniquely DC," Myers explained.[21] The idea that graffiti could be art was still relatively novel in 1991, to the point that, when a reader asked if *Whack* condoned vandalism, Myers had to clarify that they did not, asking the reader to reconsider their definition of vandalism. "We'd much rather have a Cool 'Disco' Dan tag on the wall across the street than a blazing neon 'Miller' [Beer] ad, or a butt heinous looking neo-modern-deco

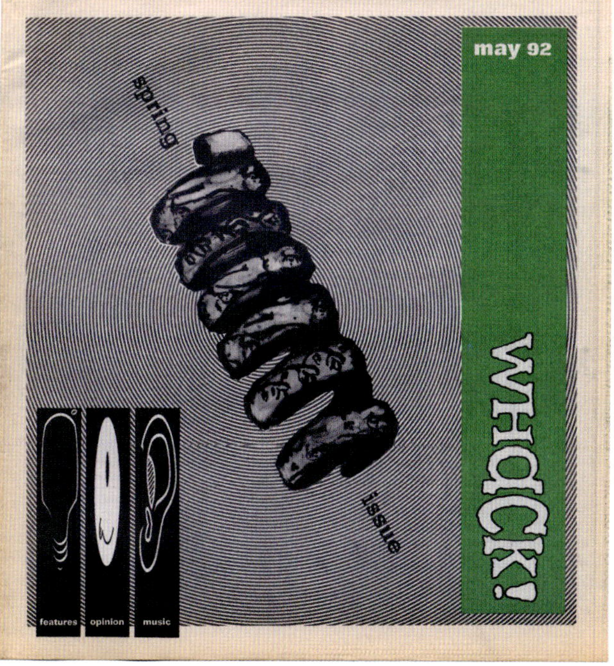

Figure 8.4 *CrackDC*, issue 1, June 1991; and *Whack*, issue 12, May 1992. Published by *CrackDC* and edited/designed by Rob Myers. Used by permission.

condominium," he wrote.[22]

Varied as *Whack*'s coverage could be, its punk and indie rock writing was among the best in DC while its monthly production schedule lent the contents an immediacy that zines with longer gaps between issues lacked. Articles on Fugazi, Positive Force, and the Fort Reno Park concert series were buttressed by coverage of some of the scene's exciting new indie labels like Simple Machines and Slumberland. Both drew inspiration from Dischord's creative spirit and business practices, but released music exploring poppier terrain, often cloaking their classic melodies in layers of cacophonous distortion to sublime effect.

Slumberland launched in 1989, releasing singles by Black Tambourine, Lorelei, and Velocity Girl, who helped forge the sound of early-1990s noise pop. Velocity Girl left for Sub Pop in 1992, finding substantial success there, particularly with their first two albums, *Copacetic* and *¡Simpatico!*[23] Slumberland moved to California in 1992 and thrives there today, but its early years in the DC area helped establish the District's noise-pop scene, a vibrant branch of the punk community outside the Dischord circuit.

Figure 8.5 Jenny Toomey and Kristin Thomson of Tsunami and Simple Machines, winter 1994. Photo by the author.

Simple Machines was started by Jenny Toomey and Derek Denckla—who collaborated in the bands Geek and Choke—along with *Nomadic Underground* fanzine editor Brad Sigal. Denckla and Sigal soon left the label, however, and musician Kristin Thomson stepped in, forming a powerful tandem with Toomey. Their new band, Tsunami, became one of the more influential bands to come out of DC's indie rock scene in the nineties. Aside from Simple Machines' ear for excellent music—usually highly melodic, clever, and unaffected indie pop—the label generated excitement and devotion behind its themed releases, creative packaging, activism, and dedication to community connection.

Whack cosponsored the cheekily dubbed Lotsa Pop Losers festival, held on October 26 and 27, 1991, and serving as an unofficial coming out party for DC's indie rock scene. Simple Machines, Slumberland, and Teen-Beat Records (whose own profile steadily rose behind outstanding new music by Unrest) organized the two concerts, which were split between an American Legion Hall in Bethesda, Maryland, and the soon-to-shutter dc space. The festival's name was a play on the Lollapalooza alternative music festival touring the United States that summer to much fanfare, an early indicator of the boom Nirvana headed months later. Lotsa Pop Losers' actual inspiration, however, came from the International Pop Underground Convention, a punk and indie rock music festival held in Olympia, Washington, that August. Organized by Candice Pedersen and Calvin Johnson of K Records, that festival (including DC-linked groups Fugazi, Nation of Ulysses, Bikini Kill, Bratmobile, Suture, and others) embodied the independent, DIY ethos of punk, extolling the pleasures of independence, unfettered creativity, and a true alternative culture.

Sparked by the events in Olympia, the DC scene got to work creating something of its own, somehow assembling the festival in only eight weeks thanks to "lots of postwork Big Gulps and late nights," Thomson joked. Toomey observed that the experience she and Thomson gained through working with Positive Force, along with booking their own concert tours, helped prepare them for organizing an ambitious event like this while simultaneously working full-time jobs. "But Lotsa Pop Losers was very different from a Positive Force show," she explained.

Figure 8.6 Top left: The Nation of Ulysses performs at Sacred Heart Church in Washington on February 15, 1991. Photo by Jamie Early. Top right and bottom: *Ulysses Speaks*, issues 0, 2, and 9, 1990–91. Published by the Nation of Ulysses. Used by permission.

"It was way more whimsical and it was a joint effort, and it was a moment [where] the newer labels were finding each other, and imagining the possibilities of what we could do together."[24] The new wave of DC indie rock groups—Tsunami, Velocity Girl, Unrest, Lorelei, Edsel, High Back Chairs, and others—was joined by like-minded bands emerging from other East Coast scenes, like Versus (New York City) and Small Factory (Rhode Island). "I remember a lot of pride," Toomey said. "It felt like this new, magical community of all your new best friends."[25]

Dominant and transformative as the Dischord and Positive Force axis still was, a successful parallel scene had emerged within the larger DC punk community. "To a great extent, if you look at Positive Force shows of that era being a bit too domineering in style and content, [Lotsa Pop Losers] was a chance for people without a narrow point of view to stretch and create a two-day DC event that was every bit as interesting and DIY [as Positive Force]," said Don Smith, who hosted a radio show on the University of Maryland's WMUC-FM in addition to his coediting duties on *Teenage Gang Debs* fanzine. "I'd talk to Positive Force people about setting up shows, and they'd want to vote on them and essentially 'vote them out.' Here, the indie crowd could take what we had experienced already from Positive Force, but create an experience that was important and unique."[26]

Ulysses Speaks

The optimism members of the Nation of Ulysses expressed in their *Interrobang?!* interview from late 1989 was well placed as the 1990s dawned. The band's volcanic music—described by *CrackDC* as "glossolalia and frenzied guitar fuzz, guaranteed to break a few hearts, guitars, eardrums, and amps"[27]—moved them to the front of the DC punk scene. The albums they released on Dischord Records during their brief time together—1991's *13 Point Program to Destroy America* and 1992's *Plays Pretty for Baby*—are posthardcore classics, influential through their music and ideology, but especially in the flair with which the band communicated its identity. The group debuted as a quartet named Ulysses in 1988, adding Tim Green on second guitar and becoming Nation of Ulysses by 1990.

The new moniker was a conspicuous nod to the Nation of Islam, a Black nationalist political and religious group headquartered in Chicago. The Nation of Islam was at the forefront of American consciousness during this period, platformed by pop culture trendsetters like hip-hop group Public Enemy and film director Spike Lee. Nation of Ulysses' vocalist, Ian Svenonius, described his band as "a nation concept—a broad, community concept. . . . We basically want to create a new sense of who we are community-wise. A nation of youths."[28] Svenonius would again borrow from the Nation of Islam when naming his band's new zine. Appropriating the erstwhile title of the Nation of Islam's official newspaper, *Muhammad Speaks*, Svenonius unveiled *Ulysses Speaks*, which ran for several issues before the band split later in 1992.[29]

The zine was rife with manifestos and sly humor. Whether extolling their own music or decrying baby boomers, baggy T-shirts, and the state of pop music, *Ulysses Speaks* made a lasting mark on punk culture. "*Ulysses Speaks* was probably the first DC zine that I saw and I loved it," zine editor and Bratmobile vocalist Allison Wolfe said. "They were so thin and little, and filled with smarty-pants like . . . whatever," she laughed. "I probably couldn't even understand most of it but I thought it looked cool, and I liked that it was politicized, or at least pseudo-politicized."[30] Its provocative pronouncements were on behalf of the band, yet were written by Svenonius. "I think there was some discussion about what was written, but obviously, it was all Ian's writing," Green explained. "I helped out with the layout on some pages, but it was Ian's baby, more than anything. It was all stuff [band members] agreed with, . . . and identified with."[31]

Aside from their growing profile within punk, the Nation of Ulysses attracted surprising interest from the mainstream young women's magazine *Sassy*, which memorably named vocalist Ian Svenonius the "Sassiest Boy in America" in October 1990. *Sassy* flouted numerous norms of teen magazine coverage, becoming a pivotal instrument in the dissemination of zine culture, feminism, and punk perspectives in the early 1990s, touting fanzines and bands unmentioned in other widely circulated publications. *Sassy* writer and editor Christina Kelly's article detailing the magazine's tongue-in-cheek "Sassiest Boy in America" contest declared Svenonius was "kooky, smart, creative, cute, and he doesn't do drugs." Svenonius' contest application included his pitch for why he felt he was the "Sassiest Boy in America," written in his "trademark crypto-intellectual rhetoric," as *Sassy* historians Kara Jeseller and Marisa Meltzer described it.[32] "Not to take; partake of illegal drugs," he wrote in a manifesto-style portion of his application, "as they are part of a murderous commerce, chaired by the government, and will be used as an excuse to strip away our last vestiges of freedom."

The *Washington Post* excitedly profiled Svenonius in the wake of the *Sassy* article—under the cringeworthy headline "Here's One Too Cool Total Babe"—where he explained entering the contest "to indoctrinate youth gone astray. Youth who have embraced the guise and stance of earlier generations. There seems to be a real propensity for baby-boom generation people to present their youthfulness as an epoch or an apex and present kids now as nothing. There are so many kids dressing like Grateful Dead people. It's kind of tedious." The *Post* seemed unthreatened by the choleric, revolutionary tenor of Svenonius's writings and performances, punning he was "a genial rebel without the caustic," before blithely dropping the coup de grâce: "Imagine Tom Hanks doing James Dean."[33]

Svenonius's frenetic stream of urgent, politically radical writing in *Ulysses Speaks* borrowed liberally from leftist political movements, the Situationist International's clever subversion, and punk fanzines' disdain for dominant musical trends. "The Nation of Ulysses really started as an ideological program before we ever struck a note of music," he later said: "We were really different. . . . We had a gang sensibility. We all lived together. It was more of a cult than a band. It was explicitly a political party. We were explicitly modeling ourselves on something like the Vice Lords, a gang from Chicago that became a political party."[34]

New issues of "the visual accompaniment to the soundtrack to the revolution," as *Ulysses Speaks* referred

Figure 8.7 *Teenage Gang Debs*, issue 3, January 1991; and *Action Teen*, issue 1, 1991. Published by Erin and Don Smith. Used by permission.

to itself, appeared intermittently. They consisted of one or two letter-sized sheets of paper, photocopied in landscape orientation and folded in half. Text was mostly typewritten, adorned with handwritten flourishes and clip art featuring French New Wave films, Italian Futurists from the 1910s, and Girl Groups from the 1960s. References within the text similarly careened from Situationist writer Raoul Vaneigem to the contemporary pop group New Kids on the Block to actress Winona Ryder, emphasizing the urgency and intelligence racing through the band's creative veins.

Ulysses Speaks, much like the highly caffeinated liner notes to the band's albums, was an integral part of expressing the quintet's professed ethics of disruption and revolt. "Nobody really believed that Nation of Ulysses were a terrorist group, but the *Ulysses Speaks* zines really created another mystery around the band," recalled Jeff Winterberg, a California-based photographer and musician, whose band Antioch Arrow bore Nation of Ulysses' influence. "It was the first zine I saw that was intentionally confusing. I wrote a letter asking for a T-shirt and they replied 'We don't sell T-shirts, only armaments.'"[35]

Teenage Gang Debs and *Action Teen*

No DC-area zine epitomized the fandom in fanzines more than *Teenage Gang Debs*, published by siblings Erin and Don Smith. The Bethesda, Maryland–rooted pair blended their love for the pop culture of their childhoods with the spirit of the punk subculture they were immersed in, starting with its first issue in summer 1989 and running until a fifth issue in May 1993. Unjaded, offbeat, and ebullient, *Teenage Gang Debs* was at the vanguard of a wider reappraisal and appreciation of 1960s and 1970s pop culture occurring in the 1990s. Some mainstream revisitation of that era's culture was drenched in irony and cynicism, mining the sweetness of shows like *The Brady Bunch* and *The Patty Duke Show* for laughs at the programs' expense. *Teenage Gang Debs*, however, was a pure encomium to youth's vitality and the innocent charms of that period's popular culture. The zine was named after a 1966 cult movie about juvenile delinquency that was rich with kitsch appeal, thanks to its inexpert acting and overheated premise. That said, it made an apt avatar for a zine that celebrated, even defended, art frequently dismissed as frivolous bubblegum.

Few, however, took popular culture more seriously than the Smith siblings, whose veneration of old sitcoms, pop music, and punk culture was infectious. "I think it's always important to never forget how to be a fan, and if you're going to be a fan, do it full-on," Erin said. "I don't know how to do it halfway."[36] She started the zine as a student at Walt Whitman High School and Don, four years older and a student at the University of Maryland, joined as coeditor from the second issue on. "I think it was to look at TV in a reverent way, in a different kind of way," Erin said of the zine's mission. He continued: "In a fun way. In a way that was a study, but not in a way of making fun of things. So, a real reverence for vintage TV. There were a lot of people making dumb jokes about bell bottoms, but that's not what we were looking at with *The Brady Bunch*. We were thinking about it in a deeper way. And that was really new."[37]

The Brady Bunch was a particular focus of fandom for *Teenage Gang Debs*, with most covers featuring one of the child actors from the show and its pages filled with detailed interviews with cast members Eve Plumb and Robbie Rist. In 1991, the Smiths drove for hours to reach a playhouse in the Poconos where Plumb performed in a production of the musical *South Pacific*. Plumb gamely answered their questions throughout the lengthy interview, seemingly perplexed but ultimately pleased by their interest. Not everything was porkchops and applesauce in the early part of the interview, however, as Don's compliment that Plumb's *Brady Bunch* character, Jan, "always represented how I felt as a kid" hit a wall. "I was just doing my job, I didn't have any input," she responded crisply. "I was really unaware of a lot of the things that people like to extrapolate from this whole thing. It's like, you know, it was a TV show. Let's get real." Don added an editorial aside in the printed interview: "Suddenly, I realize Eve might not be keen on my incessant Jan-analyization Bummer." By interview's end, however, Plumb giggled at the pair's jokes and was clearly won over by their genuine love for a show she still seemed ambivalent about.

Erin and Don traveled to Manhattan in 1992 for a taping of *The Sally Jessy Raphael Show*—a popular syndicated tabloid talk program—when *Brady Bunch* stars Barry Williams and Florence Henderson sat on a panel of past sitcom stars. Raphael briefly interviewed the Smiths out in the audience—showing an onscreen still of issue three's cover—asking them to explain their devotion to a program often minimized as dated fluff. "I think it's a really well-written show and it's like a community thing that we all grew up with these episodes," Don asserted. "In Washington, DC, it was aired twice a day for years when I was a very young kid." Williams and Henderson broke into smiles as Erin reiterated Don's appreciation for the program. "It's like the perfect show," she said. "It has six kids, all different ages, you can relate to any of the kids and the plots, I think, are really well-written and stand up really well today."

Teenage Gang Debs' layout was a combination of typed text with handwritten flourishes, illustrated with clippings of "dated first-aid books, old magazines, *Brady Bunch* coloring books, or any other humorously anachronistic items salvaged from garage sales," as one contemporary profile on the Smiths described it.[38] Photocopied at the Kinko's in Bethesda, circulation typically topped one thousand copies. Despite the relatively modest level of distribution, "the right people read it," as Erin said, and word spread through the larger media.[39] "All these journalists were there looking for things to write about," she recalled of the coverage *Teenage Gang Debs* received in the *Washington Post*, *Village Voice*, *Washington City Paper*, and numerous other outlets.

Mentions in *Sassy* particularly spread awareness of *Teenage Gang Debs*, thanks to the former's wide circulation and tastemaking status. *Sassy*'s Christina Kelly picked up an issue at New York City zine shop See Hear and was enamored with the fanzine's tone and aesthetic. *Sassy*'s reach was so broad that after Kelly wrote favorably about *Teenage Gang Debs* during the autumn of 1990, mail orders came in to the Smiths for years. Erin joined *Sassy* as

Figure 8.8 Bikini Kill performs at Saint Stephen and the Incarnation Episcopal Church in Washington on November 16, 1991. Photo by Brad Sigal. Visible in the audience are the zine creators Erin and Don Smith, Charlie Moats, and Billie Rain-Shadid. Used by permission.

an intern in summer 1991 and later became Washington Bureau chief for the magazine in 1994. "They were amazing people and very forward thinking," she said, "but if it was weird, underground, and happened between '91 and '94, it could have been easily something I wrote, photographed or suggested."[40]

Teenage Gang Debs occasionally included punk content—a Nation of Ulysses interview was a highlight of issue three—but the Smiths unveiled a one-off zine in 1991 venturing fully into punk fandom. *Action Teen* appeared between issues three and four of *Teenage Gang Debs,* and packed in interviews, a tour diary, and plenty of the Smiths' characteristic cleverness and sincerity. The Smiths were clearly friends with the bands they covered in *Action Teen,* which gave the lengthy interviews with Beat Happening and Fugazi a warm, disarming tone.

That connection allowed them to reveal elements of the bands' personalities often obscured by narratives dominating coverage in other zines. "A lot of people did Dischord-oriented type magazines, but nobody sort of remembers that Fugazi are funny," Erin observed. "A lot of people are scared of them, but they're actually just really funny, and fun, and nice. I think this kind of made them seem a little more real."[41] Don and Erin's interview with Brendan Canty and Guy Picciotto of Fugazi is loose and familiar, full of love for the DC scene and old television shows like *Ultraman* and *Kung Fu.* A page including playful paper dolls of Canty and Picciotto—"Brendan's ready for the beach and Guy's all set for a Halloween party with these Fugazi paper dolls"—flipped the group's ultraserious reputation.

The Smiths' work on *Teenage Gang Debs* and *Action Teen,* along with Erin's influence on *Sassy* as Washington Bureau chief, were a profound enough legacy already. However, it was Erin's role as guitarist for Bratmobile—a punk trio that helped spark the Riot Grrrl movement—that was her most momentous contribution. Despite the influence of her music, Erin's heart remained with fandom. "I kind of like being a fan more than a musician, really," she explained. "That's really what I am."

Riot Grrrl and *Bikini Kill*

An article in the September 1991 issue of *CrackDC* titled "Invasion of the Riot Grrrls!" was among the earliest coverage of both a zine and an eponymous punk feminist movement that became arguably the most widely influential development connected to DC punk. Longtime DC scene contributor Mark Andersen wrote the article, describing a new zine, *Riot Grrrl,* and a significant new group of musicians in town. Andersen described *Riot Grrrl* as "brimming with provocative wit, naked emotion, good fun, and serious thought."[42] Accurate words, but *Riot Grrrl's* impact and the punk feminist movement it inspired were still of a gravity impossible to grasp, let alone convey, at that early stage.

Figure 8.9 *Riot Grrrl,* issues 3 and 4, 1991. Published by Riot Grrrl DC. Used by permission.

Riot Grrrl's origins were in the DC arrivals of two bands—Bikini Kill and Bratmobile—who recently formed elsewhere but were based out of the District in parts of 1991 and 1992. The Olympia, Washington, quartet Bikini Kill became friendly with the Nation of Ulysses—band member Tobi Vail first learned of NOU from the *Interrobang?!* interview—whose members urged the group to stay on in DC when their joint tour ended in June 1991.[43] The rapt reception Bikini Kill received at the tour's conclusion on June 27 at dc space helped

Invasion of the Riot Grrls!

I'm not sure what I expected when I picked up my first copy of *Riot Grrrl*, but I'm sure I didn't expect to be overly impressed. It was, after all, fairly humble-looking fare—a small (1/4 page), xeroxed, partly hand-lettered mini-zine, the kind you pick up, flip through, set down and forget about, all in about thirty seconds.

But this fanzine wasn't like the rest. What I found inside was a delicious alternative to the bonehead macho, empty predictability or cynical cool that dominates much of our "alternative scene." Brimming with provocative wit, naked emotion, good fun and serious thought, *Riot Grrrl* was a burst of fresh air in the oppressive heat of DC's "Victory" summer.

The story of *Riot Grrrl* ("grrrl" being roughly translatable as "angry girl") is partly the story of friendship and a "Grrrl Punk" network that extends from Washington, DC to Washington State. Though two of the three orginators of *Riot Grrrl*–Kathleen Hanna and Molly Neuman–spent significant portions of their earlier life in DC and its suburbs, it was in Olympia, Washington that they and Allison Wolfe became friends and began to find their voice through punk bands and fanzines. In the heady aftermath of the Mt. Pleasant riots, Jennifer Smith, a DC friend who lived in the riot zone, wrote to Allison wishing for "a girl riot" to transform the DC scene.

The idea took hold. Molly, Allison and Kathleen returned to DC in early summer with their bands–Bikini Kill and Bratmobile–and a vision of what could be. Taking a name inspired in equal parts by Jennifer's letter and the angry "grrrl" zines of the West Coast, they set out to use their summer to do their part to revolutionize the DC punk scene..."girl-style."

Riot Grrrl was the result. It's very much about punk rock, its power...and its failures. Punk initially gained its fame and adherents by venting its rather considerable spleen at idiocy and injustice in society. But, as time passed, punk came to reflect more than reject society. This was hardly surprising–as Allison notes, "How can we be totally free of our socialization?" Molly agreed, adding "We all come into punk with our own histories." Still, "for women to come into the alternative scene and feel excluded...or silenced...is really fucked up," says Kathleen. It was time, once again, for a change–a revolution.

Revolution is what *Riot Grrrl* preaches, but not exactly the grim, grey "male" version that might first come to mind. The revolution "grrrl-style" is a very open and human one, imbued with the iconoclastic spirit of Emma Goldman (her credo: "If I can't dance, I don't want to be part of your revolution") and more than a little bit of humor. A list of revolutionary advice" in RG #3 ranges from "be a dork, tell your friends how you really feel" and "cry in public" to "selectively ignore all oppressive laws" and "make amendments to this list and think about why you don't agree with some of what I've written."–hardly your typical political manifesto.

The feminism they espouse is similarly sly and sassy but still substantive. "Feminist rhetoric can be really alienating," admits Allison, "especially for punk girls." *Riot Grrrl* departs from the feminist orthodoxy with its reclamation of the word "girl," a deviation they defend as both more fun and more inclusive than the generic "woman" favored by old-line feminists.

Inclusion is a very central theme in their purposely flexible revolutionary agenda, especially inclusion of traditionally marginalized groups such as women. Since such inclusion, of course, is not likely just to "happen" on its own, RG #3 announced "an all-girl meeting... about the ways to encourage higher female scene input, ways to help each other learn to play instruments," and to, above all, provide support and help to break down isolation.

Ultimately, this was a rallying call for women/girls to assert their creative potential within the punk community, to form bands, write fanzines, to claim their rightful equal place on stage and beyond.

That call has been heard–and answered. Each of the four weekly meetings held thus far at the Positive Force House in Arlington has attracted between one and two dozen "grrrls", ranging in age from mid-teens to mid-twenties. Taken on their own terms, the meetings seem to be successful. "We don't have any big agenda of taking over the world," Kathleen insists. "We just said, 'let's have a meeting', to talk and see what happens." Topics as seemingly mundane as slamdancing or sharing of musical or other skills, or as deep as personal experiences of sexism or sexual abuse have been discussed. To Molly, "What's inspiring to me is that it seems so vital to the younger girls to have this environment to talk about what's important to them...it's like we're all so relieved to hear each other speak."

> **"Some people think little girls should be seen and not heard but I think... Oh Bondage Up Yours!!"**
> **X-Ray Spex, 1977**

While it is easy to see how people, especially men, could be threatened by all of this, according to the *Riot Grrrls*, DC has been a remarkably supportive atmosphere thus far. While some of the younger grrrls have faced some open opposition, generally resentment has only surfaced in what Allison describes as "the subtle little shut-me-ups".

When asked how men can help with this, a long, impassioned discussion ensues. Allison: "Listen...and support us in what we do." Kathleen: "Educate yourselves, don't expect us to educate you...read books about feminism. We've been reading books by and about men for our whole lives." Molly: "Musical skills sharing is something boys can do"–if it's done with a maximum of patience and a minimum of patronizing. While the central role in the *Riot Grrrl* plan for empowerment is female, it is also clear that males have an important part to play as well.

All of this aside, it would be fair to ask how much *Riot Grrrl* has actually accomplished–especially since at least Molly and Allison plan to return to school in Washington State by the end of August. What will happen with *Riot Grrrl* and the meetings once they are gone? "I think the girls in the group right now will keep it going," asserts Kathleen. "And if they don't, there'll be a good reason for it." RG #4 itself issues a kind of sign-off challenge: "*Riot Grrrl* exists in the face of boring nowheresville fanzinedom to confront as well as be something fun. Those of us who have been working on these past four issues might not do them again, but this name is not copyrighted...so take the ball and run with it!" Judging by the impressive contributions of some of the newer recruits, *Riot Grrrl* is in good hands.

Whatever happens, this summer leaves the rumblings of a long-overdue grrrl revolution hanging in the all-too-stagnant air of DC punkdom. For someone like myself, weaned in the mid to late seventies on Patti Smith, The Slits, Poly Styrene and the Avengers, such tremors are a hopeful, even heart-warming sign. Near the end of our interview, Molly said she felt that "an incredible seed has been planted" by *Riot Grrrl* over the past summer. Just wishful thinking? Maybe–but let's hope not.

To correspond, write *Riot Grrrl* at 1830 Irving Street NW, WDC 20010. Molly and Allison can be reached at PO Box 1473, Olympia WA, 98507, Kathleen at 1023 S. Adams, Apt 1196, Olympia WA 98501. Communication is encouraged!

Mark Andersen

ROMANIA

Appearing Live
Sunday September 15th
Grog & Tankard
8 P.M.
Synth+Bass

"In a truly free society, style is the only means of distinction." –Jean Cocteau

PHANTASMAGORIA
RECORDS, TAPES & COMPACT DISCS
CASH PAID FOR USED LP'S, CD'S & CASSETTES
▸ NEW, USED & OUT OF PRINT RECORDS
▸ 20,000 VINYL LP'S AND 12" IN STOCK
▸ HUGE NEW/USED CD SELECTION
301·949·8886
11308 GRANDVIEW AVE., WHEATON, MD 20902
ONLY 2 BLOCKS FROM WHEATON METRO
MON-SAT 10AM-9PM
SUN 12 NOON-6PM
VISA/MC

CRACK! 13

Figure 8.10 Mark Andersen's article on Riot Grrrl, in issue 4 of *CrackDC*, 1991. Used by permission.

convince them DC might be worth a longer stay. "I was completely enthralled by the band, especially Kathleen [Hanna], who could deliver songs with such emotion, yet be concerned that the girls had room up front," Tsunami's Kristin Thomson remembered. "It was really inspiring."[44] Bikini Kill distributed fliers at its shows including its powerful, cathartic song lyrics and a list of aphorisms crystallizing their desire to make positive changes inside and outside punk, leading with: "The revolution starts here and now within each one [of] us."

Bratmobile—with Allison Wolfe singing and Molly Neuman on drums—was formed in Eugene, Oregon, in 1990. The duo's live debut occurred on a bill with Bikini Kill and Some Velvet Sidewalk in Olympia, Washington, on February 14, 1991.[45] Wolfe and Neuman also collaborated on a zine they called *Girl Germs*, which mixed intriguing essays on feminism, politics, and culture with occasional band interviews. Neuman was from the DC area and, while home for winter break from college, attended a Nation of Ulysses show at dc space on December 26, 1990. K Records head Calvin Johnson introduced Neuman to Erin Smith that night and the pair agreed to trade zines, leading to a friendship cultivated through letters and long-distance calls.[46] Neuman returned to DC, joined by Wolfe, for spring break in 1991 and asked Smith if she wanted to play music. The trio was initially joined by Jen Smith and Christina Billotte (the latter of the DC group Autoclave and, eventually, the outstanding Slant 6) in a band they called Bratmobile DC, but Jen Smith and Billotte departed within months. Wolfe, Neuman, and Erin Smith continued on as Bratmobile, playing their first show as a trio at Fort Reno Park in July.

Another important event in *Riot Grrrl*'s development occurred in May 1991, when protests shook DC's Mount Pleasant neighborhood. The police shooting of Daniel Enrique Gonzalez, a Salvadoran man, during an arrest on May 5 left Gonzalez paralyzed. The incident inflamed tensions between police and DC's Salvadoran immigrant community. Protests continued for days, with a number of punks participating. Jen Smith—a Mount Pleasant resident who, aside from Bratmobile DC, played in the band Rastro! and soon published the zine *Red Rover*—was inspired by the protests' intent, but felt uneasy about the thrill seeking she noticed her non-Salvadoran punk friends engaging in during the unrest. When some of her housemates joined the conflict, she stayed home. "I thought it was not cool to go up, because I didn't feel like I knew enough about [it]—I wasn't going to be an ally. And the people from our house weren't going to be allies to Salvadorians; they're just there for the ruckus."[47] Despite this, seeing her Salvadoran neighbors push back against an oppressive system motivated her to bring the same energy to feminist activism. The words "girl riot" ran through her head in the following days and, in a letter to Wolfe, she mentioned the phrase alongside her desire for change that summer.[48]

With Bikini Kill and Bratmobile in town and activist energy coursing through the humid DC air, *Riot Grrrl*'s elements coalesced. Wolfe explained in 2017 that the *Riot Grrrl* zine was born out of a desire for the West Coast arrivals to connect with other women in the DC scene, like Billotte, Jen Smith, Melissa Klein, Sharon Cheslow, and photographer Cynthia Connolly. "All these guys like Ulysses and Fugazi have their whole scene, and that's cool and everything, but we just sort of felt like, well, in Olympia, the girls absolutely ran the scene," Wolfe recalled. "Guys were so secondary [laughs] at least in our minds. And, so, it was weird to kind of all of a sudden be in this [DC] scene that was pretty male-dominated. I'm not saying like it was really sexist and macho or anything. It wasn't like that. But it was just sort of different for us, and bigger and whatever. I think that we just were like, 'We want to reach out and get to know more of the women in town and see what are they doing' and stuff like that."[49]

Knowing zines' power of communication within a subculture, Wolfe, Neuman, Hanna, and Jen Smith met in early July 1991 to craft a document as immediate as it was lasting. The first issue of *Riot Grrrl* was assembled quickly, its name derived from Smith's "girl riot" phrase and an alternative, tongue-in-cheek spelling of "girl" that Vail had used in her influential fanzine *Jigsaw* as a reference to the numerous reimaginings of "women" that feminists had utilized ("womyn," "wimmin") to rebuke patriarchy.[50] Vail had published *Jigsaw* in Olympia since early 1989, offering up smart, passionate writings rich with punk's spirit of celebration and critique.

Riot Grrrl's first issue was photocopied in Neuman's father's office during off hours. Its cover featured a cut-and-pasted clipping of pop singer Madonna, arms raised triumphantly. Next to the image was a succinct, typewritten summary: "*Riot Grrrl* is a free weekly mini-zine. Please read and distribute to your pals." The first copies were disseminated at a Fourth of July party in Erin Smith's backyard and the zine's introduction, credited to "the riot girl [*sic*] gang," observed that "there has been a proliferation of angry grrrl zines in recent months, mainly due to the queasy feeling we girls get in our stomachs when we contemplate the general lack of girl power in society as a whole, and in the punk rock underground specifically."

Another issue was turned around the next week and distributed at Bratmobile's Fort Reno show, with two more issues published in subsequent weeks. "Different people would contribute, and write one little thing that was only one quarter of a page of an 8.5 x 11 [sheet]," Wolfe said, adding: "So, you'd write one little thing like that. Some people wrote more. [Hanna] was always a really good writer, and she would write stories and do more. I think that disposable nature of it is what's really interesting. It was just made to kind of be quick—make it, fold it up, hand it out—and then the next week there's something new."[51]

Hanna realized that creating a space and time where women in DC's punk scene could gather regularly might be an effective way to draw the community closer. A meeting was held on the evening of July 24 at the Positive Force house in Arlington, Virginia, in a room adjacent to where Jenny Toomey and Kristin Thomson ran Simple Machines.[52] Hanna initially asked the fifteen to twenty attendees about their interest in joining her to work on a magazine about women in music. Soon, however, Hanna recalled that the conversation moved into attendees sharing their "horror stories" about sexism and rape.[53] The meeting was a cathartic experience that Hanna described as "vital and alive" and, the following week, the group reconvened for another meaningful discussion. Before long, others began to call participants in the meetings "Riot Grrrls," presumably due to the zine creators' involvement in the meetings. Hanna felt the tag "was annoying, but we didn't have another name, so we went with it."[54]

Hanna, Wolfe, and Neuman sat for the interview with Andersen, which ran in September's *CrackDC*. "We don't have any big agenda of taking over the world," Hanna said. "We just said, 'let's have a meeting,' to talk and see what happens." Neuman spoke on the impact Riot Grrrl meetings had simply by offering women a space for communication and connection, reifying the intangibles of a zine. "What's inspiring to me is that it seems so vital to the younger girls to have this environment to talk about what's important to them," she said. "It's like we're all so relieved to hear each other speak."[55]

At the end of that summer's fourth issue of *Riot Grrrl*, the authors noted they might hand the zine over to newer contributors. "This name is not copyrighted," they wrote, "so take the ball and run with it!" New issues continued to be published, albeit at a slower place, with contributors like Erika Reinstein,[56] May Summer, Kristin Thomson, and others writing about feminism, punk, rape culture, and the daily struggle for space within punk and mainstream cultures where patriarchy and misogyny were intrinsic elements. Soon, Riot Grrrl chapters cropped up around the world, affiliated in spirit but without formal connections. "As a movement, Riot Grrrl was amorphous and nonhierarchical in structure, with no elected leaders or central organization headquarters," scholars Kristin Schilt and Elke Zobl write. "This decentralization allowed participants in Riot Grrrl to actively direct the activities and meanings of their local chapter."[57]

Bikini Kill released the first issue of their eponymous zine while still in Olympia, publishing a follow-up later in 1991 during their DC tenure. That second issue clarified the punk feminist ethos of both the band and the Riot Grrrl movement taking shape. The fervent tone and righteous enumerations of *Ulysses Speaks* were an acknowledged influence on *Riot Grrrl* and Bikini Kill (both band and zine), but Ian Svenonius's manifestos seemed to be delivered with a wink—intentionally or not—often leaving puzzled readers asking, "is he serious?" The manifesto-like list of what "Riot Grrrl is" in *Bikini Kill* issue two inspired no confusion, its points clear and devoid of irony. Its ongoing relevance and power rest in its radically simple sincerity and common sense. The bracing, inspiring list starts with the declaration that "us girls crave records and books and fanzines that speak to US, that WE feel included in and can understand in our own ways" and concludes with the prophetic point that Riot Grrrl is "BECAUSE I believe with my

Figure 8.11 *Fake,* issue 0, 1992. Published by Irene Chien.

holeheartmindbody that girls constitute a revolutionary soul force that can, and will, change the world for real."

Numerous *Riot Grrrl*–inspired zines soon appeared around the world, indicating the zine's spirit resonated with young women demanding to be heard and treated with respect within both punk and the mainstream world. The new publications were steeped in punk culture, but often took a different course in their writings and presentation, when compared with earlier zines. "These 'zines became a means of feverish expression and collaboration," writer and zine editor Melissa Klein explained:

> *They employed a format traditionally used to review records and conduct band interviews, not only to spotlight female musicians but also to share insights, ideas, and information (such as how to induce a late period through herbal teas), to rant and reflect, and to tell personal stories—some humorous, some horrifying, some uplifting. Like other means of expression, fanzines embodied an attempt to process a wide variety of past and present images of femininity. Illustrations ran the gamut from photographs hyping girls currently involved in music, to cartoon sex kittens, to torrid lesbian pulp-fiction covers, to hilariously wholesome advertisements from old* Life *magazines. Fanzines helped girls form a network with each other, not only between towns such as Olympia, DC, and San Francisco, but also among other places, smaller places, suburbs. Hardcore enabled young suburban boys to vent their anger at the world; Riot Grrrl allowed young suburban girls to vent their anger at the world of suburban boys.*[58]

Riot Grrrl DC sought to convene various participants in the growing movement at a DC conference from July 31 to August 2, 1992. The well-attended gathering was a larger realization of the *Riot Grrrl* zine's initial mission to help punk women meet, be creative, exchange ideas, and make a difference. Aside from workshops on self-defense, audio engineering, and racism, a conference session on making zines underscored how central these self-published expressions were to the Riot Grrrl ecosystem.[59] The importance of zines was illuminated further when articles on Riot Grrrl in mainstream media publications like *USA Today*, *Newsweek*, and *Seventeen* appeared in the weeks and months after the convention, often misrepresenting or referring dismissively to Riot Grrrl participants and concepts in their coverage.[60] These recuperative attempts to either co-opt or stifle Riot Grrrl's importance demonstrated the threat that radical punk and feminist action posed to mainstream hegemony.

It seemed only zines made by Riot Grrrls themselves could be trusted to accurately represent their experiences and elucidate the meaning of the movement. Erika Reinstein's *Fantastic Fanzine* was among the first Riot Grrrl zines from DC to emerge in the wake of *Riot Grrrl* and *Bikini Kill*. "What we are doing is sincere and real," Reinstein wrote in the third issue. "We are not trying to be trendy or the next big thing like we're some kind of pop band. We are a group of girls who get together for support and to network because we need each other in this society that wants to act like we don't exist."

Fake and *Who Cares?*

Irene Chien returned home to the DC suburbs in spring 1992 from her first year at Oberlin College in Ohio. Spurred by boredom, she set to work on *Fake*, a fanzine expressing her growing interest in punk rock, feminism, and identity. Bearing her parents' address in Potomac, Maryland, as the zine's home base, "issue zero," as it was numbered, came out around May and was a potent snapshot of DC punk in early 1992. "I suppose I absolutely felt like an outsider to the scene," she remembered, despite the frequency with which she attended shows. "I'm an Asian American woman, so, already not the norm that you see in the DC punk scene. Plus, I was coming from the suburbs, and I imagined—not realizing at the time that that wasn't the case—but I imagined that everybody who was going to these shows somehow was living some sort of different, less suburban life," she said with a laugh.[61]

Fake tread a rare space where more polished layouts overlapped effectively with cut-and-paste détournement

Figure 8.12 *Who Cares?*, issues 1–4, 1991–92. Published by Steve Shapero. Used by permission.

and collage. Only a few hundred copies circulated, but many came decorated with glow-in-the dark glue, stickers, and Band-Aid bandages. These personal touches reminded readers of the almost artisanal quality fanzines were capable of. The layout combined text typed on a borrowed Apple II computer with images clipped from old magazines, all assembled in late-night sessions at the Rockville Kinko's when Chien was home during school breaks. "The people who worked there were either very, very sympathetic to zine makers because they were probably working there because they also did their own zines," Chien laughingly explained of the discounts she received on copies, "or completely didn't care." She continued: "And by copies I don't mean—I didn't actually print out the [finished] zine there, but all of the different copies that you have to make in order to get the raw materials that you then assemble. Copying and enlarging this thing three times, so that you have it the right size to cut out and paste. And just spend 2:00 to 4:00 a.m. at the Kinko's."[62]

The layouts of interviews with Nation of Ulysses, Bikini Kill, and Circus Lupus were presented with a moody, artistic flair absent from most other DC zines during this period. A subdued sense of alienation, even pain, pulses through much of the issue. It is visible in several of the examples of détournement found throughout *Fake*, with Chien criticizing pervasive, stifling societal norms by recontextualizing clippings from old magazines of mid-twentieth-century American family life. The 1950s-era image on the back cover of a woman teaching young students is subtly détourned with a trio of sad little stickers teachers used to scold underperforming children on their homework—"You did not listen," "Incomplete," and "Careless." The page smolders with a quiet heartbreak borne of the pressure young people can be under to conform and perform.

Around the time of *Fake*'s creation, Chien began attending Riot Grrrl meetings, inspired by what she heard, yet on the margins of the discussions taking place. "I basically sat silently and listened," she recalled. "I was not a runner of the meetings or an active guider of the conversation. But I would go to them every week, and I would listen, and I was just deeply in awe [laughs] of the women in these meetings, like Kathleen Hanna [and] Allison Wolfe."

Chien was taken with the possibilities that Riot Grrrl presented to someone like her, who felt outside DC's traditional punk and hardcore scenes. "It just actually seemed crazy that women could be . . . angry and sexy and in public, in this particular way." As she explained further:

> *That seemed so insane to me. And young women, women that looked like my peers. So, that was thrilling to me. And it was different and pushed against this mode of the super-masculine aggro hardcore scene, which was appealing to me because of its purity and aggressiveness and, to my mind, uncompromising political views. But also seemed to completely shut me out as a girl from that. And so that's what was really exciting to me about Riot Grrrl. That you could both be a girl who wants to talk about girl things with other girls, as well as unabashedly political and angry.*[63]

Galvanizing as the Riot Grrrl meetings were, Chien realized zines were her preferred forum for sharing her voice. "I grew up being told to be quiet, and not to raise trouble, and to listen carefully, in a Chinese American household, where that's absolutely the norm for a woman," she said. "So, I did that. I listened very quietly during these meetings, but I was completely blown away [laughs] by the women who were speaking very loudly at them. So, I think because I couldn't speak out loud in person and face-to-face, it was much more appealing to me to do a zine—where I don't have to be the face and the body attached to the voice, to be able to express my ideas or my emotions about things."[64]

Aside from Riot Grrrl and its related publications, Chien also cited zines like *Teenage Gang Debs*; the influential Berkeley, California, zine *Cometbus*; and her Oberlin classmate Josh MacPhee's *Fenceclimber* as having made an impression on her.[65] "My high school [classmate], Stephen Shapero, had this zine, *Who Cares?*, which because it emerged directly from the context of our shared high school experience, was also influential to me."[66]

Shapero, who studied alongside Chien at Potomac's Winston Churchill High School in the late 1980s and early 1990s, published six issues of *Who Cares?* from

1991 through 1993. He was introduced to DC's alternative rock scene by an unlikely source—his eighth-grade English teacher, whose husband was 9:30 Club co-owner, Rich Heinecke. "I mean, this is wildly inappropriate; no one would do this now—but she got us tickets to the 9:30 Club," Shapero laughingly recalled. "It was random, what show we went to—Zodiac Mindwarp and the Love Reaction, this British, kinda silly metal band. But, it was the old 9:30 Club. And going there—I was 13—and I was just like, "*This*." [laughs] You know? It was just like, "I need to be here.'"[67]

Shapero dove into the DC punk scene, taking in shows at the 9:30 Club and its short-lived competitor, the BBQ Iguana, as well as Positive Force shows at Saint Stephen and the Incarnation Church and Sacred Heart Church. While shopping at record stores like Yesterday & Today, Smash, or the Olsson's location in Georgetown, Shapero came across zines like *Greed* and *Uno Mas*, as well as DC's alternative news weekly, *Washington City Paper*. The clean layout and more intellectual tone of those publications appealed to him. "[*City Paper*] had very in-depth coverage of the local music scene," Shapero said. "And then there was that staff photographer—Darrow Montgomery—he had a very distinctive style. And that was actually my inspiration. I wanted to make my own version of *City Paper*. I wanted it to look really good and have dope photos and really be stylized. And then I saw *Greed*, and I was like, 'What is this? This is so dope.'"

Chien and Shapero both picked up design and production skills from their time at Churchill High School's literary magazine, *Erehwon*, and Shapero credited his photography teacher with letting him print the zine's photographs in the school darkroom. Like Chien, Shapero had access to computers and desktop publishing software, enabling his vision for the clean, professional aesthetic of *Who Cares?* "I was a nerd, and my dad was a nerd, and we had a PC, a 486, . . . a very old computer," Shapero recalled. "And we got ahold of a desktop publishing program, it might have been Aldus PageMaker, I think? And I loved it. It was so fun. It made it possible that you could try to make stuff look like *Greed*, you know, or like the *City Paper*. You could really make stuff look pro."

Over six issues, *Who Cares?* captured the DC scene during its early-1990s peak, interviewing leading bands like Velocity Girl, Gray Matter, Tsunami, Jawbox, and Holy Rollers. A stilted interview with Unrest in issue four from 1992 is a low point—"I was very young and earnest and naive, and they fucked with me the entire time," Shapero remembered—but an interview with Craig Wedren from Shudder to Think was the opposite. "That guy is just so talented," Shapero said of the vocalist/guitarist. "And, so, for me as an aspiring little baby punk dude, it was just so awesome. And he was very kind, very generous."

Although the interview with Wedren was conducted a few months before Nirvana's commercial explosion, it addressed the debate already brewing among underground bands about leaving indie labels for majors. "That's such a dilemma that we have," Wedren said:

> *I mean, not really, cause nobody's offered [laughs]. But we've been thinking about that, because we all want to move forward, and progress. But the one thing that's difficult about Dischord is their lack of promotions that they do, you know they don't advertise, and that's like an integral part of their philosophy.*[68] *And I respect that. I have an immense amount of respect for Ian and Jeff, and what Dischord stands for. I don't want to lose the artistic integrity that comes along with Dischord, and the total artistic freedom that we have being on Dischord, and . . . the lack of contractual obligations. But at the same time, I want to be able to broaden our audience and, I mean, I guess it can be done. Fugazi's proved that. I really don't know; I can't answer that. It's such a difficult question.*[69]

The impact of Nirvana and other alternative rock bands soured Shapero on the scene and *Who Cares?* petered out by 1993. "I felt like it just took all the oxygen out of our scene," he said. "And remember Jawbox, Shudder to Think, they signed to majors? Nothing wrong with signing to a major, but from that local scene point of view, where it was this intimate family—like, boom, that was done, right? . . . It was like the magic of it had gone." Despite the disappointing ending to Shapero's time in the DC scene—he

Figure 8.13 Original camera-ready artwork for "Chicks Up Front" photo layout in *Not Even*, issue 4, circa 1993. Published by Daisy Rooks.

moved to Montreal for college and became immersed in electronic music and DJ culture—he eventually reconnected with what initially inspired him. "I feel like breaking up with the DC scene was like your first big breakup in a romantic relationship," he said. "I was a little scarred by it, a little bitter. But time heals all wounds, and you go back, and you're like, 'No, this was dope.' Like, 'We were onto some shit! This was a really amazing, creative community.' There's very few things that came out of there that weren't worth listening to."

Not Even

Daisy Rooks explored punk and fanzines concurrent to Chien and Shapero, and in the same suburban Maryland milieu. She and her older sister, Margaret, fell into punk in the late 1980s, motivated by "a tremendous feeling of rage, and a tremendous feeling of not feeling into the community that we lived in, and the school that we went to, and trying to find other people who were similarly weird and discombobulated socially and angry," she recalled.[70]

The Rooks sisters' concert attendance habits highlighted various wings of DC's punk scene. The pair moved between straight-edge hardcore shows at the Safari Club, Positive Force benefits at Saint Stephen's, alternative rock concerts at the 9:30 Club, and indie and punk shows at both dc space and Georgetown's short-lived Mountain Lodge. "I was really into the straight edge scene," Rooks said. "But within punk and hardcore, my musical taste was pretty broad. So, we really tried to go to every show that we could." Despite a strict curfew imposed by her parents and not possessing a driver's license for most of high school, Rooks made do. "It was kind of hard to get home on time. There wasn't Uber. . . . So, I was often at a show, home late, grounded. Go to another show, home late, grounded."

The Dischord-centered scene and the straight-edge hardcore scene within DC often operated parallel to each other by the early 1990s, but Rooks overlapped with both. "It was very clear to me, very early on, that DC was such a special place to be," she remembered. Despite being a fan of DC bands like Fugazi and Nation of Ulysses and more aligned politically with the Dischord scene, Rooks felt the straight edge scene's music moved her most. "I loved [straight-edge hardcore] music live," she said. "But that was sort of a conservative, politically, scene and a lot of those guys were so sexist. I mean, so much sexism was just expected in that world. So, I was like, 'Oh, I understand that people in other parts of the [DC punk] scene have politics that are more similar to mine. But aesthetically and culturally and music-wise, I like [hardcore] better.'"

Rooks read any punk fanzine she encountered, with a particular love for Kent McClard's *No Answers*, Chris Boarts' *Slug and Lettuce*, and *Maximum Rocknroll*, all of which were published outside DC. Soon enough, she decided to start her own, *Not Even*. "I guess I had seen enough zines at that point, even if I hadn't seen that many, to know that the bar for entrance to this medium is low," she laughed. "It does not have to be beautiful. It does not have to be pristine. And that was really cool."

Figure 8.14 *Not Even*, issue 3, circa 1992. Published by Daisy Rooks.

Not Even was very much a hardcore fanzine, yet eschewed the graffiti aesthetics prevalent throughout much of that scene's zines and record cover art. Early issues mixed typed text with flashes of handwriting, interspersing concert photography amid the reviews, essays, and the occasional interview. In her second issue, Rooks declared an interview policy ensuring *Not Even* avoided coverage of overexposed bands. "I think that certain bands have been interviewed so many times that it is not interesting to repeat what has already been said," she wrote. "To remove myself from this 'problem,' I will try to interview bands whom I either haven't seen interviewed a lot, or whom I think I can do an interesting, different interview with." Indeed, interview subjects tended to include infrequently covered locals—like the former Fire Party vocalist Amy Pickering or straight-edge hardcore band Worlds Collide—or emerging national hardcore bands like Downcast and Shelter.

Not Even's final three issues—as well as a one-off collaboration zine, *Treadmill*, she published during this period with a friend from Richmond—saw Rooks' zine creation at a high point. The aesthetics of the zine grew more evocative, with Rooks' cut-and-paste layouts masterfully, poetically framing her writings on punk, feminism, straight edge, and the myriad of issues running through her teenage mind. "This zine is a reflection of who I am, how I think, and what I'm about," she wrote in a clear-eyed description of her work. Rooks pushed the boundaries of fanzines, mingling concert photographs of Lungfish and Split Lip with essays on domestic violence or gay and lesbian life in Ancient Greece. "What appealed to me about *Not Even* was Daisy wrote these articles and she used footnotes," musician and zine editor Amanda Huron said with an admiring laugh. "I was like, '*That* is badass.' I had never seen that in a zine before."[71] Jason Roe, who edited *Kill the Robot* fanzine, was also impressed. "Zines are a lot about the personality, and Daisy Rooks had a lot of personality," he recalled in 2023. "Particularly as a young woman in the hardcore scene, which, I don't know how it is now, but it was very male-dominated then. She spoke about a lot of different subjects and is just an incredibly intelligent woman."[72]

Rooks vocally criticized sexism within the hardcore scene, serving notice that she and other young women she was friends with would not be intimidated by violent behavior at shows. The Rooks sisters and their friends dubbed themselves the "Chicks Up Front Posse," a nod to their willingness to stake out a space at the front of the stage, as well as an inversion of a sexist chant used by male activists during counterculture protests in the late 1960s.[73] "Now it sounds like a hashtag," *Fake*'s Irene Chien later observed of the informal Chicks Up Front movement, "but she and [her] female friends would defiantly stand in the very front rows of shows and protect themselves and each other from what otherwise felt like a really violent and dangerous space where women weren't allowed, and women were actively pushed out of if they stood there."[74] Norman Brannon, a musician from New York and editor of the influential emo/hardcore fanzine *Anti-Matter* in the mid-1990s, recalled that "the Chicks Up Front thing was starting to be a real force in the hardcore scene and it was inspiring to see that kind of fearlessness and reclamation of feminist space in hardcore."[75]

Several men in the hardcore community served as allies to the Chicks Up Front Posse but, unsurprisingly, there was substantial pushback. "This whole chicks up front thing is quite silly," one male hardcore fan wrote in a letter published in *Not Even* issue four. "It's not any 'boys'' fault that more girls aren't involved. There doesn't seem to be an anti-girl scene to me. I see you at shows and you have quite the attitude. This is more clear during a band playing. You seem to get mad when you get pushed. Hardcore is hardcore."

The Rooks sisters were undeterred, with Margaret circulating a flier at shows calling out "meatheads and their 'harder than you' attitude." Also included in the first issue of her zine, *Quit Whining*, which she distributed in the DC area while home from Massachusetts during college breaks, the flier pulled no punches. "Don't tell me to move to the back, asshole, 'cuz I know just as much (maybe more) about the band, their music, their record label, their longsleeves as you do," Margaret Rooks wrote. "Don't push me out of the way, 'cuz I want to be up front and sing along just like you."

The corner of the flier read "this propaganda courtesy of Margaret/Riot Grrrl." Both Rooks sisters attended Riot Grrrl meetings, though Daisy felt less connected to it than her sister did. "I followed that scene very closely and there were many ways in which it was inspirational," Daisy Rooks recalled. "And I was doing something different, frankly. My sister was much more into that scene. I think [she] liked the music more than I did, and also just has always had a little bit more of a feminine presentation of self, so it made more sense to her. Aside from Bikini Kill, it never really grabbed me. But I don't mean that in a critical way at all. We were just doing our own thing in a different way."[76]

Circulation of *Not Even* was up to 1,500 copies by the fifth and final issue, but Rooks eventually felt her energy was better directed elsewhere. Off to Barnard College in New York by later in 1993 (and then Smith College in Massachusetts in the mid-1990s), she eventually felt drained by the constant effort required to battle sexism in the hardcore scene. "It was very exhausting," she recalled:

> *You could sort of flesh out the several dozen people that were willing to consider gender in straight edge, and then you were friends with them. And then you were sort of trying to chip away at the other people, and you were like, "I'm making no progress." So, at some point, I think I decided my political work or activism—I want to put that energy somewhere else. So, I got kind of involved in domestic violence issues and alternative transportation for a few years. And then I got really interested in labor unions and class and work. And, really, by the time I had moved up to Massachusetts, that's where my energy went.*[77]

Rooks' years in hardcore punk were often challenging, but she left with the conviction that she had something valuable to say to the world. Likewise, she discovered there was much to learn from speaking directly to others about their experiences. "I always loved interviewing, and that's really the thing that stuck with me from my zine years," she said. "I went to grad school and got a PhD and became a qualitative sociologist and I interview people all the time. That's my profession. I really honed those skills in my time in the zine world." Her experiences in punk "shaped me in a really profound way," she said. "I have always carried myself throughout the world as somebody that has something to say and I think that's all about being part of that world, and being part of that zine world."

■ ■ ■

It appeared punk had been turned inside out during the early 1990s. Opportunistic mainstream powers fed off punk's alterity and élan vital, upending and forcibly redefining a subculture that prided itself on operating apart from societal conventions. Even worse, the close associations shared by punks due to their relatively limited ranks—which admittedly could teeter into insularity—were frayed by media overexposure and the glut of unschooled new arrivals to the scene. As Steve Shapero of *Who Cares?* lamented, punk's magic seemed to have gone once the mainstream was let in on the secret, at least for some.

Conversely, the new participants were an undeniable boon to the health and longevity of the culture. More people interested in punk meant more people going to shows, forming bands, and putting out records. This was certainly the case when it came to fanzines, which were also aided by the proliferation of affordable technology for zine creation and distribution. As disruptive as the events of the early 1990s were to punk's zeitgeist, the fanzine community was about to grow even larger as the decade wore on.

Notes

1. Mike Gunderloy and Cari Goldberg Janice, *The World of Zines: A Guide to the Independent Magazine Revolution* (New York: Penguin Books, 1992), 3.
2. Jennifer Bleyer, "Cut-and-Paste Revolution: Notes from the Girl Zine Explosion," in *The Fire This Time: Young Activists and the New Feminism*, edited by Vivien Labaton and Dawn Lundy Martin (New York: Anchor Books, 2004), 44.
3. Kate Eichhorn, "Copy Machines and Downtown Scenes: Deterritorializing Urban Culture in a Pre-Digital Era," *Cultural Studies* 29, no. 3 (2015): 363–78, https://doi.org/10.1080/09502386.2014.937940.
4. Much as DC bands bristled at the tag of "emo-core" and, then, "emo," which was applied to mid-1980s bands like Rites of Spring, Embrace, and Dag Nasty, the Seattle bands tagged as "grunge" were also displeased.
5. Everett True, "Ten Myths about Grunge, Nirvana and Kurt Cobain," *Guardian*, August 24, 2011, www.theguardian.com/music/2011/aug/24/grunge-myths-nirvana-kurt-cobain.
6. Country star Garth Brooks' *Ropin' the Wind* occupied the week between *Nevermind*'s two stays at the top of the album chart before bulldozing it completely with an uninterrupted eight-week run at the top of the album chart throughout the spring of 1992, putting Nirvana's chart success in some perspective.
7. People considered a part of Generation X were born, roughly, between the mid-1960s and late 1970s.
8. Rich Shupe, "Grunge: 1992–1993, RIP," *New York*, March 29, 1993, 24.
9. Ginia Bellafante, "Where's the Next Seattle?" *Time*, October 25, 1993.
10. Pierce coedited *Uno Mas* through its third issue, before moving to Texas.
11. This is not the long-running feminist publication *off our backs*, which published several of the earliest writings on Riot Grrrl in the early 1990s, but the feminist erotica magazine *On Our Backs*, which once described itself as "entertainment for the adventurous lesbian."
12. Kurt Sayenga, interview with the author, June 13, 2017.
13. Scott Crawford, "High Back Chairs," *Uno Mas*, issue 4, 5–7.
14. Scott Crawford, "A Beautiful Day for a Funeral," *Uno Mas*, issue 3, 6–7.
15. Jack Rabid, "Fugazi: Surviving on a Steady Diet of the Do It Yourself Ethic," *Noise Works*, issue 3, September–October 1991, 22–23.
16. Scott Crawford, interview with the author, December 19, 2017.
17. Crawford, interview.
18. Englert, who died in 2020, was a prolific restaurateur who played a significant role in the growth of DC nightlife from the 1990s into the twenty-first century.
19. Joe Brown, "Heaven, Hell for Odd Souls: Nightlife," *Washington Post*, June 7, 1991.
20. Christe later made his name as a music journalist, and author, as well as founder of the publishing house Bazillion Points.
21. Paul Hendrickson, "Mark of the Urban Phantom," *Washington Post*, October 9, 1991.
22. Rob Myers, "Letters," *Whack*, issue 5, October 1991, 3.
23. The group split after its third album, *Gilded Stars and Zealous Hearts*, in 1996. It would occasionally reunite in the years since.
24. Gail O'Hara, "Lotsa Pop Losers 30 Years Later!" *Chickfactor*, October 20, 2021, https://www.chickfactor.com/tag/lotsa-pop-losers/.
25. Brandon Gentry, "Lotsa Pop Losers Festival: An Oral History," *Washington City Paper*, March 27, 2013.
26. Gentry.
27. Jeff Bagato, "Nation of Ulysses," *CrackDC*, issue 4, September 1991, 17.
28. Sharon Cheslow, "(The Nation of) Ulysses." *Interrobang*, issue 1, 1989, 11.
29. *Muhammad Speaks* was renamed multiple times before settling on *Muslim Journal*.
30. Allison Wolfe, interview with the author, June 15, 2017.
31. Tim Green, "The Nation of Ulysses: *13 Point Program to Destroy America*," podcast produced by Brian Gathy, *End on End*, MP3 audio, WNYC, June 30, 2022, www.wnycstudios.org/podcasts/radiolab/segments/91518-goat-on-a-cow.
32. Kara Jesella and Marisa Meltzer, *How Sassy Changed My Life: A Love Letter to the Greatest Teen Magazine of All Time* (New York: Faber & Faber, 2007), 73.
33. Roxanne Roberts, "Here's One Too Cool Total Babe," *Washington Post*, September 22, 1990.
34. Brandon Gentry, "The Nation of Ulysses: *13 Point Program to Destroy America*," in *Capitol Contingency: Post-Punk, Indie Rock, and Noise Pop in Washington, DC, 1991–1999* (New Orleans: Garrett County Press, 2012), 10.
35. Nathan Nedorostek and Anthony Pappalardo, *Radio Silence: A Selected Visual History of American Hardcore Music* (New York: MTV Press, 2008).
36. Erin Smith, interview with the author, January 20, 2023.
37. Smith.
38. David Rose, "Attack of the Teenage Gang Debs," *Diamondback*, November 26, 1991, 7.
39. Smith, interview.

40. Erin Smith, email interview with the author, January 26, 2023.
41. Erin Smith, interview with the author, January 20, 2023.
42. Mark Andersen, "Invasion of the Riot Grrrls," *CrackDC*, September 1991, 13.
43. Julia Downes, "Riot Grrrl: The Legacy and Contemporary Landscape of DIY Feminist Cultural Activism," in *Riot Grrrl: Revolution Girl Style Now*, edited by Nadine Monem (London: Black Dog, 2007).
44. Sara Marcus, *Girls to the Front: The True Story of the Riot Grrrl Revolution* (New York: HarperPerennial, 2010), 76.
45. Allison Wolfe, "Music," https://www.allisoncwolfe.com/music.
46. Portia Sabin, "Part One," in *Girl Germs*, podcast, MP3 audio, December 5, 2018, 19:56.
47. Jen Smith, interview with the author, January 2, 2019.
48. Marcus, *Girls to the Front*, 78–79.
49. Wolfe, interview.
50. Marcus, *Girls to the Front*, 80.
51. Wolfe, interview.
52. Marcus, *Girls to the Front*, 89; Kathleen Hanna, *Rebel Girl: My Life as a Feminist Punk* (New York: Ecco, 2024), 161–62.
53. Hanna.
54. Hanna.
55. Andersen, "Invasion," 13.
56. Reinstein's name is now Billie Rain-Shadid, but is referred to here by the name that they wrote under at the time.
57. Kristin Schilt and Elke Zobl, "Connecting the Dots: Riot Grrrls, Ladyfests, and the International Grrrl Zine Network," in *Next Wave Cultures: Feminism, Subcultures, Activism*, edited by Anita Harris (New York: Routledge, 2008).
58. Melissa Klein, "Duality and Redefinition: Young Feminism and the Alternative Music Community," in *Third Wave Agenda: Being Feminist, Doing Feminism*, edited by Leslie Heywood and Jennifer Drake (Minneapolis: University of Minnesota Press, 1997).
59. K. Dunn and M. S. Farnsworth, "'We Are the Revolution': Riot Grrrl Press, Girl Empowerment, and DIY Self-Publishing," *Women's Studies* 41, no. 2 (2012): 136–57.
60. Marcus, *Girls to the Front*, 212–15.
61. Irene Chien, interview with the author, November 21, 2017.
62. Chien.
63. Chien.
64. Chien.
65. MacPhee, Chien, and Rebecca Parker also collaborated on a zine distribution called Junglegym circa 1992–94. MacPhee left Oberlin during this period and moved to DC, where he helped launch the Beehive record store and community space.
66. Chien, interview.
67. Steve Shapero, interview with the author, December 11, 2020.
68. Dischord advertised extensively in punk fanzines, but not in larger music magazines. The label's in-house publicist, Cynthia Connolly, particularly built strong connections between the label and fanzine creators, supporting them through advertising and providing review copies.
69. Steve Shapero, "Shudder to Think," *Who Cares?* issue 4, 1991, 12.
70. Daisy Rooks, interview with the author, December 22, 2020.
71. Amanda Huron, interview with the author, January 18, 2019.
72. Jason Roe, interview with the author, November 30, 2023.
73. As journalist Mary Wiegers explained in 1970 about the phrase "chicks up front," it was used by male activists urging women to move to the front lines of a protest. "The cops, presumably, would be less likely to bop a woman over the head than a male," she wrote. "And if they did, there would be more sympathy for the cause if television viewers saw burly policemen roughing up a girl. Whether this tactic worked or not on police, it soon worked on the women. They got mad. They had gone into the civil rights, peace, and campus radical movements expecting to be treated as equals." Mary Wiegers, "Women's Work among the Radicals: Second of Four Articles," *Washington Post*, March 9, 1970.
74. Chien, interview.
75. Norman Brannon, email to the author, June 5, 2018.
76. Rooks, interview.
77. Rooks.

9

Crazy Town, 1993–1999

PUNK'S COMMERCIAL SUCCESS and cultural creep accelerated into the mid-1990s. Nirvana disbanded after Kurt Cobain's death in April 1994 but, in the weeks ahead, another branch of punk rock—headed by the California bands Green Day and the Offspring—surprisingly scraped the pop charts' upper reaches. These groups mined the same lyrical topics of mental health, drug use, and societal alienation that Nirvana had, but with more collegiality and willingness to mug for mainstream cameras. While Green Day had left an independent punk record label—Berkeley, California's, Lookout! Records—for a major label, the success of the Offspring was a surprising, even encouraging story. Their initial success came on an independent label—Southern California's Epitaph Records, founded by members of the punk band Bad Religion—selling 6 million copies in the United States alone of their 1994 album, *Smash*. Labelmates Rancid and NOFX released platinum and gold records of their own, respectively, on Epitaph during the mid-1990s. Regardless of the heated debate populating zines at this time about the artistic and ethical merits of those bands, the Offspring and their successful ilk demonstrated huge audiences could be reached without signing to a major label.

The move to major labels several DC bands pondered in the early 1990s came to fruition by 1994. Jawbox released the *Savory + 3* EP and *For Your Own Special Sweetheart* album for Atlantic Records, in January and February 1994, respectively, while Shudder to Think followed later that year with *Pony Express Record* for Epic Records. Even Unrest had morphed into a tight, catchy—though still idiosyncratic—guitar-driven pop band. *Perfect Teeth*, their 1993 full-length album on the British label 4AD, was distributed in North America by Warner Brothers Records, an affiliation unthinkable when they issued their earliest *outré* recordings in the 1980s. As the 1990s progressed, more DC indie bands—Tuscadero, Edsel, and the Dismemberment Plan—signed with major labels but, across the board, none succeeded enough commercially to be retained long. Most disbanded in the wake of their major label terminations, but the Dismemberment Plan retreated to their previous label, DeSoto, and created their best and most commercially successful work in the late 1990s and early 2000s. "To me, it's not a major versus a minor," musician and *Chickfactor* fanzine coeditor Pam Berry explained in 1996. "Just find me a cool label. It's that most major labels suck."[1]

Despite some DC bands striking up business relationships with corporations—an act that could easily have disconnected them from the city's DIY punks—little changed regarding their ongoing participation in the scene, aside from Shudder to Think's relocation to New York City. Members of bands on major labels remained linked to the community, releasing singles on indie labels and performing at punk-rooted venues like the Black Cat and the 9:30 Club. Despite earlier fears about the impact that bands moving to majors would have, the midpoint of the 1990s saw a stable, thriving, musically diverse DC punk scene that continued drawing new participants.

Figure 9.1 Jawbox performs at the Black Cat in DC, circa 1995. The author observes, seated on the left in an Edsel T-shirt. Photo by Jim Saah. Used by permission.

"You knew something special was happening," recalled Hal Miller, a University of Maryland student who published two issues of the fanzine *New Traffic Pattern* during this period. "The city had a supportive, growing community of creative, forward-thinking people playing inspiring and interesting music. I feel extremely fortunate to have been in the right place at the right time. It was a great time to discover music and go out and see bands. Bands whose members you'd see out and could hang out with."[2] Jeff Bagato, who edited *Mole* fanzine, also remarked upon the accessibility of the scene's more popular bands. "There was none of that kind of star thing in DC like there was possibly in other cities, where people were getting signed and then, suddenly, they're millionaires [and] they're not going to talk to the hoi polloi," he recalled. "It was kind of a cool scene because you could just go up and talk to people."[3]

The influx of cash to successful national indie labels like Epitaph, Sub Pop, Lookout!, and Matador meant more resources for releasing and promoting new music. The desire to exude authenticity endured within the world of punk and indie, so continuing to advertise in fanzines with minute print runs indicated that a larger punk label—some now entertaining or even accepting offers to team up with major labels for distribution and funding—had seemingly not lost touch with their roots. I was a DC punk fanzine editor during this era—publishing six issues of *Slanted* from fall 1993 to spring 1995 and starting another fanzine, *Held Like Sound*, in 1997—and was perpetually bemused by the ongoing support I received from larger punk labels whose releases I typically reviewed negatively. More positively, within the DC scene, labels like Simple Machines, Teen-Beat, and Dischord created a symbiotic relationship with

Figure 9.2 Left: *Slanted*, issue 4, summer 1994. Right: *Held Like Sound*, issue 3, summer 1998. Both published by the author.

fanzines, lending advertisement support and setting up interviews with bands, who generally saw extensive coverage of the sort larger magazines did not provide. When Simple Machines agreed to place a half page advertisement—for ten dollars—in the first issue of *Slanted*, I was stunned that an as-yet unpublished fanzine edited by an unknown teenager would enjoy that level of trust.

Zines reached a saturation point by the mid-1990s, with R. Seth Friedman of *Factsheet Five*—a widely read publication covering zines, packed with hundreds of brief reviews each issue—estimating that as many as fifty thousand titles were publishing by then.[4] "After Xerox machines became widely accessible and before the explosion of the internet," the writer Jennifer Bleyer explained, "there was a brief moment during which people realized that they could make their own rudimentary publications on copy paper, fasten them with staples, and send them out along the zine distribution thoroughfares that coursed across the country, without any permission or guidance whatsoever."[5]

Scores of zines were published in the DC area during the middle to late 1990s. Long-running titles like *Uno Mas* and *Sweet Portable You* thrived, while newer titles gained notice, such as *Chickfactor*, *Punk Life*, *Torpedo Dialogues*, and *Brickthrower*. Never mind the dozens of short-lived, but still engaging, zines like *Yeah*, *Jaded*, *Beautiful Decay*, *Faceless*, *Things Fall Apart*, *Xanadu*, and many more. DC's zine culture was never bigger than during this time, and the various voices gave a fuller idea of how DC's scene had grown since zine editors in the 1980s decried DC punk's homogeneity. By the second half of the 1990s, exhortations to broaden punk's sound had undeniably been heeded, even if some musicians objected to the term "punk" being used to describe their music. The punk community included bands playing hardcore metal (Damnation AD, Darkest Hour), dub-influenced emocore (Hoover, the Crownhate Ruin, Regulator Watts), lo-fi noise (Rake, Wingtip Sloat), straight-edge hardcore (Battery, Good Clean Fun), clever indie rock (Smart Went Crazy, the Dismemberment Plan), highly melodic punk (Trusty, Chisel, My Life in Rain), post-hardcore (Kerosene 454, Frodus, the Most Secret Method, Bluetip), throat-shredding screamo (pg. 99, Majority Rule), jazz and funk-inflected post-rock (Sea Tiger, the Sorts), avant-garde postpunk (Meltdown, Meta-matics, the Crainium, All-Scars) and humorous indie pop (Blast Off Country Style, Tuscadero), along with more traditional punk bands like the Suspects, Crispus Attucks, and the Goons. That small sampling of the scores of bands active in the scene during that period—I did not even get to Slant 6, Pitchblende, the Make-Up, Trans Am, Crom-Tech, the Monorchid, the Warmers, the Impossible Five, Burning Airlines, and so many more—indicated how, by then, punk's hallmark was as much about spirit as it was a musical aesthetic.

Despite print zines' growth in popularity, the middle to late 1990s proved to be their last days as the dominant medium for punk fans to share musical opinions. The incoming century saw the internet become the primary forum for communication within the punk subculture, first with webzines and online message boards and, soon, through blogs and social media. "In many ways, zines

Figure 9.3 Fred Erskine and Chris Farrall of Hoover perform at the Black Cat in DC in early 1994. Photo by the author.

Likewise, *Uno Mas* continued mixing thoughtful band interviews with literary magazine sensibilities. Conversations with musicians remained a fixture—DC's Ian MacKaye, Edsel, and Liquorice, as well as Guided by Voices and the former *Zone V* contributor Thurston Moore of Sonic Youth were a few—but, as *Uno Mas* established from its earliest issues, readers could equally expect poetry, still life photography, linocut art, and sit-downs with authors. Writers of the moment like T. C. Boyle (*The Road to Wellville*), David Sedaris (circa "Santaland Diaries"), and Frank McCourt (*Angela's Ashes*) spoke with *Uno Mas*, although the latter might not have realized he was talking with a small-run fanzine. "When I asked [McCourt's] publisher for an interview and I told her what our circulation was like, there was just this pregnant pause," Saah remembered between laughs. "And then she lied to him, 'cause she told me, "Don't tell him what your circulation is!"[8]

predicted what would soon happen on the web," Bleyer wrote. "Although the comparison is akin to that between a firecracker pop and a nuclear bomb, they helped pave the way for a culture that would allow anyone with anything to say, to say it." Music writer Richard Gehr also cited zines as an important predecessor to internet culture, noting that they "were instrumental in effecting the shift to highly personalized culture (or the 'micro-politics of identity') that now thrives on the internet."[6]

Uno Mas and *Sweet Portable You*

Most fanzines of any genre disappear after a few issues but, remarkably, *Uno Mas* and *Sweet Portable You* each published steadily throughout the 1990s. Patrick Foster and his colleagues churned out more than fifty issues of *Sweet Portable You* during the 1993–99 window, maintaining the signature blend of surreal prose and astute musical criticism it forged from its earliest issues. "I did find a lot of rock criticism at the time pretty limiting," he recalled. "It was nice that we stayed right on our rail and kind of didn't veer away from it, and remained right until the end as absurd."[7]

Silver Spring, Maryland–based author George Pelecanos made a name for himself through the 1990s as an author of DC-set crime novels, before attaining even greater creative and professional success in the twenty-first century for his novels and, particularly, as a television producer and writer on shows like *The Wire* and *The Deuce*. He, too, was interviewed for *Uno Mas*—musician and journalist Eric Brace profiled him in issue ten in 1995, just as Pelecanos's writing career took off—but his connection to the zine went beyond the publicity circuit. Pelecanos and Saah befriended each other in the early 1990s at Chuck & Dave's, an independent bookstore in Takoma Park, Maryland.[9] "[Saah] was an artist but not precious about it," Pelecanos recalled:

> *We ended up collaborating on a photojournalism project that was pretty interesting, back when I was riding midnights with the MPD.*[10] *Jim and I are friends to this day. Anyway, I liked his magazine. I*

felt it was a cut above the other zines I was checking out at places like Phantasmagoria, the great record store near the Wheaton Triangle, where I used to buy my vinyl. The writing was better, and Uno Mas *had the quality of a coffee table book, with beautiful cover photography by Saah. He asked me to write for him, and I wanted to be a part of it.*[11]

Pelecanos contributed film criticism to the twelfth issue of *Uno Mas* in 1997, reviewing the types of film noir and blaxploitation movies clearly embedded in his creative psyche. The mood, common themes, and bracing dynamics of the similarly disposed film genres intertwined throughout the incisive, gritty novels he published during this period. Likewise, punk's energy and affect left a mark on the young writer. "These bands fired my own ambitions," he later wrote:

My background and state-school education told me I would never be admitted to that group of writers whose privileged lives were described on countless book flaps ("He divides his time between Martha's Vineyard and a brownstone on the Upper West Side. This is his first collection of short stories"). I had never taken a writing class when I attempted to write my first book. Hell, I had never even met a novelist. To me, authors were "other people." But bands like Fugazi and the [Replacements] and Hüsker Dü told me, by example, that my lack of pedigree meant nothing relative to my potential for creativity. These people picked up guitars and played, and in the process made a kind of organic, volcanic art. I didn't have the aptitude for instrumentation. But I thought I could do something similar with a pen. At the very least, these bands assured me I had the right to try.[12]

Figure 9.4 *Uno Mas*, issue 12, 1996. Published by Jim Saah. Used by permission.

Sweet Portable You's Foster also committed to incorporating punk's egalitarian, nonprescriptive principles into his publication. Freedom of thought was as prioritized for the zine's readers as much as for the writers. Abstract reviews of recordings and concerts allowed readers to project their personalities onto the criticism, much as *Sweet Portable You*'s critics did when assessing a creative work. "In the same way that I definitely wanted people to be able to write [reviews] without any restriction, I also felt it was really important to interpret without any restriction as well," he said.

Foster concluded print production of *Sweet Portable You* in 2000, focusing instead on raising his young family and building a career as a writer, which, among other assignments, led him to cover music for the *Washington Post* and *Spin*. "I think [*Sweet Portable You*] fulfilled a part of me that was really lacking, and it really kind of solidified that I was good enough or I had enough intellectual currency about music to be able to have a discussion with people I respected," he said. He continued:

That sense of direction and purpose and authenticity that it gave to my life at that time, and my ability to create, that really has stuck with me for a long time. I don't know what would have happened or

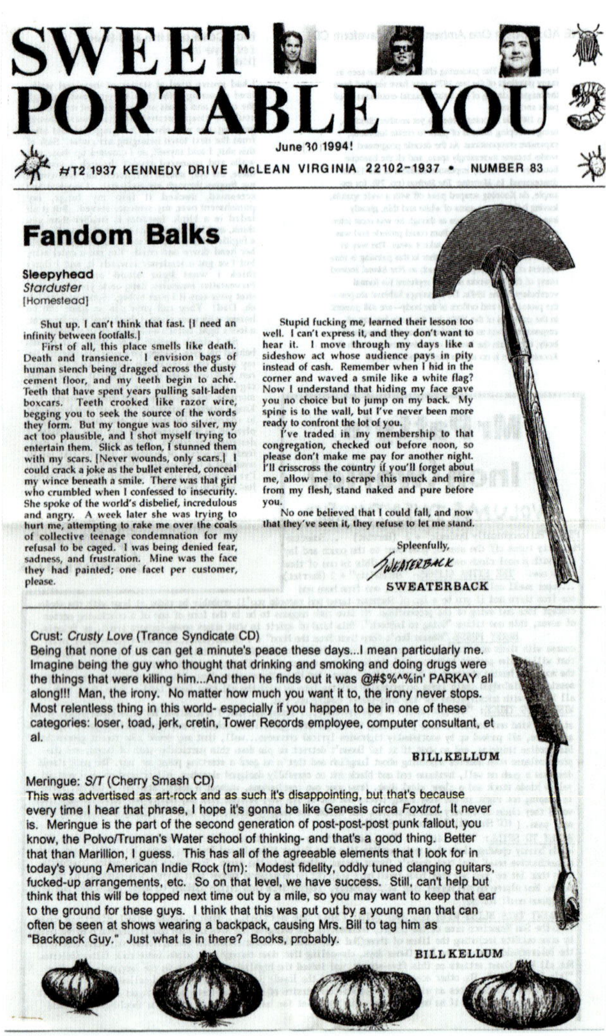
SWEET PORTABLE YOU

June 30 1994!

#T2 1937 KENNEDY DRIVE McLEAN VIRGINIA 22102-1937 • NUMBER 83

Fandom Balks

Sleepyhead
Starduster
[Homestead]

Shut up. I can't think that fast. [I need an infinity between footfalls.]

First of all, this place smells like death. Death and transience. I envision bags of human stench being dragged across the dusty cement floor, and my teeth begin to ache. Teeth that have spent years pulling salt-laden boxcars. Teeth crooked like razor wire, begging you to seek the source of the words they form. But my tongue was too silver, my act too plausible, and I shot myself trying to entertain them. Slick as teflon, I stunned them with my scars. [Never wounds, only scars.] I could crack a joke as the bullet entered, conceal my wince beneath a smile. There was that girl who crumbled when I confessed to insecurity. She spoke of the world's disbelief, incredulous and angry. A week later she was trying to hurt me, attempting to rake me over the coals of collective teenage condemnation for my refusal to be caged. I was being denied fear, sadness, and frustration. Mine was the face they had painted; one facet per customer, please.

Stupid fucking me, learned their lesson too well. I can't express it, and they don't want to hear it. I move through my days like a sideshow act whose audience pays in pity instead of cash. Remember when I hid in the corner and waved a smile like a white flag? Now I understand that hiding my face gave you no choice but to jump on my back. My spine is to the wall, but I've never been more ready to confront the lot of you.

I've traded in my membership to that congregation, checked out before noon, so please don't make me pay for another night. I'll crisscross the country if you'll forget about me, allow me to scrape this muck and mire from my flesh, stand naked and pure before you.

No one believed that I could fall, and now that they've seen it, they refuse to let me stand.

Spleenfully,
Sweaterback
SWEATERBACK

Crust: *Crusty Love* (Trance Syndicate CD)
Being that none of us can get a minute's peace these days...I mean particularly me. Imagine being the guy who thought that drinking and smoking and doing drugs were the things that were killing him...And then he finds out it was @#$%^%in' PARKAY all along!!! Man, the irony. No matter how much you want it to, the irony never stops. Most relentless thing in this world- especially if you happen to be in one of these categories: loser, toad, jerk, cretin, Tower Records employee, computer consultant, et al.

BILL KELLUM

Meringue: *S/T* (Cherry Smash CD)
This was advertised as art-rock and as such it's disappointing, but that's because every time I hear that phrase, I hope it's gonna be like Genesis circa *Foxtrot*. It never is. Meringue is the part of the second generation of post-post-post punk fallout, you know, the Polvo/Truman's Water school of thinking- and that's a good thing. Better that than Marillion, I guess. This has all of the agreeable elements that I look for in today's young American Indie Rock (tm): Modest fidelity, oddly tuned clanging guitars, fucked-up arrangements, etc. So on that level, we have success. Still, can't help but think that this will be topped next time out by a mile, so you may want to keep that ear to the ground for these guys. I think that this was put out by a young man that can often be seen at shows wearing a backpack, causing Mrs. Bill to tag him as "Backpack Guy." Just what is in there? Books, probably.

BILL KELLUM

Figure 9.5 *Sweet Portable You*, issue 83, June 30, 1994. Published by Patrick Foster. Used by permission.

> *where I would have ended up if I hadn't, in March of '89, decided to pursue this. So, I wince at some of the very early writing, but if I hadn't done it, who knows where I would be.*[13]

Mole and Brutarian

Like *Sweet Portable You*, Jeff Bagato's fanzine *Mole* seemed as fascinated with outsider culture as it did the DC punk scene, if not more so. Bagato published *Mole*'s first two issues while living in Florida, then migrating in 1990 to Herndon, Virginia—a suburb about 20 miles outside DC—unveiling an impressive run of zines concluding with issue thirteen in fall 2000. Music coverage was swaddled in comics, experimental poetry, bizarre clip art, and letters to the editor from the likes of the arch transgressive punk GG Allin.[14] "I think I developed a pretty elaborate thing—outsider art, crackpot thought, other music, and the counterculture," Bagato recalled. "Part of that's just because as the 1990s wore on, music got a lot less interesting. I was just getting tons of stuff, and every band sounded the same. Grunge killed the underground, it was terrible."[15]

Bagato excelled at blending punk and indie rock fandom with the gleeful weirdness of the *Weekly World News* and other lurid tabloids popular at the time straddling the line between satire and exploitation. The table of contents for issue four from 1991 trumpets *Mole*'s skewed sense of humor. "I Was a Muzak Zombie Wannabe" squawks one headline, while another chortles "Jesus, LSD, and Me." Even that issue's interview with Fugazi's Ian MacKaye gets refracted through *Mole*'s prism, focusing solely on MacKaye's love for the mainstream newspaper comic strip, *Mark Trail*. MacKaye seems almost relieved to get a break from his usual interview regimen of hashing out the evils of major labels and whether or not he was still straight edge. Instead, he luxuriates in his fandom of the strip's eponymous environmentalist hero. "I just called [to complain] once, but I did a phone tree," MacKaye told Bagato of efforts he and his friends made to resurrect *Mark Trail* after the *Washington Post* canceled it:

> *I called every [punk] group house I knew. Each house that had a subscription called and they called everyone they knew who had subscriptions. It just went house by house. I would never have expected* The Post *to bring it back. We were on tour and we get this message from here saying "Mark Trail's coming back." When I read the story about it, it was so great. I think twelve thousand calls were made complaining about the comics. . . . I had no idea anyone else read the thing, so I thought there wasn't a chance in hell it would show up again. We were just into the eccentric nature of the strip and I thought everyone else would think it was stupid. Actually, it is stupid.*

Figure 9.6 *Mole*, Issue 4, 1991. Published by Jeff Bagato. Used by permission.

Bagato's interview, lighthearted as it was, stands out by illuminating MacKaye's sense of humor, which weightier discussions often obscured in interviews. "Keep an eye on *The Family Circus*," MacKaye warned wryly of the popular, straitlaced comic strip. "Bil Keane is a twisted motherfucker in how many references to death there are [and] how many ghosts show up from time to time. It's a weird thing to put in a comic strip."

Most issues of *Mole* were ornamented with covers copied onto vivid Astrobright paper, which Bagato sourced directly from a paper supply store. "[I'd] get a better deal on the paper, and bring [the copy shop] the paper for the covers, and then they would do the interior. They would print it all, but they would have their own paper for the interior."[16] Bagato, with occasional help from a friend, collated and stapled the earlier issues himself, putting countless hours into the assembly process. Earlier print runs in the triple digits soon rose to three thousand copies by later issues, as Bagato's fruitful relationship with national zine distributors like Tower Records and Desert Moon necessitated more copies.

Mole continued blending coverage of alternative and indie bands like L7, Scrawl, and Crash Worship with Bagato's customary blend of humor and love for the idiosyncratic. One highlight from outside punk coverage was a 1998 interview in issue twelve with Vanilla Ice, a rapper whose 1990 track "Ice Ice Baby" was the first hip-hop song to top *Billboard*'s Hot 100 chart.[17] Ice's career had stalled by 1998, however, and his name was a perpetual punchline for jokes about the inauthenticity of many white rappers like him. Bagato was offered a chance in 1998 to speak with Ice—then attempting a rebrand with a metal-rap crossover sound—but was less interested in "Ice Ice Baby" or the rapper's humiliating fall from grace than he was something he saw in the background of Ice's promotional photo.

Coral Castle is a peculiar stone structure located in South Florida assembled in the early twentieth century by Edward Leedskalnin, a notable American eccentric. This work fit right in with Bagato's taste for outsider art, so after seeing Coral Castle in Ice's publicity photo, he spent the interview asking about it. "He had grown up [in the area], and he knew all about it," an impressed Bagato recalled. "You think, 'Oh, the guy that did 'Ice Ice Baby' is a moron' [but] this guy was no moron. He was a really nice guy, really smart. He knew exactly what he was doing at the time." Much like the interview with MacKaye, *Mole*'s talk with Ice offered readers an underexplored facet of a thoroughly covered musician to meaningful effect.

By *Mole*'s final issue in late 2000, distribution contracted in the wake of the internet's growth and larger print runs that so recently made sense swiftly became a millstone. Bagato remembered wondering how he would ever distribute the "boxes and boxes in the basement" of *Mole*, which he ultimately held on to for decades. Overstock lingered so long that Bagato left behind dozens of old copies of *Mole* after attending the 2014 DC Zinefest, much to the organizers' consternation. "Yeah, they got mad at me," he admitted. "I was just like, 'I've got to try to unload this stuff. Maybe ten, twenty years later, it'll actually find its audience.'"

Asked why *Mole* ended, Bagato cited the grind of regularly producing issues, as well as the lack of feedback that zine editors often encounter. "It's thankless," he said. "After a while, it's like, 'I kind of did this. I've learned everything I'm going to learn about this, and it's time to move on. It's time to focus on my creative work rather than trying to document other people's creative work. That's what I need to do.'" Aside from writing for numerous other publications, Bagato curated a series of experimental electronic music from 2003 to 2010 called "Electric Possible." Freed from the responsibilities of publishing *Mole*, Bagato was able to harness his creative energies to build a legacy as a prolific poet, writer, visual artist, and electronic musician.

Another Northern Virginia–based publication, Dom Salemi's *Brutarian*, reveled in the unusual, much as *Mole* did. *Brutarian*, however, was as cheerfully smutty as it was smart, covering creative works dismissed by many as trash as if they were canonical. Its sweet-and-sour mix of literary magazine elements—fiction was a regular feature, often from established authors like Dennis Etchison and Jack Ketchum, as well as poetry—ostentatiously vulgar comics, and shrewd music criticism almost felt like a funhouse mirror version of *Uno Mas*, as if edited by cult film director John Waters. Seemingly for *Brutarian*, the profane was sacred.

Salemi and artist Jarrett Huddleston launched *Brutarian* in June 1991, naming it after the French artist Jean Dubuffet's art brut ("raw art") movement valorizing the creative works of the outsider.[18] *Brutarian* quickly grew in popularity, and its more professional characteristics—glossy color covers, wide distribution through Desert Moon and Tower Records—could lead to it being labeled a prozine, a term for publications lacking the amateur essence of a fanzine. Still, unabashed fandom of art on the fringes was obviously what propelled *Brutarian*.

Its entertaining interviews included fairly unsurprising subjects like psychobilly acts the Cramps and Reverend Horton Heat, but also artists from the world of horror

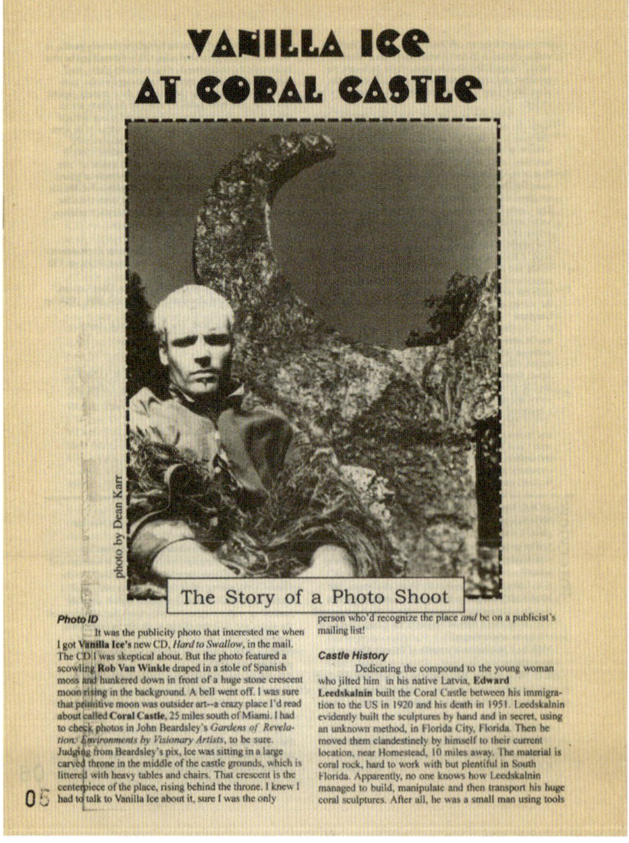

VANILLA ICE AT CORAL CASTLE

photo by Dean Karr

The Story of a Photo Shoot

Photo ID

It was the publicity photo that interested me when I got **Vanilla Ice's** new CD, *Hard to Swallow*, in the mail. The CD I was skeptical about. But the photo featured a scowling **Rob Van Winkle** draped in a stole of Spanish moss and hunkered down in front of a huge stone crescent moon rising in the background. A bell went off. I was sure that primitive moon was outsider art--a crazy place I'd read about called **Coral Castle**, 25 miles south of Miami. I had to check photos in John Beardsley's *Gardens of Revelation: Environments by Visionary Artists*, to be sure. Judging from Beardsley's pix, Ice was sitting in a large carved throne in the middle of the castle grounds, which is littered with heavy tables and chairs. That crescent is the centerpiece of the place, rising behind the throne. I knew I had to talk to Vanilla Ice about it, sure I was the only person who'd recognize the place *and* be on a publicist's mailing list!

Castle History

Dedicating the compound to the young woman who jilted him in his native Latvia, **Edward Leedskalnin** built the Coral Castle between his immigration to the US in 1920 and his death in 1951. Leedskalnin evidently built the sculptures by hand and in secret, using an unknown method, in Florida City, Florida. Then he moved them clandestinely by himself to their current location, near Homestead, 10 miles away. The material is coral rock, hard to work with but plentiful in South Florida. Apparently, no one knows how Leedskalnin managed to build, manipulate and then transport his huge coral sculptures. After all, he was a small man using tools

05

Figure 9.7 *Mole*, issue 12; and Vanilla Ice article, 1998. Published by Jeff Bagato. Used by permission.

Figure 9.8 *Brutarian*, issue 19, 1996. Published by Dom Salemi. Used by permission.

films and books, such as John Carpenter, Clive Barker, and Herschell Gordon Lewis. The comics found in each issue were especially piquant, pushing boundaries and buttons without hesitation. Mike Diana, a cartoonist who was the first artist convicted of obscenity in the United States, was a contributor, alongside Huddleston, Gary Leib, and others. "Shock value is not our purpose," Salemi told the *Washington Post*, "but we do put in stuff that's not quite politically correct in hopes of provoking a dialogue."[19]

Salemi referred to *Brutarian* as "a labor of love" that, due to the security of his job as an attorney for the United States Patent and Trademark Office, he felt no pressure to compromise on. Print publication ran intermittently up through 2012, shifting online under the new name *Beatsville* and ongoing as of 2024. As Salemi explained in a 2001 "statement of purpose," *Brutarian* always championed "art made by the innocent, the naive, the hopelessly insane. Idiots, madmen, and geniuses compelled to unloose their visions on an unsuspecting and uncaring world."[20]

Scorpion

In the early 1990s, Willona Sloan was a high school cheerleader in suburban Herndon and, like most of her peers, enjoyed rock, hip-hop, go-go, and popular music. "I was on board with American mainstream culture," she recalled. "But I also knew there was something different. I was one of the only African American students at my high school. I felt like I was fitting in, but I just always felt a little bit on the outside, even though I was on the inside."[21] Her older brother was off at college in Richmond and, immersed in the thriving punk scene there, sent his sister mixtapes bursting with exciting sounds.

Sloan ventured further into punk through attending concerts by the Virginia band Avail at the Reston Community Center and Fugazi at DC's Fort Reno Park. The blend of activism and kinetic music at each was just what she had sought, but the Fugazi concert was particularly formative. Her parents disapproved of her attending punk shows downtown that ran late into the night, but the Fort Reno concert series' early evening start time and location in DC's bustling but relatively genteel Tenleytown neighborhood made it an easier sell when asking for permission to go. Her parents relented, allowing her to catch a ride with a group of older friends down to the show.

Entering the park that summer evening, Sloan's feeling of not quite fitting in was at the front of her mind. Instead of encountering the standoffish scene she feared, however, she felt at home. "I remember walking in and it was just like all this energy," she said. "All these people who just—maybe people would have said they looked different—but to me, it was just like, 'These are my people!'"

As she explored punk culture further, Sloan learned of the Boston-area punk fanzine *Suburban Voice*, which opened her mind to the possibilities inherent in a print expression of fandom. "I loved the energy of the interviews," she recalled. "I started to get really anxious. I was like, 'I have to do this.' Like, 'I'm really shy. I don't know how I'm going to do this. I don't know how I'm going to call people up. I don't know how I'm going to ask them. But I *have* to do this. And I also have to listen to this music.'"

Sloan sent a letter to Al Quint, editor of *Suburban Voice*, hoping she might be able to write for his zine. Within, she described her life to Quint, "being Black, being punk, and finding my way," she remembered. Quint responded encouragingly, explaining the value of her perspective by urging her to create her own fanzine. Around this same time, Sloan was an intern at the Women's Institute for Freedom of the Press in DC. A mentor there learned of Sloan's interest in publishing and tasked her with putting together an instructional pamphlet on how to start a magazine.

These experiences gave her the confidence to start her own fanzine when she returned to the University of Virginia in the fall of 1995. The zine's name was drawn from Sloan's astrological sign, Scorpio. "It's really important to me," she explained. "I feel like it is a defining characteristic of my personality." *Scorpion* ran for six issues, lasting into 2001.

The debut explored Sloan's growing interest in intersectional feminism, making for a zine she described as "really personal. It was basically the things that I was interested in, that I was learning about." She involved her friends in the zine—many from outside the punk subculture—asking them to write about life from their own perspective. "I really didn't think anyone was going to read it, other than these people that I lived with, so I wanted them to be involved," she said. "So, it was more personal, feminist, at that time, with a punk-like feel, just because *I* was punk."

Later issues broadened to include interviews with participants in the DC punk subculture, such as bands and musicians like the Warmers, Ian MacKaye, Natalie Avery, and Machetres and individuals like photographer Cynthia Connolly and filmmaker Jem Cohen. Writings within *Scorpion*, however, still focused on more than music. Sloan included riveting articles on everything from campus sexual assault to the overlooked role of women of color in feminism. The artful writings shine with her intelligence, unpretentiousness, and idealism.

Sloan actively sent out review copies to other fanzines, attempting to spread the word on her work. "I got a lot of bad reviews," she remembered of the early response to *Scorpion*, chuckling over the "hardcore guys" confused about how the zine qualified as punk. Before long, however, she sensed a shift in reviewers' receptions. "I never fit in one category," she said. "A personal zine wouldn't totally get it, and a punk zine wouldn't totally get it, but then I think people got used to me. So, they would just kind of give it a fair review and be like, "This may not be my thing, but I like her take on this, or I like the interview on that." This outreach led to an increase in mail orders for *Scorpion*—her primary distribution method, rather than record stores or tabling at shows—as well as zine exchange friendships with titles from all over the world like *Clamor, It's Alive, Fracture, Hanging Like a Hex, Academiad Punk Rock,* and her early

Figure 9.9 Left: *Scorpion*, issue 2, circa 1996. Published by Willona Sloan. Used by permission. Right: Sloan at the Women's Institute for Freedom of the Press in Washington, 1995.

inspiration, *Suburban Voice*.

The inability of some hardcore zine editors to grasp *Scorpion*'s punk essence underscores the unique, intangible charms of Sloan's zine, which felt almost effortlessly original in its blend of interests. "I will say that one of the things I'm extremely proud of as a female, as a woman of color [is that] there just weren't a lot of other zines doing what I was doing," Sloan said. "I felt like that was a space that I could inhabit, and I was really happy to see people come around to that and understand what I was trying to do, even though it didn't fit into the little categories of zines that people read. A lot of people read the same types of zines. Mine kind of crossed a couple different genres, so I was really pleased to see people kind of getting into it."

Scorpion's sixth and final issue was published in 2001, but Sloan's feelings toward ending the zine were mixed. She was fatigued from the work that went into producing new issues, but her passion for music and zines remained. Sloan moved into professional writing, writing articles for the *Washington Post*, *Paste*, and numerous others. Likewise, she organizes and leads writing workshops and literary events around the world. Her ongoing love for punk and alternative culture manifested in a 2012 publication she distributed electronically as a PDF. *Come to our Show: Punk Show Flyers from DC to Down Under* was a mash note to the subculture, presenting an array of fliers Sloan gathered during her years publishing *Scorpion*.

Chickfactor

Gail O'Hara and Pam Berry befriended each other around 1990 as coworkers at the *Washington City Paper*, DC's alternative newspaper. O'Hara moved to New York City in February 1992 to take a job at *Spin Magazine*, but she frequently returned to DC on weekends where, between "going vintage shopping and eating tacos or whatever," she and Berry set to work on what would become one of indie rock's longest-lasting fanzines, *Chickfactor*.[22]

The idea was sparked by an interview O'Hara conducted—including numerous questions contributed by Berry—with David Gedge of the British indie band the Wedding Present for *Spin*. When only a small portion of the interview wound up in the final article in *Spin*, O'Hara and Berry decided to make their own publication.[23] The first issue of *Chickfactor* appeared in fall 1992, and few other publications could match its writing, graphic design, humor, and shrewd musical taste. The layout was clean and professional—albeit unconventionally oriented horizontally like a calendar—yet bore more than enough handmade flourishes and amiable banter between the coeditors to convey *Chickfactor*'s fanzine heart. Berry and O'Hara settled on the zine's name after hearing another DC-area musician comment disparagingly that Velocity Girl's success was due to their "chick factor" and that fans were more interested in the physical attractiveness of the band than their music.[24] In the punk tradition, Berry and O'Hara inverted the dismissive commentary on their friends and reclaimed the term for their own.

Comics by contributor Shawn Belschwender—also of *Washington City Paper*—lampooned concertgoer stereotypes at different venues around DC, critiquing the increasingly rote sartorial trends in early-1990s alternative culture. Needling further, Belschwender's "Pavement Boy" series of comics in *Chickfactor* mocked Mark Ibold, bassist for the ascendant New York City via Stockton, California, indie rock band Pavement, much to Ibold's displeasure.[25] "Can't pee without getting Pavement Boy wet," the comic's headline in issue four from fall 1993 teased, skewering Ibold for his apparent ubiquity at indie hotspots throughout New York City like Kim's Underground, Wetlands, and Knitting Factory. This was niche humor at its most granular—precisely what made fanzines special.

O'Hara and Berry's rapport and complementary skills were remarkable, as their friendship and fandom emanated from the page. "We do *Chickfactor* because we are madly in love with music," O'Hara declared in the debut issue's opening editorial. *Chickfactor* emerged from the scene of indie pop and indie rock fans and musicians centered on Slumberland Records, the label that released the debut single from Berry's band, Black Tambourine. That scene was overshadowed within DC in its early days by the success of Dischord Records and its bands but, by the mid-1990s, labels like Simple Machines, Slumberland, and Teen-Beat established DC as a stronghold for melodic, buzzy pop that expanded DC punk's parameters. *Chickfactor* was a key part of indie rock's ascent locally and broadly, putting DC musicians like Bridget Cross of Unrest and Trisha Roy of Heartworms on its cover, while blending in coverage of musicians from elsewhere like the Magnetic Fields, Yo La Tengo, the Spinanes, and Heavenly.

The zine's broad impact was paid tribute through an eponymous paean performed by one of indie rock's most popular bands. "The 1990s birthed innumerable zines rhapsodizing about countless songs," journalist Jay Ruttenberg noted. "*Chickfactor* is the rare publication to flip this formula and creep into a subject's song—namely, Belle and Sebastian's 'Chickfactor,' a misty-eyed New York postcard that testifies to the magazine's impact and chatty allure."[26] The namecheck did not go unnoticed by the zine's creators. "It was like a fricking dream come true," O'Hara recalled. "It was shocking and awesome. . . . It was a huge honor and a privilege, and it means everything. Especially, it's on probably one of the greatest albums they ever made, too."[2728]

Figure 9.10 Top: Pam Berry and Gail O'Hara, 1997. Bottom: *Chickfactor*, issue 7, 1994. Published by Pam Berry and Gail O'Hara. Used by permission.

O'Hara and Berry partnered on the zine until the latter departed the publication following issue nine in spring 1995, bringing the DC–New York City coproduction era of *Chickfactor* to an end. In her farewell editorial, Berry quipped that she'd always thought of the zine as a balance between her and O'Hara, therefore "without me it will be . . . well, you know, at the printer on time!" She later reflected in a 2012 interview that "*Chickfactor* was one of the most fun projects I've ever been a part of, and doing the mag together gave me and Gail an excuse to yap with people we revered, tell people about records we were digging, set up shows with a gazillion bands on the same bill, and keep in touch after she left *Washington City Paper*, where we worked, and moved to NYC."[29]

Intriguingly, O'Hara interviewed Berry for issue ten, which did not appear until fall 1996. The warm exchange was tinged with bittersweetness, as it seemed clear that O'Hara would have preferred for the pair to continue collaborating, but the enduring friendship at the center of *Chickfactor* remained on display during the lengthy conversation. As the interview opened, Berry acknowledged that *Chickfactor* had become bigger than she anticipated, admitting how much she despised writing record reviews. Quickly, however, the discussion moved from an interview to a vérité document of two friends completely in the moment—trading jokes, opinions, and stories as if they were hunkered together in a diner booth on their third cup of coffee.

"Like much of 1990s zine culture, *Chickfactor*'s influence is paradoxical," the critic Lindsay Zoladz observed. "Looking back, they may seem secondary to the music they boosted. But their editorial DNA lives on in the long-form interview style and enthusiastic, buttoned-down tone of sites like *Pitchfork*, *Stereogum*, and *The Quietus*, whose impact is far greater than *Chickfactor*'s ever was."[30] *Chickfactor* outlasted nearly all of its peers, as O'Hara continues to publish new print issues intermittently out of her current home of Portland, Oregon. "I want funny, smart writing," she explained. "That's what I want, and it doesn't have to be long-winded or super intellectual. I just want it to be fun and interesting. . . . I want someone to pick up [*Chickfactor*] in five years, and it's still gonna seem like an interesting read. I don't want it to be about the new album. I don't want any of those questions that are time-specific. I just want it to be a long-term thing that you wanna hang on to."[31]

Restaurant Fuel and *Punk Life*

Enlivened by *Chickfactor* and like-minded indie pop fanzines like New York City's *Power Toot*, as well as the thriving scene around Simple Machines and Teen-Beat Records, another pair of DC area pop fans created a memorable fanzine in the second half of the 1990s. Jeff Barrus and Tina Henry Barrus were recently married and mulling over publishing their own zine when inspiration from Go! Compact Discs' Indie Rock Flea Market in 1995 moved them to start *Restaurant Fuel*.

Go! Compact Discs was a key record store in the mid-1990s DC punk ecosystem, hosting concerts from locals like Jawbox and the Most Secret Method, as well as national bands like Helium (featuring once-and-future DC resident Mary Timony) and the Spinanes. As soon as it opened, Go! tapped into the indie rock energy thrumming through its base of Arlington, Virginia, evoking the scrappy creativity and endearing ingenuity of Arlington-based labels Simple Machines and Teen-Beat.[32] In summer 1994, Go! organized the first Indie Rock Flea Market in Arlington's Lyon Park Community Center, bringing together record labels, zines, and others in the indie community to peddle their wares in the park while bands like Frodus, Tuscadero, and Blast Off Country Style performed inside the sweltering community center. The event was so well received that a second flea market was held in July 1995, this time in the spacious parking lot of a recently shuttered Sears department store.[33]

Amid the sea of indie rockers baking on the summertime blacktop—attendance was later estimated to have been around four thousand five hundred people[34]—the young couple sparked up a friendship with the creators of *Power Toot* and decided to run with that zine's bespoke charm. "It's not printed, it's like handmade [and] hand designed," Jeff Barrus recalled of *Power Toot*'s allure in 2020. "They put in a lot of effort. It's like a piece of art in addition to being like a zine. [Tina and I] wanted to do that with ours."[35] Barrus and Henry Barrus set to work on their own zine, its name pulled from a highway sign bearing the words "Restaurant" and "Fuel," which, in addition to its humble instructions about roadside amenities, struck Barrus as a meaningful zine title. As he wrote in the first issue's opening editorial, *Restaurant Fuel* "describes the American consumer culture that so dominates our lives. That, in the 1990s, almost everything exists not for our health and benefit, but so that we'll buy it. . . . To put it more bluntly, McDonald's exists not to feed us, but to feed off of us."

Barrus and Henry Barrus resisted those cultural forces by emphasizing the human touches they could bring to their zine. Whether that was binding issues with neatly trimmed duct tape instead of saddle-stitching or tucking a minizine they called *Rack Focus* in a resealable plastic bag within the larger issue of *Restaurant Fuel*, the couple cleverly reified their passion for craft and connection wherever possible. The first two issues featured color copied covers, which, along with the higher quality printer and scanner they invested in for the zine—as well as a record label they launched called Hub City—took a financial toll that ended *Restaurant Fuel* after four issues. "We spent all of this money on it and lost so much money," Barrus said. "[We] put so much of it on credit cards, [we] were paying for it for years after the fact. . . . So, it just became too costly for us to keep it going."

Despite its limited run, *Restaurant Fuel* made an impression as a zine that bucked the cynicism and careerism sapping much of indie culture's vitality by the end of the 1990s. The role of human connection as a tenet of punk fandom could get lost during this period as bands departed indie labels for majors and fans got mired in angry exchanges about whether or not a band had sold out on the online chat boards beginning to appear on punk websites throughout the decade. *Restaurant Fuel*, however, remembered that punk's egalitarian ethos was about kinship and accessibility, not prestige or elitism. "We wanted to tell stories, not just about the music we were listening to, but [also] the culture and things that we cared about at the time," Barrus remembered. He continued:

Figure 9.11 Left: *Restaurant Fuel*, issue 1, 1996. Published by Jeff Barrus and Tina Henry-Barrus. Used by permission. Right: Flier for the 1995 Indie Rock Flea Market organized by Go! Compact Discs in Arlington, Virginia.

> *I wanted to do stories about real people. . . . Who are real people? What are their lives like? It frustrated me that the music media or just media more generally didn't tell stories about real people. They always told stories about "important" people who were doing "important" things. But I wanted to talk to people who were sort of ordinary, everyday people, and do the kind of feature about them the way that someone else would do a feature about someone important in, like,* Rolling Stone *or something like that.*

While lacking some of the tactile personal touches that *Restaurant Fuel* employed, Don Irwin's *Punk Life* was similarly idiomatic, providing detailed journals of a young punk's life in the DC area. Irwin's sincere love for punk was as appealing as his willingness to delve into the subtly amusing details of his life: "Last night the train driver was annoying," Irwin kvetched about the very DC detail of how Metro subway drivers possess idiosyncrasies of their own. "He kept saying 'Orange Line to Vi . . . en . . . aaaaaah' and all these lame things.[36] Then he was riding the brakes [so] hard I wanted to vomit."[37] Irwin invited readers into the details of his life in a way that presaged twenty-first-century internet personalities, yet without the vanity or self-absorption. His writings genuinely felt like an attempt at human connection as he processed the vagaries of modern life.

Punk Life never reached the wider popularity of the similarly diaristic punk zine, *Cometbus*, from Berkeley, California, but few zines anywhere could match *Punk Life*'s longevity or importance in offering an extended cross-section of, well, punk life in the United States. After the first issue in July 1992, Irwin published *Punk Life* into the twenty-first century, intermittently creating new issues detailing not just his love for punk, but other genres like go-go and gamelan. Irwin laughingly acknowledged in 2019 that "you don't do a fanzine for recognition," but the engine that powered *Punk Life* for decades was always fueled by a hope for personal connection. "I still have that imagery of, you know, leaving fanzines at the record store for people to pick up, but inevitably knowing that they're going to get thrown out in the trash when people clean up at the end of the day," he explained. "Or someone's going to pick up the fanzine, look at it, put it in their bag, and never pick it up again. I guess the reason you do it is because—just that one person, maybe, that might get inspired from it. Years later, someone might find it."[38]

Brickthrower

Brickthrower was among the most compelling zines published in DC during this period, focusing less on musical fandom and more on activism and the city's political landscape through a punk lens. The zine was crafted by members of the Stigmatics, a punk band whose lone 7-inch EP from late 1997 was a co-release between Dischord and their own label, Brickthrower Records. Guitarist/vocalist Natalie Avery and drummer Amanda Huron had both been involved in DC's punk community since the 1980s—Avery most notably through her role as guitarist in the Dischord band Fire Party—but did not meet until summer 1996, after Huron returned from college in Minnesota. The bassist Cristina Calle introduced the pair and, soon, the trio commenced writing music.

The band lived in DC's Mount Pleasant neighborhood—a base for many of the city's punks—and sensed inharmony between the revolutionary rhetoric and focus on fashion of their punk peers and the real world needs of the majority of their neighbors, many of whom emigrated from El Salvador over the past two decades. "I was in graduate school, and I was taking a class on urban social movements, and a lot of what I was learning and thinking about was just so manifested in Mount Pleasant," Avery explained in 2018:

> *It was also during a period of time where a lot of the music and the bands was very highly stylized, like*

Figure 9.12 Top: Don Irwin in Chicago, April 10, 1996. Photo by Cynthia Connolly. Bottom: Joe McRedmond of Hoover on the cover of *Punk Life*, issue 4, 1993. Published by Don Irwin. Used by permission.

the Make-Up and Delta 72 and some of those. A lot of the fashion stuff was really alluring to me, but it was also a little alienating, because it was so stylized. For me, it seemed a little out of touch with the strife that was happening in the neighborhood and in the lives of the people in the neighborhood where we all had our cheap group houses with practice spaces. And that was kind of what I was reading and thinking about, that sort of disconnect, where we were like, "Oh, we're these revolutionary punk rock rebels" but we just sort of went from outpost to outpost and didn't think about what was happening in our neighborhood.[39]

Huron, too, felt motivated to push her punk peers to put the subculture's ideals into practice by addressing the systemic oppressions in their midst. "Our experience of DC in the mid-1990s was one of thinking about gentrification and all these [US Immigration and Naturalization Service] raids, people getting deported, and [President Bill] Clinton ending welfare as we knew it," she recalled. "We were really concerned with the gentrification we saw happening in Mount Pleasant at the time, which was definitely going on even though so many other parts of the city were so devastated then. We were talking a lot about that." As potent as their music could be as an outlet for disseminating their ideas, Avery and Huron realized that a zine could be an additional tool in their arsenal. "Natalie and I both like to write and Cristina was an artist," Huron said, "so it seemed like, 'OK, this could be a good thing to do.'"[40] Joined by their friend, Andrea Blatchford—who later played with Avery and Huron in the group Scaramouche—the Stigmatics published a zine, *Brickthrower*, to coincide with their show at Fort Reno Park on June 30, 1997.

The zine was named after one of their songs, exploring the story of a man they learned of through the often-sordid reality television program, *Cops*. "[He] got arrested for vandalizing a Burger King he'd been fired from," the band, writing collectively, explained in the second issue. "*Cops* gave his action no context—it just portrayed him as a one-dimensional pariah to be loathed and jailed. We wondered what his story was and what it would be like if his story was told." The urgency that *Brickthrower* brought to its analysis of the painful realities many DC residents faced was electric and motivating. Few other zines from DC ever came as close to crystallizing punk's ostensible mission as this one did.

Brickthrower centered issues throughout its five issues that were rarely, if ever, broached in earlier DC punk zines: Welfare, housing, immigrants, public education, fair access to radio broadcasting, and challenging others in the Mount Pleasant community to step up and support their neighbors. "In a neighborhood where the gap between rich and the poor gapes so starkly, one might expect great outpourings of outrage from the community's more fortunate dwellers," Avery wrote in the fourth issue, published for the band's tour of the midwestern United States. "Of outrage, there is plenty but, for many, its target is not poverty or homelessness, but the poor and the homeless themselves. At community meetings, attended mainly by homeowners, constant reference is made to the need to 'reclaim' our streets and parks."

The group distributed zines at their shows and around their neighborhood, giving them away to anyone interested. Thanks to a like-minded neighbor who worked at a corporate copy shop, the group was typically able to churn out five hundred copies of each issue free, unburdening them from concerns about duplication and distribution. "We were passing [zines] out to a much broader variety of people who would have been at [a punk] show," Huron recalled. "But yeah, in general, the audience would be punks. It would be people—activist types who were living not necessarily in Mount Pleasant, but in DC."

Both the Stigmatics and the zine wound down when Huron entered graduate school. "Just kind of life taking you in different paths," Avery recalled, asserting that the friends' collaborations were never about a specific outlet like a band or a zine. "It was so much about a friendship and a community and everything was just [about] doing all these different things." The zine's exhortations to think critically and interrogate your own actions remain timeless, however. "A more radical response to co-optation involves not only pushing the limits of your creativity, but building and maintaining underground subcultures where

Figure 9.13 *Brickthrower*, issues 1 and 5, 1997–99. Published by the Stigmatics and friends. Used by permission.

people can create culture that resists instead of serves prevailing (and unjust) power relations," Avery wrote amid fears that mainstream forces were siphoning punk's vitality. "In these places, we can make culture where value is collectively determined and not simply driven by corporate spreadsheets. So, *Brickthrower* is about how we can make radios out of ourselves instead of just absorbing the frequencies of the status quo."[41]

Queer Punk Zines in Bloom

Although there were examples of queer voices in 1980s DC punk zines like Gordon Ornelas's *Enola Gay*, they particularly came to the fore in the 1990s. This was buoyed by the emergence of riot grrrl, as well as the growth of queercore, a movement celebrating and emphasizing queer identities within punk through music, zines, art, and other creative expression. Two zinemaking participants in Riot Grrrl DC—Erika Reinstein (*Fantastic Fanzine, Marika, Wrecking Ball*) and May Summer (*Jaded, Marika, Star Gang*)—founded Riot Grrrl Press in spring 1993. Fellow zinesters and riot grrrls Mary Fondreist (*Discharge, Wrecking Ball*) and Joanna Burgess (*Cherub, Star Gang*) soon joined them to help distribute riot grrrl zines springing up around the country, several of which explored issues of queer sexuality and identity.[42]

Working out of Arlington, Virginia, and calling upon that ever-important accomplice in punk zine-making of a friendly Kinko's employee who doled out free copies, Riot Grrrl Press printed and distributed more than sixty zines in

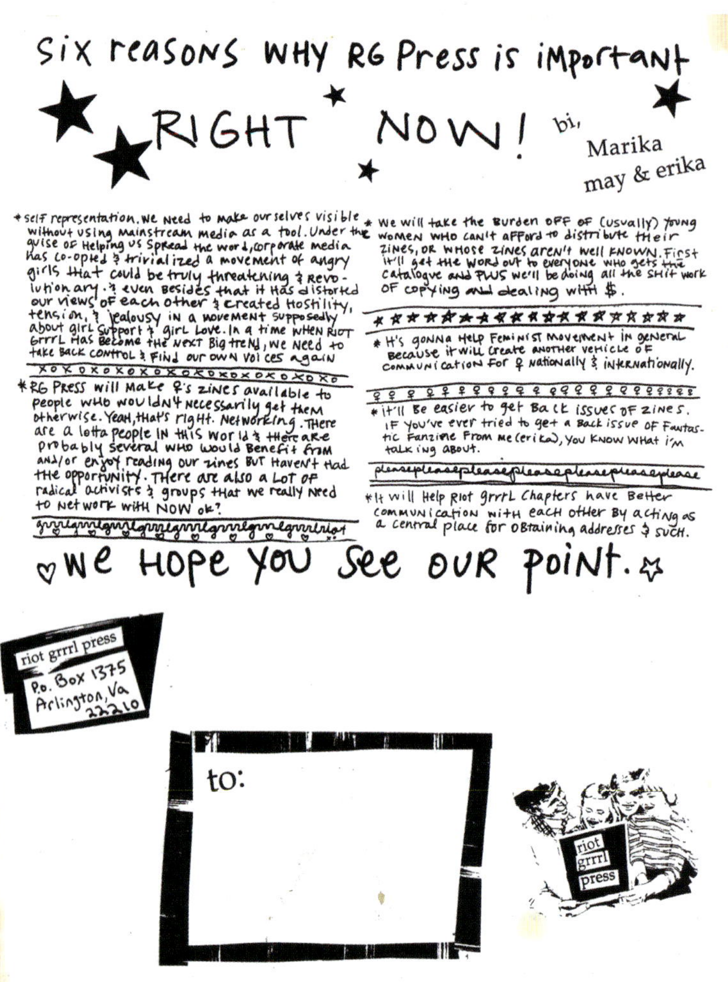

Figure 9.14 Riot Grrrl Press mailer, circa 1993. Published by Riot Grrrl Press. Used by permission.

1993, though it would move to Chicago the following year and, again, to Olympia, Washington, before folding later in the 1990s. "The importance of self-representation was the most valuable lesson of Riot Grrrl Press," Summer later wrote in an article cowritten with her fellow scholar, Kevin Dunn. "Self-representation through alternative media sources is not a luxury of some privileged group, but rather a necessity for all those wishing to challenge the destructive social forces—from patriarchy to corporate-controlled capitalism—within society at large."[43]

Hardcore punk had often been a homophobic space, as reflected in some zines from the 1980s. Despite a new generation of hardcore participants in the early 1990s, old attitudes remained. Queer visibility in hardcore, however, slowly took hold. Jason Roe's fanzine *Kill the Robot* launched in 1992 and ran for eight issues into the mid-1990s. Within those pages, Roe unflinchingly described his life as a young gay man in DC's straight-edge hardcore scene, beginning with high school life in Rockville, Maryland, and shifting to semesters away at college in Yellow Springs, Ohio. Through all of it, Roe wrote with honesty and clarity about his fears, desires, disappointments, and hopes in a way that commanded readers' attention.

Like so many other twentieth-century zine creators in DC punk, Roe was introduced to the music and subculture by an older sibling, fortified by visits to Yesterday & Today Records in Rockville and Vinyl Ink in Silver Spring. "As I listened to the music and I read the lyric sheets and everything, [it was] just really eye-opening to me, just different ways of being and thoughts that I had been having as a young teen, and they were aligned with those thoughts or expanding upon those thoughts," Roe explained. "[Punk was] just really something that was there at that time of my life that I absolutely needed and I would say, even to this day, are an influence on my decisions and the way that I live and how I operate and all of that."[44] He came across national zines like *Maximum Rocknroll*—"just a major, *major* influence," Roe recalled—as well as Jess Row's Baltimore-based zine *A Plea For Sanity*, fostering an infatuation with punk that led to making a zine of his own.

Kill the Robot's title was derived from Roe's love for *The Illuminatus! Trilogy*, Robert Anton Wilson and Robert Shea's satirical science fiction saga. From the trilogy, Roe gleaned the lesson to "be your real self," he recalled:

> *Throw off those expectations from high school or whatever you think you're supposed to be, and be who you really are. And you know, as a young queer kid, a young gay guy, particularly in the 1990s, particularly growing up in the age of AIDS and HIV coming out—not having anything like we have now*

Figure 9.15 *Kill the Robot*, issue 1, circa 1994. Published by Jason Roe. Used by permission. Some black tape is also visible on the cover, which had been used to keep the magazine closed during its mailing to the recipient.

> *with Instagram and TV—you know, there was nothing. There was nothing for me. And particularly a person like me, there was nothing there. So really just, how do you be—I guess what they say now—"your authentic self." So [laughs], it's like, how do I be me? How do I really be me? You know? That was really kind of the idea, to be my true self.*

Roe's writing could be confessional, irreverent, and often funny—as when he joked in issue two that he was "in love with myself and I am now crowning myself the sissiest boy in America," mischievously détourning the title teen magazine *Sassy* had recently bestowed on the Nation of Ulysses' Ian Svenonius. Among the most meaningful features in *Kill the Robot*, which typically did not include interviews, was a roundtable discussion moderated by Vique Martin of the British zine *Simba*. Roe and other queer punks from the national straight-edge hardcore scene—Adam Tanner of *Dance of Days* fanzine, Sean Capone of *Positron* fanzine, and Demian Johnston of the band Undertow—gathered after a concert in Syracuse, New York, and candidly discussed their sexuality, homophobia, and the challenge of merging their identities as queer people and straight-edge hardcore punks. "I think [that] was pretty amazing at the time," Roe recalled of the published article. "I mean, it's hard to understand *now* the lack of diversity or lack of understanding or lack of even, with gay or queer or whatever, how many people there are. Certainly in hardcore, where there was still a level of violence that could occur. When I was growing up, there was still gay-bashing in Dupont Circle."

For Roe, attending punk shows meant interacting with a space that was simple in its joys of connection and purpose, yet complicated in its emotional and physical vulnerability. "I think it was like a cross between total liberation—of just like I can't believe this, I'm here, I'm around people that think a similar way to me, certainly with straightedge and all of the political ideas that I learned from there," Roe said. He continued:

> *[But] also just the frickin' terror of walking across the floor and [laughs] having the eyes on you. You're still a little kid in a lot of ways, and just not wanting to stand out. Wanting to stand out, not wanting to stand out, trying to make friends. Having a hard time but also connecting with people and having an openness. Just even now, I run into people and it's just having that common frame of reference to share with other people. There's so much you don't even have to say, you know? There's a lot [about] why we ended up there that you don't really understand at the time, like the difficulties at home or in school or whatever. You're there with all these people, and—for me, for sure, I don't think I understood exactly that, at the time, but now looking back, I'm like, "Oh, yeah, of course!"*

Complex as it might have been for a young person to process the shifting social sands of a crowded punk show, Roe knew it was where he belonged. "I just wanted to go *all* the time," he remembered. "I just felt great when I was there, and just—alive. Felt really super alive." That sense of purpose was evident throughout the pages of *Kill the Robot*, a moment in time that still resonates for Roe. "I was terrible in school, and honestly [producing the zine] gave me a skill that I was able to turn into working," he explained. "I don't know what I would be doing otherwise. So, every day I feel the impact of it."

As Roe recalled, "I was one of the first of the guys like me that were coming out and saying certain things, particularly around sexuality and stuff like that, that I think had a pretty nice impact on people. So, that's something to feel good about, certainly." Indeed, *Kill the Robot*'s influence radiated out into the punk scene; its humor, queer sensibilities, love for hardcore punk, and dedication to honest expression made it a beacon for fanzine readers tired of cynicism. Norman Brannon of the New York City–based *Anti-Matter* felt that *Kill the Robot* was one of the standout zines from DC during this period. "That one was exciting because there was a wave of hardcore kids coming out and a new wave of queer hardcore zines [like national zines] *Positron* and *Dance of Days* that were all coming out of straightedge and I never thought I'd see that day come."[45] *Not Even* fanzine editor Daisy Rooks viewed Roe and *Kill the Robot* as her compatriots in "pushing back about how heteronormative [hardcore] was, and how homophobic it was," she said. "I saw us as doing some similar work, often trying to use humor and . . . poking fun at various sexist and homophobic elements of that scene."[46]

Hugh McElroy and Eve Tushnet, were among the more prolific zine producers in DC during this period, publishing

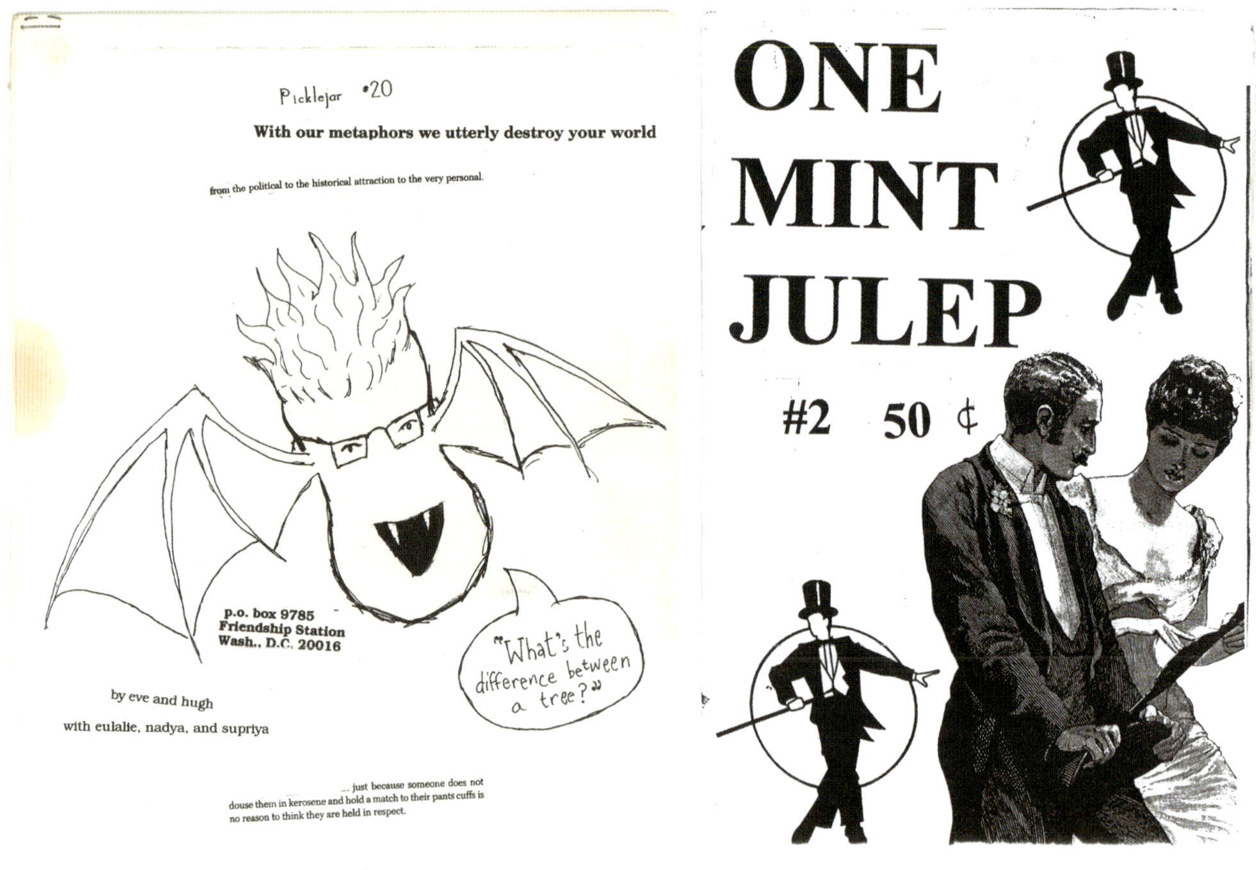

Figure 9.16 Left: *Picklejar*, issue 20, circa 1995. Published by Hugh McElroy and Eve Tushnet. Right: *One Mint Julep*, issue 2, circa 1996. Published by Hugh McElroy. Used by permission.

twenty-seven issues of their zine *Picklejar* from 1992 to 1996. According to McElroy, the pair met as sixth-graders, eventually dating in eighth grade before both came out at the end of the school year. Despite breaking up, their friendship persisted and they soon discovered DC's punk rock scene. "We ran into two older girls from school in Georgetown one day after school," McElroy recalled. "They told us they had just sold some zines to Smash! [Records, then located in Georgetown] and encouraged us to buy copies so that the store would take more. We did and liked their zine and pretty quickly decided, in grand punk tradition, that we could totally do this too."[47]

McElroy and Tushnet, along with numerous contributions from friends—including Marcus—gathered an intriguing spectrum of art, punk culture, essays, comics, fiction, and criticism. The breadth of creativity and intellect on display, never mind the prolificity of the publication schedule, belied the youth of *Picklejar*'s contributors, serving as a repudiation of the way young people in the 1990s were frequently portrayed as aimless slackers, bereft of the purpose that Baby Boomers unleashed on the world in the 1960s. "Eve wrote a wide range of essays on topics ranging from Jewish identity to scars to experiences of illness," McElroy explained. "She also wrote a long form serial novel, much of which appeared in the zine across many issues. I contributed a 'rant' every issue and wrote about Haitian Vodou, body image, teen queer identity, getting jumped by skinheads, and other stuff. . . . [We] tried to point people toward authors/musicians/filmmakers/artists that inspired us, especially ones outside of white hetero-/homo-normativity."

As *Picklejar* wound down, McElroy moved on to publish two issues of a solo zine, *One Mint Julep*, in 1996, while Tushnet created her own zine, *The Femme Skunk*. Tushnet proceeded to a career as a writer on the intersection of her Roman Catholic faith and queer sexuality, with her work appearing regularly in a number of conservative outlets. In addition to building a career as a scholar and educator, McElroy cofounded the band Black Eyes in 2001, releasing two albums of innovative and cathartic music on Dischord Records, inventively blending punk, jazz, and dub reggae with lyrics boasting the same poetic intellect his zine writings first revealed. "There is a direct through line from what I was working on then to Black Eyes and all the other music I've done," he said. "The academic work I do, especially producing teaching materials, is a direct outgrowth of the zine work. I am not afraid of opening up any copier and finding jammed paper, no matter how deep in the guts it is stuck, which happens a lot in my teaching work."

Across the DC area in the 1990s, queer punks asserted their space at the heart of the scene. Through zines, their voices could be heard, connecting them with like-minded people in the community and laying plain that punk's queer roots were immutable and undeniable. "The zine world is about the sense of community," Roe explained. "I think community is *so* important. It's really the entire point of it, right? Community and then also togetherness and expressing yourself. Really, that sharing and, also, boosting each other."

Life Amid the New Wave of Teenage Suburban Punk Fanzines

Harsh urban settings were central features in punk iconography, serving as the backdrop in cover art by the Ramones, the Clash, Dead Boys, and other foundational punk bands. The suburbs, however, also became synonymous with the subculture by the turn of the 1980s. Many notable early American punk fanzines were rooted in urban centers like New York City (*Punk Magazine*, *The Big Takeover*, Thurston Moore's *Killer*, Richard Kern's *Valium Addict* and *Dumb Fucker*), Los Angeles (*Slash*, *Lobotomy*), and San Francisco (*Search and Destroy*, *Damage*, *Maximum Rocknroll*), but punks living in the suburbs increasingly and, eventually, predominantly became the scene's chroniclers through fanzines.

Scholar Kate Eichhorn observed that "zines enabled people living in suburbs and small towns and even rural and remote locations to do more than passively bear witness to what was happening in the downtown scenes they were unable to experience firsthand." She continues: "With the spread of zine networks, they could become active participants in scenes or subcultures rooted in an urban landscape. It was as if zines picked up and made mobile the aesthetics of downtown city streets by transporting a little piece of downtown across the continent—a piece that could in turn be easily reproduced and recirculated on copy machines."[48]

Of course, the suburbs themselves were fertile ground for punk inspiration, and not just a reenactment of downtown rebellion. The tenor of the music was unique, whether it was the conformity amid Southern California's sprawl that the Descendents mocked on 1982's "Suburban Home" or in the "Suburban Wasteland" that DC's Artificial Peace sang about on the 1982 DC hardcore compilation *Flex Your Head*. "Living in a suburban wasteland, sterile walls close in on me," vocalist Steve Polcari growled. "Prefab junkyard, suburban wasteland. I can't get out, I can't get free." *Who Cares?* fanzine editor Steve Shapero remarked that growing up in suburban Potomac, Maryland, "was a nightmare. Like, I hated it. It was soulless, in my opinion. I get why my parents did it, but it sucked."[49]

DC's earliest punk fanzines were typically published out of the suburbs, with Northern Virginia's *It's Only a Movie*, *Descenes*, and *Discords*, and early issues of *Vintage Violence* and *The Infiltrator* coming out of Maryland. The pattern continued through the 1980s with zines like *Thrillseeker* from Bowie, Maryland; *Yet Another Unslanted Opinion* from Burke, Virginia; and early issues of *Truly Needy* carrying a Rockville mailing address. The substantial growth of fanzine culture in the 1990s, however, led to an even greater stream of zines by teenagers coming out of DC's suburbs during this period. The sheer volume of zines that my peers put out during this period was such that there is no way to offer a concise, comprehensive history, but I *can* accurately share some of the zines that came into my orbit during these years when I was a high school and college student in the DC area.

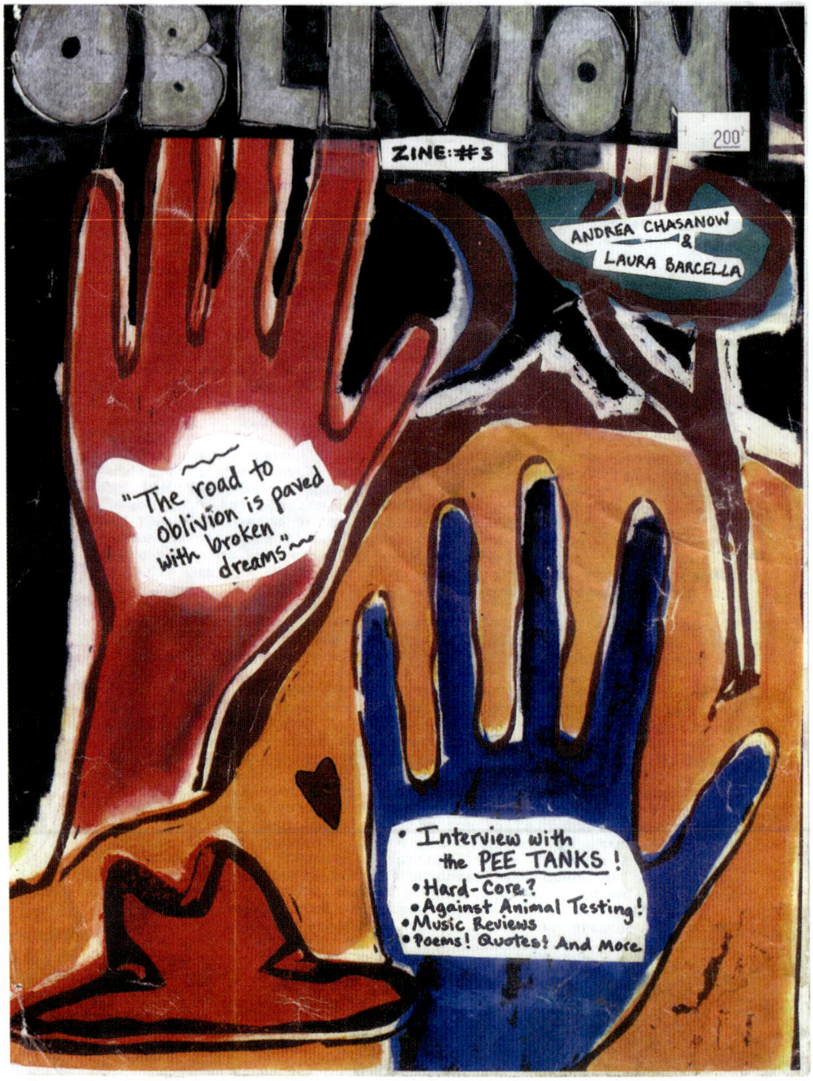

Figure 9.17 *Oblivion*, issue 3, circa 1994. Published by Laura Barcella and Andrea Chasanow. Used by permission.

My own experiences creating fanzines started in 1993, when I tracked down a phone number for Guy Picciotto from Fugazi and cold-called him, asking for an interview. Incredibly, he agreed, and we met in the shadow of the Washington Monument, hours before the band performed there on August 7. He patiently answered my dull questions about selling out and tattoo inspiration, even taking time a few days later to mail me photos of Fugazi I could use for my first issue. Much as when I received the advertising support from Simple Machines on faith, it felt so meaningful to be supported by the musicians whose music I was in awe of.

Laura Barcella and Andrea Gentle (née Chasanow), who published five issues of *Oblivion* fanzine out of Chevy Chase, Maryland, and upper Northwest DC from 1992 through 1995, shared my astonishment that bands willingly spoke to them for their fanzine. "I feel like when we approached bands, they were very receptive, surprisingly so, to being interviewed by high school kids," Gentle recalled. Her zine partner Barcella laughingly concurred: "Like, 'Oh, these children are approaching me. These two 14-year-old girls want to sit on the grass for an hour.' It's just so hilarious."[50]

Access was a central part of the DC punk scene's pull. No matter who you were, with only a few exceptions, others in the scene would talk to you about your zine or, perhaps, help your band find a show. Fugazi or Velocity Girl were bands that meant as much to me as the enormously popular mainstream bands I had grown up listening to yet, unlike an REM arena concert, I could usually clamber onto the side of the stage to watch DC punk bands or approach a band member after the show to ask for an interview. The youth and inexperience of that time of life meant that I did not really think to question my every move with making a zine or deliberate on what readers were going to think. Barcella, now an author and journalist, recalled a similar sense of abandon: "We were just like, 'Fuck it, who cares? Let's just do it.' I think that attitude was kind of refreshing, and that's not something that you always carry through as an adult. I think, as adults, we have to kinda be more measured and weigh out decisions, and we have less energy, we're tired. You're like, 'I don't wanna sit down and write a bunch of stuff or plan [a zine] out.' We were young, so we had a lot of time and more energy."

My inspiration to create a zine came from reading Steve Shapero's *Who Cares?* and Irene Chien's *Fake* fanzines, which I came across as a younger high school classmate of theirs in Potomac. Visually, their zines were fantastic and the writing inspiring. As relatively slick as their zines were, what Chien and Shapero did felt attainable, so I gave it a try, mimicking their layout and editorial styles without shame, as it all felt like part of a community continuum. Creating a zine allowed me to strike up conversations with the bands I was interested in, as well as build relationships with record labels, allowing me to hear the newest music and participate in spreading the word on the good things I heard. Among the most exciting moments in life for me then was heading to pick up my mail from my zine's post office box at White Flint Mall in Rockville, where I usually walked out with a bin filled with packages of promotional records and letters from readers. Typically, I would not even wait to get home before ripping into what was sent, so I took over a bench at the mall or a table in the food court to spread out and see what the latest music was from Sub Pop, Matador, Jade Tree, and other indie labels.

"I loved going to the post office," Laris Kreslins of *D Magazine* recalled. "I loved picking up mail [and] I loved mailing copies [of *D*] to people. The process of going and actively interacting with people at the post office was always super cool to me."[51] Aside from the exposure to new music from record labels, the post office was a tool for connection. "It was this magical access to these people in other scenes and other places, or other parts of Maryland, or into DC and Virginia," Kreslins said: "I was writing people all over the place. I was writing to people in Europe. . . . Because this was before email. I felt like we were limited by what we had access to, music and culture content wise, that just sending a letter to somebody would open up that world that much more, and then you could kind of keep on expanding and building and opening out your world. That was really super exciting to me."

Like me, Kreslins started his zine as a teenager in Montgomery County in the early 1990s. He learned about punk from his older brother, Kristaps, who was already involved in the DC scene. "We'd always be figuring out ways to get to DC and going to either all-ages shows or stores like Smash and stuff like that," he said. "[We were] so hungry for anything relating to punk and indie music." Kreslins and his brother's friend, Adam Kahan, found themselves talking about music often, which led to the idea of creating a zine together. "We were just like, 'Let's just sit down and cut and paste a bunch of shit together, and then pass them out at shows,'" Kreslins remembered. "Another part was like, 'oh, this is the best way that we can connect with record labels or bands we like. If we make something, then they'll think

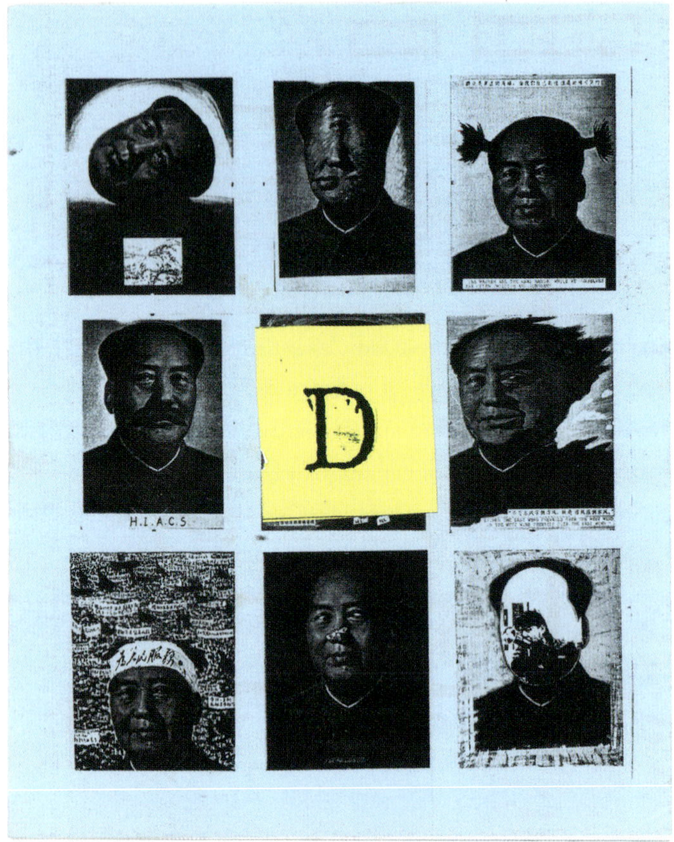

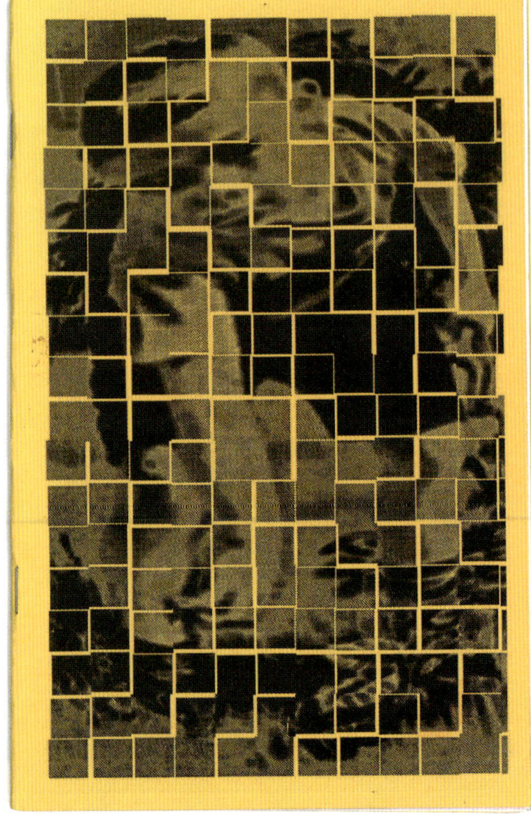

Figure 9.18 *D Magazine*, 1993–94, published by Laris Kreslins and Adam Kahan. Used by permission.

we're relatively legitimate, and we would get promos or get guestlisted for shows or something like that.'"

The pair set to work on *D Magazine*, utilizing access to a free photocopier at Kreslins' godmother's office to pump out copies after hours, typically around one hundred copies per issue. "That's how I learned how to paginate and put together my own zines," he said. "Adam and I would write everything, and then I'd be more on the design end of stuff, and then I'd be the assembler of everything. . . . Later on, we started using a regular offset printer, especially for the covers, if we wanted better printing quality."

I learned of *D Magazine* while standing in line in 1992 to meet Henry Rollins at the Tower Records in Rockville.[52] When my friends and I talked about a recent Fugazi concert and, unknowingly, loudly mispronounced Guy Picciotto's name as "guy picky-otto," one of us received a tap on the shoulder. It was Kahan, standing behind us, who then correctly declared, "no! It's pronounced "ghee pi-cho-toe!" This led to a conversation about music during which Kahan gave us a copy of *D Magazine*. Along with the other zines I had recently learned about in high school, *D* showed me that you could air your fandom in ways that were funny, sincere, irreverent, and honest. After leaving the DC area, Kreslins went on to publish some of the most notable magazines to come from alternative culture in the late 1990s and into the twenty-first century—*Sound Collector* and *Arthur*, among others—citing lessons he learned from his first efforts with *D Magazine*.

As frequently as in-person connections happened through trading zines at shows or hanging out at record stores, I also came across zines from further out in the DC area through some of my earliest experiences on the internet. Using the then-new technology of an online bulletin board, I would post messages asking for pen pals or zine trades with anyone into DC punk. Most memorably for me, this led to finding out about zines from Northern Virginia like *Nerd Gerl* from Alexandria and *A Piece of Zine* from Chantilly, whom I contacted and traded issues with.

Eleana Whitesell's *Nerd Gerl* was a particular favorite of mine, as her writings so often jibed with things I felt about the indie scene at the time, whether it was our shared love for the music of labels like Simple Machines and Teen-Beat, an unexpected paean to the author Willa Cather ("word up, this girl can write. Or rather, could"), or her essay against moshing, which I was deeply sympathetic to. The act of moshing—also known as slam dancing—involved careening into other concertgoers near the front of the stage, whether they liked it or not. A once-novel dance expression in the 1980s had become a shibboleth of alternative culture, a rote tool of MTV-inspired conformity in the post-Nirvana 1990s. That is at least how it felt to me then, so Whitesell's 1994 essay "Mosher Monsters" in the first issue of *Nerd Gerl* was gratifying, particularly when she pointed out the absurdity of moshers in the crowd at a Velocity Girl show. "This seems ridiculous to me," she wrote of slam dancing to a "fuzz pop" band not known for its hardcore energy. "I could see some relevance (very little) at some cheesy hard rock show, but not at Velocity Girl. Plus, it's old. And dumb. So, if you're an offender, stop—'cause you look dumb."

Sara Marcus was a high school student in North Potomac, Maryland, in the early 1990s who was puzzled when she heard her friends Tara Osborne and Joan West talk about starting a zine. As she recalled in 2018, "I was like, 'Zine? What's a zine?'" A short time later, she and her friends congregated outside of her high school at lunchtime "with the kids who smoke at lunch," where she was handed a copy of Jason Roe's *Kill the Robot*. Years later, she still remembered her reaction to the zine: "This is brilliant!"[53] Galvanized by *Kill the Robot*, Marcus and her friends published several issues of *Out of the Vortex* from about 1992 to 1995, which served as a forum for their intelligent, passionate writings on punk culture, feminism, and politics. Marcus continued creating zines after that, publishing three issues of *Kusp* as a college student, its title reflecting her stage of life, moving from a teenager into adulthood. In 2010, Marcus wrote *Girls to the Front*, a detailed history of riot grrrl that exhilaratingly conveyed, among other things, the importance of zines in the feminist punk movement's development. "[There was a] magnificent moment between 1994 and 1995 when so many young women would be at shows at the Black Cat with vintage lunch boxes full of zines, getting to shows super early, and getting right up close to the stage, and knowing that anyone with a lunch box, you could trade zines with them, and how much fun that was," she recalled.

"It's one of the strongest sensory memories I have, of being a person who made a zine in DC in the mid-1990s."

Forbes Graham first engaged with punk and hardcore in the early 1990s thanks to friends at Silver Spring's Montgomery Blair High School, who used mixtapes to expose him to bands from the riot grrrl scene, Dischord Records, and the city's burgeoning second wave of hardcore, like Ashes. From that latter scene, Graham learned of Dave Brown's zine, *Blood Ties*, which precipitated his closer involvement with DC's hardcore and emo scene in the mid-1990s. "It was [at] shows where I was exposed to more zines, because you would just meet people and then they'd be like, 'Oh, here's my zine,'" Graham explained. "People were pretty much just giving them away, practically, or trading them or whatever. If they were a dollar, that would have been like, 'Whoa, that's a dollar!'"[54]

Graham, who also sang for the hardcore band Amalgamation in the late 1990s, observed that zines were particularly the currency of connection within the emo scene he gravitated toward. "I think in the scene I was in, I wouldn't say *everybody* did a zine, but *almost* everybody did a zine, at some point," he said. He continued:

> *I kind of was dipped in a bunch of scenes, but I was more in the emo hardcore scene. So, you were supposed to indulge people in your feelings, and writing was a way to do that. Especially, again—like not to harp on, "Oh, we were before the Internet," but you know, in the internet now, everybody can say what their feelings are. Whether anyone cares or should is a different matter, but they can. . . . Again, in the normal world [during the 1990s], the idea that you would express yourself and tell people what you were thinking and feeling was not particularly normal, so having an avenue to do that was really special.*

Graham's zines, *Arcadia of my Youth* and *Invisible Man*, combined elements like concert photography, handwritten reports on DC-area vegan options, and writings that reflected Graham's positive mind-set. This outlook extended to columns he contributed to another fanzine I published, *Held Like Sound*, which launched in 1997 and continued until 2002. Graham's columns often critiqued and challenged punk's tenets and trends, but always did so without pretense or smugness. Approaching fellow participants in the punk subculture with respect was a cornerstone of Graham's mien, rooted in his reverence for hardcore, which he deemed "almost like a mini religion" for him. "I always felt like sincerity was probably the

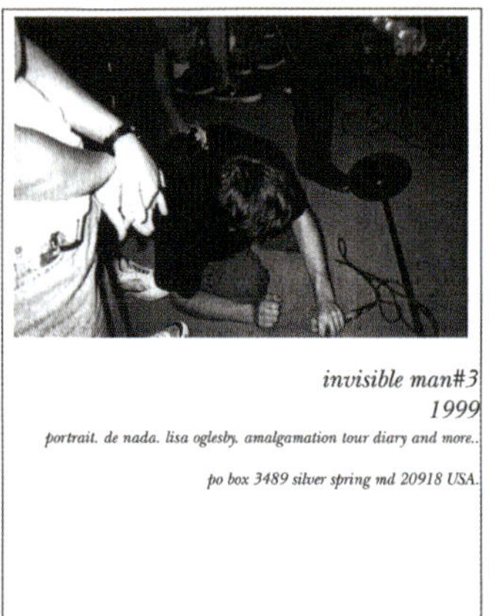

Figure 9.19 Top left: *Nerd Gerl*, issue 3, 1994, published by Eleana Whitesell. Top right: *Out of the Vortex*, issue 5, summer 1994, published by Sara Marcus and Joan West. Bottom left: *Invisible Man*, issue 3, 1999, published by Forbes Graham. Bottom right: *Torpedo Dialogues*, issue 1, summer 1997, published by Chris Richards. All used by permission.

biggest thing in hardcore, and it was the thing that kind of went through every style [of hardcore]. Like every style was in a sense built off of 'you mean what you say.'"

As a Black person, Graham was frequently confronted with the privilege his white peers in the hardcore scene possessed. "It's funny, I never actually read the Ralph Ellison novel *Invisible Man,* but I did name [the zine] for pretty much the same kind of reason. I touched on some of those themes of race a little [in the zine], but I was never a person that really beat that horse a lot. That just wasn't my style." Upon re-reading his zine after twenty years, however, Graham observed that "I wrote about these things that we're still talking about almost twenty years later in society."

One such moment occurred outside of a hardcore show where numerous white punks openly consumed alcohol on the street in front of the venue "and no one's going to bother them. The police are not going to come and make their lives miserable," he pointed out, bringing to mind generations of Black Americans that endured police harassment for similarly minor infractions, as they still do today. Likewise, a raucous outdoor hardcore concert at a festival that went on past 1:30am drew police attention, yet officers left without incident. "I was across the street and I'm thinking, 'Man, when the cops come, they gonna kill these people,'" Graham recalled:

> *Like, "They have a show going on, on the lawn at 1:30. They're going to kick everybody's ass up and down the street." So, the first cops come on their bikes. I walked off. I immediately left. [laugh] I was like, I do not want to be here when these cops come and beat the shit outta all these people. So, I ran into a friend of mine the next day. I said, "So, what happened when the cops showed up?" He said—because he had a front-row seat—"Oh, well, the first couple cops came on bikes. They said 'What's going on here?' I said, 'I don't know.' Then they left. Then the next set of cops came up. Same thing. They said, 'What's going on here?' I said, 'I don't know.' They left." And that was it! I was dumbfounded! I was like, "That was it?! Nothing else happened?!"*

Despite those reminders that Graham's race presented threats from society that so many of his white peers in hardcore could blithely ignore, he still felt a sense of gratitude for the community he was in. "It was a special time for me in my life," he said. "If I had not been in the hardcore [scene], there was a lot of experiences that I never would have had. So, I'd never take that back for anything. . . . There were a lot of problems with that scene, but there were a lot of things people tried to do that were really worthwhile and valuable. So, you know, I'm glad I was there."

Chris Richards, then a high school student in Arnold, Maryland—about 30 miles east of DC, near Annapolis—later recalled one of the forces that drove him to create his zine, *Torpedo Dialogues,* in 1997. "When I was a teenager, I found a sense of power in skepticism—the idea of being skeptical of what's around you and what's being presented to you, and the way you're encouraged to live your life in American society," he said:

> *These weren't things I was thinking of really consciously at the time, but I think when you are a kid growing up in the suburbs and the school system unfolds a certain way, and the government acts a certain way, and your parents expect certain things of you, there's a lot of power in doubt. And I think that's what resonated with me, with punk rock, in one way. Because it was sort of an articulation of that skepticism in this really incredible, energetic way.*[55]

Over three issues of *Torpedo Dialogues,* Richards cast an enthusiastic eye toward the new generation of DC bands emerging, like the Better Automatic, Free Range Pilgrim, and the Most Secret Method.[56] An avid zine reader, Richards was inspired by the bold graphics of the popular Chicago fanzine *Punk Planet,* as well as other national zines like Jessica Hopper's *Hit It or Quit It,* Josh Hooten and Tony Leone's *Commodity* and, particularly, Keith Werwa's *Number Two.* Werwa's writing style mystified Richards, who described it as "difficult to penetrate, [but] I thought it kind of spoke to the mystery of music." He continued:

> *I'm also realizing in my adulthood too that I think mystery, cultivation of mystery, engagement with mystery—these are things that really keep me tethered tightly to music. The sort of unknowing and what can't be known. [Werwa] had this great zine that [had] a really strong graphic design sensibility, but some of the writing was just very confusing to me, [laugh] at that age.*

The first issue of *Torpedo Dialogues* was photocopied and bound with tape—an idea Richards lifted from *Restaurant Fuel*—but the second issue from later in 1997 was printed on newsprint. "*Punk Planet* was [printed on] newsprint and they also had like a one-color cover, and it was like, 'OK. They mean business.' And I don't think it was actually the tactile thing. It was the suggestion that enough people care about what I'm talking about that I printed five hundred copies of this," he said, before adding with a laugh, "or which means one hundred people care about this and I have four hundred copies in my parents' basement right now."

Torpedo Dialogues folded after a third issue in 1998, but Richards went on to play guitar and sing in the Dischord Records band Q and not U—for whom I was the drummer—from 1998 to 2005. He has continued to write about music, most notably as the Pop Music Critic for *The Washington Post* since 2009. "It's really impossible, I think, to communicate what music really is in writing," he explained:

> *That's the reason music exists. It communicates something that can only be communicated that way. And I still think of music writing—when I'm really stuck or frustrated by the idea, and kind of knowing this thing is futile—"What am I doing?" At the end of the day, it's like, well, you're just trying to help get people to the light. You're trying to be the sort of vehicle that gets them to the airplane so they can take off in this music. You're transporting them there. And that's what I think fanzines ultimately did.*

So much of this period in the 1990s, as teenagers making zines in and around DC, was about trying to find an identity, a space to belong and be heard. The persistent power of zines is that it offers a reliable, flexible, understood template to project yourself onto. The lesson that Riot Grrrl Press sought to convey, that self-representation was critical, was an example that any punk fanzine maker—any zine creator, period—could follow: I am here and this is what I think of music, politics, art, life, or just about anything else one could think of. The conclusion of the 1990s also served as the ending for an era of zinemaking in the DC punk subculture. What started in the mid-1970s as a handful of fans self-publishing analog serials and then exploded in the 1980s and 1990s changed dramatically in the early twenty-first century. The ease of digital publishing through webzines, blogs, and social media led most fans to abandon print fanzines throughout the 2000s, but the print format would unexpectedly see new life as the twenty-first century lurched forward.

Notes

1. Gail O'Hara, "Pam Berry," *Chickfactor*, issue 10, Fall 1996–Spring 1997, 4–7.
2. Hal Miller, email to the author, January 18, 2019.
3. Jeff Bagato, interview with the author, March 7, 2023.
4. Richard Gehr, "Zines," in *Alt. Culture: An A-to-Z Guide to the '90s: Underground, Online, and Over-the-Counter*, first edition, edited by Nathaniel Wice and Steven Daly (New York: HarperPerennial, 1995), 280–81.
5. Jennifer Bleyer, "Cut-and-Paste Revolution: Notes from the Girl Zine Explosion," in *The Fire This Time: Young Activists and the New Feminism*, edited by Vivien Labaton and Dawn Lundy Martin (New York: Anchor Books, 2004), 44–45.
6. Gehr, "Zines."
7. Patrick Foster, interview with the author, July 18, 2018.
8. Jim Saah, interview with the author, June 11, 2018.
9. Saah also met his future wife, an employee of Chuck & Dave's, at the shop during this period. "I actually can credit *Uno Mas* in finding my wife, 'cause I went into Chuck & Dave's to sell it. She started looking at it and [noticed] J. Robbins had some artwork in it—and she was like, 'Oh, I know him! I live with him!' And (laughter) he's in the back room 'cause he worked at Chuck and Dave's, too. . . . We had so many mutual friends, [and] we placed ourselves at many shows, but I never really met her. And that's when we started hanging out, trying to sell my fanzine."
10. As part of his research when writing a new book, Pelecanos rode along with Washington police officers during their late-night shifts to observe the way they worked and the types of situations they encountered.
11. George Pelecanos, email to the author, February 17, 2018.
12. George Pelecanos, "Review of 'Our Band Could Be Your Life,'" no date, www.george-pelecanos.com/pelecanos-writers/review-of-our-band-could-be-your-life-scenes-from-the-american-indie-under-ground-1981-1991/.
13. Foster, interview.
14. Allin was a New England–area punk infamous for his provocative antics, devotion to the scatological, and threats of onstage suicide. Allin was an

avatar for many of punk's darkest impulses and built an enduring cult following. He died from a drug overdose in 1993. Allin's postcard to *Mole* was sent from prison, declaring that "my only concern is my own fucking mission" and advising Bagato that "maybe you should dedicate some space to me in your next issue."

15. Bagato, interview.
16. Bagato.
17. Andrew Unterberger, "In Honor of the 30th Anniversary of Rap's First Hot 100 No. 1, a List of Hip-Hop Hot 100 Firsts," *Billboard*, November 4, 2020, www.billboard.com/pro/hip-hop-hot-100-firsts-vanilla-ice/.
18. Dom Salemi, "*Brutarian* Magazine: It's *Beatsville* Now . . . ," *Beatsville*, March 2019. www.beatsville.net/2019/03/brutarian-magazine-brutarian-was-pseudo.html.
19. Peter Gilstrap, "The Magazine Reader: Missives from the Basement," *Washington Post*, July 21, 1992.
20. Salemi, "*Brutarian* Magazine."
21. Willona Sloan, interview with the author, May 2, 2018.
22. Gail O'Hara, interview with the author, December 12, 2023.
23. "Chickfactor 25: An Interview with Gail O'Hara—Freeform Portland," no date, www.freeformportland.org/2017/11/28/chickfactor-25-an-interview-with-gail-ohara/.
24. O'Hara.
25. Lindsay Zoladz, "For Ex-Zinesters Only: On *Chickfactor*'s Influence in the Digital Age," *Washington City Paper*, April 4, 2012, https://washingtoncitypaper.com/article/419313/for-ex-zinesters-only-on-chickfactors-influence-in-the-digital-age/.
26. Jay Ruttenberg, "Chickfactor 30," no date, *New Yorker*, www.newyorker.com/goings on about town/night life/chickfactor 30.
27. "Chickfactor" appeared on Belle and Sebastian's 1998 album *The Boy with the Arab Strap*.
28. Jason Cherkis, "*Chickfactor*: The Little Zine That Shaped Indie Music Culture," *HuffPost*, June 18, 2018, www.huffpost.com/entry/chickfactor-zine-indie-music_n_5b23e1dfe4b0a0a5277b1fa4.
29. Alison Baitz, "Black Tambourine Quotes: *Chickfactor* Magazine Interview," *Refinery29*, April 5, 2012, www.refinery29.com/en-us/black-tambourine-pam-berry.
30. Zoladz, "For Ex-Zinesters Only."
31. Cherkis, "*Chickfactor*."
32. Go! Compact Discs called Arlington home until late 1996, when it briefly moved into the basement of DC's Black Cat nightclub, before closing for good at the end of January 1997. "I remember thinking of [the relocation to DC] as a last, desperate move to keep afloat," I wrote in the first issue of my fanzine, *Held Like Sound*, published a few months after Go! went out of business. "There was some optimism after that move, but it quickly faded as everyone seemed to realize that Go's boat was sinking fast."
33. A third Indie Rock Flea Market occurred on August 10, 1996. The event was again held in the parking lot of a closed-down Sears department store on Clarendon Boulevard in Arlington. "I guess there's some sort of a need for something this fun and intimate," Go! co-owner Jimmy Cohrssen told the *Washington Post* about the Indie Rock Flea Market. "Kids go to the Dischord table to see Ian working."
34. Brace, "Night Watch: Republic Gardens, Cultivating Cool," *Washington Post*, August 9, 1996.
35. Jeff Barrus, interview with the author, January 2, 2020.
36. The Vienna stop in Northern Virginia is the western terminus for the Orange Line on Washington's Metro subway system.
37. Don Irwin, *Punk Life: Notes from the Underground*, unnumbered issue, c. 1997, 10.
38. Don Irwin, interview with the author, January 6, 2019.
39. Natalie Avery, interview with the author, November 2, 2018.
40. Amanda Huron, interview with the author, January 18, 2019.
41. Natalie Avery, "Brickthrower Radio," *Brickthrower*, issue 2, 1997, 4.
42. Kevin Dunn and May Summer Farnsworth. "'We Are the Revolution': Riot Grrrl Press, Girl Empowerment, and DIY Self-Publishing," *Women's Studies* 41, no. 2 (2012): 136–57, https://doi.org/10.1080/00497878.2012.636334.
43. Dunn and Farnsworth.
44. Jason Roe, interview with the author, November 30, 2023.
45. Norman Brannon, email to the author, June 5, 2018.
46. Daisy Rooks, interview with the author, December 22, 2020.
47. Hugh McElroy, email to the author, January 29, 2024.
48. Kate Eichhorn, *Adjusted Margin: Xerography, Art, and Activism in the Late Twentieth Century* (Cambridge, MA: MIT Press, 2016), 106.
49. Steve Shapero, interview with the author, December 11, 2020.
50. Laura Barcella and Andrea Chasanow Gentle, interview with the author. April 13, 2023.
51. Laris Kreslins, interview with the author, November 21, 2023.
52. The line stretched all the way outside the store and down the sidewalk. We had stood there for hours when word circulated that Rollins needed to leave for a sound check at his show that night. Cries of protest came from the waiting crowd, and Rollins agreed to stay until he talked with everyone. Not realizing that I was supposed to bring something for him to autograph, when my turn at the front of the line came, I asked him to sign the shoulder of the Sonic Youth T-shirt I was wearing, which he politely did—"Hello from Rollins." I still have the shirt packed away somewhere today.
53. Sara Marcus, interview with the author, August 10, 2018.
54. Forbes Graham, interview with the author, December 28, 2019.
55. Chris Richards, interview with the author, May 7, 2018.
56. Members of the latter had their own publication, *Back*, a comics zine highlighted by the drummer Ryan Nelson's illustrations, which became a key part of DC punk iconography in the late 1990s and the early twenty-first century.

10

DC Punk Fanzines in the Twenty-First Century

CHANGE CAME SWIFTLY with the new century, as the internet's hold on attention grew from the supplemental explorations of the 1980s and 1990s to, for many, an indispensable tool for communication and activity. An enormous shift occurred within popular culture in 1999, with the debut, and almost immediate rise to dominance, of peer-to-peer file-sharing networks like Napster. These enabled fans to share and download music files free, notably reducing album sales while, conversely, making it easier for a band's recordings to be heard—whether they liked it or not. However, when the popular heavy metal band Metallica sued Napster for copyright infringement, the backlash from fans against the band damaged Metallica's reputation and served as a warning to other musicians who might push back against file-sharing. Purchasing a compact disc from a major label band in the late 1990s frequently cost somewhere from fifteen to twenty dollars, so it was an easy choice for many music fans to make when presented with a free option to acquire music. Punk fans now spent hours on the internet trolling for mp3 files of music to download, so the idea of staying online to find music news and connect with other punk fans became increasingly palatable.

Web browsers like Netscape and Microsoft Internet Explorer circulated by the mid-1990s, making it easier for a zine to project its form onto computers. This potential was highly appealing, as the prospect of not having to spend hundreds or thousands of dollars to print and distribute your zine led numerous zine creators to make websites—often called webzines—in parallel to their print fanzines. Many twentieth-century print zine publishers emphasized how obtaining free photocopies from family members' workplaces or friendly copy shop employees were a necessity for publishing their zine. With the internet, though, anyone with access to a computer and an internet connection could broadcast their fandom, no Kinko's hookup required. Soon, many abandoned print altogether, shifting to the seemingly unlimited possibilities of the internet.

Several zines from DC repositioned to a wider web presence, with most then discontinuing print versions. Before long, however, it was clear that the ineffable charm of print zines was nearly impossible to replicate online. "I realized that I couldn't put my arms around the internet in the way that I could around the punk scene or the zine scene," Wilona Sloan of *Scorpion* said:

> *I knew who was in [the punk scene, but] I couldn't just have internet people come to my house, you know? So, it just didn't feel as inclusive to me, and it wasn't as fun. Getting random spammy comments wasn't quite the same high as going to my post office box, and seeing a letter in there and getting postcards. I remember I used to write the lead singer from Avail all the time. I don't know why; I just did. And he would send me postcards from the road, or pictures, and I'm like, "You don't get that on the internet."*[1]

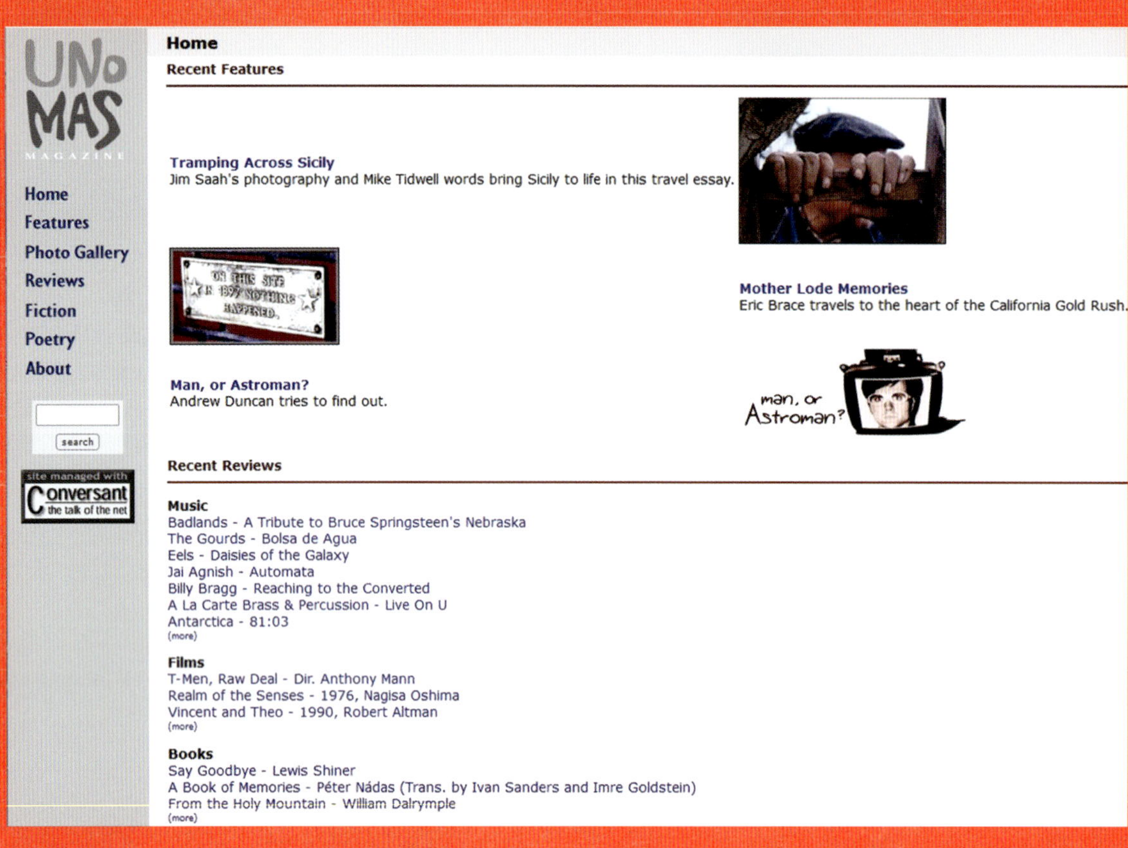

Figure 10.1 Screengrab of Unomas.com, the early-2000s internet presence for *Uno Mas* fanzine. Published by Jim Saah and Greg Pierce.

Uno Mas and *Sweet Portable You* each moved to the internet after publishing their final print issues, but Foster echoed Sloan's concerns about the transition to pixels. "It just didn't feel right, and it seemed like it lost a lot of the immediacy," he recalled. "I loved putting [print zines] in envelopes, folding them up, and sending them out and getting appreciative notes back from people who I respected. And I loved getting the packages in the mail, and I could sort of see that all not happening anymore."[2]

For Don Irwin of *Punk Life*, internet zines were too disruptive to one's attention to recreate either the magic of print zines or their practical purpose as a tool to spread information. "You're always going to be distracted by the next hyperlink that you're going to click and you don't have that with a fanzine or a record," he explained. "You're just overloaded with information. And having too much information isn't good, because your brain can still only absorb so much." For Irwin, online zines suffered in comparison with "having a hard copy and being able to see and touch a photo, and *not* having the option of moving on to the next hyperlink, [thereby] making you read all of the record reviews, so hopefully you could find something buried in there."[3]

As the 2000s proceeded, punk fan writings occurred on blogs, websites that users could typically create for free to present diaristic entries on whatever they chose. Blogs reasonably seemed like a successor to print zines at the time, allowing fans to share their thoughts on a platform that nearly anyone could view. Author and critic Marc Masters grew up in Northern Virginia and published the print zine *Crank* in the 1990s while at college in Williamsburg, Virginia. When the new technology presented itself, he felt optimistic that blogs could merge the discrete personal sensibilities of zines with an easy, cheap way to publish them. "There was a sweet spot there in the early

2000s where [blogs seemed like] a great way to do it and a lot of people managed to get their blogs around pretty well [yet] still keep a sense of 'This is my one-person or two-person voice' and it's not been co-opted by anything or it's not here for 'clicks,'" Masters said. Like other zine creators, however, he felt that the promise of online zines and blogs flickered out quickly. "Blogs were kind of like that for a while but, now, as everything on the internet has sort of re-conglomerated, the only things that can survive are things that get a lot of publicity or a lot of readership. It does seem like zine style and the culture has been pushed out of the internet a little bit now."[4]

Librarian and zine creator Jenna Freedman keenly illuminated a furtive truth underlying the move of zine content to a blog platform. "Blogs seem to be self-published, but ultimately the blogger is responsible to someone other than him, her, or hirself," she observed:

> *While blogs can be a very empowering medium, there aren't many people out there capable of fully hosting their own blogs. Therefore, there is usually an internet service provider that has the power to pull the plug on something it deems offensive, be it because of politics, sex, religion, copyright, or anything else. It's also much more difficult for the average blogger to be truly anonymous than it is for a zinester. Being able to violate copyright and readers' ethics or sensibilities have their good and bad points. Part of what makes zines what they are and what makes them so great is the total freedom not afforded to, but taken by the zinester.*[5]

Nationally, punk and indie rock blogs like *BrooklynVegan* and *Stereogum* became enough of a powerhouse that a subgenre—blog rock—was invented to describe the mostly

Figure 10.2 Left: *To Hell with Good Intentions*, issue 10, circa 2010. Published by Jack Abok and Trisha Georgino. Right: *Give Me Back*, issue 1 (aka #51), February 2007. Published by Fil Baird. Used by permission.

banal indie rock bands that came and went amid brief torrents of hype on blogs during the mid to late 2000s. Meanwhile, a Chicago-based indie rock website named *Pitchfork* employed the webzine concept and rose to prominence in the 2000s, significantly influencing the commercial rise of indie rock through its tastemaking powers. *Pitchfork*'s record reviews were little different than the kind found in fanzines—at their worst, they were uninformed and capricious in their dismissals of bands whose careers subsequently suffered—but the popularity of *Pitchfork* at its peak vastly outstripped that of print zines.

Print punk fanzines never went away during this era of blogs and webzines, but they became scarce toward the end of the 2000s and into the 2010s. Still, DC had its holdouts like *Milkshake*, *Korrupt Yrself*, and *To Hell with Good Intentions*, among others, while several musicians in the scene, like Beck Levy (of Turboslut and Hand Grenade Job) and David Combs (Max Levine Ensemble, Spoonboy, and Bad Moves), were active zine creators. As ever, zines could be found at DC area record stores like Smash (which moved from Georgetown to Adams Morgan in 2006) and Crooked Beat, as well as tables at DIY concerts, but there was a feeling then that the form's necessity as a tool of punk communication—something just a few years in the rearview mirror during the 2000s—was ending in the internet's wake.

A standout DC punk fanzine from this relatively fallow period was *Give Me Back*, Fil Baird's paean to a just-passed era that published its first issue in February 2007. The zine meaningfully shared its name with both the Embrace song from the mid-1980s *and* a compilation from the early 1990s on Kent McClard's California-based hardcore/emo label, Ebullition Records. *Give Me Back*'s visual and thematic traits leaned heavily on McClard and Lisa Oglesby's then-recently defunct *HeartattaCk*, a smart and serious black-and-white newsprint punk zine running from 1994 to 2006. Baird assisted with *HeartattaCk* shortly before it ended and his new fanzine carried on the lessons learned. *Give Me Back* ran for several issues, its newsprint pages jammed with interviews, columns, and record reviews, serving as a beacon for those who still felt the allure of print punk zines. Levy was a key contributor to getting the zine off the ground, as was the musician and cofounder of Exotic Fever Records, Katy Otto. In a time when blogs seemed like the future of learning about bands and the briefly ascendant social media site MySpace was the novel way to interact with other punks, print punk zines still had meaning. "This is a learning process," Baird wrote of the zine in its first issue.[6] "Part of the appeal is that I don't know what I'm doing. I just know I want it to be intentional and relevant."

Although it was clear that the internet was now the dominant way for punks to communicate, a sturdy niche for print remained. "Blogs did not kill the zine because they are incapable of usurping the exact function of zines, a function that may have expressed cultural and societal yearning for 'networks' of a kind, but which has yet to be answered in any way by the internet and blogs," the scholar Sheila Liming wrote in 2010:

> *Blogs, for their own part, represent a harsh, indissoluble duality: on the one hand, a return to the idea of the author, of privileged individuality and singular voice, and, on the other hand, the eradication of authorial presence from all written material. . . . The stakes of authorship have decreased dramatically with the rise of the internet, the result of which is not an enlarged, multivoiced public sphere but, instead, a deafening cacophony through which only the voices of the rich and powerful—the updated versions of twentieth-century mainstream media, now digitized—can be heard. . . . Where zines were a conscious turn away from traditional modes of print authorship, blogs are a remodeling of the most problematic facets of those old modes.*[7]

By 2011, zines maintained enough of a community in DC to inspire the first DC Zinefest, an annual gathering of creators demonstrating the persistent appeal of the format. Many of those zines still came from participants in the punk community, yet fewer focused on fandom, instead consisting primarily of personal zines ("perzines") and comics. By 2022, DC Zinefest was large enough that it drew more than twelve hundred attendees to browse tables filled with zines.[8] "DC Zinefest is the best day of the year," enthused

Figure 10.3 Left: Flier for DC Zinefest 2014, designed by Solomon J. Brager. Right: *Vinyl Vagabonds*, issue 9, summer 2018. Published by Eric and Sara Gordon. Used by permission.

J. C. Parker, a librarian and zine creator (*Tributaries*, *Collide*), as well as one of DC Zinefest's organizers.

Vinyl Vagabonds, often represented at DC Zinefest, was rooted in music fandom, particularly the culture surrounding vinyl LPs and their collectors. Eric and Sara Gordon started blogging about their love of vinyl in 2010, soon incorporating a print zine into their output. "We have a lot of things that we're just compelled to talk about, and some of it's humorous, farcical, just being silly," Eric Gordon explained. "[Sometimes] we're just super passionate about a band or a particular record, and we want to sing it from the rooftops."

Another DC Zinefest tabler was Evan Keeling, whose engaging *DC Punk* series of zines in the mid-2010s moved origin stories for several Dischord bands into the frames of a comic strip. Keeling's illustrated histories of Fugazi and the Nation of Ulysses were more expected, considering their large role in DC punk history, but the retelling of the founding of the Warmers, a lesser-known trio from the mid-1990s, was a welcome surprise. "I wanted to make these comics a narrative, not just a string of facts and I remembered in [the graphic novel] *From Hell* how Alan Moore had extensive end notes that told page by page what he made up [and] what lines were taken from different writings and such," Keeling said:

> *I thought that would be a great way to get the information out and still have a narrative. There are also a lot of people and places that are going to appear in the stories. I didn't want to crowd the pages with informative text boxes or have awkward introductions like "Hello, Christina Billotte from Slant 6" or "Let's go to independent music venue, dc space." Nobody talks like that and I want the conversations to be as natural as possible.*[9]

Keeling recounted an interaction with Ian MacKaye at the 2015 DC Zinefest, which led to Dischord's distribution support for *DC Punk*. "His partner Amy Farina was the drummer in the Warmers and I had sent her a copy of the book, so, he knew about the comic and wanted to pick some up for some other folks," Keeling said. "I had a bunch of misprints that I had cut out to make buttons of people's faces from the book and Ian had his and Amy's son with him so they were having fun digging through the buttons and grabbing ones of people they recognized." MacKaye subsequently arranged for the *DC Punk* comics to be sold through Dischord's website, a relative seal of approval that pleased Keeling. "It's pretty exciting to be distributed there because if someone

Figure 10.4 *DC Punk Presents: Nation of Ulysses, Volume 2, '90–'91,* 2016. Published by Evan Keeling. Used by permission.

were to go to the Dischord site and look up the Warmers, my comic is listed right there along with their albums."

DC Zinefest co-organizer and *Phlegm Fatale* zine publisher Ariana Stone explained in 2014 that, despite the complexity of putting on the annual gathering, "each of us does this because we're super pumped about zines." She continued:

> *A lot of times when I'm tabling for [DC Zinefest] or telling people about it, they'll mention that they thought zines disappeared around, like, the era of the Monica Lewinsky scandal. The international zine community is not as active as it was in decades prior, but we're in the middle of a resurgence, for sure. Cities like Chicago and DC have resurrected long-dead zinefests, zinesters like Mimi Nguyen[10] have started publishing zines again after years of silence, and new zines, zinefests, and distros are emerging at rates that we haven't seen since the early 2000s.*[11]

Many zines moved away from being outlets for punk fandom, but the medium's ongoing power as a tool for individual expression persisted. Likewise, they operated as a respite from and, often, a rebuke of technology's increasingly pervasive role in our lives. "For me, reading a zine is a way to step back from all the white noise of technology, but for someone who started doing zines in the early 1990s, it was a way to initiate social contact that was missing," Stone said. "Reading a zine—I associate it with relaxation. It's my way to disconnect and put down my phone, turn off the TV, curl up in my bed or in the tub with a nice thick zine and relax."[12]

Fewer in number than other types of zines, a spate of outstanding punk fanzines developed from the early 2010s on into the 2020s, many of which dovetailed with a revival of hardcore punk in DC. By the mid-2010s, "a new crop of young, hungry DC punk bands unleashed a series of generally excellent albums upon a city where hardcore punk is written into the genetic codes of dejected suburban youth and city stalwarts alike," wrote NPR's Ron Knox. "The nickname that has stuck to the new scene—the New Wave of DC Hardcore—somehow feels like an important marker in the anthropological sense, a name that makes the scene cohesive and preserves its existence."[13]

Mosher's Delight was published by John "Crucial John" Scharbach and Zachary Wuerthner, vocalists for the hardcore bands Give and Intent, respectively. Their fanzine launched in 2012, consisting of a single page with one side of record reviews and an interview on the other. *Mosher's Delight* crackled with the economy and energy of the hardcore punk Scharbach and Wuerthner obsessed over. The layout "was strictly cut and paste, and it was meant to kind of look like old fanzines that inspired us, like early UK, DC, and NYC zines, classic 1980s-type stuff," Scharbach explained.[14] "Very crude but, also, it kind of just looks good. You can read everything and the pictures are clear."[15]

Mosher's Delight evolved into a prolific record label that issued dozens of releases—almost all in the cassette format that also was revived in the 2010s—from hardcore bands throughout the country, including DC's Give, Red Death, and Stand Off. A fifth issue of *Mosher's Delight* compiled the previous four single-page issues into a brief anthology, with another four single-page issues to follow before coming to an end. "In short, I learned a whole lot about creative expression, networking, production, business, etc.," Wuerthner reflected on *Mosher's Delight's* end in 2017. "But looking at the bigger picture, I realized that it's possible to inspire an entire generation of younger hardcore kids to form their own bands, create their own scenes and everything that comes along with that simply through what we've done as a label, fanzine, and idea. That's more than enough for me to feel fulfilled."[16]

Scharbach harnessed his distinctive graphic design acumen and infectious enthusiasm for punk into other projects, including the *Strawberry Dreams* zine and *Shining Life*, a zine and publishing label. *Strawberry Dreams* was a collaboration between Scharbach, Paula Martinez, and photographer Farrah Skeiky that published its debut issue in August 2015. Initially, Scharbach and Martinez were acquaintances from the punk scene who followed each other on social media until Scharbach unfollowed her, sparking an unlikely origin story for their zine. "This story is humorous, but it's so of the time," he recounted in 2018:

> *Her boyfriend asked me "Why did you stop following Paula? She took offense to that." So, then I was like, "Oh, I need to rectify this." I messaged her, and I was like, "Yeah, sorry I stopped following you, but..."*

PROTESTER

5 RECORDS WITH CONNOR DONEGAN

SSDECONTROL - GET IT AWAY
Anyone who knows me knows that this is my favorite Hardcore record of all time. It embodies everything I love about the style. The music hits the perfect sweet spot of being straight forward and downright bizarre. Somewhere in between the unhinged approach of the almighty Bad Brains and the neanderthal-like simplicity of fellow Bostonians D.Y.S. The lyrics are confrontational and powerful. Even the Buzzcocks cover at the end is unique and strong in it's own way! In other words, everything about it is perfect. Every Protester song I've ever written has been an attempt to create my own version of what SSD did.

NEGATIVE APPROACH - TIED DOWN
I feel like I couldn't make a list of the most influential records for Protester and not include Negative Approach... What can I say? They're the greatest of all time! Needless to say, John Brannon is arguably the best Hardcore vocalist to ever do it and is a constant source of inspiration for me when I'm behind the mic. On the record we're writing right now I've been telling Robin to do a lot of beats with no cymbal hits - very directly inspired by Negative Approach. I always loved that. I also really love that Negative Approach were never afraid to let their Rock n' Roll influences shine (specifically on tracks like "Evacuate" and "Dead Stop"). That shamelessness definitely helped influence the intro of "Can't Hang On" on our last record. Both of their records are flawless but if I had to choose a favorite I'd have to go with Tied Down.

AGNOSTIC FRONT - VICTIM IN PAIN
AF has always been a big influence on Protester. When we started out I had the idea of only doing Agnostic Front covers for the entire existence of the band. We've definitely done at least 5-6 AF tracks over the years. Wish I would have stuck with that plan. Anyway, Victim In Pain is what I would show somebody who had never heard Hardcore before to to give them an idea of what they're in for. Painfully simple but instantly memorable songwriting, steamroller-like drumming, and unmatched brutality in Roger's vocals make this record a perfect example of what I think Hardcore should be. 100% unmatched.

POISON IDEA - KINGS OF PUNK
Definitely about as far away from Straight Edge as you can get, but Poison Idea will always be one of my #1 influences when it comes to Hardcore songwriting. Those boys could really write a goddam tune! All their 80's stuff is untouchable, but Kings Of Punk is probably my favorite record of theirs. It's the perfect mix of the straightforwardness of Pick Your King and the more "mature" stuff they did later on. I feel like I always end up using the "Poison Idea scale" when I write Protester songs unless I make a conscious effort not to. One of my favorite bands ever.

CONFRONT - PAYDAY
As far as late 80's Straight Edge Hardcore goes, Confront is easily my favorite. Payday reminds me a lot of Get It Away in certain ways. Mainly how bizarre (stupid?) some of the song structures are and how unapologetically hateful they sound. That's a winning combination in my book. Despite his... uh... interesting political views, Mean Steve had one of the best voices in Hardcore and it really shows on this record. Have to include "One Life Drug Free" and "Our Fight" too since those are Confront's two best songs. Jay Of Today > Art Blakey

Figure 10.5 Top: *Shining Life*, issue 11, 2018. Published by John Scharbach. Used by permission. Bottom: *Mosher's Delight*, issue 5, 2013. Published by John Scharbach and Zachary Wuerthner.

ISSUE 2 JOIN THE STRAWBERRY SCENE

STRAWBERRY DREAMS

OCTOBER 2015

SCREAMING FEMALES

NUCLEAR AGE

THIS IS STRAWBERRY DREAMS

This is a place for girls from all over with all different interests to come and express ourselves. This is where we send our paintings/ drawings/ photographs/ whatever we want. This is where we can send writing and talk about what we love or hate. This is where we can talk about our experiences as a girl and how they've made us feel.

THIS ZINE IS AN ACT OF RESISTANCE

When we create something new-- art, media, dialogue, dynamics-- we are resisting meeting what is expected of us. When women (especially women who are brown, queer, trans or differently abled) attend basement shows full of suburban white males, we are resisting the expectation that we will stay in the back and stay quiet. When you print out this zine and share it with your friends, your class, your coworkers, you are resisting the division and competition that comes with being a woman. Resistance has many faces, and it means different things to different people. So does feminism. When I was first introduced to the idea of this zine, I was immediately against it. A separate zine for women sounded like more of the same-- men make zines or music and everyone is expected to enjoy them, but women make zines or music and the resulting art is seen as a "girl thing." I've always fought for inclusiveness and just wanted to see more women in zines that already existed. But this is where resistance comes in. Suburban white boys are not going to make room for you. Their idea of inclusiveness is narrow and shaped by their own experiences, not yours. Women and girls in this world have to fight for our space. We can resist by showing up. We can resist by making space for ourselves and other women, too. We can resist by being cheerleaders for each other's music, art, projects, and passions; rather than competing to fit the mold of "just one of the guys" that's expected of us. You can resist by declaring your femininity as powerful and punishing, not a weakness. Realizing that this zine is an act of resistance is what changed my mind. We declare the contents of this zine to be our priorities, problems and opinions, and that they are relevant to EVERYONE. There can be disagreement in its pages, and that doesn't make it any less valid. This zine is beyond paper. It's a space for us to be as powerful as we want to be. It's what you make of it.

Farrah Skeiky

FARRAH PAULA CRUCIAL JOHN NIRVA

ALL PHOTOS BY FARRAH SKEIKY UNLESS OTHERWISE NOTED

Figure 10.6 Top left: *Strawberry Dreams*, issue 2, 2015. Published by Paula Martinez, Farrah Skeiky, and John Scharbach. Top right: *Neighborhood Life*, issue 1, 2014. Published by Ambrose Nzams. Bottom: *Demystification*, issues 3 and 4, 2021 and 2024. Published by Paula Martinez and Ambrose Nzams. All used by permission.

> *We started talking about zines for some reason and she was really into Bikini Kill and riot grrrl stuff. I proposed to patch up the bad blood that had seemingly been between us—"Why don't we do a zine?"*

Figure 10.7 *Potion for Bad Dreams*, issue 2, September 2020. Published by Jack Lustig. Used by permission.

The mission of *Strawberry Dreams* was to publish only female-identifying contributors, highlighting the works and thoughts of those who, despite decades of pushback, still had to fight for space in male-dominated punk fanzines. Scharbach enlisted Skeiky to help guide the zine, but the latter was initially skeptical. "I was just like 'OK, this is a girl zine, this is gonna be *great*,'" she remembered. "I was being really sarcastic about it because I really like to focus on the inclusiveness of things. My ideal is always, 'Why doesn't every zine just have more female contributions?'"[17] Skeiky reconsidered and brought her extraordinary photography—as good as any in DC punk's long history—to the zine. Scharbach questioned whether or not it was his place, as a man, to have a creative stake in a zine centered otherwise exclusively on women contributors. Encouraged by Skeiky and Katie Alice Greer—vocalist for Priests, a flagship band for DC punk in the 2010s—Scharbach proceeded to design the zine, while Martinez directed the content. "I think it's really good that [Scharbach] was part of this idea because he's just being a really good male ally to women in the scene," Skeiky said. "He's setting a really good example—he's not using his voice in the scene, which is a pretty strong one, to decide what should be in it. He's using his voice [for] something everybody should be reading regardless of their gender."[18]

Strawberry Dreams published two issues, a project that Martinez later described as "a really fun project of doing stuff for my friends and also doing a lot of things that promoted my self-expression. I did all the art for it and . . . it just had an aesthetic that I was interested in exploring at that time."[19] Scharbach turned his attention to *Shining Life*, consisting of one-to-two-page zines focusing on a single topic. Often, it would consist of DC hardcore bands like Laughing Corpse, Protester, or Brain Tourniquet or of twentieth-century hardcore bands like Bold, Verbal Assault, or Swiz. Some issues, however, focused on topics that Scharbach was similarly fascinated with, whether it was the *Teenage Mutant Ninja Turtles* characters or the Toy Machine skateboard company. "I'm kind of always wondering, like, when am I going to stop being so obsessive," he said. "I don't know if that will ever go away."[20] Scharbach's ongoing work remains an utterly pure and inspiring distillation of fandom, both of punk and the pieces of popular culture comprising his character.

After *Strawberry Dreams*, Martinez collaborated on a zine called *Demystification* with Ambrose Nzams, a punk fanatic from Montgomery County, Maryland. Nzams' 2014 zine, *Neighborhood Life*, blended intelligent writing, fervent fandom, and a cut-and-paste aesthetic to make one of the more memorable DC punk zines of the decade. Much like his earlier peers in zinemaking, Nzams spent hours at a FedEx Office (formerly known as Kinko's, but rebranded in the 2000s) using photocopiers, scissors, and adhesive to piece together *Neighborhood Life*'s layout. "The text was typed in [Microsoft] Word, printed out and, then, if I needed to resize anything, I would do it on the copy machines," Nzams later explained. "None of it was laid out on a computer. I didn't know how to do that and, in some ways, I still don't."[21] Considering the insight and pure fandom evident in *Strawberry Dreams* and *Neighborhood Life*, it was no surprise when Martinez and Nzams combined to push *Demystification* into new territory, crafting a punk fanzine rooted in the genre, yet with its vision set for the future.

Starting with its first issue in November 2018, *Demystification*'s striking, colorful covers signified the care and imagination that Martinez and Nzams invested in each issue. Its canny coverage of the disparate elements animating contemporary punk sensibilities include detailed articles on the link between hardcore and Nike's Air Max 95 athletic shoes, the development of the "Hooded Mosher" character in hardcore iconography, and an oral history of the long-gone New York City fanzine shop See Hear. These lengthy, granular explorations run alongside interviews with artists and coverage of new music, merging with skillful, but not slick, graphic design to make a defining modern punk fanzine. As California punk fanzine *Razorcake* remarked on *Demystification*, "a zine like this, with a fresh perspective, doesn't come around often. So great."[22]

Jack Lustig's *Potion for Bad Dreams*—its title culled from an unreleased album recorded by Void, one of the hardcore bands putting the DC scene on the map in the early 1980s—published two issues in 2019 and 2020. Among its DC punk zine contemporaries, it had the most throwback qualities with its crowded, even chaotic, cut-and-paste layout. Printed in black and white, these pages mingled disparate aesthetic styles from throughout hardcore's history, like the occasional bubbly, graffiti-style logos of the early 1990s and the more frequently employed metal-influenced crosses and skulls favored by bands like Void and their followers. *Potion for Bad Dreams* conjured the neat trick of actually feeling like a newsprint zine without being one. Its voluminous black ink and shadowy photographs implied that one's fingers would be inkmarked by issue's end—traditional ink often transferred off newsprint onto readers' hands—but the modern digital printing kept the reader's digits clean. Lustig's hand numbering of each issue underscored the unadulterated fannish nature of *Potion for Bad Dreams* further. This was for fans, by fans, and not meant for mass consumption.

In limited, but meaningful fashion, print punk fanzines persisted through the 2010s and into the next decade. Just as back when Howard Wuelfing of Nurses and the Slickee Boys published zines in the late 1970s and early 1980s, musicians like Scharbach, Wuerthner, Lustig, and others were at the heart of DC punk zine publication in the 2020s. Jack Abok, vocalist for Des Demonas and Ecstatic International, returned to zinemaking several years after discontinuing his previous title, *To Hell with Good Intentions* (which he copublished with Trisha Georgino). The new fanzine *Bad Vibes* featured Agwelt's forthright opinions on music written out by hand, a very human tonic in light of most music criticism living online, scrolled through momentarily before the next nugget of information crowds it out. Abok's unfiltered editorial voice was equally refreshing, gleefully taking the piss out of bands around the DC scene, while extolling the virtues of others. His list "Bands I Hate" at the end of issue four, published in 2023, pleasingly recalled *The Infiltrator*'s "What We Hate" section from its final issue in 1981, demonstrating a persistent thread of blurry sarcasm that has continued unspooling through punk for decades. Abok's deadpan humor often makes it hard to tell when his disapproval is cheeky or genuine (or both simultaneously), but within that ambiguity lies much of *Bad Vibes*' generous appeal.

Amanda Huron, who copublished *Brickthrower* in the late 1990s and drummed for the Stigmatics, continued making urgent music in the bands Puff Pieces and Sensor Ghost, who were among the city's best in the twenty-first century. As Abok wrote in *Bad Vibes* of Sensor Ghost's spiky, eccentric postpunk sounds in 2023, "You can't dance to this shit, but you could beat the shit out of someone to it. Believe." Huron, like Abok, continued zinemaking in the 2020s with *Probation Area*, analyzing punk life with the same perceptive eye she brought to *Brickthrower* nearly three decades prior.

Issue three of *Probation Area*, in 2023, included Huron's essay critiquing the decision to build a statue honoring Dave Grohl. The former Scream drummer remained vocal about the love and connection he still felt for his hometown DC punk scene years after achieving mainstream success elsewhere with his bands Nirvana and

Foo Fighters. The relatively abstract statue of Grohl was unveiled in May 2023 at the opening of the Atlantis, a new venue owned by IMP, a successful DC-based concert promotion and production company that had also operated the 9:30 Club since buying it from Dody DiSanto and Jon Bowers in 1986.[23] The new version of the Atlantis was named after Paul Parsons' club from the late 1970s, which evolved into the original 9:30 Club in 1980. When Foo Fighters performed at the 9:30 Club in September 2021, Grohl excitedly told the audience, "They're going to open up a place that's an exact replica of the old 9:30, right next door." IMP's communications director, Audrey Fix Schaefer, seconded the notion in 2021 that "the new club promises to look just like the original."[24]

Ultimately, the new Atlantis featured a glowing, multistory facade meant to invoke the design of the Atlantic Building, which housed the original 9:30 Club. Other details dotted throughout the club were meant to stir memories of the old location, most prominently in the decorations of the rooftop bar. Ersatz storefronts covered in graffiti, vintage newspaper boxes, and other period touches sought to impart the feel of the old 9:30 Club's neighborhood at 9th and F Streets NW. This deeply nostalgic gesture was well intentioned, but it drifted too far into theme park territory. "It's a glorying in the roughness of the old days, the sense that things back then were a bit out of control and also cooler, when everyone, also, coincidentally, was younger and discovering things for the first time," Huron wrote in *Probation Area* of the replication attempt. To her, the decision to decorate the club with an eye on the past was "riding a punk nostalgia wave . . . that just gets bigger and stronger and more moneyed and more all-encompassing as the years pass by and we all watch death approach ever closer on the horizon. I guess it's created some jobs, at least."

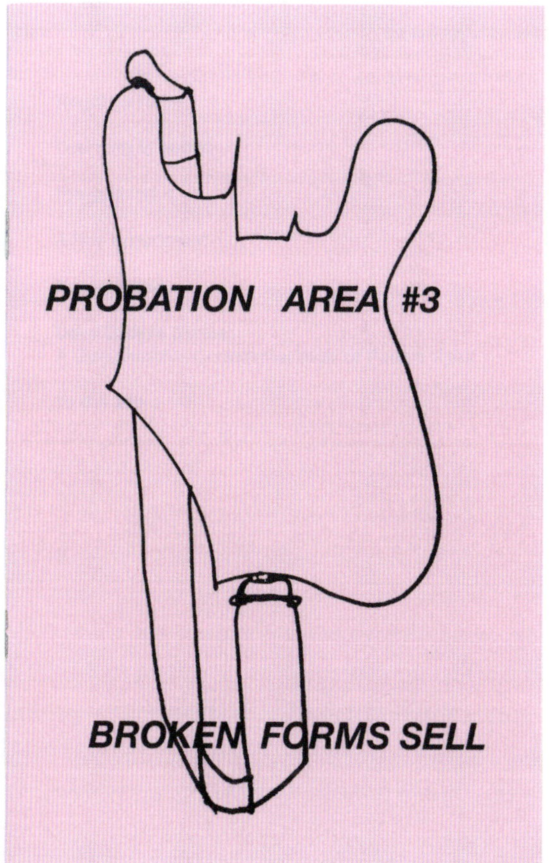

Figure 10.8 Left: *Bad Vibes*, issue 4, 2023. Published by Jack Abok. Right: *Probation Area*, issue 3, winter 2024. Published by Amanda Huron. Used by permission.

Figure 10.9 *Debussy Ringtone*, issue 2, 2019. Published by Chris Richards. Used by permission.

As for the statue dedicated to Grohl, Huron wondered in her essay why Grohl was chosen over others from the community for the purported honor, as well as why he would permit "this statue of his likeness to be built and publicly displayed." To Huron, the entire spectacle was a reminder for "the ongoing joy of and gut-level need to rebel against convention, even—especially?—against the conventions of thought that have arisen out of my own tribe's collective cultural making over the years."

Huron followed her essay in *Probation Area* with one generated by ChatGPT, an artificial intelligence (AI) chatbot that surged in popularity in the early 2020s. Huron prompted the chatbot to "write a very short essay critiquing Dave Grohl for allowing a statue of himself to be built to commemorate the opening of the new replica 9:30 Club. Include memories of the old 9:30 Club and a critique of punk nostalgia." The AI-written essay scolded Grohl more directly than Huron did, opining that his approval of the statue "not only contradicts punk's rejection of idolatry but also elevates personal achievement above the values of inclusivity and rebellion that punk aimed to embody." The juxtaposition of human and AI writings was not only amusing; its inclusion also served as another deft criticism of the faux-downtown simulacra at the new Atlantis. As Huron joked darkly once the ChatGPT essay concluded, "who needs to learn to write anymore, am I right?"

Chris Richards, who published *Torpedo Dialogues* in the late 1990s, remained active musically in the new century and also returned to the zine medium in 2018 with *Debussy Ringtone*.[25] His new zine offered a stream of short, astute writings on art, life, and music—covering jazz, hardcore punk, hip-hop, go-go, R&B, and whatever else captured his interest. Its spare, colorful abstract covers conveyed the idea that the words within were free of dogma and up to the reader to absorb and interpret. Like *Demystification*, *Debussy Ringtone* was a punk zine for the new era. Catholic in its artistic fascinations, while resolutely punk in spirit.

The choice in the late 2010s to print your zine rather than strictly distribute it as a digital object was an intentional gesture in a time when the internet's hold on society grew tighter. "In this digital climate, you obviously want to differentiate yourself, and how things look really, really matters," Richards explained in 2018. "I'm really waiting for the internet to catch up to design on the printed page. And I don't mourn print the way that a lot of people do, [although] it's very difficult to argue that things look better online than they did in the print era. And I think that's going to have to come around at some point."[26]

Elizabeth von Oehsen's *PaperJam* also took to the revitalized print format, publishing five issues from 2021 through 2023, including interviews with participants in the DC punk subculture like G. L. Jaguar (Priests, Ecstatic International), Adriana Lucia-Coates (Mock Identity), Catherine Ferrando (co-owner of the Black Cat club and vocalist for the Owners), and Ray Brown (concert promoter and drummer for Snail Mail). Like those of several peers in this period's DC music zine scene, *PaperJam* had a broad approach to its coverage. "It's been an art and music zine from the

Figure 10.10 *PaperJam*, issue 4, 2022. Published by Elizabeth von Oehsen. Used by permission.

beginning," von Oehsen said:

> *I have always been trying to honor my love for DC music and the community here. And it's not just a punk zine. In fact, it's not a punk zine. We have covered go-go and jazz musicians, a lot of indie stuff, [the DJ collective] Black Rave Culture, electronic music. I've tried to make it a zine that is a little bit more overarching and not so specific because [of my] not truly identifying as a punk, I'm more of an indie kid. I didn't feel like I had the authority to make a punk zine, specifically. [laughs]*[27]

PaperJam intriguingly incorporated touches of the digital world into its print format. This manifested not only through its crisp laser printing and von Oehsen's talents for modern graphic design, but also by using a QR code in each issue that sent readers who scanned it with their smartphone to an online playlist of new music. "Yeah, it's sort of this unbroken cycle between the digital and print realms," they explained:

> *It's like, "Okay, I am making a print, music, and art zine. But it is the 2020s. I'm not going to pretend that we don't all have phones." Having a QR code in the back that links to the Linktree that links to all the content just makes sense. And it's also kind of cool. I've played around with some VR [virtual reality] software, and you can do stuff where you look at the cover through your phone, and then it animates. I would love to do something like that. It would just take so much time, and I don't have any time. I'm now, like, in two bands, I have this very demanding job, I also try to have a social life,*

Figure 10.11 Left: DC punk archival collections on shelves at the University of Maryland's Special Collections in Performing Arts. Photo by the author. Right: *Maximum Preservation*, issue 1, 2014. Published by the DC Public Library. Used by permission.

and I'm in a [Dungeons and Dragons] campaign, so I don't have the time. But I would love to do more stuff like that, where it's bridging the digital and physical spaces. And the Instagram [social media account]: We put effort into those photos and those posts because not everyone's going to get the zine, and I want people to hopefully look at it and be like, "This is kind of cool-looking. Let me look into this." From the beginning, I wanted it to be a no-gatekeeping kind of project because the only reason that I am hip to any DC music stuff is because people were not gatekeeping with me.

The return of print zines in the 2010s could indicate dissatisfaction with the assumption many made at the start of the century that the internet was the successor for airing fandom. Print zines have persisted so far throughout the twenty-first century, offering a welcome alternative to scrolling through social media on one's phone or desktop. However, a palpable hesitation lingers when it comes to declaring print zines as "back" or even a sustainable alternative to the internet's dominance. "Social media, as a whole, has made the world feel smaller in a way that zines made the world feel bigger, which is a weird thing," Nzams said. "I'd say I don't know if [print zines] went away and came back as much as they're less and less necessary, [other than for] the people who are upholding it, or people who believe in it, you know?"[28]

Jeff Barrus, who copublished *Restuarant Fuel* in the 1990s and has continued to follow punk culture, observed that "when the internet came, it sort of made zines an anachronism in a lot of ways." He went on:

I do think modern zines are sort of anachronistic and a little nostalgia-focused. Like, the basic concept of a zine in 2020 is it's almost this thing that's not really part of the culture anymore. When we did zines [in the 1990s], it was a real vehicle for regular people to have their voices heard. But now, that's changed. Now it has moved on to the internet. And I see the same kind of spirit that I saw with zines with streamers on Twitch or YouTube. I see the same kind of desire to connect with people and to tell stories about yourself or tell stories about things that you like. It's not the same form, and it's way more commercialized than zines ever were, but it is still, I think, kind of the same spirit that drove us at the time.[29]

In a new afterword to the 2018 edition of his book *Notes from the Underground*, zine scholar Stephen Duncombe asked the question "Are print and paper zines merely an exercise in nostalgia?" Answering in the affirmative, he asserted that "zine producers have historically embraced new technology," yet this century's print zines often embrace vintage approaches like cut-and-paste layouts. However, he acknowledged that "there's something missing from the blogs, the fan sites, and the social networking pages—and I think this something has everything to do with democratization." Duncombe pointed out that "the world of self-publishing on the internet is not an alternative culture. There is no cultural price of admission into the digital realm, there are no arcane rituals to master or rules to follow (or even debate). The result is a multiplicity of voices and values. There is nothing wrong with this; indeed there is a lot that is good. But this diversity does not constitute a community, and as such, there are no coherent community values."[30]

This sense of fellowship, of people writing about and for each other, is an essential aspect of punk fanzine culture. It has coursed through DC punk since its inception in the mid-1970s and continues today, even as the notion of what constitutes punk evolves. Many of those fanzines now reside in acid-free folders and boxes in archives at the DC Public Library and the University of Maryland, two institutions that assembled vast collections of materials related to DC punk throughout the 2010s and into the 2020s. "From a historian's perspective, [fanzines] are precious documents," Positive Force DC's Mark Andersen explained. "They are a time capsule from within the community itself."[31]

Since its beginning in 1976 and up through the present, DC punk has been about creative expression, community, passion, purpose, and connection. DC punk fanzines embody those traits, from *It's Only a Movie* and *Vintage Violence* in the 1970s to *Demystification*, *Shining Life*, and

Probation Area in the 2020s. Those characteristics are not specific to DC, of course, but few scenes anywhere have excelled like DC's has at effectively telling its own stories from creation to the archive. DC never had a leading national fanzine like San Francisco's *Maximum Rocknroll* in the 1980s or Chicago's *Punk Planet* in the 1990s, but its role as one of punk's most influential scenes through bands like Bad Brains, Minor Threat, and Fugazi or movements like straight edge and Revolution Summer was fortified and influenced by local fanzines. Some circulated beyond the city—*Descenes, Thrillseeker, Truly Needy, Uno Mas*—while others had press runs limited to a handful of copies circulating through DC-area show spaces, record stores, and high school hallways. Through both avenues, fanzines played a critical role in maintaining and growing the community and culture of DC punk. They serve as a material reminder to fans that their own creative impulses and opinions are worthy of sharing, just as those of musicians are.

This all holds true today, even if fanzines are no longer central sources for communication. Discussing the ongoing appeal of print punk zines in the 2020s, Nzams remarked that "to some, it feels [like a] novelty but, to me, it doesn't. I love to get a zine, I love to hold one, I love to see it. I believe that that physical beauty is important. I feel like it's important to keeping our culture alive, whatever that is, you know?"[32]

Notes

1. Willona Sloan, interview with the author, May 2, 2018.
2. Patrick Foster, interview with the author, July 18, 2018.
3. Don Irwin, interview with the author, January 6, 2019.
4. Marc Masters, interview with the author, December 12, 2018.
5. Jenna Freedman, "Zines Are Not Blogs," Barnard Zine Library, no date, https://zines.barnard.edu/zines-are-not-blogs.
6. This was an unmissable homage to *HeartattaCk*, which ended after its fiftieth issue; the first issue of *Give Me Back* was numbered "#51" on its cover.
7. Sheila Liming, "Of Anarchy and Amateurism: Zine Publication and Print Dissent," *Journal of the Midwest Modern Language Association* 43, no. 2 (Fall 2010): 121–45.
8. Michelle Goldchain, "How DC's Zine Culture Is Thriving," WTOP, September 14, 2023, https://wtop.com/dc/2023/09/how-dcs-zine-culture-is-thriving/.
9. Matt Dembicki, "ComicsDC: Q&A: Keeling on His '*DC Punk*' Series," *ComicsDC*, September 12, 2015, https://comicsdc.blogspot.com/2015/09/q-keeling-on-his-dc-punk-series.html.
10. Mimi Thi Nguyen is an accomplished scholar and influential zine creator active since the early 1990s. Her papers can be found in the Feminist Theory Archive at Brown University.
11. Christine Stoddard, "Capital Zinesters," *Quail Bell*, January 19, 2014, www.quailbellmagazine.com/the-real/interview-dc-zinefest.
12. Arielle Milkman, "DC's Zinesters Prove the Art Form Is Alive and Well, Even in the Digital Age," *Elevation DC*, June 24, 2014, www.elevationdcmedia.com/features/dczines_062414.aspx.
13. Ron Knox, "The State of DC Hardcore," NPR, March 24, 2016, www.npr.org/sections/therecord/2016/03/24/470744767/the-state-of-d-c-hardcore.
14. John Scharbach, email to the author, August 19, 2024.
15. John Scharbach, interview with the author, May 3, 2018.
16. Anonymous, "Fulfilled: A Farewell Interview with Tape Hardcore Punk Label Moshers Delight Records," *Idioteq*, November 21, 2017, https://idioteq.com/fulfilled-farewell-interview-tape-hardcore-punk-label-moshers-delight-records/.
17. Alison Baitz, "'*Strawberry Dreams*' Is a New Feminist Punk Zine Out of DC," *Bandwidth*, September 11, 2015, http://bandwidth.wamu.org/index.html%3Fp=56338.html.
18. Baitz.
19. Paula Martinez, interview with Colin Atrophy Hagendorf, Life Harvest Radio, podcast, May 25, 2020.
20. Scharbach, interview.
21. Ambrose Nzams, interview with the author, January 13, 2025.
22. Michael T. Fournier, "Demystification #3," *Razorcake*, July 20, 2021, https://razorcake.org/demystification-3-12-8%c2%bd-x-11-glossy-128-pgs/.
23. IMP has its roots in the DC punk scene, going back to the first concert it produced on May 29, 1980. That concert, at the Ontario Theatre in DC's Adams Morgan neighborhood, was a screening of *The Punk Rock Movie* along with performances by Tex Rubinowitz and the Slickee Boys. The Cramps were the advertised headliner but dropped out before the show.
24. Jason Fontelieu, "Foo Fighters Played the 9:30 Club and It Was Quite a Scene," *Washingtonian*, September 10, 2021, https://www.washingtonian.com/2021/09/10/foo-fighters-played-the-930-club-and-it-was-quite-a-scene/.
25. After the breakup of Q and Not U in 2005, Richards was a part of the projects Ris Paul Ric, Street Stains, TK Echo, and Paint Branch (the latter was a collaboration with this author). He also ran a long-running series of new age music DJ nights under the title "Glide."
26. Chris Richards, interview with the author, May 7, 2018.
27. Elizabeth von Oehsen, interview with the author, December 16, 2022.
28. John R. Davis, Jennifer Fox-Thomas, and Ambrose Nzams, "Persistent Vision: A Roundtable Discussion on DC Punk Fanzines," panel discussion, University of Maryland, December 2, 2022.
29. Jeff Barrus, interview with the author, January 2, 2020.
30. Stephen Duncombe, *Notes from Underground: Zines and the Politics of Alternative Culture*, 3rd ed. (Portland: Microcosm, 2017), 218–19.
31. Greta Weber, "Zines Deserve a Bigger Place in DC Punk History: Here's Why," *Washingtonian*, August 4, 2016, www.washingtonian.com/2016/08/04/zines-deserve-a-bigger-place-in-dc-punk-history-heres-why/.
32. Davis, Fox-Thomas, and Nzams, "Persistent Vision."

AFTERWORD: THIS ZINE COULD CHANGE YOUR LIFE

Yancey Strickler

Art is both an expression of a worldview and a lens through which others are invited to see the world. An artist creates a frame or perspective for us to look through and get a sense of what it means to see the world through their eyes. A unique transference of perspective occurs.

Though they're not the first format people think of when considering forms of art, zines are one of the most effective means to express a coherent worldview available to us all. Zines allow us to document, express, and propagate a scene or culture. They let us express how we see the world, which, crazily enough, changes how others see the world, and which, craziest of all, can change the world itself.

Keep Your Ear to the Ground is a testament to this. The growth of hardcore, emo, and punk rock music were all hugely enabled by zines. Indie rock bands were underground and strident in comparison with major label music, and the zines were similarly rougher, handmade, and small run. What indie rock bands and zines lack in reach, they gain in freedom. By virtue of being small and of limited (or nonexistent) commercial aspirations, there's no need to conform to the editorial standards or voice of the mainstream. A zine and a great indie rock band can stand in their own world.

From straight-edge to hardcore to Revolution Summer to feminism and antiracism, zines and their makers have been the perfect counterpart to musicians in establishing the larger scene. Yes, punk and hardcore are about the music and the feeling and the tempo, but the scene also represents something much bigger: a respite from the mainstream; a counterculture that refuses to conform; an alternative life path available to everyone.

My own life changed when I intersected with these worlds in the early 1990s as a teenager growing up in Southwest Virginia. The band Nirvana was my gateway to the underground, and soon Pavement, Archers of Loaf, Sebadoh, and other early '90s classic bands dominated my listening. Weekly visits to the local record store (Record Exchange in Blacksburg, Virginia, RIP) unlocked deeper worlds. It is where I first encountered Fugazi, which I saw play a show in a community center not long after. I was hooked.

My love of music combined with an existing love of writing caused me to make my own high school zine (which, mercifully, ran just one issue), and to later become one of the first writers for *Pitchfork*. (My time there was brief—they let me go.) Not long after that, I met John Davis, then playing in one of my favorite bands, Q and Not U, who ran a zine I loved called *Held Like Sound*. After a couple of earnest fan emails, I was writing for the same zine.

As I soon learned, this is how the DC scene works. In the following years, when I had the good fortune to interact with a number of folks throughout the DC scene, I always found an openness of spirit. The line between band and fan wasn't totally erased, but it was very blurry.

In the decades since my entry into this world, the internet happened and the world changed many times over. The indie music scene still exists as a half-corporatized but still very DIY space, yet its cultural power and meaning are not what they once were. The music hasn't fallen out of favor—in some cases, it's more popular than ever. The increasing noise in the world in general has made it hard for anything to stay meaningful and hard to keep the scene strong and together.

In the years since writing for *Held Like Sound,* I went on to work as a music critic for almost a decade and to start a tiny record label of my own. Though I didn't think of them this way, these projects were naturally entrepreneurial, and they became a training ground for future projects: Kickstarter—the pioneering crowdfunding platform; the Creative Independent—a resource of practical and emotional advice for creative people; and, my current project, Metalabel—a release platform for creative people. Zines, I now realize, have been a constant presence across all these projects. Many zines were funded on Kickstarter, and we at Kickstarter made zines to express our beliefs. The Creative Independent made multiple zines, covering everything from how to make a living as an artist to dealing with creative anxiety. Metalabel has already been used to publish several dozen zines, with many more on the way.

As we are deluged with more and more culture material, zines and other forms of intentionally small-scale and DIY creations are making a comeback. Zines are once again creating space outside the mainstream to tell new stories and create new spaces.

The internet once felt like a cyberpunk future, and now it's turned into a mall, where larger forces battle for power and surveillance is rampant. As a result, new undergrounds are being formed away from the "clearnet" of the mainstream internet and are moving into what I once wrote about as "Dark Forests of the internet"—places where we could safely come together with like-minded people.

Like the many countercultures in history, Dark Forest groups use zines and zine-like methods of communication—handmade and collage-y, self-referential with insider language, things made for us by us—as a way of expressing identity, attracting new people, and drawing a clear line between themselves and mainstream society. Some of these zines are physical, printed objects, and some are digital—even PDFs and ZIP files are now used to spread ideas in ways to create new spaces of the makers' own.

Can these internet-based scenes ever replicate the past scenes in DC, Berlin, London, and New York? Of course not. There is no replication. What lies ahead will not be better or worse, simply different.

It's not the zine format that's so magical, but the invitation a zine provides: a space for us to define our world and ourselves, and to explore who we really are (or who we play like we are). Zines provide a place to play, and play helps unlock things we naturally love and are curious about to unlock the kind of energy that attracts others who feel the same way.

This is the raw power of the zine: a conduit for new cultural ideas, a place of deep curiosity, and the resulting transformation that unfolds when a small group of people come together around the values they share.

INDEX

JOHN R. DAVIS

is a musician, writer, and certified archivist from the Washington, DC, area. He is also the curator of Special Collections in Performing Arts in the Michelle Smith Performing Arts Library at the University of Maryland.